Katakana

ア	イ	ウ	エ	オ				
カ	キ	ク	ケ	コ		キャ	キュ	キョ
サ	シ	ス	セ	ソ		シャ	シュ	ショ
タ	チ	ツ	テ	ト		チャ	チュ	チョ
ナ	ニ	ヌ	ネ	ノ		ニャ	ニュ	ニョ
ハ	ヒ	フ	ヘ	ホ		ヒャ	ヒュ	ヒョ
マ	ミ	ム	メ	モ		ミャ	ミュ	ミョ
ヤ	(イ)	ユ	(エ)	ヨ				
ラ	リ	ル	レ	ロ		リャ	リュ	リョ
ワ	(イ)	(ウ)	(エ)	ヲ				
ン								

ガ	ギ	グ	ゲ	ゴ		ギャ	ギュ	ギョ
ザ	ジ	ズ	ゼ	ゾ		ジャ	ジュ	ジョ
ダ	ヂ	ヅ	デ	ド				
バ	ビ	ブ	ベ	ボ		ビャ	ビュ	ビョ
パ	ピ	プ	ペ	ポ		ピャ	ピュ	ピョ

Yookoso!

ようこそ

SECOND EDITION

Yookoso!
Continuing with
Contemporary Japanese

Yasu-Hiko Tohsaku

University of California, San Diego

よ
う
こ
そ

McGraw-Hill
College

Boston   Burr Ridge, IL   Dubuque, IA   Madison, WI   New York   San Francisco   St. Louis
Bangkok   Bogotá   Caracas   Lisbon   London   Madrid
Mexico City   Milan   New Delhi   Seoul   Singapore   Sydney   Taipei   Toronto

McGraw-Hill

A Division of The McGraw·Hill Companies

This is an ⟨EBI⟩ book.

Yookoso! Continuing with Contemporary Japanese

This book is printed on acid-free paper.

2 3 4 5 6 7 8 9 0 VNH VNH 9 0 3 2 1 0 9

ISBN 0-07-013697-1

Editor-in-Chief: Thalia Dorwick
Senior sponsoring editor: Leslie Hines
Development editors: Peggy Potter and Patricia Murray
Senior marketing manager: Karen Black
Project manager: Natalie Durbin
Production supervisor: Pam Augspurger
Designer: Adriane Bosworth
Cover designer: Francis Owens
Cover art by: Sally Vitsky
Illustrators: Akiko Shurtleff and Rick Hackney
Photo researcher: Diane Austin
Compositor: Interactive Composition Corporation
Typeface: Shinsei kaisho
Printer: Von Hoffmann

Library of Congress Cataloguing-in-Publication Data

Tohsaku, Yasuhiko.
    Yookoso!   : continuing with contemporary Japanese / Yasu-Hiko
Tohsaku. — 2nd. ed.
      p.   cm.
    ISBN 0-07-013697-1 (alk. paper)
    1. Japanese language—Textbooks for foreign speakers—English.
2. College readers.   I. Title.
PL539.5.E5T641999b
495.682'421—dc21   98-55103
                                                         CIP

http://www.mhhe.com

 Contents

Topics / Vocabulary	Grammar

Culture Notes

Reading and Writing

Skills Practice

Topics / Vocabulary	Grammar

Topics / Vocabulary	Grammar

Culture Notes	Reading and Writing	Skills Practice

Preface

Welcome to the Second Edition of ***Yookoso!* Continuing with Contemporary Japanese.** This is Book 2 in a complete package of instructional materials for beginning and intermediate Japanese. When the first edition of ***Yookoso!*** was published five years ago, the response was so overwhelming that we knew we had something special. The program struck a chord with instructors around the world who were looking for a text that matched what they were doing in the classroom. ***Yookoso!*** was the first Japanese series to integrate the teaching of all four language skills (listening, speaking, reading, writing) and to promote interaction in the classroom.

The ***Yookoso!*** approach has been used by thousands of beginning and intermediate Japanese students. ***Yookoso!*** integrates grammar in a more useful and flexible way to accommodate various approaches to language teaching and different learning styles. In our experience, students' proficiency in Japanese develops better and faster when grammar is used as a tool for developing language proficiency rather than as the focal point of learning.

Changes in the Second Edition

In responding to feedback about the first edition of ***Yookoso!***, our goal has been to make suggested changes that will enhance instruction, while at the same time retaining the key features that were praised by reviewers and that set ***Yookoso!*** apart from other beginning and intermediate-level Japanese programs. The visual *Guided Tour Through **Yookoso!*** explains all major features, some of which are new.

Enhancements to the Second Edition of Book 2 include the following:

- The text has been streamlined by reducing slightly the amount of content with no loss in the number of vocabulary and grammar topics and activities.
- The presentation of vocabulary and grammar has been reorganized so that related vocabulary and grammar are grouped together in sections. Each chapter now has three such Vocabulary and Grammar sections.
- Certain oral activities now appear after the grammar explanations to which they are related. Students and instructors will find grammar-related oral activities in a logical sequence.
- Some grammar points have been revised to provide more clarity.
- Some oral and written activities have been either revised or replaced in order to make them more accessible to students.

- Many cultural notes have been updated.
- A list of functional objectives appears at the beginning of every chapter. A similar checklist appears at the end of each chapter so students can check their progress.
- Chapter vocabulary lists and **kanji** lists have been moved to the end of each chapter and now follow the Language Skills section of Reading and Writing, Functions and Situations, and Listening Comprehension.
- The first edition's review chapters, which appeared only twice in the book, have been replaced by a two-page review section following each chapter.
- The font size for Japanese characters has been increased for easier readability.
- Exciting new ancillaries have been added to the program. They include new CD-ROMs and a Web Site (see "Program Components," below, for a description of all the ancillaries).

Objectives of the *Yookoso!* Program

- To teach the listening skills needed to understand basic everyday conversations
- To teach the oral skills needed to express oneself in a variety of everyday situations in Japanese
- To teach skimming, scanning, and intensive reading skills
- To teach basic writing skills, including descriptions and some functional writing tasks, such as letter writing
- To provide grammar explanations that help students acquire functional skills more readily
- To provide sociocultural information useful to beginning and intermediate-level Japanese language students

Methodology

Yookoso! was developed based on the results of recent research into second language acquisition and language pedagogy. All activities and exercises have been designed so that students develop proficiency in Japanese rather than simply acquiring grammatical knowledge.

- The main purpose of *Yookoso!* is to teach students how to use Japanese in real-life situations for different communicative purposes. Since activities involving interaction promote communicative abilities, *Yookoso!* includes a variety of activities that serve as a starting point for communicative interaction in the classroom.
- Current research has shown that the role of explicit grammar instruction in language learning is less important than previously believed. The study of

grammar is neither a sufficient nor a necessary condition for learning to communicate, and it is best learned through self-study outside of class. For this reason, grammar is presented in simple terms and via charts whenever possible. Easily understood explanations and abundant examples make it possible for students to study grammar on their own. Thus, instructors can devote precious class time to more meaningful communicative, interactive activities.

- The *Yookoso!* approach to orthography expects students to master the reading and writing of **hiragana** and **katakana** while working with Book 1. Throughout the text, **hurigana** accompany a **kanji** in the chapter in which it is first presented and in the following two chapters. Thereafter, as a general rule, no **hurigana** are provided for that **kanji.** The materials in the grammar exercises also follow this rule of thumb, but students need not use **kanji** that have not yet been presented for active learning, and they may write these words in **hiragana.**

- In each chapter, all activities are related to the main theme, and students can practice listening, speaking, reading, and writing about this theme in an integrated way.

- Topics and contents in the textbook have been selected for their relevance to the life and interests of college students. Topically based organization presents meaningful contexts for language learning and raises students' motivation for learning the language.

- For successful language acquisition, learners must be exposed to meaningful input. Activities throughout the text are designed to encourage instructors and students to engage in meaningful interactions.

- The acquisition of vocabulary is of great importance for achieving proficiency, and intermediate students need to expand their vocabularies beyond the comfortable elementary level. For this reason, a relatively large number of vocabulary items is presented throughout the text.

- Language acquisition takes place when learners attempt to comprehend a conveyed message. Also, students must be able to comprehend before they can produce language of their own. Priority is given to the development of comprehension abilities over production abilities. In order to facilitate students' language acquisition, the activities are sequenced from comprehension activities to simple production activities to creative, personalized production activities.

- Reintroduction of vocabulary, grammar, and language functions at regular intervals facilitates the development of students' proficiency. The cyclical organization of this textbook helps students review materials consistently and repeatedly.

- Group work encourages interaction and communication. For this reason, *Yookoso!* includes a variety of pair work, small-group work, and interviews, during which students can practice using Japanese in a stress-free, non-threatening atmosphere.

Guided Tour Through *Yookoso!* Book 2

Organization of the Textbook

Do You Remember?

Yookoso!: Continuing with Contemporary Japanese, Second Edition, (Book 2 of *Yookoso!*), begins with a comprehensive review chapter called Do You Remember? The activities of this introductory chapter provide an enjoyable but thorough reintroduction to spoken and written Japanese. Do You Remember! provides a handy mid-course review going all the way back to the beginning.

CHAPTERS 1-7

The opening page of each chapter lists the functional goals of the chapter and contains a photo related to the theme of the chapter. This can be used as a starting point for oral activities or class discussion.

1. Vocabulary and Oral Activities is intended for vocabulary building and oral communication practice in the classroom. Activities in this section are designed so that students can build up their knowledge of vocabulary and practice using it in natural communicative situations in an integrated fashion.

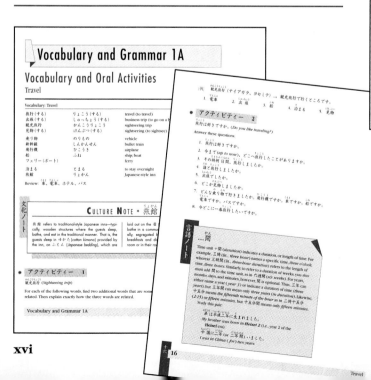

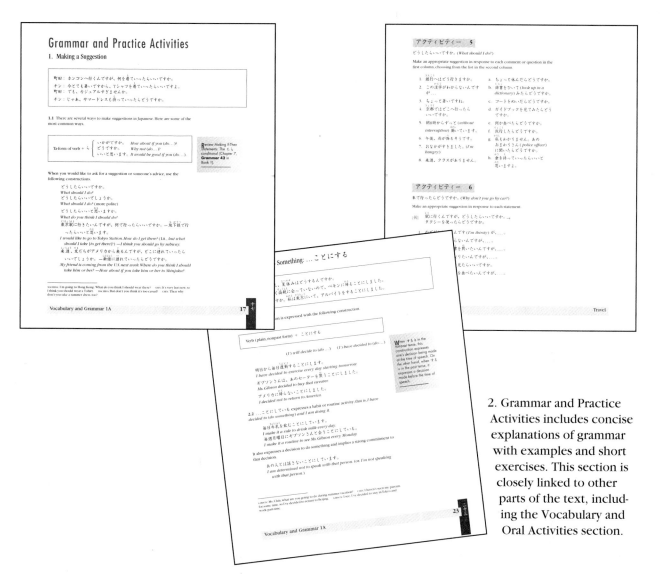

2. Grammar and Practice Activities includes concise explanations of grammar with examples and short exercises. This section is closely linked to other parts of the text, including the Vocabulary and Oral Activities section.

The sequencing of Vocabulary and Oral Activities directly before related Grammar and Practice Activities makes it possible to use *Yookoso!* in linear fashion.

The Language Skills part of each chapter includes instruction and practice with reading, writing, speaking, and listening.

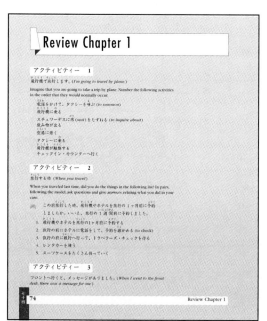

A two-page Review follows each chapter. Each review includes oral and written activities that combine, recycle, and review vocabulary, grammar, and language functions presented in the preceding chapter.

CULTURE

Culture notes provide information on Japanese culture that is important or pertinent for understanding vocabulary and facilitating oral or written activities.

Some of the marginal notes offer sociolinguistic information, and many language notes provide linguistic information that can help students use the language more effectively and communicate smoothly in a variety of real-life situations.

…泊 is a counter for overnight stays. 三泊 means *three overnight stays*, and 一泊する means *to stay over one night*. 泊 has different pronunciations depending on what number precedes it.

言語ノート

持っていく versus 持ってくる

In Japanese, *to take (things)* and *to bring (things)* are expressed with the te-form of 持つ (*to hold, to have*) followed by 行く and 来る, respectively. It may help to remember the literal meaning: 持って行く means *to go holding*, that is, *to take*.

プレゼントにネクタイを持って行きました。
I took a necktie as a gift.
高田さんはすしを持って来ました。
Mr. Takada brought sushi.

Realia, photos, and line drawings may serve as a starting point for oral and written activities, and all are intended to expose students to real culture.

A cast of characters appears throughout the text. The main characters are foreign students who are studying Japanese language and culture at the University of Tokyo. These people reappear in dialogues, grammar examples, reading materials, and listening comprehension activities. The characters are meant to illustrate the social relationships in Japanese culture that determine speech style and the use of honorifics. They also help students better understand the contexts in which the conversations take place.

John Kawamura Linda Brown Heather Gibson Toshiko Yokoi

LANGUAGE SKILLS

The series of activities in Vocabulary and Grammar begins with contextualized mechanical drills and proceeds through meaningful, communicative exercises to creative, free-answer sequences. This enables students to begin with the basics and move gradually on to more thoughtful communication as they gain skill and confidence with the vocabulary and grammar being learned.

Many language notes present brief information on grammar that is helpful for conducting oral activities or understanding reading materials. Study hints provide advice about how to acquire language skills: how to learn vocabulary, kanji, verb conjugations, and so forth.

The Reading and Writing section contains two sets of reading materials and writing tasks.

- Reading selections are based on authentic materials such as magazine articles, personal messages, and advertisements. They are preceded by activities that facilitate students' comprehension and help develop good reading strategies. Post-reading activities are mostly comprehension-oriented; in some cases, students apply their reading skills to related materials.

- Writing exercises are extensions of the preceding reading activities. Students write a response to the content of the reading selection, write a similar passage on their own, or write about their own lives and ideas by using the chapter vocabulary and grammatical structures.

In the Language Functions and Situations section, students learn how to express themselves in specific real-life situations. They study dialogues that illustrate functional language and situations related to chapter themes, then practice interacting in role plays that engage them in real communication in meaningful contexts.

In the Listening Comprehension section, students practice comprehending the general content of conversations or narratives related to chapter themes. They receive training in listening for meaning and perform tasks based on their listening. The section is the basis for a variety of interactive oral activities in class. A cassette with the listening comprehension selections is part of the Audio Program; a transcript of the selections appears in the Instructor's Manual.

Program Components

Available to adopters *and* to students:

- *Main text.* (See "Organization of the Textbook," below.)
- *Workbook/Laboratory Manual to accompany* **Yookoso!: Continuing with Contemporary Japanese.** The *Workbook/Laboratory Manual* is intended to (1) help students review the grammar, vocabulary, and language functions presented in the main text and (2) practice writing hiragana, katakana, and kanji. There are three sections for each of the seven main chapters.

    1. *Listening Comprehension Activities* (coordinated with the *Audio Program*). The activities in this section develop listening comprehension through dialogues, interviews, and narratives. Pronunciation exercises are also included.
    2. *Kanji Practice and Exercises.* This section consists of a list of newly introduced **kanji,** including the pronunciations, meanings, examples of use, and stroke order, followed by exercises. This section also includes some interesting and useful notes about **kanji** and the writing systems of Japanese (for example, the radicals, the principles of stroke order). A feature in Book 2 of the Workbook/Laboratory Manual is *Kanji in Everyday Life,* a set of context-based exercises that teach intelligent guessing and other skills necessary for reading unfamiliar materials.
    3. *Writing Activities.* This section provides additional vocabulary and grammar practice through a variety of activities, from controlled, mechanical exercises to creative, free-response activities. Several activities in this section are realia-based, and many of them can also be used for speaking practice.

- *Audio Program to accompany* **Yookoso!: Continuing with Contemporary Japanese.** Corresponding to the laboratory portion of the *Workbook/Laboratory Manual,* the *Audio Program* contains all of the recorded dialogues from the main text as well as additional dialogues and aural texts for reviewing vocabulary, passages for extensive and intensive listening practice, and guided pronunciation practice.
- *CD-ROM.* A new CD-ROM, developed for each level of the **Yookoso!** program, provides students with a wealth of additional dialogues, vocabulary and grammar practice, cultural readings, and video clips.
- *Web site.* This new web site, developed exclusively for **Yookoso!**, allows students to explore topics related to the chapter themes by jumping from **http://www.mhhe.com/japanese** into selected Japanese web sites as well as to do on-line activities that practice the vocabulary and structures of each chapter.

Available to adopters only:

- *Instructor's Manual/Testing Program/Tapescript.* Revised for ***Yookoso!: An Invitation to Contemporary Japanese,*** Second Edition, this practical guide includes a general introduction to the communicative approach to language teaching and learning, general guidelines for using the textbook, a sample lesson plan and syllabus, sample semester and quarter schedules, suggestions for using and expanding the text materials, additional exercises, models for vocabulary introduction and expansion, other teaching hints and techniques, answer key for student text activities, and transcript for the Listening Comprehension section of each chapter. A transcript of the listening comprehension activities from the *Audio Program* and an answer key for the Workbook/Laboratory Manual are also included.
- *Video to accompany **Yookoso!*** This 30-minute video includes some of the situations and dialogues presented in the textbook and others related to chapter topics. The majority of segments were filmed in Japan and include a variety of interactions in natural settings.

Acknowledgments

Many people have contributed to the process of developing the second edition of *Yookoso!* First of all, I would like to thank the following language-teaching professionals and friends whose valuable suggestions and feedback contributed to the preparation of this revised edition. The appearance of their names does not necessarily constitute the endorsement of this textbook or its pedagogical approach.

Tom Abbott
  (*California State University, Monterey Bay*)
Mark Blum
  (*Florida Atlantic University*)
Yoko Collier-Sanuki
  (*University of British Columbia*)
Tamaye Csyionie
  (*Scottsdale Community College*)
Carl Falsgraf
  (*University of Oregon*)
Fumiko Foard
  (*Arizona State University*)
Yumiko Guajardo
  (*U.S. Air Force Academicy*)
Suzuko Hamasaki
  (*University of California, Irvine*)

Jean Hanna
  (*Windward Community College*)
Kyoko Hijirida
  (*University of Hawaii at Manoa*)
Yasuko Ito-Watt
  (*Indiana University*)
Akiko Kowano Jones
  (*Bowling Green State University*)
Akiko Kakutani
  (*Earlham College*)
Akiko Kamo
  (*Episcopal School, Baton Rouge, Louisiana*)
Hiroko Kataoka
  (*California State University, Long Beach/Japana Foundation and Language Center*)

Toshiko Kishimoto
(*Clemson University*)
Ryuko Kubota
(*University of North Carolina*)
Junko Kumamoto-Healey
(*University of Melbourne*)
Toshiyumi Kumashiro
(*University of California, Irvine*)
Yoshiko Kuno
(*Colorado State University*)
Keiji Matsumoto
(*California State University at Fullerton*)
Yukari McCagg
(*American School in Japan*)
Takiko Morimoto
(*El Camino College*)
Akemi Morioka
(*University of California, Irvine*)
Mutsuko Motoyama
(*Illinois Wesleyan University*)
Hiromi Muranaka
(*University of Western Sydney, Nepean*)
Mariko Nakade-Marceau
(*Franklin and Marshall College*)
Makoto Nishikawa
(*University of Alaska at Anchorage*)
Emi Ochiai Ahn
(*Mesa Community College*)
Kaoru Ohta
(*University of Washington*)
Toyoko Okawa
(*Punaho School, Honolulu*)

Tamae Prindle
(*Colby College*)
Yoko Pusavat
(*California State University, Long Beach*)
Christopher M. Rich
(*Northern Arizona University*)
Eunhee C. Roth
(*University of Delaware*)
Kyoko Saegusa
(*University of Colorado, Boulder*)
Yoshiko Saito
(*California State University, Monterey Bay*)
Yosei Sugawara
(*Pima Community College*)
Yasuko Takata
(*Ohio University*)
Naoki Takei
(*Tokyo Institute of Technology*)
Yuzuru Takigawa
(*University of Minnesota in Akita, Japan*)
Noriko Vergel
(*American School in Japan*)
Yuko Yamada
(*Nebraska Weslyan University*)
Hilofumi Yamamoto
(*University of Tsukuba*)
Toshiko Yokota
(*University of California, Irvine*)

Student feedback played a crucial role for the revision, too. My thanks go to all the students who sent me their comments while using the first edition.

I also would like to express my appreciation to many people at McGraw-Hill and their associates for their excellent work on this complicated project, their patience, and perseverance: Peggy Potter, Patricia Murray, Karen Sandness, Karen Judd, Francis Owens, Margaret Metz, Natalie Durbin, Pam Augspurger, Sally Vitsky, Rick Hackney, Chris de Heer, Cristene Burr, Bill Glass, and Leslie Hines. In particular, I owe much to Gregory Trauth for his tireless work and insightful ideas for this project. Special thanks are due to Chieko Altherr, who checked the linguistic accuracy and cultural authenticity of the text.

This project could not have been completed without the generous support, assistance, and encouragement of the people at the University of California, San Diego: all of my colleagues at the Graduate School of International Relations and Pacific Studies, especially, Peter Gourevitch and Miles Kahler, Sherman George, Ron Quilan, Gary Hoffman, Hifumi Ito, Denise Kelliher, Masao Miyoshi, Christena Turner, Jennifer Schroeder, Linda Murphy, Masato Nishimura, Noriko Kameda, Yutaka Kunitake, Noriko Knickerbockers, and Mayumi Mochizuki. I especially thank my former and current assistants, Sheri Brusch and Alejandrina Quintero-McCluskey, without whose daily help and encouragement I could not have finished this project.

A word of warmest thanks is due to Hiroko Kataoka for her steadfast friendship, patient criticism, helpful advice, insightful suggestions, and constant encouragement, all of which were indispensable to me at various stages of the development of this text.

I would like to extend my deepest gratitude and appreciation to Thalia Dorwick, for her constant support for *Yookoso!*, her enthusiasm for and commitment to developing an innovative Japanese language text, her encouragement, generosity, patience, thoughtfulness, and care. Her insights, creativity, dedication, wisdom, and expertise have been a constant source of inspiration to me and have been my guiding light throughout this project.

I thank Umechiyo and Takechiyo for their unconditional affection and positive spirit.

A final simple but very sincere appreciation goes to my wife, Carol, for her inspiring love, spirit, understanding, patience, and support beyond the call of duty. I thank you for giving so much as well as putting up with me during the revision of *Yookoso!* This text is dedicated to Carol as well as to my parents, Morio and Ritsuko Tohsaku.

Yasu-Hiko Tohsaku
ytohsaku@ucsd.edu

Dear Student,

You probably already know that **Yookoso** means *welcome* in Japanese. I am delighted to welcome you to Book 2 of this program for learning contemporary Japanese. By the time you finish the program, you'll be able to communicate in Japanese even better than you do now if you take to heart the hints below.

- Your classroom is probably the only place you have to interact with other people in Japanese. Your instructor is your major resource and your classmates are your other contacts. Attend class regularly and make an effort to interact as much as possible with all of them.

- Keep up with daily assignments. They are essential if you are to be able to participate and learn in class.

- Use all of the supplementary materials that accompany the text. Use the Workbook/Laboratory Manual to review vocabulary and grammar in listening, speaking, reading, and writing, and to practice Kanji. Use the Audiotape, Videotape, and CD for listening and speaking practice and to develop a stronger cultural knowledge. Regularly check the *Yookoso!* home page (http://www.mhhe.com/japanese/yookoso.html) for study hints, additional activities, and cultural information.

- Don't force yourself to memorize all the vocabulary words for a chapter at the start. Learn and use vocabulary necessary to express yourself first. Then, since the acquisition of vocabulary is of great importance for achieving proficiency in language, learn as much as you can of the other vocabulary as well, to broaden your ability to express ideas.

- Before starting each chapter, review the learning objectives found on the opening page. At the end of each chapter, use the checklist on the last page to check you progress.

- Familiarize yourself with the organization of the text.

    The Characters: You will meet a cast of characters who will appear throughout the text. Some of them are students at the university and others are their neighbors and families.

    Vocabulary and Grammar: Every chapter has three sections that start by introducing and practicing new vocabulary and then present grammar explanations and activities that use the grammar in meaningful context with previously presented vocabulary.

    Language Skills: Once you have learned the grammar and vocabulary of the chapter, you can practice them as you strenghten your abilities with the four language skills. In Reading and Writing, you will learn to read for content, guess contextually, and understand the gist of what you read. Then you'll build on what you have read as you write. Language Functions and Situations help you develop your ability to cope with many daily contexts and situations through speaking. The activities in Listening Comprehension help you develop listening abilities for everyday contexts.

    Vocabulary and Kanji: At the end of each chapter is a list of vocabulary and Kanji (Chinese characters). Use this list as a reference for review, reading, and writing activities.

    Review Activities: These activities offer a final review of the chapter's vocabulary and grammar.

- Keep studying little by little every day; don't wait until just before a test. Language learning takes time and is a gradual process. If you work at it day by day, you will become a proficient user of Japanese.

Now, let's see what you remember.

Yasu-Hiko Tohsaku

About the Author

Yasu-Hiko Tohsaku is a Professor at the University of California, San Diego, where he is Director of the Language Program at the Graduate School of International Relations and Pacific Studies and Coordinator of the Undergraduate Japanese Language Program. He received his Ph.D. in Linguistics from the University of California, San Diego, in 1983. He is the author of numerous articles on second-language acquisition and Japanese-language pedagogy. In addition, he has been involved with the development of Japanese-language teaching videos, computer-assisted language-learning programs, and Web-based training programs for language teachers.

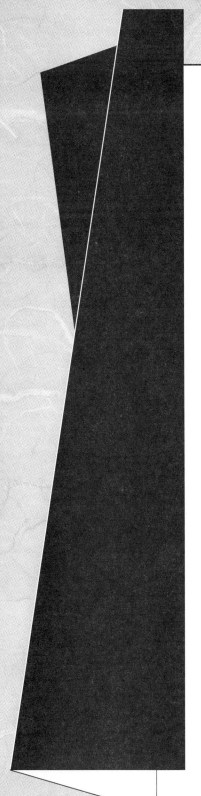

Do You Remember?

Before going on with Book 2 of *Yookoso!*, let's see how much you remember from Book 1.

アクティビティー　1

ご紹介（しょうかい）します。(*I'm going to introduce someone to you.*)

1. Your instructor will briefly describe two students, A and B. Fill in the following table with the information that your instructor gives.

Refer to Chapter 1, Book 1.

	(A) STUDENT A	(B) STUDENT B	(C) YOUR PARTNER
Name			
Age			
Birthplace			
Nationality			
School			
Grade (year)			
Major			
Courses currently taken			
Residence			
Telephone number			
Other information (hobbies, etc.)			

2. Work in pairs. Do not look at each other's charts, but compare the information you have written down with the information that your partner has written down by asking questions in Japanese.
3. Now ask your partner questions about himself/herself in Japanese and fill in column C with the answers. (You may fill in the table in English.)
4. If time permits, introduce your partner to the class in Japanese, basing your introduction on the information in column C.

Refer to Chapter 1, Book 1, for how to introduce friends.

アクティビティー　2

どこにありますか。(*Where is it?*)

1. Your instructor will describe the locations of nine places on the accompanying street map. Write in the appropriate lot numbers (e.g.,"22" for the coffee shop) on the following chart.

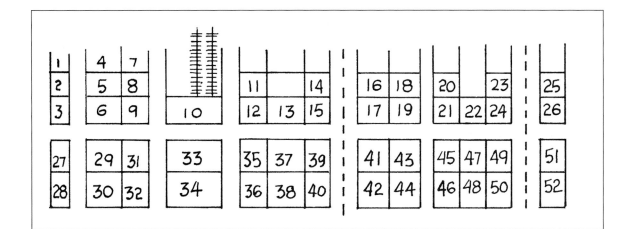

	PLACE	LOCATION
a.	喫茶店	
b.	図書館	
c.	スーパー	
d.	バス停	
e.	駅	
f.	デパート	
g.	映画館	
h.	ガソリンスタンド	
i.	ホテル	

2. Work in pairs. Without looking at each other's maps, check the accuracy of your answers by asking each other how to get from one location to another on the map.

3. At which of the places on the map do you think you would hear the following comments or questions?

a. 今日はバナナが安いですよ。

b. シングル・ルームはありますか。

c. アイスコーヒーをお願いします。

d. タイヤをチェックしてください。

e. 次のバスは駅まで行きますか。

f. ブラウスは何階ですか。

g. 東京行きの電車は何時ですか。

h. 暗くなりました。始まりますよ。

i. ヘミングウェイの本を読みたいんですが、...

アクティビティー 3

週末の予定 (*Weekend plans*)

1. Working in pairs, practice the following scenario.

STUDENT 1	STUDENT 2
Invite your partner to see a movie on Friday afternoon or evening.	Politely turn down the invitation by explaining why you cannot come.
Find out if your partner plans to do anything on Saturday or Sunday.	Explain what you will be doing on both days. But tell your partner that you are free on Saturday evening.
Invite your partner to a party at your home on Saturday evening. Tell him or her who is coming to the party.	Accept your partner's invitation. Ask what time everyone is arriving at the party.
Tell your partner what time everyone is coming.	Thank your partner. Tell him or her that you will see each other on Saturday evening.

Reverse roles, and practice a conversation in which Student 1 invites Student 2 to some other event or activity.

2. You have invited a couple of classmates to dinner at your house. One of them has asked you to write down the directions to your house and leave them in his or her campus mailbox. Write a note that includes the following instructions.

Get off at JR Higashiyama Station. Go out the east exit. There is a bank across from the exit; go straight down the street that runs alongside the bank. Turn right at the second traffic light (about 250 meters from the bank to the second traffic light). Turn left at the first light (about 100 meters from the previous light). Walk straight for 50 meters. My house is on the right-hand side next to a coffee shop. It has a red roof and a large gate. If you call me from Higashiyama Station, I can meet you there.

アクティビティー 4

世界各地のお天気 (*Weather all over the world*)

Following are transcripts of TV weather reports from Japanese-language radio programs in London, Honolulu, Tokyo, and Sydney. Read them, and fill in the following table.

Refer to Chapter 4, Book 1.

1. ...
   朝から晴れていて、いいお天気ですが、ちょっと寒いです。今、気温はマイナス２度です。私は今、駅のホームにいますが、神社や、お寺にお参りに行く人でいっぱいです。着物を着た女性がいますから、ちょっと...

   いっぱい *full*

2. ...
   12月に入っていい天気が続いていましたが、今日はちょっと雨が降っています。今日の最高気温は25度で、暖かい一日でしょう。私のいるところからオペラハウスが見えますが、...

   最高気温 *highest temperature*

3. ...
   今の気温はマイナス1度。くもりです。えー、私は今テムズ川のそばにいますが、霧が濃くて、何も見えません。ヒースロー空港は朝から閉まっています。

   濃い *thick, dense /* 空港 *airport*

4. ...
   現在、気温は30度で、とても暑いです。いい天気で雲一つありません。ワイキキ・ビーチは、人でいっぱいです。

PLACE	WEATHER	TEMPERATURE
London		
Honolulu		
Tokyo		
Sydney		

アクティビティー 5

趣味・余暇についてインタビューしましょう。(*Let's do an interview about hobbies and free time.*)

Refer to Chapter 5, Book 1.

Work in pairs. One of you is doing research on how people spend their leisure time. Interview your partner using the following survey sheet. Skip any questions that are not applicable to your partner's situation, and go on to the next relevant question. Report the survey results to the class.

1. 趣味
   a. 趣味はありますか。どんな趣味ですか。
   b. その趣味はいつから始めましたか。
   c. その趣味に一週間に何時間ぐらい、時間を使いますか。
   d. その趣味にどれくらいお金を使いますか。
   e. それを趣味としているのは、なぜですか。
   f. (Add your own question) _____
      _____

2. 音楽
   a. 音楽は好きですか。
   b. どんな音楽が好きですか。
   c. 好きな歌手は誰ですか。
   d. どんな音楽が嫌いですか。なぜですか。
   e. コンサートによく行きますか。
   f. 最近、CDや、テープを買いましたか。
   g. CDや、テープに一ヵ月いくらぐらい使いますか。
   h. 何か楽器が演奏できますか。
   i. (Add your own question) _____
      _____

3. テレビ
   映画
   a. テレビをよく見ますか。
   b. 先週は何時間くらいテレビを見ましたか。
   c. どんな番組を見ますか。
   d. 嫌いな番組はありますか。
   e. 映画をよく見ますか。
   f. 最近、どんな映画を見ましたか。
   g. どんな映画が好きですか。
   h. 好きな俳優 (actor) は誰ですか。
   i. (Add your own question) _____
      _____

4. 読書
   a. 最近、どんな本や雑誌を読みましたか。
   b. 先月一ヵ月で、何冊 本を読みましたか。
   c. どんな本を読みましたか。
   d. どんな本が好きですか。
   e. 好きな作家は誰ですか。
   f. 一週間に何時間くらい、本を読みますか。
   g. (Add your own question) _____
      _____

After a class discussion on the survey results, write a short paragraph about the overall class results for one section of the survey.

アクティビティー　6

いろいろな家庭 (*Many kinds of households*)

Each of the following paragraphs describes an individual or family. Match each paragraph with the accompanying drawing of the household that it describes.

efer to Chapter 5, Book 1.

1. 伊藤武夫さんとひとみさん御夫妻は、結婚してまだ9ヵ月です。子供はまだいませんが、あと3ヵ月で子供が生まれます。武夫さんは男の子をほしがっていますが、ひとみさんは女の子をほしがっています。

2. 吉村利夫君の家族は両親とお兄さんとお姉さんと妹さんと弟さんです。利夫君は弟さんと同じ部屋で寝ていますが、早く自分一人の部屋がほしいと言っています。

   自分一人の *one's own*

3. 岡崎邦年さんと鈴木まり子さんはまだ結婚していませんが、いっしょに暮らしています。これは日本では「同棲」といいます。岡崎さんは、来年結婚したいと思っていますが、鈴木さんはまだ結婚したくありません。

   同棲 (する) *unmarried couples living together (to live together)*

4. 竹村里志さんと洋子さんの御夫妻は結婚して10年になります。8歳の息子さんと、6歳と3歳の娘さんがいます。家が小さいので、もう子供は作らないつもりです。

5. 池田荘太郎さんと恵子さんは結婚して42年になります。お孫さんが5人います。時々、お孫さんが遊びに来ます。

6. 花村節子さんは離婚して、お嬢さんの舞さんと二人で住んでいます。前の御主人と会うことはもうありません。

   離婚 (する) *(to get a) divorce*

7. 花村孝さんは離婚して、一人で暮らしています。お嬢さんは前の奥さんといっしょに住んでいますが、二人に会うことはもうありません。寂しい時はパチンコ屋に行きます。

   寂しい *lonely*

8. 河原はなさんは今年76歳です。御主人は去年亡くなりました。今は息子さん御夫婦と三人のお孫さんといっしょに住んでいます。

   亡くなる *to die*

七

7

アクティビティー　7

<ruby>食<rt>た</rt></ruby>べ<ruby>物<rt>もの</rt></ruby> (Food)

In each of the following groups, one word does not belong to the same category as the others. Identify it, and tell why it is different. Then, if you can, add one more word that *does* belong to the category.

Refer to Chapter 6, Book 1.

1. いか、まぐろ、たこ、<ruby>魚<rt>さかな</rt></ruby>、マトン
2. ぶどう、みかん、りんご、ジュース、メロン、レモン
3. ワイン、<ruby>水<rt>みず</rt></ruby>、コーヒー、<ruby>紅茶<rt>こうちゃ</rt></ruby>、ミルク
4. <ruby>皿<rt>さら</rt></ruby>、ナイフ、フォーク、コップ、<ruby>冷蔵庫<rt>れいぞうこ</rt></ruby>、スプーン
5. <ruby>甘<rt>あま</rt></ruby>い、<ruby>塩<rt>しお</rt></ruby>、<ruby>辛<rt>から</rt></ruby>い、まずい、おいしい
6. <ruby>味噌汁<rt>みそしる</rt></ruby>、すきやき、そば、<ruby>卵<rt>たまご</rt></ruby>、てんぷら
7. <ruby>調味料<rt>ちょうみりょう</rt></ruby>、<ruby>醤油<rt>しょうゆ</rt></ruby>、<ruby>砂糖<rt>さとう</rt></ruby>、<ruby>胡麻<rt>ごま</rt></ruby>、<ruby>夕食<rt>ゆうしょく</rt></ruby>
8. <ruby>肉屋<rt>にくや</rt></ruby>、<ruby>八百屋<rt>やおや</rt></ruby>、<ruby>家具屋<rt>かぐや</rt></ruby>、<ruby>魚屋<rt>さかなや</rt></ruby>、<ruby>酒屋<rt>さかや</rt></ruby>

アクティビティー　8

レストランで (*At a restaurant*)

1. Work in pairs. Practice ordering the items on the following menu by taking turns being the server and the customer.

オードブル・前菜サラダ・スープ
Appetizers/Soups

スモーク名古屋コーチンのオニオンサラダ……	¥	940
帆立貝のチーズ焼き ………………………	¥	720
チーズとり合わせ …………………………	¥	740
季節野菜のマリネ …………………………	¥	650
ローストビーフサラダ ……………………	¥	850
シーフードサラダ …………………………	¥	850
シェフサラダ ………………………………	¥	850
ポタージュ …………………………………	¥	480

サンドウィッチ
Sandwiches

ミックスサンドウィッチ …………………	¥	850
クロワッサンサンドウィッチ ……………	¥	850
コールドローストビーフサンドウィッチ …………	¥	850
フレンチバケットサンドウィッチ ………………	¥	850

仔牛肉と茄子のスパゲッティ

小海老のトマト風味スパゲッティ

‥ スパゲッティセット ¥1,310

お好みのスパゲッティ
プティサラダ
コーヒー または 紅茶

ピラフ・カレー・オムライス
Pilaff/Curries/Omelette Rice

ミックスピラフ サラダ添 …………………	¥	980
シーフードパエリア サラダ添 ……………	¥	980
ビーフカレー サラダ添 ……………………	¥	980
シーフードカレー サラダ添 ………………	¥	980
オムライス パラドール風 サラダ添 ………	¥	980

‥ サンドウィッチセット ¥1,180
（コーヒー または 紅茶付）

パスタ料理
Pastas

海の幸のスパゲッティ ……………………	¥	980
仔牛肉と茄子のスパゲッティ ……………	¥	980
森のきのこスパゲッティ …………………	¥	980
小海老のトマト風味スパゲッティ …………	¥	980
ツナとベーコンのスパゲッティ …………	¥	980

2. As seen in the accompanying illustration, Heather Gibson and Masao Hayashi are talking to a waiter at a restaurant. Complete the following dialogues, giving one line each to Gibson, Hayashi, and the waiter.

Refer to Book 1, Chapter 6, for expressions to use when dining out.

[例]れい
　A: このスープ、ちょっとぬるいんですが、...
　B: どうもすみません。
　C: ええ、僕ぼくのスープもちょっとぬるいです。

a.　A: _____
　B: 御注文ごちゅうもんは。
　A: _____
　C: _____

b.　A: _____
　B: _____
　C: コーヒーをお願ねがいします。

c.　A: どんなデザートがありますか。
　B: _____
　C: _____
　A: _____

d.　A: _____
　B: _____
　C: あのテーブルの人ひとたちがちょっとうるさいんですが ...

アクティビティー　9

店みせ (*Shops and stores*)

Following the example, tell where you can buy the items listed. Then name more items that are available at the same store.

Refer to Chapter 7, Book 1.

[例]れい　フレンチ·ロール、クロワッサン、サンドイッチ →
　　　パン屋やで買かえます。サワドーブレッドも買かえます。

1. ソファー、椅子いす、テーブル
2. ハイヒール、ブーツ、サンダル
3. アスピリン、風邪薬かぜぐすり、目薬めぐすり
4. スイートピー、カーネーション、チューリップ
5. ペン、ノート、カレンダー
6. テレビ、冷蔵庫れいぞうこ、ステレオ

7. バービー人形、ビデオ·ゲーム、プラモデル

8. ブラウス、スカート、スカーフ

アクティビティー 10

買い物 (*Shopping*)

Work in pairs, but do not look at each other's prepared written materials. Student 1 should write a very specific shopping list of four common items that are available in stationery stores: pens, pencils, notebooks, paper, envelopes, and so on, specifying the size, color, price range, and perhaps brand name of the items.

Student 2 should prepare an inventory list of the same types of items, including a wide variety of sizes, colors, prices, and brand names. When you have completed your lists, Student 1 should play the part of a customer, asking whether Student 2 has the desired items. Student 2 should answer based on the inventory list that he or she has written. Student 1 should come to a decision about what to purchase and then buy the items.

アクティビティー 11

服 (*Clothing*)

What would you wear on the following occasions? Or what did you wear on the following occasions in the past? Describe your clothing as shown in the example.

Refer to Chapter 7, Book 1.

[例] 夏、海へ行く時
　　去年の夏、家のそばの海に毎日行きました。その時はいつも半袖のTシャツを着て、ショートパンツをはいていました。むぎわら帽子 (*straw hat*) をかぶって、サングラスもかけました。時々、サンダルをはきましたが、ほとんど裸足 (*barefoot*) でした。

1. 結婚式 (*wedding ceremony*) に行く時
2. 仕事の面接 (*job interview*) の時
3. スキーに行く時
4. 雨が降って寒い時

アクティビティー 12

夏期クラスを取りたいのですが、... (*I would like to take a summer course,...*)

1. Work in pairs. One of you has been awarded a fellowship to take a summer course (夏期クラス) in the Japanese language in Japan this summer. (Congratulations!) You have just found that Saitama College

offers a good Japanese course, so you phone the college and obtain information about the course. The other student plays the role of the academic coordinator of Saitama College's Japanese course. The academic coordinator can refer to the English brochure shown here, making up additional details if necessary.

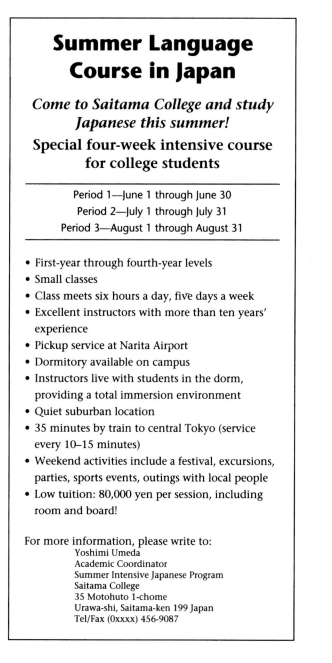

Summer Language Course in Japan

Come to Saitama College and study Japanese this summer!

Special four-week intensive course for college students

Period 1—June 1 through June 30
Period 2—July 1 through July 31
Period 3—August 1 through August 31

- First-year through fourth-year levels
- Small classes
- Class meets six hours a day, five days a week
- Excellent instructors with more than ten years' experience
- Pickup service at Narita Airport
- Dormitory available on campus
- Instructors live with students in the dorm, providing a total immersion environment
- Quiet suburban location
- 35 minutes by train to central Tokyo (service every 10–15 minutes)
- Weekend activities include a festival, excursions, parties, sports events, outings with local people
- Low tuition: 80,000 yen per session, including room and board!

For more information, please write to:
Yoshimi Umeda
Academic Coordinator
Summer Intensive Japanese Program
Saitama College
35 Motohuto 1-chome
Urawa-shi, Saitama-ken 199 Japan
Tel/Fax (0xxxx) 456-9087

2. Saitama College has sent you a brochure and an application form. After reading the brochure, you decide to go there for your summer course in Japanese. Fill in the following application form in Japanese.

Useful Vocabulary: 志願者 *applicant,* 出願理由 *reason for applying,*
氏名 *full name,* 現在 *present, current,* 学習 *study, learning,*
推薦状 *recommendation,* 国籍 *nationality,* 厳封のうえ *sealed,*
その他 *other,* 提出（する）*submission (to submit),* 能力 *ability*

埼玉学院夏期日本語コースの入学願書

志願者氏名	生年月日：　　　年　　　月　　　日
	性別　　　　　　男・女

住所
電話番号：（　　　　　　）

国籍	高校卒業：　　　　　年　　　月
日本語の学習期間	大学：
高校：　　　　　　年間	住所：
大学：　　　　　　年間	
その他：	
日本語能力：	現在の日本語の先生または出身校の教員からの推薦状を厳封の上、提出すること
会話：	
漢字：	推薦者の氏名：
出願理由：	住所：
	電話番号：

志願者のサイン：＿＿＿＿＿＿＿＿＿＿＿＿＿＿＿　　年　　　月　　　日

1

第
一
章

旅
行
りょこう

Travel

新幹線のホーム
しんかんせん

Objectives

In this lesson, you are going to

- Talk about travel, transportation, and sightseeing
- Talk about travel planning and travel schedules
- Learn to make a suggestion
- Learn to say whether something occurred before or after
- Learn to use と conditionals
- Learn to use the command form of verbs
- Learn to express prohibition and obligation
- Learn to scan travel information and travel guides
- Learn to make a hotel reservation
- Learn to buy a train ticket

Vocabulary and Grammar 1A

Vocabulary and Oral Activities
Travel

Vocabulary: Travel

旅行(する)	りょこう(する)	travel (to travel)
出張(する)	しゅっちょう(する)	business trip (to go on a business trip)
観光旅行	かんこうりょこう	sightseeing trip
見物(する)	けんぶつ(する)	sightseeing (to sightsee)
乗り物	のりもの	vehicle
新幹線	しんかんせん	bullet train
飛行機	ひこうき	airplane
船	ふね	ship; boat
フェリー(ボート)		ferry
泊まる	とまる	to stay overnight
旅館	りょかん	Japanese-style inn

Review: 車、電車、ホテル、バス
くるま でんしゃ

文化ノート

CULTURE NOTE • 旅館
りょかん

旅館 refers to traditional-style Japanese inns—typically, wooden structures where the guests sleep, bathe, and eat in the traditional manner. That is, the guests sleep in ゆかた (*cotton kimono*) provided by the inn, on ふとん (*Japanese bedding*), which are laid out on the 畳 [たたみ] (*reed-mat flooring*); they bathe in a communal bath (usually two baths, actually, segregated by sex), and they eat Japanese breakfasts and dinners served in a central dining room or in their rooms.

❋ アクティビティー　1

かんこうりょこう
観光旅行 (*Sightseeing trip*)

For each of the following words, find two additional words that are somehow related. Then explain exactly how the three words are related.

[例]　観光旅行（ナイアガラ、ヨセミテ）→　観光旅行で行くところです。

1. 電車　　　2. 出張　　　3. 船　　　4. 泊まる　　　5. 見物

❋　アクティビティー　2

旅行は好きですか。(*Do you like traveling?*)

Answer these questions.

1. 旅行は好きですか。
2. 今まで(*up to now*)、どこへ旅行したことがありますか。
3. その時何日間、旅行しましたか。
4. 誰と旅行しましたか。
5. 出張でしたか。
6. どこか見物しましたか。
7. どんな乗り物で行きましたか。飛行機ですか。車ですか。船ですか。
　　電車ですか。バスですか。
8. 今どこに一番旅行したいですか。

言語ノート

...間

Time unit ＋間 (*duration*) indicates a duration, or length of time. For example, 三時 (lit., *three hour*) names a specific time, *three o'clock,* whereas 三時間 (lit., *three-hour duration*) refers to the length of time, *three hours.* Similarly, to refer to a duration of weeks, you also must add 間 to the time unit, as in 六週間 (*six weeks*). For years, months, days, and minutes, however, 間 is optional. Thus, 三年 can either name a year (*year 3*) or indicate a duration of time (*three years*), but 三年間 can mean only *three years (in duration)*. Likewise, 十五分 means *the fifteenth minute of the hour* as in 二時十五分 (*2:15*) or *fifteen minutes,* but 十五分間 means only *fifteen minutes.*

　　Study this pair:

　　　弟は平成二年に生まれました。
　　*My brother was born in **Heisei 2** (i.e., year 2 of the*
　　　***Heisei** era).*
　　　中国に二年 (or 二年間) いました。
　　I was in China (for) two years.

Grammar and Practice Activities

1. Making a Suggestion

町田：ホンコンへ行くんですが、何を着ていったらいいですか。

チン：今とても暑いですから、Tシャツを着ていったらいいですよ。

町田：でも、カジュアルすぎませんか。

チン：じゃあ、サマードレスも持っていったらどうですか。

1.1 There are several ways to make suggestions in Japanese. Here are some of the most common ways.

Ta-form of verb + ら
- いかがですか。 *How about if you (do…)?*
- どうですか。 *Why not (do…)?*
- いいと思います。 *It would be good if you (do…).*

Review Making If-Then Statements: The たら conditional (Chapter 7, **Grammar 42** in Book 1).

When you would like to ask for a suggestion or someone's advice, use the following constructions.

どうしたらいいですか。
What should I do?
どうしたらいいでしょうか。
What should I do? (more polite)
どうしたらいいと思いますか。
What do you think I should do?
東京駅に行きたいんですが、何で行ったらいいですか。—地下鉄で行ったらいいと思います。
I would like to go to Tokyo Station. How do I get there? (Lit., but what should I take [to get there]?) —*I think you should go by subway.*
来週、友だちがアメリカから来るんですが、どこに連れていったらいいでしょうか。—新宿に連れていったらどうですか。
My friend is coming from the U.S. next week. Where do you think I should take him or her? —How about if you take him or her to Shinjuku?

MACHIDA: I'm going to Hong Kong. What do you think I should wear there?   CHIN: It's very hot now, so I think you should wear a T-shirt.   MACHIDA: But don't you think it's too casual?   CHIN: Then why don't you take a summer dress, too?

連れていく、連れてくる

To take someone and *to bring someone* are expressed with the te-form of 連れる (*to accompany*) plus いく and くる respectively. Thus, 連れていく means *to take someone* (lit., *to go, accompanying someone*), whereas 連れてくる means *to bring someone* (lit., *to come, accompanying someone*). Use 持っていく and 持ってくる only for inanimate objects.

> デパートに行くんだったら、私も連れていってください。
> *If you are going to the department store, please take me, too.*
> 今夜は高田さんを連れてきました。
> *I brought Mr. Takada along tonight.*

Don't use these verbs if the accompanied person is your social superior, because it would sound impolite to do so. In such a case, you should use 一緒に行く or 一緒に来る instead.

> 今日は先生と一緒に来ました。
> *Today I came with my professor.*

1.2 In colloquial speech, the endings of these constructions are often unexpressed. In these cases, the ends of the sentences are pronounced with a rising intonation.

> 明日のパーティー、何を着ていったらいい？ —赤いワンピースを着ていったら、どう？
> *What should I wear to the party tomorrow? —How about wearing (your) red dress?*
> この漢字が読めないんだけど... —町田さんに聞いてみたら？
> *I can't read this Chinese character ...(What should I do?) —How about asking Ms. Machida (to see if she can help you)?*

> ...だけど is a colloquial form of ...だけれども.

アクティビティー 3

ダイアログ：旅行したらどうですか。(*How about going on a trip?*)

山口：カワムラさん、来週は学校が休みなんでしょう？

カワムラ：ええ、24日まで休みなんです。

山口：じゃあ、京都へでも旅行したらどうですか。

カワムラ：ううん、それはいい考えですね。前から京都へ旅行したいと思っていたんです。

YAMAGUCHI: Mr. Kawamura, your school is closed for vacation next week, isn't it?   KAWAMURA: Yes, I am off until the twenty-fourth.   YAMAGUCHI: Then why don't you take a trip to Kyoto or somewhere like that?   KAWAMURA: Oh, that's a good idea. I've wanted to take a trip to Kyoto for some time (lit., *from before*).

Practice the preceding dialogue, substituting the following phrases (altered as appropriate) for the underlined portions.

1. 東京見物でもする
2. 上野の美術館にでも行く
3. 新幹線にでも乗ってみる

言語ノート

でも

でも in the dialogue in Activity 3 means *something/somewhere/someone like that.* It is frequently used when making suggestions or offering things to others. With でも, the speaker implies that the hearer can choose from options other than the one specified and thereby avoids giving the impression of being too pushy or insistent.

ケーキでも食べませんか。
Would you like some cake? (Lit., *Won't you eat cake or something like that?*)

ブラウンさんにでも電話しましょう。
Let's call Ms. Brown (lit., *or someone*).

Note that でも replaces the particles は, が, and を but is appended to other particles.
で is the te-form of the copula (だ／です), and も is the particle meaning *also, even.* In other contexts, でも means *even.*

私でもわかります。
Even I understand.

Do you remember how でも attaches to interrogatives? (If not, review Chapter 5, **Grammar 24** in Book 1.)

アクティビティー 4

手紙を書いたら... (*How about writing a letter?*)

Turn the following sentences into suggestions, using たらどうですか.

1. お母さんに手紙を書く
2. あと十五分、三村さんを待つ
3. もう少し早く起きる
4. あのレストランで食事をする
5. 山本さんと話してみる
6. 毎日ジョギングをする
7. お酒をやめる (*quit*)
8. 水を飲む
9. ここに来る
10. 村山さんに会う

アクティビティー　5

どうしたらいいですか。(*What should I do?*)

Make an appropriate suggestion in response to each comment or question in the first column, choosing from the list in the second column.

1. 銀行へはどう行きますか。
2. この漢字がわからないんですが...
3. ちょっと暑いですね。
4. 京都ではどこへ行ったらいいですか。
5. 朝8時からずっと (*without interruption*) 働いています。
6. 午後、雨が降るそうです。
7. おなかがすきました。(*I'm hungry.*)
8. 来週、クラスがありません。

a. ちょっと休んだらどうですか。
b. 辞書をひいて (*look up in a dictionary*) みたらどうですか。
c. コートをぬいだらどうですか。
d. ガイドブックを見てみたらどうですか。
e. 何か食べたらどうですか。
f. 旅行したらどうですか。
g. 私もわかりません。あのおまわりさん (*police officer*) に聞いたらどうですか。
h. 傘を持っていったらいいと思いますよ。

アクティビティー　6

車で行ったらどうですか。(*Why don't you go by car?*)

Make an appropriate suggestion in response to each statement.

[例] 駅に行くんですが、どうしたらいいですか。→
タクシーを使ったらどうですか。

1. のどがかわいたんです (*I'm thirsty*) が、...。
2. この問題がわからないんですが、...。
3. いい日本語の辞書を買いたいんですが、...。
4. 日本語が上手になりたいんですが、...。
5. この町ではどこを見たらいいですか。
6. おいしい日本料理を食べたいんですが、...。

道南（洞爺・札幌）3日間

札幌
洞爺湖　千歳空港

添乗員同行／2朝食・2昼食・1夕食　　　　　●募集人員35名（最少催行人員20名）

日次	コース（★印の箇所は下車観光となり、それ以外は車窓観光となります）	食事
1	（07:00〜10:00頃） 羽田空港------→千歳空港　　★ノーザンホースパーク 　★支笏湖（昼食）　　★登別クマ牧場　　　洞爺湖（泊）	― 昼 夕
2	洞爺湖　　★昭和新山　　　倶知安　　　　　余市 　★小樽（昼食・北一硝子・運河等）　　札幌市内（泊）	朝 昼 ―
3	（出発迄フリータイム） 　　　　　　　　（各自） 札幌市内―――――――千歳空港――――――――→羽田空港 　　　千歳空港集合　　　　　　　　　　　　（17:00〜21:00頃）	朝 ― ―

※出発日により往復の利用航空便の時間帯が変更になる場合があります。

宿泊地・利用予定ホテル

第1日目：洞爺湖温泉／洞爺湖プリンスホテル湖畔亭、洞爺観光ホテルなど
第2日目：札幌／チサンホテルすすきのなど

●出発日： 4月 24
　　　　　 5月 16
　　　　　 7月 17

●旅行代金（お一人様）

タイプ	出発日	4/24	5/16	7/17、8/23
お と な	4名以上1室（B〜E）	55,800円	68,800円	86,800円
	3名1室（A）	57,800円	70,800円	88,800円
	2名1室（A）	59,800円	73,800円	91,800円
こ　ど　も		おとなと同じ	おとなと同じ	各16,000円引

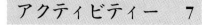
どこで泊まりますか。(*Where are you going to stay?*)

These are advertisements for various types of lodging. How much information, and what kind, can you get from them? Look at them again after you have finished studying Chapter 1.

Vocabulary Library

Travel

旅行者	りょこうしゃ	traveler
国内旅行	こくないりょこう	domestic travel
海外旅行	かいがいりょこう	travel abroad
団体旅行	だんたいりょこう	group travel
一人旅	ひとりたび	traveling alone; solo travel

Sightseeing and Vacations

ツアー		package tour
観光（する）	かんこう（する）	sightseeing; touring (to sightsee; to tour)
観光客	かんこうきゃく	sightseer; tourist
観光案内所	かんこうあんないしょ	tourist information center
名所	めいしょ	sights (lit., *famous place*[*s*])
温泉	おんせん	hot spring
休暇	きゅうか	vacation; holiday
民宿	みんしゅく	Japanese-style bed and breakfast

Loanwords: チャーター、ツアーコンダクター、ヒッチハイク、ユースホステル、リゾート

2. Deciding to Do Something: ...ことにする

> ギブソン：チンさん、夏休みはどうするんですか。
> チン：しばらく両親に会っていないので、ペキンに帰ることにしました。
> ギブソン：そうですか。私は東京にいて、アルバイトをすることにしました。

2.1 A personal decision is expressed with the following construction.

> Verb (plain, nonpast form) ＋ ことにする

(I) will decide to (do ...)   *(I) have decided to (do ...)*

明日から毎日運動することにします。
I have decided to exercise every day starting tomorrow.

ギブソンさんは、あのセーターを買うことにしました。
Ms. Gibson decided to buy that sweater.

アメリカに帰らないことにしました。
I decided not to return to America.

When する is in the nonpast tense, this construction expresses one's decision being made at the time of speech. On the other hand, when する is in the past tense, it expresses a decision made before the time of speech.

2.2 ...ことにしている expresses a habit or routine activity; that is, *I have decided to (do something) and I am doing it.*

毎日牛乳を飲むことにしています。
I make it a rule to drink milk every day.

毎週月曜日にギブソンさんと会うことにしている。
I make it a routine to see Ms. Gibson every Monday.

It also expresses a decision to do something and implies a strong commitment to that decision.

あの人とは話さないことにしています。
I am determined not to speak with that person. (or, I'm not speaking with that person.)

GIBSON: Ms. Chin, what are you going to do during summer vacation?   CHIN: I haven't seen my parents for some time, so I've decided to return to Beijing.   GIBSON: I see. I've decided to stay in Tokyo and work part-time.

2.3 Noun + ...にする means *to decide on (something).*

何にしますか。
What will you have (lit., choose)?
タクシーにしますか。バスにしますか。
Shall we go by taxi or bus?

アクティビティー 8

クラスを休むことにしました。(*I decided to skip class.*)

Fill in the blanks with an appropriate verb from the following list.

Suggested Verbs: 食べる、起きる、休む、買う、帰る

1. 今日は頭が痛い (*my head hurts*) ので、学校を（　　）ことにした。

2. おなかがすいた (*I'm hungry*) ので、昼ごはんを（　　）ことにします。

3. 毎日朝 6 時に（　　）ことにしています。

4. 今日は娘の誕生日 (*birthday*) なので、早く家に（　　）ことにします。

5. 横井先生がすすめる (*recommend*) ので、その辞書を（　　）ことにしました。

アクティビティー 9

毎日テレビニュースを見ることにしている。(*I make it a rule to watch the TV news every day.*)

Complete the following sentences with a phrase ending in ことにした or ことにしている.

[例] 日曜日は... →
日曜日は12時に起きることにしている。or デパートへ行くことにした。

1. 私は毎日...
2. 来週の木曜日...
3. 夏休みに...
4. 毎週土曜日...
5. 友だちと...
6. つかれた (*I'm tired*) ので、...
7. 雨が降っているので、...
8. あのレストランはおいしそうなので、...
9. 私の趣味は読書で、...
10. 私はサラダが大好きで、...

アクティビティー 10

コーラにします。(*I'll make it a Coke.*)

Answer these questions using にします, based on the background information in parentheses.

[例] カーテンの色は赤にしますか。グレーにしますか。(はでな色はあまり
好きじゃありません。) → グレーにします。

1. ホットコーヒーにしますか。アイスティーにしますか。(今日は暑い
です。)

2. カーティスさんの誕生日 (*birthday*) のプレゼントは本にしますか。CD
にしますか。(カーティスさんの趣味は読書だそうです。)

3. 夏休みの旅行は北海道にしますか。九州にしますか。(去年北海道へ
行きました。)

4. お風呂にしますか。夕ごはんにしますか。(おなかがすいています。
[*You are hungry.*])

5. ビールにしますか。ジュースにしますか。(アルコールはだめなん
です。)

✴ アクティビティー 11

ダイアログ: 観光バスに乗ることにします。(*I will take a sightseeing bus.*)

カワムラ: 京都でいろいろなところを見たいんですが、...。
山口: 京都は広いので、歩くのは大変ですよ。観光バスに乗ったらどう
ですか。
カワムラ: それはいい考えですね。じゃ、観光バスに乗ることにします。
山口: いろいろなコースがあって、便利ですよ。

KAWAMURA: I would like to see many different places in Kyoto, but .... YAMAGUCHI: Kyoto is large, so it's
hard to walk everywhere (lit., *so walking is awful*). How about taking a sightseeing bus?
KAWAMURA: That's a good idea. Then I will (lit., *have decided to*) take a sightseeing bus.
YAMAGUCHI: There are a variety of sightseeing routes, so it's convenient.

Practice the preceding dialogue, then do the following exercise with a classmate as in the example. (s1 = Student 1, and s2 = Student 2.)

[例] おいしい日本料理を食べたいんですが、...。→

s1: おいしい日本料理を食べたいんですが、...。
s2: 大学の前の和食の店に行ったらどうですか。
　　何でもおいしいですよ。
s1: そうですか。じゃ、そのレストランに行くことにします。

1. おいしいコーヒーを飲みたいんですが、...。
2. スペイン語のテープを聞きたいんですが、...。
3. この大学のTシャツを買いたいんですが、...。
4. 何か食べたいんですが、あまりお金がありません。どうしたらいい
　　ですか。
5. 日本語の宿題がたくさんあるんですが、...。
6. アルバイトを探しているんですが (am looking for)、...。
7. ボーイフレンド（ガールフレンド）を探しているんですが、...。
8. 日本語をもっと練習したいんですが、...。

Vocabulary and Grammar 1B

Vocabulary and Oral Activities

Transportation and Schedules

Vocabulary: Transportation and Schedules

Buying Tickets

時刻表	じこくひょう	timetable
切符	きっぷ	ticket
予約（する）	よやく（する）	reservation (to make a reservation)

Preparation for a Trip

保険	ほけん	insurance
荷物	にもつ	luggage
つめる		to pack

Transportation

空港	くうこう	airport
港	みなと	harbor, port
停留所	ていりゅうじょ	bus or tram stop
待合室	まちあいしつ	waiting room
乗る	のる	to ride
降りる	おりる	to get off
乗り換える	のりかえる	to transfer
発つ	たつ	to leave
着く	つく	to arrive
遅れる	おくれる	to be late, to be delayed

During a Trip

借りる	かりる	to rent (e.g., a car, bicycle, etc.)
おみやげ		souvenir
雇う	やとう	to hire (e.g., a guide, driver, interpreter, etc.)

Loanwords: トラベラーズ・チェック、スーツケース、パスポート、ビザ、ガイドブック、レンタカー、ガイド

Review: 駅、タクシー、バス停

アクティビティー 12

何ですか。(*What is it?*)

Fill in the blanks with an appropriate word from list that follows the sentences.

1. 電車が遅れているから、(　　　)で待ちましょう。
2. 日本で弟の(　　　)にラジカセを買いました。
3. シカゴでワシントン行きの飛行機に(　　　)つもりです。
4. (　　　)で何時のバスがあるか調べてみましょう。
5. ギブソンさんは空港についたら、車を(　　　)そうです。
6. ホテルを(　　　)するため、電話しました。
7. そんなにたくさん(　　　)を持って、どれくらい日本へ行くんですか。
8. バスに乗る前に、(　　　)を買いましょう。

a. 切符
b. おみやげ
c. 乗り換える
d. 待合室
e. 荷物
f. 予約
g. 時刻表
h. 借りる

Grammar and Practice Activities

3. Saying Whether Something Occurred Before or After:

前 and 後
まえ　　　あと

ギブソン：今日の予定はどうなっていますか。

林：ええと、まず上野へ行きます。上野で買い物をした後、
浅草へ行きます。浅草でお寺を見た後、日光へ行きます[1]。

ギブソン：昼ごはんはどこで食べますか。

林：日光へ行く前に、浅草で食べましょう。おいしい天ぷら屋が
あるんですよ。

3.1 To say that something happens before or after something else, use the
following patterns.

BEFORE
Noun の
Verb (dictionary form) } → 前に
まえ

AFTER
Noun の
Verb (ta-form) } → 後で
あと

Note that 前 (*before*) is
also used to refer to
location (*in front of*) and
that the Chinese character
後 is read
うし (ろ)— 後ろ—when it
is used in a positional
sense (*behind*). (See
Book 1, Chapter 2,
Grammar 8.)

海外旅行の前に、パスポートを取った。
かいがいりょこう　　　　　　　　　　　と
Before my trip abroad, I got a passport.

GIBSON: What is scheduled for today?　HAYASHI: Uh, first we will go to Ueno. After we shop in Ueno, we
will go to Asakusa. After seeing a temple in Asakusa, we will go to Nikko.　GIBSON: Where will we eat
lunch?　HAYASHI: Let's eat in Asakusa before we go to Nikko. There is a good tempura restaurant there.

[1]Asakusa is an area of Tokyo. Nikko, known for its brightly colored Toshogu Shrine, is located north of
Tokyo.

その旅館を予約する前に、ガイドブックで値段を調べて (*check*)
みましょう。

Before making a reservation at that inn, let's check the price in the guidebook.

昼ごはんの後で、その町を見物した。

After lunch, we went sightseeing in that town.

クラスが終わった後、駅に切符を買いに行った。

After class was over, we went to the station to buy tickets.

3.2 As you studied in Chapter 4, Grammar 49.2 in Book 1, the te-form of a verb + から has a meaning similar to the ta-form of a verb + 後 (で).

切符を買ってから、ホームへ行った。

After I bought a ticket, I went to the train platform.

3.3 前 and 後 are also used with time expressions. When it directly follows a time expression, 後 can be read ご.

Time expression	+	前 (に)…ago, …before 後 (に)…later, …after, in …

いつ北海道へ行ったんですか。—二ヶ月前に行きました。(or 二ヶ月前です。)

When did you go to Hokkaido? —We went there two months ago. (or, Two months ago.)

いつペキンに帰るんですか。—三週間後に帰ります。

When will you return to Beijing? —I'll return in three weeks.

> ヶ月 (pronounced かげつ) is a counter for counting (not naming) months. (See Chapter 2, **Grammar 9** in Book 1.)
> 週間 is a counter for weeks.

3.4 前に and 後で can be used adverbially, meaning *before* and *later*.

そこには前に行ったことがあります。

I have been there before.

その問題は後で話しましょう。

Let's talk about that issue later.

アクティビティー 13

起きてからすぐ出ました。(*I left soon after getting up.*)

Choose either the *before* or *after* phrase, whichever best completes the sentence.

1. 席(*seat*)に、(座る前に、座ってから)、シートベルトをしめました。
　　(しめる = *to fasten*)
2. 切符を予約 (する前に、した後)、旅行のプランをたてました。
　　(プランをたてる = *to make a plan*)
3. 朝(起きる前に、起きた後)、オレンジジュースを飲んだ。
4. 夜(寝る前に、寝た後)、テレビを見ます。
5. ホテルにチェックイン(する前に、した後)、部屋(*room*)に行きました。

アクティビティー　14

前ですか。後ですか。 (*Before or after?*)

Combine the sentences using the time expressions given (前に、後、or
〜てから). Make any necessary changes to the verb endings.

　　前に
1. (ホテルに行く)(明日の飛行機の予約をしましょう)
2. (日本に来る)(町田さんに手紙を書きました)
3. (家に帰る)(家内に電話することにしています)
　　後
4. (切符を買う)(フライトがキャンセルになった)
5. (日本語を一年勉強する)(日本に来た)
6. (パスポートを取る [*get a passport*])(トラベラーズ・チェックを
　　作りました)
　　〜てから
7. (ハワイから帰ってくる)(病気になった)
8. (レンタカーを借りる[*rent*])(町を見物しました)
9. (日本を発つ)(ブラウンさんと話しました)

アクティビティー　15

一年前... (*One year ago...*)

Answer these questions using the information given in parentheses.

1. いつ日本に来ましたか。(one year ago)
2. いつアメリカに帰りますか。(three months later)

> **R**eview how to count
> days in Chapter 2,
> **Grammar 9** in Book 1,
> if necessary.

3. いつ町田さんに会いましたか。(four days ago)

4. いつヨーロッパに発《た》ちますか。(two weeks later)

5. いつ朝ごはんを食べましたか。(thirty minutes ago)

✸ アクティビティー 16

後《あと》ですか。前《まえ》ですか。(*Is it after or before?*)

Connect the two clauses using 前 or 後 so that the resulting sentence represents a logical sequence.

[例] （旅行《りょこう》に行く）（トラベラーズ・チェックを買う）→
旅行《りょこう》に行く前に、トラベラーズ・チェックを買います。
（ホテルをチェックアウトする）（駅《えき》へ行く）→
ホテルをチェックアウトした後、駅《えき》へ行きます。

1. （旅館《りょかん》に着《つ》く）（お風呂《ふろ》に入る[*take a bath*]）
2. （新幹線《しんかんせん》に乗《の》る）（切符《きっぷ》を買《か》う）
3. （お寺《てら》に着《つ》く）（写真《しゃしん》をとる）
4. （ハワイへ行く）（新《あたら》しい水着《みずぎ》を買《か》う）
5. （旅行《りょこう》に出る）（ガイドブックを買《か》う）
6. （寝《ね》る）（家族《かぞく》に絵《え》はがき[*picture postcard*]を書く）
7. （ガイドを雇《やと》う）（町を見物《けんぶつ》する）

文化ノート

CULTURE NOTE • みどりの窓口《まどぐち》

Trains are the most popular mode of travel in Japan. An extensive, well-developed national network of train lines run by Japan Railways (JR) plus numerous other private railways make it more convenient to travel by train than by any other means of transportation.

If you travel in Japan, sooner or later you will need to visit the みどりの窓口 (lit., *green window*) that is found at major stations on JR lines. There you can buy JR tickets for long-distance trips one month in advance of the day of travel. In addition, you can purchase commuter passes, package-tour tickets, and plane tickets, and even make hotel reservations.

旅行のスケジュール。(*Travel itinerary*)

Following is the itinerary for Linda Brown and Heather Gibson's ongoing three-day trip. At the end of the first day, they wrote down what they had done and what they planned to do for the rest of the trip. Describe what they did or will do in Japanese.

[例] 今日12時に東京駅を新幹線で発ちました。会津若松に着いた後、
タクシーで猪苗代湖に行きました。夕ごはんを食べる前に、
温泉に入りました。

TODAY

12:00	bullet train	Left Tokyo
2:45 P.M.		Arrived at Kooriyama
		Got off the train and transferred
2:50 P.M.	electric train	Left Kooriyama
4:20 P.M.		Arrived at Aizuwakamatsu
	taxi	Went to Lake Inawashiro
5:30 P.M.		Arrived at Inawashiro Inn
6:00 P.M.		Took a hot spring bath
7:00 P.M.		Had dinner in their room
10:00 P.M.		Went to bed

TOMORROW

7:00 A.M.		Get up
8:00 A.M.		Have breakfast at the hotel cafeteria
9:00 A.M.		Go fishing
4:00 P.M.		Go to Hotel Lake Hibara
		Stay at Hotel Lake Hibara

あさこ

THE DAY AFTER TOMORROW

9:00 A.M.	sightseeing bus	See Lake Hibara area
1:17 P.M.	bus	Leave for Hukushima
4:36 P.M.		Arrive at Hukushima Station
4:49 P.M.	bullet train	Leave Hukushima
7:06 P.M.		Arrive in Tokyo
8:00 P.M.		Arrive home

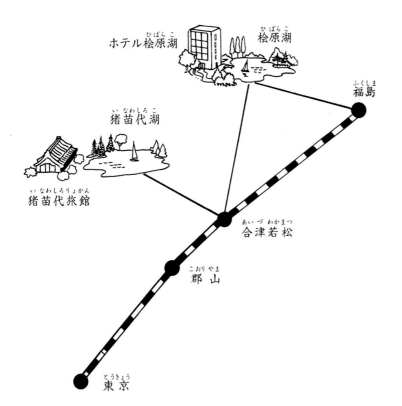

ホテル桧原湖 <ruby>桧原湖<rt>ひばらこ</rt></ruby>

<ruby>桧原湖<rt>ひばらこ</rt></ruby>

<ruby>福島<rt>ふくしま</rt></ruby>

<ruby>猪苗代湖<rt>いなわしろこ</rt></ruby>

<ruby>猪苗代旅館<rt>いなわしろりょかん</rt></ruby>

<ruby>合津若松<rt>あいづわかまつ</rt></ruby>

<ruby>郡山<rt>こおりやま</rt></ruby>

<ruby>東京<rt>とうきょう</rt></ruby>

Now make up your own questions to ask your classmates.

Vocabulary and Grammar 1C

Vocabulary and Oral Activities

Sightseeing and Travel Planning

Vocabulary: Sightseeing and Travel Planning

Travel by Train

特急	とっきゅう	express
普通列車	ふつうれっしゃ	local train
ホーム		platform

車掌	しゃしょう	conductor
乗客	じょうきゃく	passenger
私鉄	してつ	private railway
運賃	うんちん	fare
券売機	けんばいき	ticket vending machine

Lodging

客室	きゃくしつ	guest room
1泊2食付き	いっぱくにしょくつき	one night's lodging with two meals

Loanwords: キャンセル、シングル、スイート、チェックアウト、チェックイン、フロント、ルームサービス、ダブル

Travel by Plane

飛ぶ	とぶ	to fly

Loanwords: スチュワーデス、スチュワード、パイロット、フライト、カウンター

アクティビティー　18

でんしゃ
電車で旅行しますか。(*Are you going to travel by train?*)

Imagine that you travel from Tokyo to Kyoto by train and stay at a hotel. Number the following activities in the order you would normally do them.

京都までの運賃を調べる
東京駅に行く
ホテルにチェックインする
ホームに行く
電車を降りる
ルームサービスをたのむ
ホテルまでタクシーに乗る
京都までの切符を買う
電車に乗る
部屋で荷物をあける

Grammar and Practice Activities

4. と Conditionals

カワムラ： すみません。赤坂神社はどこでしょうか。

通行人： あの角を右に曲がると、銀行があります。銀行の横の道を
まっすぐ行くと、左側にあります。

カワムラ： どうもありがとうございます。

通行人： どういたしまして。

ブラウン： コンサートのチケットは、どこで買えますか。

林： デパートのチケットのプレイガイド[1]に行くと、買えますよ。

ブラウン： 学生割引はあるんですか。

林： ええ、学生証を見せると、安くなります。

Besides たら (review Chapter 7, **Grammar 42**, Book 1), と can be used to mark the end of a conditional clause.

CONDITIONAL CLAUSE (C1)		
Noun ＋ だ／でない I-adjectives (plain, nonpast form) Na-adjectives ＋ だ／でない Verbs (plain, nonpast form)	と、	＋ RESULTANT CLAUSE (C2)

The と conditional can be interpreted in either of two ways, depending on whether the second clause is in the present tense or the past tense. In a present-tense sentence, a と conditional expresses the idea that the second clause is a natural or expected consequence of the first clause. It often translates into English as *if* or *when(ever)* and is used in statements about general principles or recurring events and situations.

KAWAMURA: Excuse me. Where is Akasaka Shrine?   PASSERBY: Turn right at that corner, and you will see (lit., *there is*) a bank. Go straight down the street next to the bank, and the shrine will be on your left. KAWAMURA: Thank you very much.   PASSERBY: You are welcome.

BROWN: Where can I buy a concert ticket?   HAYASHI: If you go to the Playguide counter in a department store, you can buy one.   BROWN: Is there a student discount?   HAYASHI: Yes, if you show your student ID, your ticket will be cheaper.

[1]プレイガイド is an event ticket sales service, akin to Ticketron in the U.S., with outlets throughout Japan.

まだ学生だと、あのバーに入れません。
If you are still a student, you cannot enter that bar.
アパートが駅から遠いと、歩くのは大変でしょう?
*If the apartment is far from the station, it would be hard to walk
(there), wouldn't it?*
こんなに不便だと、誰も来ませんよ。
If it's this inconvenient, no one will come.
冬になると、雪がたくさん降ります。
When winter comes (when it becomes winter), it snows a lot.

In the last sentence, ~たら would also be grammatical, but the meaning would
change slightly. The version with と can be only a general statement of fact; it
cannot describe a specific winter. The version with ~たら, on the other hand,
would allow the interpretation that the speaker is talking about a specific winter,
most likely this coming winter: *When (this) winter comes, it will snow a lot.*
Unlike ~たら, however, と cannot be used if the second clause is a command,
request, invitation, prohibition, or expression of will.

宿題が終わると、映画に行きましょう。(ungrammatical)
宿題が終わったら、映画に行きましょう。(grammatical)
When the homework is finished, let's go to the movies.
宿題が終わると、部屋を片付けてください。(ungrammatical)
宿題が終わったら、部屋を片付けてください。(grammatical)
When the homework is finished, please straighten up the room.

In spite of this restriction, it is possible to make suggestions using a と
construction, usually to express some general principle or guideline.

このガイドブックを読むといいですよ。
It would be good if you read this guidebook.
電卓 (calculator) を使うと便利ですよ。
It's (more) convenient if you use a calculator.

When used in a past-tense sentence, と is similar to ~たら, translating as the
English *when.* Unlike ~たら, however, と is used when the second clause is an
event or situation outside the speaker's control. For this reason, it is often used to
describe unexpected events.

その喫茶店に行くと、チンさんがいた。
When I went to the coffee shop, Ms. Chin was there.
家に帰ると、三村さんが来ていた。
When I returned home, Mr. Mimura had (already) come.
角を曲がると、子供が車の前に飛び出してきました。
When I turned the corner, a child came dashing out in front of my car.

✳ アクティビティー　19

ダイアログ：青山神社（あおやまじんじゃ）にはどうやって行きますか。(*How do I get to Aoyama Shrine?*)

カワムラ：すみません。青山神社（あおやまじんじゃ）にはどうやって行きますか。

通行人（つうこうにん）：ええと、この道（みち）をまっすぐ行って、二本目（め）の道（みち）を右に曲（ま）がります。

　　　　　しばらく行くと、左側（がわ）にあります。

カワムラ：どうもありがとうございます。

通行人：どういたしまして。

言語ノート

…目（め）

As you have learned, when you count people and things in Japanese, you have to use a counter suffix. Streets, for example, are counted with 本, the counter for long, thin objects: 一本の道 [いっぽんのみち] (*one street*), 二本の道 (*two streets*), etc. Adding 目 to this combination of numeral plus counter allows you to express ordinal numbers (in English, first, second, third, etc.): 一本目の道 (*the first street*), 二本目の道 (*the second street*), and so on. Street corners, by the way, are counted with the Japanese ～つ numerals. Thus, *five corners* is 五つの角 [いつつのかど], and *the fifth corner* is 五つ目の角. Here are a few more ordinal numbers: 五人目 [ごにんめ] (*the fifth person*), 四軒目 [よんけんめ] (*the fourth building*), and 一番目 (*the first one*).

アクティビティー　20

バスで行くと10分です。(*When you go by bus, it's ten minutes.*)

Join sentences from the two columns using the と conditional.

[例]　夜（よる）になります。暗（くら）くなります。→ 夜（よる）になると、暗（くら）くなります。

1. 春（はる）になります。
2. カワムラさんの家に行きました。
3. 二十（はたち）になりました。
4. 寒（さむ）くなりました。

a. 電車（でんしゃ）がもう来ていました。
b. 誰（だれ）もいませんでした。
c. セールをしていました。
d. 少し暖（あたた）かくなります。

KAWAMURA: Excuse me. How do I get (lit., *go*) to Aoyama Shrine.　PASSERBY: Uh, go straight up this street, and turn right at the second corner. Keep going, and you will find it on your left (lit., *Go for a while, and it will be on the left*).　KAWAMURA: Thank you very much.　PASSERBY: You're welcome.

5. デパートへ行きました。

6. ホームへ行きました。

7. 電車に乗りました。

8. あの角を曲がります。

e. お酒が飲めます。

f. セーターを着ます。

g. すぐ (immediately) 席 (seat) にすわりました。

h. スーパーがあります。

アクティビティー　21

右に曲がると... (If you turn right, ...)

Give directions from the station to Ms. Tanaka's house by using the と conditional and the following expressions.

1. この道、まっすぐ、信号 (traffic light)

2. 右に曲がる、すぐ、スーパー

3. 左に曲がる、少し行く、銀行

4. 公園のとなりの道、まっすぐ、大学

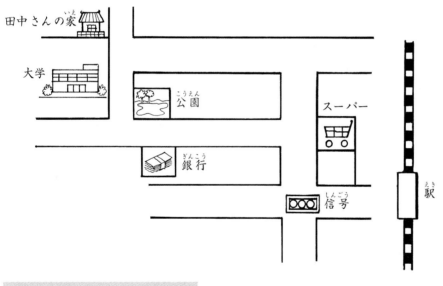

アクティビティー　22

冬が来るとスキーができます。(When winter comes, you can ski.)

Complete these sentences.

1. 冬が来ると、

2. 雨が降ると、

3. 3時になると、

4. 図書館へ行くと、

5. ここをまっすぐ行くと、

6. マクドナルドへ行くと、

7. 暑いと、

8. 電車を降りると、

道をたずねる (*Asking the Way*)

ASKING FOR DIRECTIONS

すみません、駅へ行く道を教えてください。

Excuse me, but please tell me how to get to the station (lit., please tell me the way to the station).

すみません、駅にはどうやって行ったらいいんでしょうか。

Excuse me, how do I get to the station (lit., how should I go to the station)?

駅はどちらでしょうか。

Where is the station?

歩いて何分くらいかかるでしょうか。

About how many minutes does it take on foot?

GIVING DIRECTIONS

この道をまっすぐ100メートルほど行くと右側にあります。

Go straight up this street about 100 meters, and it will be on the right side (of the street).

二つ目の交差点を右に曲がって、しばらく行きます。

Turn right at the second intersection, and go (straight) a bit (lit., for a while).

この道をまっすぐ行って、つきあたりを左に曲がります。

Go straight down this street, and turn left at the intersection.

橋(道)を渡って、左に行きます。

Cross the bridge (street), and go left.

歩いて5分くらいです。

It takes about five minutes on foot.

私もそちらへ行きますから、一緒に行きましょう。

I am going in that direction, so let's go together (and I will show you where it is).

すみません。誰かほかの人に聞いてください。

I'm sorry. Please ask someone else.

ASKING WHERE TO GET OFF

美術館へ行きたいのですが、どこで降りたらいいでしょうか。

I would like to go to the art museum. Where should I get off?

16番のバスに乗って、4つ目の停留所で降ります。

You take a number 16 bus, and get off at the fourth stop.

Vocabulary and Grammar 1C

地図 (Map)

Look at the map, and explain how to get from point X to the following places.

1. 伊勢丹デパート
2. 丸井旅館
3. 中央公園 (Central Park)
4. 東宝劇場 (Toohoo Theater)
5. 三島神社
6. 仁徳寺
7. 現代美術館 (Modern Art Museum)

Travel

観光案内所 (*Tourist Information Center*)
（かんこうあんないしょ）

You are working at a tourist information center. Answer these tourists' questions based on the information in the box.

1. 吉野寺はどのように行きますか。
（よしのでら）

2. おみやげを買いたいんですが、...

3. 歌舞伎を見たいんですが、...
（か ぶ き）

4. レストラン・ローマに行きたいんですが、...

5. モダン・アート・ギャラリーへ行く道を教えてください。
（みち）（おし）

Sightseeing and Shopping Guide

東急デパート　　Walk straight down the road in front of the Tourist
（とうきゅう）
Information Center, and you will find it on your left. They sell a lot of good souvenirs.

レストラン・ローマ　　Take a number 30 bus from the bus stop across the street from the Center, and get off in front of Aoyama Post Office. The restaurant is to the left of the post office. Their pasta is the best in town.

モダン・アート・ギャラリー　　It's a fifteen-minute walk to the left, down the street in front of the Center; look for a red and green building on your right.

吉野寺　　It's about twenty minutes by taxi from the Center; it's the most
（よしのでら）
popular tourist attraction in town.

明治劇場　　Take a number 52 bus across from the Center, and get off at
（めい じ げきじょう）
Ginza. It's the brown building across from the Ginza stop. You can see Kabuki theater there.

シティー・ファッション・センター　　Cross the street in front of the Center, and go left for five minutes; they sell inexpensive clothes.

Vocabulary and Grammar 1C

5. Commands

山口ゆり子：さとみ、起きなさい。
山口さとみ：お母さん、今何時？
山口ゆり子：もう7時よ。
山口さとみ：まだ7時？

山口ゆり子：大助、部屋の掃除はした？
　山口大助：まだだよ。
山口ゆり子：まだ？早く掃除しなさい。洋子さんが来るんでしょう？
　山口大助：うん、今するよ。

5.1 Commands to subordinates can be expressed by the following construction.

Conjunctive verb form + なさい

書く → 書き
食べる → 食べ
する → し
来る → 来
} + なさい

もっと野菜を食べなさい。
Eat more vegetables.

わかった人は手を上げなさい。
Those who have understood, raise your hands.

答えはここに書きなさい。
Write your answer here.

This is the command form used by parents talking to children, teachers talking to students, and other authority figures giving orders to subordinates.

YURIKO YAMAGUCHI: Satomi, get up.　SATOMI YAMAGUCHI: Mom, what time is it now?
YURIKO YAMAGUCHI: It's already 7:00.　SATOMI YAMAGUCHI: Only (lit., *still*) 7:00?

YURIKO YAMAGUCHI: Daisuke, did you clean your room?　DAISUKE YAMAGUCHI: Not yet.
YURIKO YAMAGUCHI: Not yet? Clean it quickly.　Yooko is coming, isn't she?　DAISUKE YAMAGUCHI: Yes, I'll clean it now.

5.2 The plain equivalent of the なさい command is formed as follows.

CLASS 1 VERBS	CLASS 2 VERBS	CLASS 3 VERBS
Root + the e-column **hiragana** corresponding to the dictionary ending	Root + ろ	Irregular
買う → 買え 書く → 書け 話す → 話せ 立つ → 立て 死ぬ → 死ね 読む → 読め 乗る → 乗れ 泳ぐ → 泳げ	食べる → 食べろ 見る → 見ろ	する → しろ 来る → 来い

u-column	→ e-column
う	→ え
く	→ け
す	→ せ
つ	→ て
ぬ	→ ね
む	→ め
る	→ れ
ぐ	→ げ

This command form, which is called the imperative, sounds very blunt and harsh, so non-Japanese learners would be well-advised to avoid using it for commands and requests. Female speakers do not use it at all.

おい、早く食べろ。
Hey, eat quickly! (not-so-well-educated or angry father to son)
ビールを持って来い。
Bring me beer! (chauvinistic husband to wife; drunk customer to bartender)

When you quote someone's command indirectly, you can use the plain command + と言う. It does not matter what form the original command was in. Even though this command form sounds harsh and masculine when used by itself, its use within indirect quotations is completely acceptable, for female speakers as well as male.

彼は早く起きろと言いました。
He said to get up quickly.
父は息子にもっと勉強しろと言った。
The father told his son to study more.

アクティビティー 25

何か言いなさい。(*Say something!*)

What do you say to the following people who are subordinate to you? Answer using ...なさい。

[例]　a student who doesn't come to school every day → 毎日学校に来なさい。

1. a child who doesn't drink milk
2. a student who doesn't study at all
3. a child who doesn't go to bed
4. a student who doesn't go back home after class
5. a child who doesn't read books at all
6. a student who looks not at the chalkboard, but at a pretty student next to him
7. a child who stays out after 8:00 P.M.

アクティビティー　26

父が言った . . . (*Father said . . .*)

Rewrite these sentences using the plain command form ＋ と言った.

[例]　名前を書く → 名前を書けと言った。

1. ここに来る
2. 学校に行く
3. 本を読む
4. 勉強する
5. お金をはらう
6. これを買う
7. お茶を飲む

6. Admonishment and Prohibition:
〜てはいけない／...な

カワムラ：ここで写真を取りましょうか。

林：ええ。あっ、芝生の中に入ってはいけませんよ。

カワムラ：中に入っちゃいけないんですか。

林：ほら、「立ち入り禁止」の立て札があるでしょ。

林：あっ、湯船の中で体を洗ってはいけません。

カワムラ：あっ、そうですか。

林：日本のお風呂では、体は湯船の外で洗います。

カワムラ：あっ、あのおじいさんは？

林：おじいさん、湯船の中で入れ歯を洗ってはだめですよ。

入っちゃ is a colloquial form of 入っては.

KAWAMURA: Let's take a photo here.　　HAYASHI: Yes. Oh, you have to keep off the grass.
KAWAMURA: Can't I go onto the grass?　　HAYASHI: Look! There is a sign saying "Keep Out."

HAYASHI: Oh, you mustn't wash your body inside the bathtub.　　KAWAMURA: Oh, really?
HAYASHI: In Japan, we wash ourselves outside the bathtub.　　KAWAMURA: How about that elderly man?
HAYASHI: Sir! You mustn't wash your dentures in the bathtub.

おじさん、おばさん、おじいさん、おばあさん

In Chapter 5 of Book 1, you studied the above words, which mean *uncle, aunt, grandfather,* and *grandmother,* respectively. These words are used not only to refer to family members or relatives but also to refer to or address middle-aged and older people in informal speech. おにいさん and おねえさん are used to refer to young men and women. If you go to Japan during your student years, don't be surprised when small children address you as おにいさん or おねえさん.

6.1 Admonition or warning is expressed by the following constructions.

Te-form of verb ＋ は ＋	{	いけない（いけません） ならない（なりません） だめだ（だめです） こまる（こまります）

You must not (do...)

ここに車を止めてはならない。
You mustn't park (stop) the car here.
お酒を飲みすぎてはだめですよ。
You mustn't drink too much sake.

...いけない、...ならない and ...だめだ have a similar meaning, but the sense of prohibition is most strongly expressed by ...だめだ, followed by ...ならない and ...いけない in this order. ...こまる expresses prohibition indirectly by saying that the hearer's action will inconvenience the speaker.

6.2 A negative command is expressed as follows.

Dictionary form of verb ＋ な

Don't ....

ここにごみをすてるな。
Don't throw your garbage here.
そんなばかなことはするな。
Don't do such a stupid thing.

The negative command form sounds harsh and strong. It is used only in public signs and by males speaking to family members, close friends, or subordinates. As with the plain command, you may use . . . な in front of と言う, no matter what the original form of the negative command was, without any unpleasant connotations.

父は私にそんなにたくさん食べるなと言いました。
Father told me not to eat that much.
彼にあまりテレビを見るなと言いましょうか。
Shall I tell him not to watch TV so much?

アクティビティー　27

そうしてはいけません。(*You mustn't do that.*)

Rewrite the following sentences using てはいけません.

1. ここでサッカーをする
2. ごみをすてる
3. ロビーをスリッパで歩く
4. ここで泳ぐ
5. たばこをすう (*to smoke a cigarette*)
6. 水を飲む
7. 大きな声 (*voice*) で話す

アクティビティー　28

こうしてもいけません。(*This isn't allowed either!*)

What is forbidden in these situations? Complete the following using てはいけません.

1. 教室 (*classroom*) の中で
2. ホテルの部屋の中で
3. 飛行機の中で
4. 日本では
5. アメリカでは
6. 食事の時

7. The Adverbial Use of Adjectives

林：チンさん、昨日はクラスに行きましたか。

チン：ええ。でも、早く帰ったんです。

林：どうしたんですか。

チン：頭が痛かったんです。

山口ゆり子：大助、部屋の掃除したの？

山口大助：うん、したよ。

山口ゆり子：これで掃除したと言うの？

山口大助：うん。

山口ゆり子：もっときれいに掃除しなさい。

Sentence-Final の

The sentence-final particle の, used mainly, but not exclusively, by female speakers and children, indicates (1) mild affirmation, (2) asking a question or asking for an explanation（の is spoken with a rising intonation）, (3) persuasion, and (4) explanation. It is one of the informal forms of the ...んです construction.

何をするの？
What are you going to do?
もっと勉強したらどうなの？
Why don't you study more?
お金がないの。
I don't have any money.

The sentence-final particle よ, which is used to give new information, to impose one's opinion, or to emphasize information, may follow の.

何をするのよ。
もっと勉強したらどうなのよ？
お金がないのよ。

HAYASHI: Ms. Chin, did you go to class yesterday?   CHIN: Yes, but I left early.   HAYASHI: What happened?
CHIN: I had a headache.

YURIKO YAMAGUCHI: Daisuke, did you clean your room?   DAISUKE YAMAGUCHI: Yes, I did.

YURIKO YAMAGUCHI: Do you call this a clean room? (Lit., *This is the condition you call cleaned?*)

DAISUKE YAMAGUCHI: Yes.   YURIKO YAMAGUCHI: Clean more thoroughly.

Male speakers usually use のだ instead of sentence-final の, and female speakers may occasionally use のだ, too, especially if they are trying to sound "tough."

You can make adverbs from adjectives in the following way.

ADVERBIAL FORM OF ADJECTIVES

| I-adjectives | Root + く | 小_{ちい}さい → 小_{ちい}さく
安_{やす}い → 安_{やす}く |
| Na-adjectives | Root + に | きれい → きれいに
静_{しず}か → 静_{しず}かに |

もう少し小さく切_きってください。
Please cut it into smaller pieces.
このソックスはセールの時_{とき}に安_{やす}く買_かいました。
I bought this pair of socks cheaply when there was a sale.
ナイフとフォークをきれいに並_{なら}べてください。
Please arrange the knives and forks neatly.
ここでは静_{しず}かに歩_{ある}きなさい。
Walk quietly here.

アクティビティー　29

早く飲みなさい。(*Drink it quickly.*)

Fill in the blanks with an appropriate form of the following adjectives.

Suggested Adjectives: 遅_{おそ}い (*late*), きれい (な), 静_{しず}か (な), 早_{はや}い, 上手_{じょうず} (な), 大きい, 長_{なが}い (*long*)

1. 仕事_{しごと}が終_おわったら、（　　　）うちに帰_{かえ}るつもりだ。

2. （　　　）ごはんを食べなさい。

3. ちょっとこれは小さすぎますね。もう少し（　　　）書いてください。

4. きたない手 (*hands*) ですね。(　　　) 洗いなさい。
5. 昨日は仕事がたくさんあって、(　　　) うちに帰った。
6. 妹 はいつもお風呂に (　　　) 入っている。
7. カワムラさんは日本語を (　　　) 話せますね。

✳ アクティビティー　30

ダイアログ：早く行きなさい。(*Go now!*)

山口ゆり子：早く行きなさい。電車に遅れるわよ。
山口さとみ：じゃあ、行ってきます。[1]
山口ゆり子：あまりお金を使ってはダメよ。
山口さとみ：うん、わかってるわ。

> This is a conversation between mother and daughter. わかってる is a shortened form of わかっている (the い is dropped). This shortened form of ている is frequently used in informal speech.

✳ アクティビティー　31

両親の忠告 (*Parents' advice*)

Imagine that you are a parent of a twenty-year-old who is going on a trip to Japan with a friend for the first time. Would you give the following pieces of advice? Why or why not?

1. 毎日、うちに電話しなさい。
2. 生水 (*unboiled water*) を飲んではいけません。
3. 毎日うちに手紙を書きなさい。
4. 毎日ビタミンCを飲みなさい (*take*)。
5. お金をたくさん使ってはいけません。
6. 日本人の男の人に気をつけなさい (*watch out for*)。
7. 生の (*raw*) 魚を食べてはいけません。
8. お酒を飲みすぎてはいけません。
9. トラベラーズ・チェックを持って行きなさい (*take*)。
10. 危ない (*dangerous*) ところに行ってはいけません。

YURIKO YAMAGUCHI: Hurry up! (Lit., *Go quickly*.) You will be late for your train.　SATOMI YAMAGUCHI: Well, see you later.　YURIKO YAMAGUCHI: Don't spend (Lit., *use*) too much money.　SATOMI YAMAGUCHI: Yeah. I know.

[1]Do you remember this set phrase for saying good-bye?

8. Expressing Obligation or Duty

高田：アメリカへ行く時は、ビザはいりますか。
ブラウン：どれくらいアメリカへ行くんですか。
高田：一ヶ月です。
ブラウン：それじゃ、いりません。三ヶ月以上はビザを取らなくてはなりません。

佐野：お出かけですか。
高田：ええ、スーツケースを買わなくてはいけないんです。
佐野：旅行ですか。
高田：ええ、出張でニューヨークへ行かなければならないんです。

8.1 An obligation or a duty is expressed by the following construction.

The te-form of the negative, nonpast form (ない form) of verb + は	ならない（なりません） いけない（いけません） だめだ（だめです）

One must … One has to …

このレンタカーは6時までに返さなくてはいけない。
We have to return this rental car by six o'clock.
早く寝なくてはいけませんよ。
You have to go to sleep quickly.
もっと勉強しなくちゃだめだよ。
You have to study more.

8.2 An obligation or a duty is also expressed by the following construction.

The root of the negative, nonpast form of verbs + ければ +	ならない（なりません） いけない（いけません） だめだ（だめです）

For instance, the te-form of the negative, nonpast form 書かない is 書かなくて. Note that ない is an i-adjective and conjugates as such. Note that ならない、いけない、and だめだ are used in the construction expressing admonishment or prohibition. (See **Grammar 6** in this chapter.)

しなくちゃ is a colloquial form of しなくては.

TAKADA: When I go to the United States, do I need a visa?   BROWN: How long are you going to be there?
TAKADA: One month.   BROWN: Then you don't need one. If you stay there for more than three months, you have to get a visa.

SANO: Are you going out?   TAKADA: Yes, I have to buy a suitcase.   SANO: Is it for your trip?
TAKADA: I have to go to New York on business.

The roots of negative, nonpast forms 書かない, 食べない, しない, and 来ない are 書かな, 食べな, しな, and 来な, respectively. Note that verb forms ending in ない are conjugated like i-adjectives.

夜9時までここにいなければなりません。
I have to stay here until nine in the evening.
海外旅行にはパスポートを持っていかなければならない。
You must carry your passport when traveling abroad.
毎日、歯をみがかなければだめですよ。
You must brush your teeth every day.

> **N**ote that the root of i-adjectives can be obtained if you delete the final i from their dictionary form. むずかしい → むずかし、赤い → 赤、ない → な。

Midterm!

言語ノート

まで versus までに

In Chapter 3 of Book 1, you learned that the particle まで means *until*. までに (adding the particle に), on the other hand, means *by* or *before* and is used to indicate the time *by* or *before* which an action or an event is completed.

一時まで勉強した。
I studied until one o'clock.
三時までにうちに帰らなければならない。
I have to return home before (by) three o'clock.

レア・シュベルト

❋ アクティビティー 32

ダイアログ：朝早く起きなければなりませんね。(*We have to get up early in the morning.*)

カワムラ：金沢行きの電車は何時ですか。
林：午前6時14分です。

カワムラ：じゃあ、明日の朝は早く起きなければなりませんね。
林：ええ、遅くとも5時半には旅館を出なければなりません。

KAWAMURA: What time is the train bound for Kanazawa?　HAYASHI: It's at 6:14 A.M.
KAWAMURA: Then we have to get up early tomorrow morning.　HAYASHI: Yes, we have to leave the inn at 5:30 at the latest.

アクティビティー　33

じゃーいつか . . . . (*Maybe another time . . .*)

Following the example, create a dialogue.

[例]　（今日の午後、映画に行く）（早く家に帰る）→
　　　—今日の午後、映画に行きませんか。
　　　—すみません。早くうちに帰らなければならないんです。

1.　（来週、うちに来る）（ニューヨークに行く）
2.　（明日図書館に行く）（うちにいる）
3.　（あさって昼ごはんをいっしょに食べる）（ギブソンさんと話す）
4.　（今夜テレビを見る）（宿題をする）
5.　（そろそろ帰る）（チンさんを待っている）

アクティビティー　34

よく勉強しなくてはいけません。(*You have to study hard.*)

Complete the following using … なくてはなりません or … なくてはいけません。

1.　日本へ行く時には、
2.　バスに乗る時には、
3.　ホテルを予約する時には、
4.　ホテルをチェックアウトする時には、
5.　授業中 (*during class*) は、
6.　旅行の前には、
7.　家に帰ってきたら、

＊　アクティビティー　35

旅行の用意 (*Preparation for a trip*)

What do you have to do to prepare for your trip to Japan? Complete the following
sentences using なければなりません.

[例]　スーツケース →
　　　スーツケースがないので、買わなければなりません。*or*
　　　スーツケースを持っていかなければなりません。

Useful Vocabulary: パスポートを取る *obtain a passport,*
トラベラーズ・チェックを作る *buy travelers' checks,* 保険に入る *take out insurance*

1. パスポート
2. 飛行機の切符
3. トラベラーズ・チェック
4. 保険
5. 日本にいる友だち

6. 旅館
7. おみやげ
8. 服
9. ガイドブック

✳ アクティビティー　36

予定通りにいきませんでした。(*Things didn't go as planned.*)

Mr. Takada had several problems on his trip. Describe these problems, following the example.

[例]　予定 (*plan*)　　　　　　　実際 (WHAT ACTUALLY HAPPENED)
　　　9時の飛行機に乗る　　　　　空港へ行くバスが遅れた。
　　　　　　　　　　　　　　　　11時の飛行機に乗った。

→9時に飛行機に乗るつもりでした。でも、空港へ行くバスが遅れたので、11時の飛行機に乗らなければなりませんでした。

予定 | 実際

1. タクシーで旅館へ行く　　　　　タクシーがなかった
　　　　　　　　　　　　　　　　バスで行った

2. 旅館に泊まる　　　　　　　　　旅館が満員 (*full*) だった
　　　　　　　　　　　　　　　　ホテルに泊まった

3. 9時にお寺を見物する　　　　　10時までお寺が閉まっていた
　　　　　　　　　　　　　　　　(*closed*)
　　　　　　　　　　　　　　　　10時まで待った

4. ガイドを雇う　　　　　　　　　ガイドがいなかった
　　　　　　　　　　　　　　　　一人で町を見物した

5. 有名なレストランで昼ごはんを食べる　レストランの予約をするのを
　　　　　　　　　　　　　　　　忘れた (*forgot*)
　　　　　　　　　　　　　　　　ファースト・フードを食べた

Travel by Train

指定席	していせき	reserved seat
自由席	じゆうせき	nonreserved seat
グリーン車	グリーンしゃ	first-class (lit., *green*) car
普通車	ふつうしゃ	regular car, coach
喫煙席	きつえんせき	smoking seat
禁煙席	きんえんせき	nonsmoking seat
寝台車	しんだいしゃ	sleeping car
食堂車	しょくどうしゃ	dining car

Tickets

| 片道切符 | かたみちきっぷ | one-way ticket |
| 往復切符 | おうふくきっぷ | round-trip ticket |

Lodgings

宿泊(する)	しゅくはく(する)	lodgings (to stay, to lodge)
サービス料	サービスりょう	service charge
空室	くうしつ	vacant room

Loanwords: キャッシャー、シングル

Travel by Plane

| 離陸(する) | りりく(する) | takeoff (to take off [lit., *to leave the ground*]) |
| 着陸(する) | ちゃくりく(する) | landing (to land) |

Loanwords: ターミナル、ウイング(北ウイング、etc.)

✳ **アクティビティー 37**

どちらにしますか。(*Which one do you choose?*)

Tell which of the two options you would choose in each situation. Why?

1. 日本人の生活(*life*)をよく知りたい(*want to know*)です。ホテルにしますか。旅館にしますか。
2. 大阪で今日の午後会議があります。東京から新幹線で行きますか。バスで行きますか。
3. 明日、大阪へ行って、夜帰ってきます。片道切符にしますか。往復切符にしますか。

4. 東京から大阪まで座って行きたいです。指定席にしますか。
   自由席にしますか。

5. 一日の旅です。スーツケースを持っていきますか。持っていきません
   か。

6. 夜、電車で旅行します。ゆっくり寝たいです。普通席にしますか。
   寝台車にしますか。

7. お金があまりありません。グリーン車にしますか。普通車にしますか。

8. おなかがすきました。駅弁 (box lunch) を買いますか。食堂車に
   行きますか。

言語ノート

持っていく versus 持ってくる

In Japanese, *to take* (*things*) and *to bring* (*things*) are expressed with the te-form of 持つ (*to hold, to have*) followed by 行く and 来る, respectively. It may help to remember the literal meaning: 持って行く means *to go holding*, that is, *to take*.

プレゼントにネクタイを持って行きました。
I took a necktie as a gift.
高田さんはすしを持って来ました。
Mr. Takada brought sushi.

文化ノート

CULTURE NOTE • 駅弁 (Station Box Lunches)

One of the pleasures of traveling by train in Japan is trying the different box lunches (弁当)[べんとう] sold at each station. On major intercity express trains like the **Shinkansen,** vendors walk up and down the aisles selling standard varieties of 弁当, such as the 幕の内 [まくのうち] 弁当, which was originally sold at **Kabuki** theaters and contains rice and a variety of side dishes, such as pork, broiled fish, and pickled vegetables. The vendors also sell boxes of fried chicken or sandwiches, ice cream bars, and plastic containers of green tea.

You have the additional option of buying your lunch from one of the vendors on the station platform, and, if you are traveling on a small, local line, it is your only option. (Don't worry; Japanese regulations about food preparation and handling are very strict.) The 弁当 sold on the station platforms typically feature foods for which the region is famous.

幕の内弁当：おいしそうですね。

※ アクティビティー　38

日本旅行のスケジュール (*The itinerary of my trip to Japan*)

You are going to Asia soon. The following is your travel itinerary for the Japanese portion of your trip. Answer the questions based on your itinerary.

DATE	
May 11	Fly out of Los Angeles
May 12	Arrive in Tokyo
	Stay in the Miyako Hotel
May 13	See some friends in Tokyo
	Sightseeing in Tokyo
	Stay in the Miyako Hotel
May 14	Go to Kyoto by bullet train (first-class, reserved seat)
	Sightseeing in Kyoto
	Stay in the Higashiyama Ryokan
May 15	Sightseeing in Kyoto by bus
	Stay in the Higashiyama Ryokan
	Go from Kyoto to Izumo[1] by train (regular-class, nonreserved seat)
	Sightseeing in Izumo
May 16	Go back to Tokyo by train (sleeping car)
May 17	Leave Tokyo for Taiwan by airplane (business class)

[1]Located on the Japan Sea coast, Izumo in Shimane Prefecture is the site of Izumo Shrine, which is a famous place where people go to pray for a good marriage.

1. 何月何日に日本へ発ちますか。
2. 東京に何泊しますか。
3. 東京で何をしますか。
4. 東京では旅館に泊まりますか。
5. 東京から京都へ行く時は、
   何で行きますか。

6. 京都ではどこに泊まりますか。
7. 京都からどこへ行きますか。
8. そこへ行く時、何を使いますか。
9. 東京へは何で帰りますか。
10. いつ日本を発ちますか。
11. 日本からどこへ行きますか。

> ...泊 is a counter for overnight stays. 三泊 means *three overnight stays*, and 一泊する means *to stay over one night*. 泊 has different pronunciations depending on what number precedes it.

Language Skills

Reading and Writing

Reading 1 北海道の案内

Mr. and Ms. Sano are members of the Nakano Travel Club. Today they received an announcement of a trip to Hokkaido from the club.

Before You Read

1. What information do you think is included in a travel itinerary?

2. The announcement that you will read includes many 漢語 (*Chinese-origin words*). You may not know these words, but you can often figure out their meaning based on your knowledge of related 和語 (*Japanese-origin words*). For example, the Chinese-origin 集合 means *getting together*. The first character is found in the Japanese-origin word 集まる, which also means *to get together*. Now guess the meaning of these 漢語.

   出発　到着　朝食　昼食　夕食　乗船

3. The announcement employs the same abbreviated style you might see in an English itinerary: *You depart Tokyo at 9:00 A.M.* becomes *9:00 A.M. Tokyo departure*. Add appropriate particles and verbs to the following itinerary entries to make complete sentences. By the way, 出発, 到着, and 乗船 are nominal verbs.

   a. 午前9時東京出発　b. 午後10時中野到着　c. 観光船乗船

Useful Vocabulary: みなさん *everyone*, 知らせる *to notify*, 便 *flight number*, 羽田空港 *Haneda Airport*, 千歳空港 *Chitose Airport (near Sapporo)*, 支笏湖 *Shikotsu Lake*, 登別温泉 *Noboribetsu Hot Spring Spa*, 洞爺湖 *Tooya Lake*, 市内 *inside the city*, 料金 *fee*, 含む *to include*, 自分で *by oneself*, 払う *to pay*

Now Read It!

中野旅行クラブのみなさんへ

七月の北海道旅行のスケジュールが決まりましたので、お知らせします。

7月12日	午前8時	中野駅前に集合
	午前8時半	バスで羽田空港へ
	午前10時45分	ANA123便で千歳空港へ出発
	午後12時10分	千歳空港到着
	午後1時半	バスで札幌到着
		観光バスで札幌市内見物
	午後6時半	札幌プリンスホテルにチェックイン
7月13日	午前6時	ホテルで朝食
		朝食の後、チェックアウト
	午前8時	バスで支笏湖へ出発
	午前10時	支笏湖到着
		観光船乗船
	午後12時半	昼食
	午後2時	バスで登別温泉へ出発
	午後4時	登別温泉到着
		登別温泉グランドホテルにチェックイン
	午後7時	ホテルで夕食
7月14日	午前6時	ホテルで朝食
		朝食の後、チェックアウト
	午前8時	バスで洞爺湖へ出発
	午前10時	洞爺湖到着
	12時	昼食

	午後1時	バスで函館へ出発
	午後6時半	函館到着
		函館ホテルにチェックイン
	午後7時	ホテルで夕食
7月15日	午前9時	観光バスで見物
	午後4時	ショッピング
	午後6時18分	寝台特急「はくつる」で函館を出発
7月16日	午前7時9分	上野駅に到着

料金は一人7万8千円です。料金は13日と14日の食事を含んでいますが、12日の夕食と15日の食事は含んでいません。これは自分で払わなければなりません。

昼は暖かいですが、夜は涼しくなるので、セーターかジャケットを持って行ったらいいでしょう。

After You Finish Reading

Trace the route of the trip on the map. Write in the
form of transportation that will be used from one
place to the next place.

Answer these questions in English.

1. Where will the tour group meet on the morning of July 12?
2. Where will they take a boat ride?
3. What are they going to do in Sapporo?
4. What time will they arrive at Hakodate?
5. By what means of transportation will they return to Tokyo?
6. How much is the fee?
7. Does the fee include all meals?
8. What suggestion is made in the announcement? Why?

The Sanos decided to go on the club trip. Here is a postcard (絵はがき) that Ms. Sano sent to Linda Brown during their travels. Read it, and figure out what the Sanos did in addition to the activities described in the itinerary.

ブラウンさん、

　今、このはがきを登別温泉のホテルで書いています。おとといの朝、東京を出発、お昼ごろ千歳空港に着きました。バスで札幌市内を見物して、おとといの夜は札幌に泊まりました。昨日、札幌からバスで支笏湖に行き、観光船に乗りました。午後登別に着きました。昨日夜はホテルの温泉に何度も入りました。今日はこれから洞爺湖へ向かい、その後、函館に行きます。東京にはあさって帰ります。おみやげを買って帰りますから、楽しみにしてください。では、また。

佐野良子

7月14日朝　　　　　　　　　　　登別にて

What is the most memorable trip you have ever taken? Explain to a classmate in Japanese what you did on that trip.

CULTURE NOTE ● 温泉
おんせん

Japan is sitting on one of the most active geothermal fault zones in the world. As a result, it is home to numerous volcanoes, both active and dormant, and thousands of hot springs. These hot springs have been used for centuries for their purported ability to cure various ailments, and that tradition continues at the inns and resorts built up around the most popular springs. Today, however, most Japanese see the hot springs simply as places to soak and relax several times daily in between sightseeing, relishing local delicacies, and otherwise enjoying a hard-earned vacation. Hot spring destinations range from touristy spa towns like Atami to remote mountaintop open-air pools with no sign of civilization for miles.

If you take a traditional Japanese bath, either at an 温泉 or in a public bath or private home, you need to follow a few simple rules. First of all, you are expected to wash and rinse yourself thoroughly before entering the water. It will be extremely hot in most cases, so enter slowly, and sit very still. (If the water is too hot to touch, you may add cold water.) Get out once your body is heated through, or else you may faint. Do not bring soap into the tub or let your hair or washcloth touch the water, because that will ruin the water for everyone else. You will find that a traditional bath not only keeps you warm in the winter but also makes you feel refreshed and clean in the summer.

温泉で：いい湯だな。

文化ノート

Writing 1

1. Using the following information, write a postcard to Henry Curtis.

   You arrived in Kyoto yesterday. Today you went to temples and shrines south of Kyoto Station. Tomorrow you will see temples and shrines north of Kyoto Station. The day after tomorrow you will go to Kyushu. After traveling in Kyushu, you will return home next Wednesday.

2. Write a brief account of the most memorable trip you have ever taken.

Reading 2　トラベルガイド・札幌

Before You Read

Bring a travel guide to class, and check to see what information is included. Now match the words in the first column to related words in the second column.

1. 空港　　　　　a. 食べる
2. 特急　　　　　b. 片道
3. 往復　　　　　c. 冬
4. 旅館　　　　　d. 電話
5. 予約　　　　　e. 泊まる
6. 料理　　　　　f. 飛行機
7. 雪　　　　　　g. 駅

Answer the questions.

1. 長さ(*length*) is a noun derived from the adjective 長い (*long*). What does 高さ mean?
2. If 夏まつり means *summer festival*, what does 雪まつり mean?
3. 植物 means *plant*, and 動物 means *animal*. 植物園 means *botanical garden*. What does 動物園 mean?
4. You have seen the character 屋 at the ends of words referring to stores and shops. What do you think おみやげ屋 means?

Now Read It!

交通

　札幌は北海道の真ん中にある、人口百四十万人の美しい町だ。北海道の政治、経済、文化の中心である。東京から飛行機で千歳空港まで1時間15分。

交通 *transportation*

真ん中 *middle* / 政治 *politics*

経済 *economy* / 文化 *culture*
中心 *center*

千歳からバスで1時間。電車で45分だ。上野から寝台特急で12時間。飛行機だと、東京から往復46,000円。寝台特急は往復53,860円だ。

見どころ

見どころ *things to see*

- **大通り公園**
  幅105メートル、長さ3.8キロのグリーンベルト。冬はここで雪まつりがある。

  幅 *width*

- **中島公園**
  札幌駅から地下鉄で4分。豊平川のそばにある緑と水の公園。夏はバラが美しい。

  バラ *rose*

- **時計台**
  札幌駅から歩いて8分。札幌のシンボル。

  時計台 *clock tower*

- **円山公園**
  大通りからバスで15分。高さ220メートルの円山にある公園。動物園、スポーツセンターがある。

- **北海道大学植物園**
  札幌駅から5分

ホテル・旅館

札幌市内にはデラックスホテルからビジネスホテルまで[1]、また日本旅館などが140軒ぐらいある。ユースホステル、民宿もある。駅の中の観光案内所でホテル、旅館を探すことができる。6月から7月は観光客が多いので、三ヶ月位前から予約しなければならない。

民宿 *Japanese style bed and breakfast*

観光案内所 *tourist information center* / 探す *to look for*

味

- **ラーメン**
  札幌のラーメンは全国で有名。大通り公園のそばにはおいしいラーメン屋がたくさんある。熊さん（電話011-261-0900）、味の三平（電話011-231-0377）。

  全国 *all over the country*

- **ジンギスカン[2]**
  ビールを飲みながら、ジンギスカンが食べられるのはサッポロビール園（電話011-742-1531）

---

[1]*Business hotels* are "no frills" Western-style hotels intended particularly for business clientele. Their rooms are usually small, simply furnished singles.

[2]ジンギスカン (lit., *Genghis Khan*) is a mutton dish for which Hokkaido is famous.

■ 北海道料理
　　雪国（電話 011-221-8286）はカニとさけで有名。

北海道料理 *Hokkaido cuisine*

カニ *crab* / さけ *salmon*

おみやげ
　　北海道のおみやげと言えば、じゃがいも、アスパラガス、カニ、
スモーク・サーモンなど。札幌駅のそばにおみやげ屋さんが多い。

年中行事
■ 札幌雪まつり
　　北海道で一番大きい年中行事。全国から観光客が集まる。大きな雪の像が
大通り公園に並ぶ。

年中行事 *annual event* / 集まる *to get together* / 像 *sculpture*
並ぶ *to be lined up*

方言
旅行している時には、方言を聞くのも楽しみの1つだ。北海道方言では、
「つかれた」は「こわい」という。「気持ちがいい」は「あずましい」という。
「凍る」は「しばれる」という。

方言 *dialect*

つかれた *(I'm) tired* / 気持ちがいい *to feel comfortable, to feel at home* / 凍る *to freeze*

　　　　　　　　　　　　　　トラベル・コンサルタント田中由子

言語ノート

…と言えば

…と言えば means *speaking of,* and it is used to introduce a new topic of conversation or to change the subject.

—この本、佐野さんのですか。—ええ。ところで、佐野さんと言えば、もう北海道から帰ってきましたか。
—*Is this book Mr. Sano's? —Yes. By the way, speaking of Mr. Sano, has he already come back from Hokkaido?*

After You Finish Reading

The city of Sapporo has decided to make up an English-language brochure for foreign tourists based on Ms. Tanaka's travel guide. Please help the city officials prepare the brochure by summarizing the content of the Japanese brochure in simple, natural English. (Do not translate it directly.) Include information about transportation, things to see, seasonal attractions, locations, distances, travel time, lodging, food, and shopping.

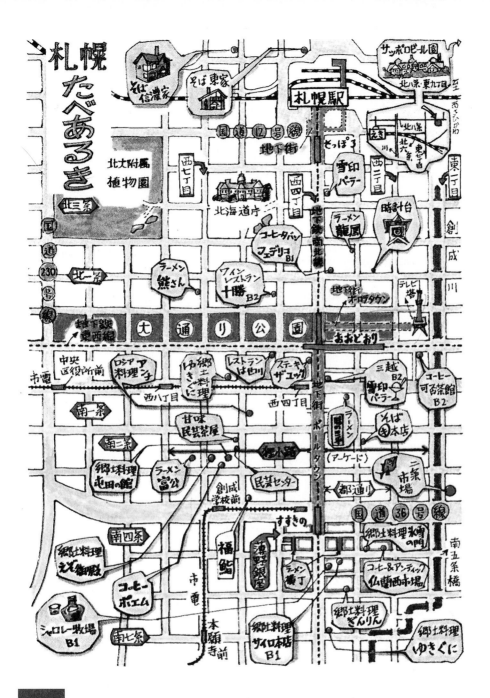

方言 (ほうげん)

The dialects (方言 (ほうげん)) of Japan differ from one another more than the various dialects of English spoken around the world, largely because of a history of geographical barriers and poor transportation. That's why you can often identify a Japanese person's home region based on his or her dialect.

Some of the differences are in pronunciation: The people of Tohoku (northern Honshu) have trouble distinguishing **shi** from **su** and **chi** from **tsu,** while the people of the Kansai (Kyoto-Osaka-Kobe) area accent words according to a pattern that is almost the exact opposite of that found in the Tokyo-Yokohama area. As in English dialects, there are many differences in vocabulary: Kansai people say おおきに instead of ありがとう and ほんま instead of 本当[ほんとう]. Tohoku people say めんこい instead of かわいい. There are even differences in grammar: Kansai people attach the ending 〜へん to the negative stem instead of using the 〜ません ending, so that わかりません becomes わからへん.

Thanks to Japan's more than 100 years of compulsory education and to the spread of mass communications in the postwar years, you don't have to worry about these differences in pronunciation and grammar in talking to people as you travel through the country. All schools teach standard Japanese (標準語 [ひょうじゅんご]), so, by and large, the standard language you are learning in *Yookoso!* should serve you well wherever you travel in Japan.

Writing 2

Write a brief description of your community or region such as might be found in a guidebook for Japanese tourists. Include the subjects in the following list. If you don't know some of the things listed, either look up the information or make something up.

1. transportation to your town
2. sightseeing locations you recommend
3. hotels you recommend
4. restaurants you recommend
5. souvenirs you recommend

Language Functions and Situations

Making a Hotel Reservation

林さんが予約係 (*reservation clerk*) に電話をかけています。

予約係： プリンセスホテルでございます。
林： 来月の13日の予約をしたいんですが。

Mr. Hayashi and a reservation clerk are talking on the phone. CLERK: This is the Princess Hotel. HAYASHI: I would like to make a reservation for the thirteenth of next month (Lit., *but...* [*could you help me?*]).

予約係：かしこまりました。どんな部屋（へや）がよろしいでしょうか。

林：ダブル・ルームはありますか。

予約係：申（もう）し訳（わけ）ありませんが、ダブルはございません。

林：では、ツインはありますか。

予約係：はい、ございます。

林：一泊（いっぱく）いくらですか。

予約係：1万3千円です。

林：では、13日に一泊（いっぱく）お願（ねが）いします。

予約係：かしこまりました。お名前とお電話番号（でんわばんごう）をどうぞ。

林：林正男（はやしまさお）です。電話番号（でんわばんごう）は 03-3654-7892 です。午後 3 時ごろ着（つ）きます。

予約係：03-3654-7892、林正男様（はやしまさおさま）、8 月 13 日一泊（いっぱく）ツインですね。お待（ま）ちしております。

様（さま）is an honorific title corresponding to さん、お待（ま）ちしております is a humble form of 待（ま）っています。

Role Play

Work in pairs. Student 1 is the reservation clerk at the Princess Hotel, and Student 2 wants to spend at least two days out of the coming four-day weekend at the hotel with his or her family.

Student1: The Princess Hotel has singles, twins, doubles, and large, Japanese-style tatami rooms. Assign each category a price ranging between ¥8,000 and ¥25,000. Then decide whether there are any rooms available in these categories on each night of the coming four-day weekend, Thursday through Sunday. If you cannot accommodate Student 2's request, suggest alternative nights or combinations of rooms.

Student 2: Decide how many people are in your family (parents, siblings, spouse, children, or other relatives) and what combination of rooms would be best. Find out whether these rooms are available on the two nights of the upcoming four-day weekend that are most convenient for your family. If the hotel cannot accommodate your first request, ask Student 1 for suggestions about other nights or combinations of rooms.

CLERK: Certainly. What kind of room do you want?   HAYASHI: Do you have a double room with one bed?
CLERK: I am sorry, but we don't have any (available on that day).   HAYASHI: Then do you have a double room with two beds?   CLERK: Yes, we do.   HAYASHI: How much is it per night?   CLERK: It's 13,000 yen.
HAYASHI: Then put me down for one night on the thirteenth.   CLERK: Certainly. May I have your name and telephone number?   HAYASHI: I am Masao Hayashi. My telephone number is 03-3654-7892.
I will arrive around three o'clock.   CLERK: Your number is 03-3654-7892, Mr. Masao Hayashi, you'll stay one night on October thirteenth, and it's a twin room, right? We are looking forward to your visit.
(Lit., *We will be waiting for you.*)

Buying a Train Ticket

東京駅で

ブラウン：あのう、次の鎌倉行きの電車は何時でしょうか。

駅員：8時21分です。

ブラウン：鎌倉に着くのは何時ですか。

駅員：10時17分です。

ブラウン：グリーン車はいくらですか。

駅員：運賃とグリーン料金合わせて、片道が1350円、
　　　往復は2500円です。

ブラウン：では、往復切符を2枚ください。

駅員：はい、5000円です。

ブラウン：何番線ですか。

駅員：3番線です。

Role Play

Work in pairs. Using the table, practice buying a train ticket.

横須賀線時刻表／料金表

行き先	発	着	番	グリーン車		普通車	
				片道	往復	片道	往復
鎌倉	8:21 9:30	10:17 11:28	3 6	1,350	2,500	980	1,760
茅ヶ崎	7:09 8:40 9:21	9:39 11:05 11:50	11 5 7	2,450	4,700	1,850	3,420
逗子	7:20 8:15 9:00	10:02 10:45 11:40	12 12 14	2,890	5,550	2,220	4,210

At Tokyo Station: BROWN: Um, at what time does the next train to Kamakura leave?   CLERK: At 8:21.
BROWN: What time does it arrive at Kamakura?   CLERK: At 10:17.   BROWN: How much is a first-class
(lit., *green*) seat?   CLERK: The total cost of the fare and a first-class seat is 1,350 yen for a one-way
ticket and 2,500 yen for a round-trip ticket.   BROWN: Then please give me two round-trip tickets.
CLERK: Yes. That will be 5,000 yen.   BROWN: Which platform does the train leave from? (Lit., *What
number track is it?*)   CLERK: Platform number 3. (Lit., *It's track number 3.*)

行き先 *destination*
片道 *one-way*
往復 *round-trip*

指 定 券 （グリーン）

大 阪 ▶ 青 森
（ 9：55発）
7月18日　白鳥号　　　4号車 10番 D席

¥＊＊＊　　　　　　　　　　　　　　　　C23

1.－7.11　東京駅旅セ－7発行
50173-02　　　　　　（2－タ）

Role Play

Here is an example of the form you must fill out when buying tickets or making reservations at the みどりの窓口. Could you fill it out yourself?

特急・寝台・指定席券申込書

必要なものを記入又つけてください。

お名前　　　　　　　TEL（　）	大人　　　枚　こども　　　枚	乗車券	片道、往復　学割　割引　その他	駅から　　　　駅まで
禁煙車希望				

小学生はこどもの欄に記入してください。

第　1　希　望		第　2　希　望		第　3　希　望	
普 通 車 グリーン車 A 寝 台 B 寝 台 二 階 席 個　　室 1人用 ┊ 2人用 3人用 ┊ 4人用	（列車名）　月　　日 　　　　　　　　号 時　　分発 駅から 駅まで	普 通 車 グリーン車 A 寝 台 B 寝 台 二 階 席 個　　室 1人用 ┊ 2人用 3人用 ┊ 4人用	（列車名）　月　　日 　　　　　　　　号 時　　分発 駅から 駅まで	普 通 車 グリーン車 A 寝 台 B 寝 台 二 階 席 個　　室 1人用 ┊ 2人用 3人用 ┊ 4人用	（列車名）　月　　日 　　　　　　　　号 時　　分発 駅から 駅まで
乗り継ぎ列車 ┊ 普 通 車 グリーン車 A 寝 台 B 寝 台 二 階 席 個　　室 1人用 ┊ 2人用 3人用 ┊ 4人用	（列車名）　月　　日 　　　　　　　　号 時　　分発 駅から 駅まで	乗り継ぎ列車 ┊ 普 通 車 グリーン車 A 寝 台 B 寝 台 二 階 席 個　　室 1人用 ┊ 2人用 3人用 ┊ 4人用	（列車名）　月　　日 　　　　　　　　号 時　　分発 駅から 駅まで	乗り継ぎ列車 ┊ 普 通 車 グリーン車 A 寝 台 B 寝 台 二 階 席 個　　室 1人用 ┊ 2人用 3人用 ┊ 4人用	（列車名）　月　　日 　　　　　　　　号 時　　分発 駅から 駅まで

Listening Comprehension

1. Mr. Kobayashi, a travel agent, is conducting a survey on what kind of vacations people would like to take. Today he is interviewing Ms. Kikuchi. Fill in the following survey sheet while listening to their conversation.

NAME _Yuriko Kikuchi_   AGE _23_

1. Which country would you most like to visit? _France_
2. Why would you like to visit that country? _School major in French_
3. How would you like to go to that country? _Big ?_
4. Which city in that country would you most like to visit? _Paris_
5. Why? _kenbutsu_
6. How would you like to travel within that country? _no driving guide, bus, train_
7. What would you like most to do in that country? _tomodachi_
8. How long would you like to stay there? _Nishukan 2weeks_
9. With whom would you like to go? _alone_
10. How often do you take a vacation?
11. How often do you travel for pleasure? _sanban ?_
12. How often do you travel on business?

---

2. Ms. Sakamoto is making a reservation for her trip at a travel agency. Write a summary of her plans, including transportation and accommodations for each day.

Vocabulary

Travel

いっぱくにしょくつき	1泊2食付き	one night's lodging with two meals
うんちん	運賃	fare
おみやげ		souvenir
きゃくしつ	客室	guest room
かんこうりょこう	観光旅行	sightseeing trip
きっぷ	切符	ticket
くうこう	空港	airport
けんばいき	券売機	ticket vending machine

けんぶつ（する）	見物（する）	sightseeing (to sightsee)
じこくひょう	時刻表	timetable
してつ	私鉄	private railway
しゃしょう	車掌	conductor
しゅっちょう（する）	出張（する）	business trip (to go on a business trip)
じょうきゃく	乗客	passenger
ていりゅうじょ	停留所	bus or tram stop
とっきゅう	特急	express
にもつ	荷物	luggage
ふつうれっしゃ	普通列車	local train
ほけん	保険	insurance
まちあいしつ	待合室	waiting room
みなと	港	harbor, port
やど	宿	accommodations
よやく（する）	予約（する）	reservation (to make a reservation)
りょかん	旅館	Japanese-style inn

Loanwords: ツアー、ガイド、ツアーコンダクター、スーツケース、トラベラーズチェック、パスポート、ビザ、チケット、スケジュール、ホーム、キャンセル、シングル、チェックイン、フロント、ルームサービス、スチュワーデス、パイロット、フライト、カウンタ

Review: ホテル

Transportation

しんかんせん	新幹線	bullet train
のりもの	乗り物	vehicle
ひこうき	飛行機	airplane
ふね	船	ship; boat

Loanwords: タクシー、フェリーボート、レンタカー
Review: 車、電車、バス

Nouns

えはがき	絵はがき	picture postcard
おふろ	お風呂	bath (*especially Japanese-style*)
おんせん	温泉	hot spring
こうさてん	交差点	intersection
ちず	地図	map
ひだりがわ	左側	left side
みぎがわ	右側	right side
よてい	予定	plan, schedule

Verbs

おくれる	遅れる	to be late
おしえる	教える	to teach, tell

Vocabulary

おりる	降りる	to get off (*a vehicle*)
かりる	借りる	to borrow, rent
たずねる	尋ねる	to ask, inquire
たつ	発つ	to leave
つく	着く	to arrive
つめる		to pack
つれていく	連れていく	to take (*people*)
つれてくる	連れてくる	to bring (*people*)
とぶ	飛ぶ	to fly
とまる	泊まる	to stay overnight
のりかえる	乗り換える	to transfer (*from one means of transportation to another*)
まがる	曲がる	to turn (*in a direction*)
もっていく	持っていく	to take (*things*)
もってくる	持ってくる	to bring (*things*)
やとう	雇う	to hire
りょこうする	旅行する	to travel
わたる	渡る	to cross
Review: 乗る の		

X を Y につめる to pack X into Y

Adverbs

いそいで	急いで	quickly
はやく	早く	early
まっすぐ		straight
よく		often, well

Grammar

あと(で)	後(で)	after
~かん	間	during, for
...ことにする		to decide on ...
~たらいいとおもいます	~たらいいと思います	I think it would be good to (do) ...
~たらいかがですか		How about (doing) ...?
~たらどうですか		How about (doing) ...?
~てから		after (doing)
~てはいけない		must not (do)
~てはこまる		It will cause trouble if you (do)
~てはだめだ		It's forbidden/inappropriate to (do)
~てはならない		must not (do)
~でも		or something like that
~なさい		*command to subordinate*
どのように		how, in what way
~なければいけない		must, have to

～なければだめだ		must, have to
～なければならない		must, have to
まえ(に)	前(に)	before
まで		until
までに		by (the time)
…め	…目	*suffix for ordinal numbers (e.g., first, second, third)*

Kanji

Learn these **kanji:**

京	早	寺
都	歩	神
社	館	地
内	乗	図
目	待	曲
所	駅	海
約	止	私
予	旅	
車	客	

チェックリスト

Use this checklist to confirm that you can now

- ☐ Talk about travel, transportation, and sightseeing
- ☐ Talk about travel planning and travel schedules
- ☐ Make a suggestion
- ☐ Say whether something occurred before or after
- ☐ Use と conditionals
- ☐ Use the command form of verbs
- ☐ Express prohibition and obligation
- ☐ Scan travel information and travel guides
- ☐ Make a hotel reservation
- ☐ Buy a train ticket

Review Chapter 1

アクティビティー 1

飛行機で旅行します。(*I'm going to travel by plane.*)

Imagine that you are going to take a trip by plane. Number the following activities in the order that they would normally occur.

電話をかけて、タクシーを呼ぶ (*to summon*)
飛行機に乗る
スチュワーデスに席 (*seat*) をたずねる (*to inquire about*)
飲み物が出る
空港に着く
タクシーに乗る
飛行機が離陸する
チェックイン・カウンターへ行く

アクティビティー 2

旅行する時 (*When you travel*)

When you traveled last time, did you do the things in the following list? In pairs, following the model, ask questions and give answers, relating what you did in your case.

[例] この前旅行した時、飛行機やホテルを旅行の 1 ヶ月前に予約 しましたか。いいえ、旅行の 1 週間前に予約しました。

1. 飛行機やホテルを旅行の1ヶ月前に予約する
2. 旅行の前にホテルに電話をして、予約を確かめる (*to check*)
3. 旅行の前に銀行へ行って、トラベラーズ・チェックを作る
4. レンタカーを使う
5. スーツケースをたくさん持っていく

アクティビティー 3

フロントへ行くと、メッセージがありました。(*When I went to the front desk, there was a message for me.*)

Complete the sentences following the examples.

[例] 駅に行くと、→ 駅に行くと、いつも駅弁を買います。
観光案内所に行くと、→ 観光案内所に行くと便利な地図がありました。

1. 日本の旅館に泊まると、　　　4. その人に道をたずねると、

2. そのお寺を見た後、　　　　　5. ホテルを予約した後、

3. 日本に行く前に、

アクティビティー　4

東京駅観光案内所 (*Tokyo Station Travel Information Center*)

With a partner, play the roles described.

Student 1: You are a tourist staying in Tokyo, and you are thinking of visiting 川崎大師 (Kawasaki Taishi Shrine), 横浜中華街 (Yokohama Chinatown), 大船撮影所 (Oohuna Movie Studio), 鎌倉大仏 (the Great Buddha of Kamakura), or 横須賀マリーンパーク (Yokosuka Marine Park). Ask your partner, who works at Tokyo Station's tourist information desk, the following questions.

1. which town to go to and what you can see/do there
2. how frequent the trains are (between 9:00 and 10:00 A.M.)
3. train departure and arrival times and fares (from Tokyo)
4. whether you have to transfer

Student 2: You work at the tourist information center in Tokyo Station. Give your partner the requested information, using the following chart.

STATION	TRAIN 23	TRAIN 26	TRAIN 41	TRAIN 56	TRAIN 58	TRAIN 60	FARE (IN YEN)
Tokyo	9:00		9:20	9:40		10:00	
Kawasaki (shrine)	9:20		9:40	10:00		10:20	210
Yokohama (Chinatown)			9:50			10:30	340
Oohuna (movie studio)		9:35	9:55		10:15	10:35	380
Kamakura (Buddha)		10:00				10:40	670
Yokosuka (Marine Park)		10:15			10:55		830

2

第二章 家(いえ)で

At Home

新(あたら)しい住宅地(じゅうたくち)

Objectives

In this lesson, you are going to

- Talk about houses, furnishings, and appliances
- Talk about household chores
- Learn to express a purpose
- Talk about giving and receiving
- Learn to express permission
- Learn to offer advice
- Learn to scan directions to houses
- Learn to scan real estate ads
- Learn to talk with real estate agents
- Learn how to invite people to your house

Vocabulary and Grammar 2A

Vocabulary and Oral Activities

Houses

Vocabulary: Houses

住宅	じゅうたく	residence; housing
マンション		apartment building; condominium
団地	だんち	public housing development; apartment complex
(二)階建て	(に)かいだて	(two-)story
住む	すむ	to reside; to live
庭	にわ	garden; yard
戸、ドア	と	door

Rooms in a House

玄関	げんかん	entry hall; foyer
廊下	ろうか	hallway
部屋	へや	room
居間／茶の間	いま／ちゃのま	living room
リビング・ルーム		living room
ダイニング・キッチン		eat-in kitchen (lit., *dining kitchen*)
客間／応接間	きゃくま／おうせつま	sitting room for entertaining guests
寝室	しんしつ	bedroom
浴室	よくしつ	bathing room (room with bathtub/shower)
洗面所	せんめんじょ	washstand (area with sink for washing hands and face)
お手洗い、トイレ	おてあらい	rest room; toilet
和室、日本間	わしつ、にほんま	Japanese-style room
洋室、洋間	ようしつ、ようま	Western-style room

Building a House

建てる	たてる	to build
建築家	けんちくか	architect
大工	だいく	carpenter
天井	てんじょう	ceiling
床	ゆか	floor
屋根	やね	roof
階段	かいだん	stairway; steps

Review: アパート、家、…階、壁、キッチン、近所、…軒、狭い、台所、広い、窓

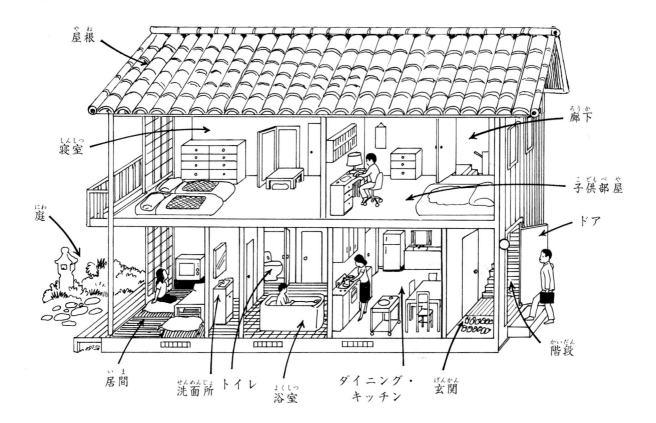

屋根（やね）
寝室（しんしつ）
庭（にわ）
廊下（ろうか）
子供部屋（こどもべや）
ドア
階段（かいだん）
居間（いま）
洗面所（せんめんじょ）
トイレ
浴室（よくしつ）
ダイニング・キッチン
玄関（げんかん）

CULTURE NOTE • 洋室（ようしつ）と和室（わしつ）

Most houses built in Japan in recent years have both Western-style rooms (洋室 [ようしつ]) and Japanese-style rooms (和室 [わしつ] or 日本間 [にほんま]). The Western-style rooms look similar to those found in houses in Western countries, although some minor features of the accessories and decor would be unfamiliar to the foreign visitor. No one may wear street shoes anywhere inside a Japanese house, so everyone wears slippers in the Western-style rooms and in the hallways.

Only stocking feet are permitted inside a Japanese-style room, however, because of the delicate **tatami** (畳 [たたみ]) mats that cover the floor. The Japanese-style room is separated from other rooms or hallways by a **husuma** (襖 [ふすま]), or opaque sliding door. **Shooji** (障子 [しょうじ]), which are made of translucent paper stretched over wooden latticework and often mounted on a sliding door,

cover the windows or other sources of light. Often there is a **tokonoma** (床の間 [とこのま]), an alcove featuring a decorative scroll and a flower arrangement suitable to the season. The furniture (described more fully in the Culture Note 日本の家具 [にほんのかぐ] that appears later in this chapter) is low to the floor and often adaptable to multiple uses.

Although Western-style hotels and recently built small apartments have Western-style bathrooms, with the toilet, sink, and bathtub all in one room, the traditional preference is for keeping the three functions separate. The room with the deep, gas-heated bathtub is called the 浴室 (よくしつ) or the お風呂 (おふろ); the room or area with the sink for washing one's hands and face is called the 洗面所 (せんめんじょ); and the room with the toilet is called the お手洗い (おてあらい) or the トイレ.

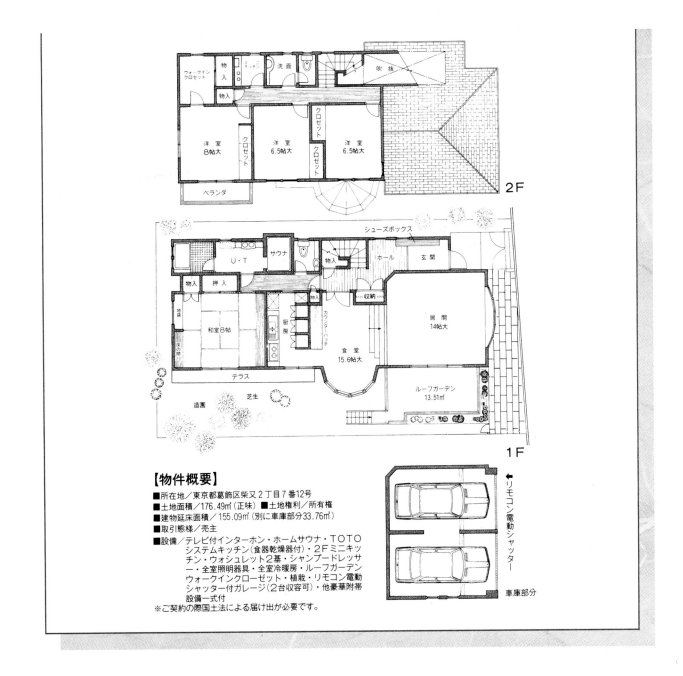

2F

1F

【物件概要】
■所在地／東京都葛飾区柴又2丁目7番12号
■土地面積／176.49㎡（正味）■土地権利／所有権
■建物延床面積／155.09㎡（別に車庫部分33.76㎡）
■取引態様／売主
■設備／テレビ付インターホン・ホームサウナ・TOTO
システムキッチン（食器乾燥器付）・2Fミニキッ
チン・ウォシュレット2基・シャンプードレッサ
ー・全室照明器具・全室冷暖房・ルーフガーデン
ウォークインクローゼット・植栽・リモコン電動
シャッター付ガレージ（2台収容可）・他豪華附帯
設備一式付
※ご契約の際国土法による届け出が必要です。

← リモコン電動シャッター

車庫部分

✳ アクティビティー　1

ここはどこですか。(*Where is this?*)

In what part of the house are the following statements typically heard?

1. 赤ちゃん (*baby*) が寝ているから、静かにしなさい。
2. 石けん (*soap*) がもうないですよ。

3. ああ、林さん、いらっしゃい。(*Welcome!*)

4. もう 8 時ですよ。起きなさい。

5. お母さん!紙!

6. きれいな花ですね。

7. どうぞ食べてください。

8. お茶をどうぞ。

Grammar and Practice Activities

9. To Do Things Like Such and Such: 〜たり... 〜たり

カワムラ：大助さん、会社の仕事のほうはどうですか。
山口：忙しかったり、暇だったりです。
カワムラ：英語の勉強のほうはどうですか。
山口：したり、しなかったりです。

KAWAMURA: Daisuke, how is your work at the company?　YAMAGUCHI: We're sometimes busy, sometimes not.　KAWAMURA: How is your English study?　YAMAGUCHI: I sometimes study (lit., *do it*) and sometimes don't.

9.1 The ～たり...～たり construction expresses such meanings as *do this, do that, and do others like them; do these things, among other similar activities.* Thus it is used to express only representative actions or states, with the implication that there are additional related actions or states not mentioned explicitly.

> Plain past verb, + り、
> Plain past i- or na-adjective + り $\Big\}$ + する or だ

Because the plain, past form of many verbs and all adjectives ends in た, this pattern is often called the たり、たり construction.

昨日は日本語を勉強したり、音楽を聞いたりしました。
Yesterday I studied Japanese and listened to music, among other things.

In most cases, two actions or states are expressed in this construction, but you can express more than two (usually three), as shown in the following examples, or only one. The tense of the actions or states is determined by that of the sentence-final する or だ, whether expressed or implicit.

休みの日は、テレビを見たり、本を読んだり、買い物をしたりする。
On my days off, I do things like watching television, reading books, and shopping.

Whatever the number of actions or states, they don't necessarily occur in the order given, unlike the ～て...～て construction.

昨日はテレビを見て、本を読んで、それから買い物をしました。
Yesterday, I watched television, read a book, and then shopped. (Also implied is that the speaker didn't do any major activities other than these.)

9.2 When you use the affirmative and negative form of a predicate in this construction, it means *sometimes yes, sometimes no.* When an inconsistent state is described, the copula だ is used in place of する after ～たり、～たり.

牛乳は飲んだり、飲まなかったりです。
I sometimes drink milk and sometimes don't.
私の作る料理はおいしかったり、おいしくなかったりだ。
The food I cook is sometimes delicious, sometimes not.

A pair of verbs with contrastive or related meanings is often used in this construction, too, implying that the two actions or states, which are usually opposites, have been alternating.

子供が何度も家を出たり、入ったりしました。
The children kept going in and out of the house.

ダイアログ：買い物をしたり、映画へ行ったりしました。(*We went shopping, went to movies, and did other things.*)

ブラウン：町田さん、先週は何をしましたか。

町田：札幌からめいが来たので、一緒に買い物をしたり、映画へ行ったりしました。ブラウンさんは？

ブラウン：私はテレビばかり見ていました。

町田：じゃあ、いい日本語の勉強になりましたね。

Practice the dialogue, substituting the following phrases for the underlined portion.

1. テニスをする、ビデオを見る
2. 話す、料理をする
3. レストランで食事する、ウインドーショッピングする
4. 音楽を聞く、ケーキを作る

言語ノート

ばかり

Noun + ばかり means *only (one thing)*, *nothing (or little else) but (one thing)*. ばかり is different from だけ, which also means *only*, in a significant way. Compare these sentences.

日本語だけ勉強した。
I studied only Japanese.
日本語ばかり勉強した。
I studied only Japanese and nothing else.

The first sentence simply states that the speaker studied only Japanese. The second sentence implies that the speaker studied only Japanese in spite of the fact that he or she should have studied other subjects; it implies that the speaker ignored other subjects. Because of this implication, ばかり is sometimes used to express unfairness, bias, or other negative meanings.

BROWN: Ms. Machida, what did you do over the weekend?　MACHIDA: Since my niece visited (lit., *came*) from Sapporo, we went shopping, went to movies, and did other things together. How about you?　BROWN: I just watched TV.　MACHIDA: Then it was good Japanese-language study.

アクティビティー　3

歌を歌ったりします。(*We do things like singing.*)

Following the example, complete the sentences using 〜たり...〜たり.
Remember to omit the incompatible activity.

[例]　東京では(東京タワーを見る、銀座へ行く、シアーズタワーへ行く)
　　　しました。→ 東京では東京タワーを見たり、銀座へ行ったりしました。

1. 冬は(海で泳ぐ、スキーをする、スケートをする)します。
2. パーティーでは(お酒を飲む、踊る、手紙を書く)した。
3. お客さんが来るので、(買い物をする、学校へ行く、料理をする)
　　しました。
4. 大学では(クラスに出る、友だちと話す、朝早く起きる)する。
5. 音楽が好きなので、(タイプする、コンサートへ行く、
　　レコードを聞く)します。
6. 自分の(*one's own*)部屋でいつも(勉強する、テニスをする、
　　本を読む)します。
7. 昨日は(晴れる、雨が降る、強い風が吹く)して、ひどい(*terrible*)
　　お天気でした。
8. リゾートでは(テニスをする、ゴルフをする、電車に乗る)すること
　　ができます。

アクティビティー　4

歩いたり、歩かなかったりです。(*Sometimes I walk, sometimes not.*)

Following the example, answer these questions.

[例]　毎日、ごはんを食べますか。→
　　　いいえ、食べたり、食べなかったりです。

1. 毎朝、ジョギングをしますか。
2. 毎週、両親に手紙を書きますか。
3. 毎週、うちに電話しますか。
4. 毎日、暇ですか。
5. あの先生はいつもやさしいんですか。
6. いつも早く起きるんですか。
7. この町はいつも静かなんですか。

Vocabulary Library

In and Around the House

門	もん	gate
塀	へい	wall
表礼	ひょうさつ	nameplate
ベル		doorbell
インターフォン		intercom
鍵（をかける）	かぎ（をかける）	key; lock (to lock)
郵便受け	ゆうびんうけ	mailbox (*for receiving mail*)
書斎	しょさい	study
勝手口	かってぐち	back (or side) door
流し	ながし	sink
車庫	しゃこ	garage; carport
物置	ものおき	storeroom
柱	はしら	pillar
煙突	えんとつ	chimney

Loanwords: ガレージ、ダイニング・ルーム、ベランダ、バルコニー

✳ アクティビティー 5

何をしますか。(*What do you do?*)

Ask a classmate what people typically do in the following places around the house.

［例］ 玄関 → 一玄関で何をしますか。
　　　　　　 一靴をぬいだり、はいたりします。or
　　　　　　 一あいさつ (*greetings*) したりします。

1. 台所
2. 勉強部屋
3. 客間
4. リビングルーム
5. 庭
6. ベッドルーム
7. 洗面所
8. ダイニングルーム
9. 浴室／お風呂

✳ アクティビティー 6

どんな家に住んでいますか。(*What type of house do you live in?*)

Answer these questions.

1. あなたの家は大きいですか。小さいですか。
2. 新しいですか。古いですか。
3. 何階建てですか。

4. いくつ部屋がありますか。
5. 寝室はいくつありますか。
6. あなたの部屋は何階にありますか。部屋は広いですか。狭いですか。
7. 部屋の天井は何色ですか。壁は何色ですか。
8. あなたの家の隣にはどんな人が住んでいますか。
9. 家のそばにどんな店がありますか。
10. 家から一番近くのバス停まで何分かかりますか。

CULTURE NOTE • Describing Living Space

Even though there are many Western-style houses and apartments in Japan today, the floor area of a room is always measured by the number of **tatami** mats that would fit into it. A standard **tatami** mat measures about 1 meter by 2 meters, enough space for one person to sleep. The size can vary somewhat by region and depending on the type of building under consideration, but the ratio of length to width is always approximately 2 to 1.

The most common standard room sizes are 1, 3, 4.5, 6, 8, and 10 mats, although larger rooms do exist. Each number of mats has a standard layout, as shown in the drawings.

Understanding this system of measurement allows you to read the real estate and rental advertisements in newspapers or in the windows of real estate agents' offices. Roman letters in advertisements refer to either a living room (L) or an eat-in kitchen (DK, from ダイニング・キッチン). A 2DK has an eat-in kitchen and two other rooms. Only the most luxurious houses have separate dining rooms.

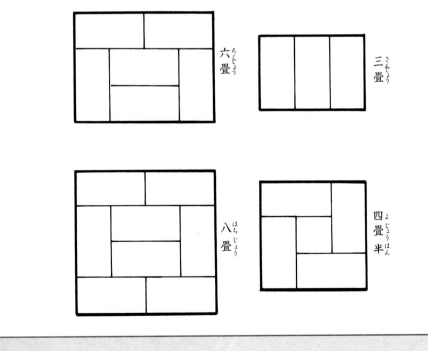

六畳　三畳　八畳　四畳半

私のうち、うちの近所 (*My house and my neighborhood*)

Work in pairs. Describe the following to your partner. If necessary, draw a
picture.

1. the floor plan of your house
2. who lives in your neighborhood
3. what is in your neighborhood

[例]

1. 玄関を入ると、右に客間、左に居間があります。...
2. うちの隣にはウイリアムさんの家族が住んでいます。...
3. 家を出て右に行くと、セブン・イレブンがありす。...

Vocabulary Library

Real Estate

不動産屋	ふどうさんや	real estate agency or agent
探す	さがす	to look for
住宅地	じゅうたくち	residential area
郊外	こうがい	the suburbs
住所	じゅうしょ	address
...部屋	...へや	counter for rooms
...間	...ま	counter for rooms
引っ越す	ひっこす	to move (from one address to another)
土地	とち	land
家主	やぬし	property or apartment owner (*formal*)
大家さん	おおやさん	property or apartment owner (*colloquial*)
借家人	しゃくやにん	tenant
貸す	かす	to rent out; to lend
借りる	かりる	to rent (from); to borrow
家賃	やちん	rent (money)
中古	ちゅうこ	secondhand; used
（お）隣	（お）となり	next-door neighbor

Loanwords: コンドミニアム、タウンハウス、モデルルーム

Vocabulary and Grammar 2B

Vocabulary and Oral Activities

Furnishings and Appliances

Vocabulary: Furnishings and Appliances

Furnishings

家具	かぐ	furniture
本棚	ほんだな	bookshelf
たんす／タンス		chest of drawers; wardrobe
鏡	かがみ	mirror

Review: 椅子、絵、カーテン、机、テーブル

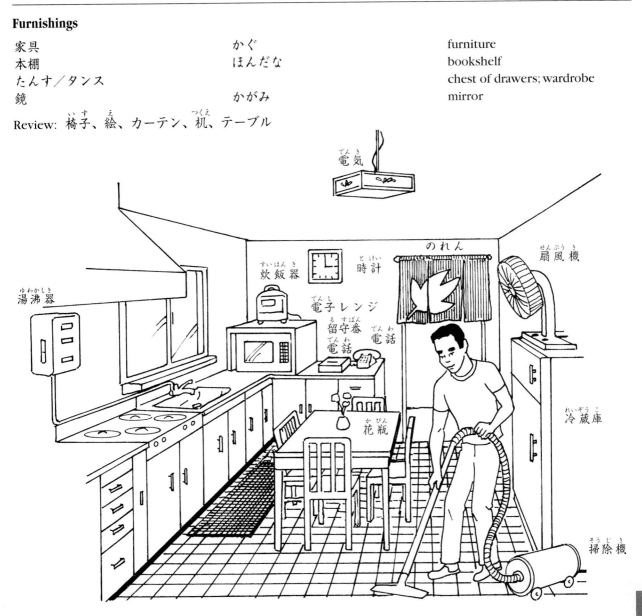

Electric Appliances

電気製品	でんきせいひん	electric appliance
留守番電話	るすばんでんわ	answering machine
電子レンジ	でんしレンジ	microwave oven
冷蔵庫	れいぞうこ	refrigerator
洗濯機	せんたくき	washing machine
エアコン、クーラー		air conditioner
スタンド		floor lamp, desk lamp
掃除機	そうじき	vacuum cleaner
炊飯器	すいはんき	rice cooker
扇風機	せんぷうき	electric fan
ミシン		sewing machine
ストーブ		space heater
電気（をつける／を消す）	でんき（をつける／をけす）	(to turn on/to turn off) a light
スイッチ（を入れる／を切る）	スイッチ（をいれる／をきる）	to turn on a switch

Review: ステレオ、テレビ、電話、時計、ラジオ

✳ **アクティビティー　8**

どんな家具がありますか。どんな電気製品がありますか。(*What kind of furniture and electric appliances are located here?*)

Tell what furnishings and electric appliances are typically found in the following places.

1. 寝室
2. 浴室
3. 居間
4. 台所
5. 勉強部屋
6. ダイニング・ルーム

Discuss the furnishings and electric appliances you have at home.

✳ **アクティビティー　9**

こんな時、何が必要ですか。(*What do you need on this occasion?*)

Tell what electric appliance you need on the following occasions.

1. 今日はとてもむし暑いです。
2. 部屋がきたないです。
3. 生の魚がたくさんあります。
4. 父がコーヒーを飲みたがっています。

5. 今夜見たいテレビの映画があります。でも、仕事がありますから、
   見られません。

6. 私のドレスがしわくちゃ(*wrinkled*)です。

7. ジョギングをしながら、音楽を聞きたいです。

8. 今日はとても寒いです。

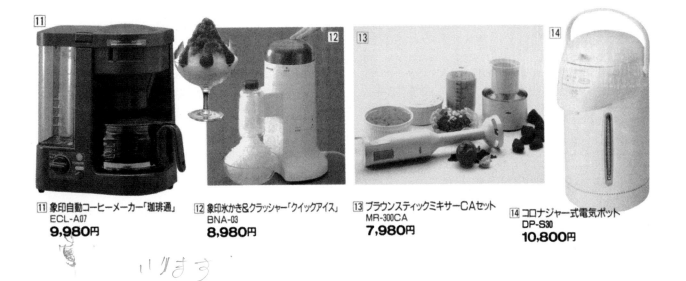

11 象印自動コーヒーメーカー「珈琲通」
ECL-A07
9,980円

12 象印氷かき&クラッシャー「クイックアイス」
BNA-03
8,980円

13 ブラウンスティックミキサーCAセット
MR-300CA
7,980円

14 コロナジャー式電気ポット
DP-S30
10,800円

Vocabulary Library

More Furnishings and Electric Appliances

屑入れ	くずいれ	wastebasket
ごみ箱	ごみばこ	trash basket
引き出し	ひきだし	drawer
棚	たな	shelf

Loanwords: カーペット、クロゼット、ソファー、ブラインド、ベッド

乾燥機	かんそうき	clothes dryer
電球	でんきゅう	lightbulb
目覚まし時計	めざましどけい	alarm clock
ガスレンジ		gas stove

Loanwords: アイロン、ウォークマン、オーブン、コーヒーメーカー、コンピュータ、シェーバー、ジューサー、トースター、ドライヤー、ミキサー、ヒーター、ビデオレコーダー、CDプレーヤー、リモコン (for TV, air conditioner, etc.)

CULTURE NOTE • 日本の家具（かぐ）

Because a traditional Japanese-style room may be used for many purposes during the day, the furniture is minimal and portable. In recent years, people in Western countries have become familiar with futon-style mattresses, but the Japanese term **futon** actually refers to the entire ensemble of bedding: the folding mattress, or 敷布団（しきぶとん）; the overquilt, or 掛け布団（かけぶとん）; and the pillow, or 枕（まくら）, which is smaller than a Western-style pillow and often filled with rice husks. During the day, the **futon** is stored in the 押入れ（おしいれ）, a closet with a sliding door and a single shelf at waist height, but on sunny days people like to air their bedding outside to prevent the growth of mildew.

In a small house or apartment, the same room that serves as the bedroom by night may serve as the living room by day. A short-legged table (座卓 [ざたく]) surrounded by large square **zabuton** cushions （座布団 [ざぶとん]） or legless chairs (座椅子 [ざいす]) is the main furniture in the room. During the cold months, the 座卓 may be replaced by a **kotatsu,** a table with an electric heating element underneath and covered by a quilt and a second tabletop. Many Japanese houses and apartments lack central heating, so the **kotatsu** and ストーブ (*space heaters running on kerosene, natural gas, or electricity*), along with layered clothing, are the principal ways to keep warm.

Many families have a small Buddhist altar (仏壇 [ぶつだん]) somewhere in the house, and some have a Shinto altar (神棚 [かみだな]) as well.

Grammar and Practice Exercises

10. Expressing a Purpose: . . . ため（に）

> ブラウン：高田（たかだ）さんはどこかへ出（で）かけたんですか。
>
> 佐野（さの）：ええ、会議（かいぎ）に出（で）るために、京都（きょうと）へ行きました。
>
> ブラウン：いつ帰（かえ）ってくるんですか。
>
> 佐野（さの）：あさってです。ブラウンさんのために、おみやげを買（か）ってくるって言っていましたよ。
>
> ブラウン：わあ、うれしい。

10.1 The combination of a noun or verb plus the noun ため forms an adverbial phrase expressing purpose.

BROWN: Did Mr. Takada go somewhere?　SANO: Yes, he went to Kyoto in order to attend a meeting. BROWN: When will he come back?　SANO: The day after tomorrow. He said that he would buy a souvenir for you.　BROWN: Wow, I'm glad to hear that.

```
┌─────────────────────────────────────────────┐
│  Noun + の                                     │
│                          } + ため (に)         │
│  Verb ( plain, nonpast)                        │
└─────────────────────────────────────────────┘
```

in order to (do something)
for the sake of (someone, something)

林さんのために、ケーキを作った。
I made a cake for Mr. Hayashi.
テレビを見るために、居間へ行った。
In order to watch TV, I went to the living room.

The following construction modifies a noun as an adjectival phrase.

```
┌─────────────────────────────────────────────┐
│  Noun + の                                     │
│                          } + ため + の         │
│  Verb ( plain, nonpast)                        │
└─────────────────────────────────────────────┘
```

for (the purpose of doing something)
intended, made especially for (someone or something)

これは子供のためのゲームです。
This is a game for children.
これはお茶を飲むための茶わんです。
This is a cup for drinking Japanese tea.

10.2 ため is a noun meaning *purpose, benefit, reason, cause.* When ため(に) is used to mean *because,* it may be preceded by plain, past, or nonpast forms of verbs and adjectives, or by the pronoun forms of the copula.

期末試験があった (or ある) ために、コンサートへ行けませんでした。
Because there was a term test, I couldn't go to the concert.
あまりにも高かったため、だれもその絵を買いませんでした。
Because it was too expensive, nobody bought that painting.
英語が下手なため、彼の言っていることがわからない。
Because he is poor at speaking English, I cannot understand what he is saying.
あまりにも静かだった (or 静かな) ため、人がいるとは思わなかった。
Because it was so quiet, I didn't think that anyone was there.

When ため is used to express reason or cause, it can be replaced with から or ので in most cases, with little change in meaning other than that ため sounds somewhat more formal.

アクティビティー　10

何のためですか。(*For what purpose?*)

Combine the two sentences using ため (に).(All questions are concerned with purpose.)

[例]　チンさんは昼ごはんを食べます。レストランへ行きました。→
　　　チンさんは昼ごはんを食べるために、レストランへ行きました。

1. フランス語を勉強します。パリへ行くことにしました。
2. 日本語を練習します。日本人の友だちをたくさん作りました。
3. 漢字の意味(*meaning*) を調べます(*to check*)。辞書を使いました。
4. 山本さんに会います。喫茶店で待ちます。
5. スキーをします。北海道へ行きました。
6. トイレを使います。デパートに入りました。
7. コーヒーを飲みます。喫茶店に入りました。

アクティビティー　11

昼ごはんを食べるために、うちに帰ります。(*I go home at noon in order to eat lunch.*)

Complete these sentences, explaining how you would accomplish each purpose or what the result of the reason given would be.

1. 日本語がまだ下手なため、
2. 夕ごはんを作るため、
3. アパートを借りる (*to rent*) ため、
4. 部屋が狭いため、
5. おいしいコーヒーを飲むため、
6. 雪が降らないため、
7. パーティーをするために、
8. 試験のために、

✳ アクティビティー　12

いつ使いますか。何のために使いますか。(*When do you use it? For what purpose do you use it?*)

Useful Verbs:　かわかす *to dry*, 縫う *to sew*

[例]　扇風機 → 暑い時、使います。
　　　コーヒーメーカー → コーヒーを作るために使います。

1. 洗濯機
せんたくき
2. ステレオ
3. カメラ
4. シェーバー
5. ヘアードライヤー
6. ワープロ
7. 掃除機
そうじき
8. トースター
9. ミシン

Vocabulary Library

In a Japanese House		
靴箱	くつばこ	shoe cabinet
押入れ	おしいれ	**futon** closet
座布団	ざぶとん	floor cushion
畳	たたみ	**tatami** (woven reed) mat
障子	しょうじ	**shoji** screen (made of translucent paper)
ふすま		sliding door of opaque paper
床の間	とこのま	alcove
こたつ		table with built-in heater

11. Giving and Receiving

高田： 昨日、村山さんの部屋へ行ったら、りんごをくれました。
たかだ　きのう　むらやま　　へや

ブラウン： 村山さんはよくいろいろなものをくれますね。
むらやま

高田： ええ、今度は私も何かあげないといけませんね。
たかだ　　　こんど　わたし

カーティス： 今年一年、大野先生にはお世話になりましたね。
ことしいちねん　おおの　　　せわ

チン： そうですね。お礼に何かさしあげましょうか。
れい

カーティス： 大野先生はお酒がお好きだから、ウイスキーをさしあげません
おおの　　　さけ
か。

チン： それはいい考えですね。
かんが

TAKADA: When I went to Ms. Murayama's place (lit., *room*) yesterday, she gave me some apples.
BROWN: Ms. Murayama always gives us various things.　TAKADA: Yes, next time I (really) must give her something too.

CURTIS: We've been well taken care of by Professor Oono all year.　CHIN: We sure have. Let's give him something as a token of our gratitude.　CURTIS: Professor Oono likes liquor, so shall we give him whiskey?　CHIN: That's a good idea.

チン：　大野先生にウイスキーをさしあげたら、とても喜んで、私たち
　　　　　に辞書を一冊ずつくださいました。

カーティス：　本当ですか。

　　　　チン：　カーティスさん、これはあなたの辞書です。

カーティス：　わあ、いただいてもいいんでしょうか。

ずつ

ずつ preceded by a number plus counter or by a word expressing quantity means *each, of each, at a time.*

女子学生と男子学生が、8人ずついます。
There are eight female students and eight male students.
   (Lit., *There are eight each of female and male students.*)

みんなにノートを一冊ずつあげよう。
I will give everyone one notebook each.

少しずつわかってきました。
I have come to understand gradually (lit., *a little at a time*).

11.1 Japanese expressions for giving and receiving are very different from those in English. Suppose that Mr. Mimura gave a book to me. Then, Mr. Mimura would be a giver and I would be a receiver. If the giver is the subject, you say

1. Mr. Mimura gave a book to me.

If the receiver is the subject, you say

2. I received a book from Mr. Mimura, or
3. I was given a book by Mr. Mimura.

11.2 In Japanese, there are five verbs corresponding to *to give* and two verbs corresponding to *to receive*. The choice of verbs to describe giving and receiving in Japanese depends on the social relationship between the giver and the receiver, specifically, whether or not they belong to the same social group (family, colleagues, etc.). The constraints on the social relationship can be summarized as follows.

1. G が R に X をあげる。 (*G gives X to R.*)

CHIN: When I gave the whiskey to Professor Oono, he was very pleased and gave a dictionary to each of us.　CURTIS: Really?　CHIN: Mr. Curtis, this is your dictionary.　CURTIS: Wow! Do you think it's all right to accept (lit., *receive*) this from him?

At Home

The Giver can be anyone (typically, speaker or in-group person). The Recipient cannot include the speaker. The Giver and the Recipient are socially equal.

私はあなた／彼にこの本をあげます。

あなたはこの本を彼にあげますか。

彼は彼女に本をあげました。

2. Gが Rに Xをくれる。(*G gives X to R.*)

The Recipient is the speaker or an in-group person, someone closer to the speaker than the Giver. The Giver is socially equal or inferior to the Recipient.

あの人は／彼は[私に]本をくれました。

彼女は私の弟に本をくれましたか。

彼もあなたに本をくれましたね。

3. RがGに(から)Xをもらう。(*R receives X from G.*)

The Recipient can be anyone. The Giver is socially equal or inferior to the Recipient.

私はあなた／彼に本をもらいました。

あなたも彼から本をもらいましたか。

彼は彼女に本をもらいました。

彼は私からその本をもらったんです。

In Pattern 1, when the Recipient is an in-group superior person or an out-group person, さしあげる is used instead of あげる. In Patterns 2 and 3, when the Giver is an in-group superior person or an out-group person, くださる and いただく are used instead of くれる and もらう, respectively.

> Because くれるand くださる always mean *give to me* or *give to my group*, you do not have to add 私に unless you are emphasizing the *to me* part.

私は先生に本をさしあげました。

I gave a book to my professor.

先生は[私に]本をくださいました。

My professor gave me a book.

私は先生から本をいただきました。

I was given a book by my professor.

In Pattern 1, when the Recipient is notably inferior to the Giver, やる is used.

> It must be noted that many Japanese consider やる to be a vulgar word, so they use あげる even in referring to dogs or flowers.

私は犬にドッグフードをやりました。

I gave some dog food to my dog.

ブラウンさんは花に水をやった。

Ms. Brown watered the flowers. (*Lit., Ms. Brown gave water to the flowers.*)

Vocabulary and Grammar 2B

95 | 九十五

11.3 Doing something for the sake or the benefit of someone else is considered in Japanese to be the same as giving and receiving a benefit. Such benefactive acts are expressed by attaching the te-form of verbs to the expressions of giving and receiving in Grammar 11.2.

Te-form of verb +	あげる、さしあげる、やる くれる、くださる もらう、いただく

The choice of verbs follows the same rules as presented earlier.

[私は] 山本さんの車を洗ってあげました。
I washed Ms. Yamamoto's car for her.

[私は] 先生のかばんを持ってさしあげました。
I carried my professor's bag for him.

弟の宿題を見てやりました。
I looked over my brother's homework.

三村さんは日本語を教えてくれました。
Mr. Mimura taught me Japanese.

私は佐野さんにアイロンをかけてもらいました。
I had Ms. Sano do my ironing.

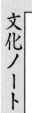

CULTURE NOTE • 義理

The word 義理 refers to the duties and obligations people have to carry out in order to maintain harmonious relations with others and fulfill their roles in society, whether they like it or not. For example, employees have 義理 toward their employers in the sense that they are expected to work hard, be honest, and always think of the company's interests; the employers have 義理 toward their employees in the sense that they are expected to treat them fairly and look out for their welfare in an almost paternalistic way. 義理 is contrasted with 人情 (にんじょう), which is what people's emotions or gut feelings tell them to do, and which is often in conflict with their social duties.

ダイアログ：このカメラ、あげましょうか。(*I will give you this camera.*)

山口： カワムラさんはカメラを持っていますか。

カワムラ： いいえ。

山口： じゃあ。このカメラ、あげましょうか。

カワムラ： 本当ですか。

山口： ええ、父から新しいのをもらったので、もうこれはいらないんです。

Practice the dialogue, substituting these items for the underlined word.

1. ワープロ　　　　　2. ウォークマン　　　　　3. ヘッドホン

アクティビティー 14

いいものをくれました。(*You gave me something good.*)

Look at the accompanying picture, and complete the following sentences, taking Masao Hayashi's point of view.

[例]　町田さんは、セーターをくれました。

1. カワムラさんは、
2. 横井先生は、
3. 母は、
4. 犬のポチに、
5. 母に、
6. 横井先生に、
7. カワムラさんに、
8. 町田さんに、

Answer these questions.

9. カワムラさんから何をもらいましたか。
10. 町田さんから何をもらいましたか。
11. 横井先生から何をいただきましたか。
12. お母さんから何をもらいましたか。

横井先生

ジュース　ノート

もらいました

町田　セーター　ラケット　カワムラ

ブラウス　林　かばん

あげました

マッサージ機　お金　ドッグフード　ポチ

母

ジャンケンポン！
あいこでしょ！

YAMAGUCHI: Do you have a camera?　KAWAMURA: No.　YAMAGUCHI: Well, shall I give you this camera? KAWAMURA: Really?　YAMAGUCHI: Yes, I got a new one from my father, so I don't need this one anymore.

Vocabulary and Grammar 2B　　　　　97　　九十七

アクティビティー 15

シェーバーをあげた。(*I gave him a razor.*)

Fill in the blanks with the most appropriate verb for giving or receiving.

1. 私は毎年クリスマスには家族にプレゼントをします。去年は父に
   シェーバーを（　　　）。母にはスカーフを（　　　）。妹にはアイロンを
   （　　　）ましたし、弟にはラジカセを（　　　）。家族のみんなも私に
   プレゼントを（　　　）。父は私にペンを（　　　）ましたし、母は時計を
   （　　　）。弟からはスニーカーを（　　　）。妹からは本を（　　　）。

2. 先日、私は友人の山下さんから今年の10月に結婚するという手紙を
   （　　　）。山下さんにはいつもお世話になっていますし、私が結婚
   した時も、トースターを（　　　）ので、何かいい電気製品を（　　　）
   つもりです。会社の佐藤さんに話したら、佐藤さんも何かいい
   電気製品を（　　　）つもりだと言っていました。

3. 先日、先生がクラスで日本の映画を見せて（　　　）。とてもおもしろい
   映画でした。それで友だちにその映画について話して（　　　）。

アクティビティー 16

もらいたいもの (*The thing I want to receive*)

Answer these questions.

1. 今年のクリスマスに一番もらいたいものは何ですか。
2. 今年のクリスマスにみんなに何をあげますか。
3. お母さんの誕生日に何をあげるつもりですか。
4. 結婚する友だちに何をあげますか。
5. 病気で寝ている友だちに何をしてあげますか。
6. 今、だれかにしてもらいたいことはありますか。

CULTURE NOTE • Gift-Giving

Gift-giving is deeply rooted in Japanese life and society. When Japanese people travel, they are expected to bring back souvenirs for virtually everyone they know—this is one reason that Japanese tourists have a reputation for being zealous shoppers. When they visit someone's home, they bring a small gift, usually sweets or some other snack food. After receiving a gift, they have to look for or create an occasion to give a return gift.

During the two big gift-giving seasons, in July (お中元[おちゅうげん]) and December (お歳暮[おせいぼ]), Japanese give presents to all the people who have done something for them, whether tangible or intangible. Thus they might give a gift to their children's teacher, their own university professor, someone who helped them get a job, their supervisor at work, or the person who introduced them to their spouse.

If you visit a Japanese home, be sure to take a small present. A small souvenir or gift-wrapped candy from your home country will be especially appreciated; or you can buy gift-wrapped packages of sweets, baked goods, or fresh fruit at department stores and special kiosks in train stations. Etiquette requires you to make some disparaging remark about the gift as you hand it over, and the recipient will most likely offer a token refusal before accepting. In contrast to the typical Western practice, some Japanese people do not open presents immediately but wait until the giver has left, often placing the present on the family's Buddhist altar (仏壇[ぶつだん]) temporarily. This way, they believe, the giver will not be embarrassed if the gift turns out to be defective or displeasing to the recipient.

✳ アクティビティー 17

誰(だれ)にもらいましたか。(*Whom did you receive it from?*)

Recently you moved into a new house and several relatives and friends gave you gifts. Using the following table, explain from whom you received what.

くれた人	ギフト
横井(よこい)先生	スタンド
林(はやし)さん	時計(とけい)
チンさん	花瓶(かびん)
おじ	炊飯器(すいはんき)
おば	トースター
大野(おおの)先生	テーブルクロス
両親(りょうしん)	テーブル
祖母(そぼ)	電子(でんし)レンジ
妹(いもうと)	コーヒーメーカー

お歳暮のシーズン (*Year-end gift-giving season*)

According to the accompanying drawing, what did each person give or receive as a year-end gift? Explain in Japanese.

部長 *department head*

伊藤部長

調味料 ↑ ↓ そば

高田さん

加山さん　ジュース →　辞書 →　ブラウンさん
　　　　　← ビール　ウィスキー ←

のり ↓ ↑ ワイシャツ

のり *seaweed*

鈴木さん

12. Expressing Permission: 〜てもいい

カワムラ：ここに座ってもよろしいですか。
女の人：すみません。連れの者が来ますので、...
カワムラ：じゃ、そちらの席に座ってもよろしいでしょうか。
女の人：ええ、こちらは空いていますよ。

KAWAMURA: May I sit here?　WOMAN: Excuse me, my companion is coming, so...　KAWAMURA: Then may I take that seat?　WOMAN: Yes, this one is free.

…中

中, attached to a noun, makes a word meaning *in the middle of* (*something*), or *in progress.* For example,

こうじちゅう 工事中	*under construction* (工事 = *construction*)
じゅんびちゅう 準備中	*in preparation* (準備 = *preparation*)
えいぎょうちゅう 営業中	*open for business* (営業 = *business operation*)
はな ちゅう 話し中	*(telephone) is busy*
しようちゅう 使用中	*in use* (使用 = *use*)
がいしゅつちゅう 外出中	*out (of the office, etc.)*

かいぎちゅう
高田はただいま会議中です。
Takada is now at a meeting.

しごとちゅう
仕事中、どうもすみませんが、ちょっとここに来てください。
I am sorry for interrupting your work, but can you come here for a while?

You often see the sign じゅんびちゅう 準備中 in front of stores and restaurants in Japan. In most cases, they are closed and no one is inside, because this sign is used to mean *closed*.

りょうり みせ まえ じゅんびちゅう
日本料理の店の前で：準備中です。

12.1 When you ask for permission, use the following construction.

Te-form of verb + も	いい？ いいですか。 かまいませんか。 いいでしょうか。 よろしいでしょうか。	in increasing order of politeness

This も may be dropped.

May I (do something)?

この辞書を使ってもいい？
May I use this dictionary?
たばこをすってもかまいませんか。
May I smoke?
2、3日休みを取ってもよろしいでしょうか。
May I take two or three days off?

The te-form of verb + も means *even if*… Thus, this construction literally means, *Is it OK even if…?*

言語ノート

Responding to a Request for Permission

このペンを使ってもいいですか。
May I use this pen?

GRANTING PERMISSION

ええ、どうぞ。
Yes, please.
ええ、けっこうですよ。
Yes, it's all right.
ええ、もちろんです。
Yes, of course.
ええ、ご自由に。
Yes, as you like it.
ええ、どうぞお使いください。
Yes, please use it.

TURNING DOWN A REQUEST

ちょっと、...
Well, …
すみませんが、ちょっと...
I'm sorry, but …
申し訳ありませんが、ちょっと...
I'm sorry (to have to say this), but …

Following are examples of the affirmative counterparts of the construction used for turning down a request, as shown in the Language Note box.

ソファーをここに動かしてもいいですよ。
You may move the couch here.

好きなだけ使ってかまいません。
Please use it as much as you like.

好きなだけ is an idiomatic expression meaning *as much as you like*.

12.2 When this construction appears before から and is followed by a wish, command, or request, the speaker is stating that he or she is accepting a possibly unfavorable limitation.

高くてもいいから、その絵がほしい。
It's OK even if it is expensive; I want that picture.

一度でもいいからあそこへ行ってみたい。
I want to try going there, even if it's just once.

12.3 Interrogatives (such as 何、だれ、いつ、どこ、どう、and いくら) plus the te-form of the verb + てもいい mean *it is all right no matter what/who/where/when/how/how much*.

何を食べてもいいですよ。
You may eat anything.

いつ帰ってもかまいません。
You may leave anytime.

ここは誰が来てもいいです。
Anyone can come here. (Lit., *It is all right whoever comes here.*)

12.4 The negative te-form of a verb followed by (も) いい means *you need not (do something)* or *you don't have to (do something)*. (Lit., *It is all right if [you don't do something]*).

ここはお金を払わなくてもいいです。
You don't have to pay here.

この仕事をしなくてもいいですか。
Is it all right even if I don't do this work?

アクティビティー 19

してもいいですか。 (*Is it all right to do it?*)

Change these sentences to requests for permission, using ～てもいいですか.

[例] クレジット・カードを使う → クレジット・カードを使ってもいいですか。

1. お風呂に入る
2. ちょっと遅れる (to be late)
3. このビールを飲む
4. ペンを借りる
5. ここに名前を書く

6. 映画に行く
7. ちょっと休む
8. 帽子をかぶる
9. 靴を脱がない
10. 町田さんと話さない

アクティビティー 20

してもいいです。(*It's OK to do it.*)

Complete the following sentences by using てもいいですよ.

1. 疲れている時は、
2. おなかがすいた時は、
3. このホテルでは、
4. 家の中では、

5. 雨が降った時は、
6. 病気の時は、
7. 電車が遅れた時は、
8. お金がない時は、

13. Negative Request: 〜ないでください

カワムラ: 林さん、じゃあ、また明日。
林: 明日？明日は休みでしょう？
カワムラ: もう忘れたんですか。明日は三村さんの誕生日パーティーが
あるでしょう。
林: ああ、ああ、すっかり忘れていました。
カワムラ: ケーキを買って来るのを忘れないでくださいね。

KAWAMURA: Mr. Hayashi, see you tomorrow.　HAYASHI: Tomorrow? Tomorrow is a holiday, isn't it?
KAWAMURA: You have already forgotten? There is a birthday party for Mr. Mimura tomorrow, isn't there?
HAYASHI: Yes, I had totally forgotten about it.　KAWAMURA: Please don't forget to buy a cake.

13.1 The following construction is used to express a negative request.

$$\text{Negative te-form of verb} + \left\{\begin{array}{l}\text{くださいませんか} \\ \text{ください} \\ \text{くれ}\end{array}\right\} \begin{array}{l}\text{in decreasing order} \\ \text{of politeness}\end{array}$$

Please don't (do something).

くれ is used only by male speakers giving orders to close friends, family members, or subordinates.

それはブラウンさんには言わないでくださいませんか。(very polite)
Please don't say that to Ms. Brown.
そこに座らないでください。
Please don't sit there.
もう電話しないでくれ。
Don't call me anymore.

13.2 In informal speech, ください is often omitted.

そこで遊ばないでね。
Please don't play here.
そんなこと言わないでよ。
Don't say such a thing.

> It is sometimes easy to confuse the negative te-form of the verb, ～ないで, with the te-form of the ～ない form of the verb, which is ～なくて. The ～ないで form is used mostly in negative commands and for the meaning of *without doing*: 勉強しないで試験を受けた means *took the test without studying*. The ～なくて form is used in other constructions, such as ～なくてはいけない、～なくてもいい, and a few others that you haven't studied yet.

どうぞ遠慮しないでください。

As you learned before, Japanese people typically refuse when they are first offered food, gifts, and favors. The person who is offering these things then says, どうぞ遠慮しないでください (*Please don't hold back,* or *Please don't hesitate*). Notice how the construction is used in these situations.

PRESENTING AND ACCEPTING A GIFT

あのう、これつまらないものですが、どうぞ。
Uh, this is a trifling thing, but please accept it.
いいえ、そんな...
No, this kind of thing ... (won't do).
どうぞ遠慮しないでください。
Please take it. (Lit., *Please don't hold back.*)

そうですか。では、ありがとうございます。
Really? Well, thank you very much.

OFFERING AND ACCEPTING A MEAL

なにもありませんが、どうぞ召し上がってください。
We don't have anything (special), but please go ahead and eat.
いいえ、どうぞおかまいなく。
No, please don't trouble yourself over me.
どうぞ遠慮しないでください。
Please help yourself.
そうですか。では、いただきます。
Really? Then I will have some.

どうぞおかまいなく is a phrase used for polite refusals, not for sincere refusals.

召し上がる is the honorific form of 食べる.

✳ アクティビティー 21

ダイアログ：ここに置いてもいいですか。(*May I put it here?*)

運送屋：スタンドはここに置いてもいいですか。

町田：いいえ、そこには置かないでください。このソファーの横に置いてください。

運送屋：じゃ、ソファーの横の花瓶はテーブルの上に動かしてもいいですか。

町田：ええ、そうしてください。

アクティビティー 22

しないでください。(*Please don't do it.*)

Where do you think you would hear these warnings or admonitions? Match the phrases in the second column to the sentences in the first column.

1. ここに車を止めないでください。　　a.　in front of a garage
2. ここに入らないでください。　　　　b.　at a filthy beach

MOVER: May I put the floor lamp here?　MACHIDA: No, please don't put it there. Please put it next to this couch.　MOVER: Then may I move the vase that is next to the couch over to the top of the table?
MACHIDA: Yes, please do that.

3. たばこを吸わないでください。　　　c.　in a hospital waiting room

4. ごみを捨てないでください。　　　　d.　on a construction site
   (*Please don't litter*.)
　　　　　　　　　　　　　　　　　　　e.　on a just-painted bench
5. 座らないでください。
　　　　　　　　　　　　　　　　　　　f.　in a park
6. ここで泳がないでください。

アクティビティー　23

まちがえないでください。(*Please don't make a mistake.*)

Change these sentences to negative commands by using 〜ないでください.

1. 教室の中で、ものを食べる　　　　5. たくさんお金を使う

2. ベッドの中で、たばこを吸う　　　6. クラスを休む

3. このセーターは洗濯機で洗う　　　7. 夜、電話する

4. ここでお酒を飲む　　　　　　　　8. うちに来る

✳ アクティビティー　24

引っ越し (*Moving*)

Work in pairs. One of you is in the process of moving into a new house. The other
is a mover. The mover asks permission from the new resident before doing
anything. The mover's job is to place the following furnishings and appliances in
appropriate places in the house represented by the accompanying floor plan.
Now get to work!

Useful Vocabulary: 置く *to put, place,* 動かす *to move (something),*
運ぶ *to carry*

ステレオ	テレビ
ソファー	電話
エアコン	テーブル
花瓶	椅子
絵	たんす
トースター	靴箱 (*shoe cabinet*)
鏡	

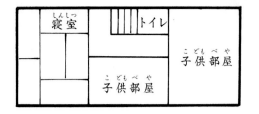

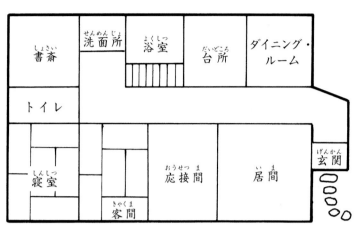

Vocabulary and Grammar 2C

Vocabulary and Oral Exercises

Household Chores

Vocabulary: Household Chores

家事	かじ	housework; household chores
掃除（する）	そうじ（する）	cleaning (to do cleaning)
磨く	みがく	to polish; to wipe clean a smooth surface
拭く	ふく	to wipe
洗濯（する）	せんたく（する）	laundry (to do laundry)
洗濯物	せんたくもの	laundry; things to be laundered
干す	ほす	to air-dry (something); to air (something) out
片付ける	かたづける	to straighten (something) up
縫い物（をする）	ぬいもの（をする）	(to do) sewing

アイロンをかける   to iron
庭いじり（をする）   にわいじり（をする）   (to do) gardening
直す   なおす   to repair; to mend
手伝う   てつだう   to help; to assist

Review: 料理（する）、洗う、皿、買い物

Note the particles: シャツにアイロンをかける *to iron a shirt.*

Note the particles: 林さんの仕事を手伝う *to help Mr. Hayashi with his work.*

アクティビティー 25

どれですか。(*Which one?*)

Which of the words listed in parentheses is most closely connected to the first word given?

[例] 家事（タイピング、コピー、洗濯、ミーティング、出張）
→ 洗濯です。家事の一つです。(*It's one of my house chores.*)

1. 磨く（ドレス、窓ガラス、テレビ、セーター）
2. 洗濯（寝室、下着、教科書、買い物）
3. アイロン（靴、下着、ドレス、帽子）
4. 庭いじり（キャンプ、ヨット、クロッカス、サーフィン）
5. 洗う（椅子、机、たんす、皿）
6. 掃除（直す、手伝う、干す、拭く）
7. 料理（客間、寝室、トイレ、台所）
8. 縫い物（コンピュータ、ミシン、冷蔵庫、掃除機）

Grammar and Practice Activities

14. Offering Advice: ... ほうがいい

山口：この部屋、昼間でもちょっと暗いんです。どうしたらいいでしょうか。
大工：ううん、この窓をもう少し大きくしたほうがいいですね。
山口：壁の色はどうでしょうか。
大工：そうですね。もう少し明るい色に変えたほうがいいと思います。

YAMAGUCHI: This room is a bit dark even during the day.   CARPENTER: Umm, it would be better to make this window somewhat larger, wouldn't it?   YAMAGUCHI: How about the wall color?   CARPENTER: Let me see. I think it would be best to change it to a brighter color.

The following construction is used to offer advice or make a strong suggestion.

Ta-form of verb
Nonpast, negative form of verb } + ほうがいい（です）

You'd better ([not] do something)
It's better for you ([not] to do something)
You'd better not; you shouldn't

電車が来ますよ。急いだほうがいいですよ。
The train is coming. You'd better hurry up.
あの窓にカーテンをつけたほうがいいでしょう。
It would be better to put a curtain on that window.
あの人とは話さないほうがいいですよ。
It's better for you not to talk with him.
あまりお酒は飲まないほうがいいんじゃありませんか。
It's better for you not to drink too much sake.

言語ノート

Responding to Advice

ACCEPTING ADVICE

ええ、そうですね。
Yes, that's right.
ええ、そうします。
Yes, I will.
それはいい考えですね。
That's a good idea.

REFUSING ADVICE

そうですね。でも…
I see, but…
ええ、そうですが、ちょっと…
Yes, that's right, but…

ダイアログ：すぐ掃除したほうがいいですよ。(*You should clean it immediately*.)

ギブソン：わあ、すごいほこりですね。

　　林：しばらく掃除していないんです。

ギブソン：すぐ掃除したほうがいいですよ。このにおいは何ですか。

　　林：しばらく皿も洗っていないんです。

ギブソン：早く洗ったほうがいいですよ。

アクティビティー　27

覚えたほうがいいですよ。(*You'd better learn it.*)

Turn the following sentences into suggestions by using …ほうがいいですよ.

1. コートを持って行く
2. 窓を閉める
3. 部屋を掃除する
4. バスに乗る
5. 早く家を出る
6. 9時前に着く
7. 古い新聞を捨てる(*to dispose of, throw away*)

アクティビティー　28

いろいろなアドバイス (*Various kinds of advice*)

Match the situation in the first column with the appropriate advice in the second column.

1. うちはとてもうるさいんです。
2. 頭が痛いんです。
3. 今夜は遅くなります。
4. 迷ってしまいました。(*We've gotten lost.*)
5. テストで0点を取りました。
6. 電車に遅れました。
7. 昨日飲みすぎました。

a. アスピリンを飲んだほうがいいですよ。
b. もっと早く起きたほうがいいですよ。
c. もっと勉強したほうがいいですよ。
d. 図書館で勉強したほうがいいですよ。
e. うちに電話したほうがいいですよ。
f. 地図を見たほうがいいですよ。
g. あまり飲まないほうがいいですよ。

GIBSON: Wow, look at this dust! (Lit., *It is terrible dust, isn't it?*)　HAYASHI: I haven't cleaned (my room) for a while.　GIBSON: You should clean it immediately. What's this smell?　HAYASHI: I haven't washed the dishes for a while, either.　GIBSON: You should wash them right away (lit., *quickly*).

Vocabulary and Grammar 2C

アクティビティー　29

こまります。(*I have a problem.*)

What kind of advice would you give? Respond to the following by
using ほうがいい.

Useful Word:　やめる　*to stop, quit*

1. 僕は勉強が大嫌いだ。
2. ハンバーガーが大好きで、一日に三つ食べるんです。
3. I hate using Japanese. I won't use Japanese even in my Japanese class!
4. 夕べ、テレビを見すぎて、寝坊しました。
5. 勉強しすぎて、疲れました。
6. 私の部屋はきたなくて...財布 (*wallet*) はどこでしょう。
7. コーヒーは一日 10 杯飲みます。

アクティビティー　30

家事！家事！家事！(*Chores! Chores! Chores!*)

What advice would you give in the following situations?

[例]　すごいほこりです。→ 掃除をしたほうがいいですよ。

1. 今夜食べるものがありません。
2. テーブルの上によごれた食器がたくさんあります。
3. 洗濯物がたまりました (*piled up*)。
4. 服がしわくちゃ (*wrinkled*) です。
5. お父さんの靴がきたないです。
6. セーターに穴があいています (*a hole has developed*)。
7. 床に本や新聞がちらかっています (*are scattered*)。
8. 窓ガラスがきたないです。

15. Expressing Different States of Actions: … ところ

ブラウン： 高田さん、何をしているんですか。
高田(たかだ)： お客(きゃく)さんが来るので、玄関(げんかん)を掃(は)いているところです。
　　　　　ブラウンさんは？
ブラウン： 美容院(びよういん)へ行くところです。
高田： ああ、そうですか。

The noun ところ (*place*), used with different forms of verbs, expresses different states of actions.

You will learn about いた ところだ in Chapter 3.

Dictionary form of verb
(nonpast, plain, affirmative)　　+　ところだ

to be about to (*do something*)

Te-form of verb + いる + ところだ

to be in the process of (*doing something*)

私(わたし)は車(くるま)を洗(あら)うところです。
I am about to wash my car.
ブラウンさんはその時(とき)、出(で)かけるところでした。
Ms. Brown was about to go out then.
私(わたし)は部屋(へや)を掃除(そうじ)しているところです。
I am in the midst of cleaning the room (or *I am just now cleaning the room*).

The ～ているところだ construction is similar to the ～ている construction, but it focuses more on the exact point in time. The ～ている form can denote long-term, ongoing processes, as in 英語(えいご)を勉強している (*I am studying English*), which allows for the possibility that the speaker is referring merely to being enrolled in a course. On the other hand, 英語(えいご)を勉強しているところだ can mean only *I am studying English at this moment.*

BROWN: Mr. Takada, what are you doing?　　TAKADA: A guest is coming so I am in the middle of sweeping the entrance. How about you?　　BROWN: I'm just about to go to the beauty salon.　　TAKADA: Oh, really?

Vocabulary and Grammar 2C

ダイアログ：部屋の掃除をしているところです。(*I am in the midst of cleaning my room.*)

カワムラ：　大助さん、何をしているんですか。
山口：　部屋の掃除をしているところです。

カワムラ：　ガールフレンドが来るんですね。
山口：　よくわかりましたね。

カワムラ：　ええ、大助さんはガールフレンドが来る時しか、部屋を掃除しませんからね。

言語ノート

しか...ない

As you already know, you can use だけ to express the concept of *only* or *just*.

> 5ドルだけあります。
> *I have just five dollars.*
> ギブソンさんだけに会いました。
> *I met only Ms. Gibson.*

Another construction, noun しか... verb ない, also expresses the idea of *only* or *just*. しか replaces the particles は, が, and を. Here are some examples of its use.

> 5ドルしかありません。
> *I have just five dollars.*
> ギブソンさんにしか会いませんでした。
> *I met only Ms. Gibson.*

There is a subtle difference between the two ways of saying *only*. The だけ construction implies that the subject has only a certain amount of something, or did only a certain thing, but that it is sufficient. For example, ギブソンさんだけに会いました implies that you met only Ms. Gibson, but she was the only person you were supposed to meet anyway.

KAWAMURA: Daisuke, what are you doing?　YAMAGUCHI: I'm in the midst of cleaning my room.
KAWAMURA: Your girlfriend's coming, right?　YAMAGUCHI: How did you know? (*Lit., You understood well.*)　KAWAMURA: Well, you clean your room only when your girlfriend comes.

The しか…ない construction, on the other hand, implies that whatever the subject did or has is insufficient. ギブソンさんにしか会いませんでした implies that you expected to meet someone else or were expected to meet someone else but for some reason did not.

If you find the negative construction confusing, you may want to think of it as meaning *except*, as in *I don't have anything except five dollars. I didn't meet anyone except Ms. Gibson.*

アクティビティー 32

すろことが多い。(*There are many things to do.*)

Following the example, practice using the ところ constructions.

[例] 家を探す (*to look for*) → 家を探すところです。
家を探しているところです。

1. 電気をつける
2. 電気を消す
3. 料理をする
4. 皿を洗う
5. 部屋を片付ける

6. ガラスを磨く
7. ラジオを直す
8. ヒーターを入れる
9. 新しいアパートに引っ越す

アクティビティー 33

三村さんは今車を洗っているところです。(*Mr. Mimura is just now washing his car.*)

Fill in the blanks, and complete the sentences.

1. 三村さんは学校で（　　　）ところです。
2. 8時に帰った時、父は（　　　）ところでした。
3. 母は台所で（　　　）ところです。
4. ブラウンさんが来た時、居間で（　　　）ところでした。
5. 町田さんが電話をかけてきた時、寝室で（　　　）でした。

料理しているところです。(*I am cooking now.*)

Work in pairs. One of you is in the place indicated doing household chores. The other walks in and asks what you are doing there. Answer, following the example.

[例] 台所 → ―台所で何をしているんですか。
　　　　　　　―料理をしているところです。

PLACE	POSSIBLE CHORES
台所	料理をする 皿を洗う
ダイニング・キッチン	テーブルの上を片付ける
居間	アイロンをかける 窓をふく 縫い物をする
洗面所	洗濯をする 鏡を磨く
庭	庭いじりをする 花 (*flower*) に水をやる 洗濯物を干す
玄関	靴を磨く 掃除をする
家の前	ゴミ (*garbage, trash*) を出す

Now practice following these examples.

　　　これから何をするんですか。
　　　家の前に水をまくところです。
　　　家の前で何をしていたんですか。
　　　水をまいたところです。

ダイアログ：洗濯をしてくれました。(*She did laundry for me.*)

三村：ブラウンさん、風邪をひいて、寝ていたそうですね。

ブラウン：ええ、一週間寝ていました。

三村：それはたいへんでしたね。

ブラウン：ええ、でも佐野さんの奥さんが洗濯をしたり、食事を作ったりして
くれました。

三村：そうですか。親切な大家さんですね。

アクティビティー　36

ダイアログ：洗濯もしてあげますよ。(*I'll also do your laundry for you.*)

佐野：ブラウンさん、私が買い物をしてあげますから、
寝ていてください。

ブラウン：でも、ご迷惑でしょう。

佐野：洗濯もしてあげますよ。

ブラウン：そんなことまでしてもらってはこまります。

佐野：ブラウンさんはゆっくり休んで、早く元気になってください。

R efer to **Grammar II** earlier in this chapter.

※ **アクティビティー　37**

何をしてあげますか。(*What are you going to do for him/her?*)

One of your classmates is sick in bed and has been unable to do any household chores for two weeks. What will you do to help out? Choose from your ill classmate's To Do list, which follows.

[例]　オルテガさんは何をしてあげますか。
洗濯をしてあげます。

MIMURA: Ms. Brown, I heard that you were in bed with the flu.　BROWN: Yes, I stayed in bed for a week.
MIMURA: That must have been awful.　BROWN: Yes, but Ms. Sano did laundry and cooked for me.
MIMURA: Is that right? She's a good landlady, isn't she?

SANO: Ms. Brown, I'll do the shopping for you, so please stay in bed.　BROWN: But it would be too much trouble for you.　SANO: I'll do your laundry, too.　BROWN: I would feel bad if you did that much for me.
SANO: Please rest up and get well soon.

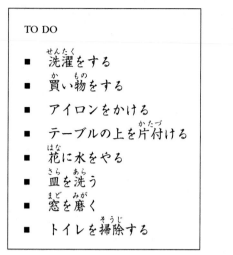

TO DO

- 洗濯をする
- 買い物をする
- アイロンをかける
- テーブルの上を片付ける
- 花に水をやる
- 皿を洗う
- 窓を磨く
- トイレを掃除する

After each member of the class offers to help, pair up, and discuss with a classmate who will do what.

[例] ―誰が掃除をしてくれますか。
　　　―ジャクソンさんに掃除をしてもらいます。

16. Describing a Preparatory Action: ～ておく

林：カワムラさん、新幹線の切符、買っておきました。
カワムラ：ぼくは旅館を予約しておきました。
林：これで旅行の準備はできましたね。
カワムラ：ええ。

16.1 The following construction means *to (do something) in advance,* or *in preparation for future use.*

Te-form of verb + おく　　　（おく itself means *to put, to place*）

to do something in advance, or ahead of time
to do something with an eye toward the future

HAYASHI: Mr. Kawamura, I bought tickets for the bullet train.　KAWAMURA: I made the inn reservations.
HAYASHI: Now (lit., *with this*) we have finished preparing for our trip.　KAWAMURA: Yes.

クラスの前に教科書を読んでおいた。
I read the textbook before class (implying preparation for the class).
映画を見る前に、コーラとポップコーンを買っておきました。
Before watching the movie, I bought cola and popcorn.
旅行に行くので、スーツケースを出しておこう。
Because I'm going on a trip, I'll get out my suitcase.

16.2 ~ておく is often contracted to ~とく or ~どく in colloquial speech.

これ食べときなさい。
Eat this ahead of time.
これ読んどいたよ。
I read this in advance.

✳ アクティビティー　38

ビールを買っておきましょう。(*I'll get the beer* [i.e., *ahead of time*].)

カワムラ：　今夜はお客さんが来るんですか。
山口：　ええ、主人の会社の人たち。ビールをたくさん買っておきましょう。
カワムラ：　ぼくが買ってきてあげましょう。
山口：　そう、助かるわ。

アクティビティー　39

先生に聞いておく。(*I'll ask the teacher.*)

Change these sentences by using ~ておく to indicate that the action is being done as preparation for something else.

1. カワムラさんに電話する
2. 高田さんと話す
3. 日本へ行く前に、日本語を勉強する
4. パーティーのためにビールを買う
5. クラスの前にテープを聞く
6. 山本さんに会う前に、写真を見る

KAWAMURA: Are guests coming tonight?　YAMAGUCHI: Yes, some people from my husband's company. I'm going to buy lots of beer.　KAWAMURA: I'll go buy beer for you.　YAMAGUCHI: Really? That would help me out.

アクティビティー 40

私が予約をしておきます。 (*I'll make the reservations.*)

Match each phrase in the first column with the most appropriate sentence ending in the second column.

1. お酒の好きなお客さんがいらっしゃるので、＿＿＿

2. 明日はテストがあるので、＿＿＿

3. パーティーの前に、＿＿＿

4. ブラウンさんに会う前に＿＿＿

5. フランスに行く前に＿＿＿

6. カワムラさんは甘いものが好きなので＿＿＿

7. 会議の前に、＿＿＿

a. レポートを読んでおいた。

b. ビールを冷やして (冷やす = *to cool*) おきましょう。

c. 電話をかけておいた。

d. ケーキを買っておいてください。

e. トラベルガイドを買っておいた。

f. 漢字を勉強しておいた。

g. ドレスにアイロンをかけておいた。

アクティビティー 41

前にしておきました。 (*She did it ahead of time.*)

Complete these sentences by using ておきました. Make as many sentences as you can.

[例] 日本語のテストの前に、→
日本語のテストの前に、漢字を勉強しておきました。
日本語のテストの前に、テープを聞いておきました。
日本語のテストの前に、教科書を読んでおきました。

1. 旅行の前に、

2. お客さんが来るので、

3. 病気にならないために、

4. 取るクラスを決める前に、

5. パーティーをするので、

6. ピクニックに行く前に、

7. 引っ越す前に、

お客<ruby>客<rt>きゃく</rt></ruby>さんが来ます。(*Guests are coming.*)

What do you do to prepare for receiving guests at home? Tell what each person in your family (or a typical family) does, choosing from the following list.

窓<ruby>まど</ruby>をふく
客間<ruby>きゃくま</ruby>を掃除<ruby>そうじ</ruby>する
テーブルの上を片付<ruby>かたづ</ruby>ける
廊下<ruby>ろうか</ruby>を磨<ruby>みが</ruby>く
料理<ruby>りょうり</ruby>をする
座布団<ruby>ざぶとん</ruby>を出<ruby>だ</ruby>す
ビールを買<ruby>か</ruby>う
ビールを冷蔵庫<ruby>れいぞうこ</ruby>に入<ruby>い</ruby>れる

Language Skills

Reading and Writing

Reading 1　石黒<ruby>いしぐろ</ruby>さんの新<ruby>あたら</ruby>しい家

Before You Read

What factors go into your decision to rent an apartment or house? Which factors in the following list are important to you?

a. 静かな住宅 街<ruby>しず　じゅうたくがい</ruby>にある。

b. いいレストランがそばにある。

c. 公園<ruby>こうえん</ruby>がある。

d. 寝室<ruby>しんしつ</ruby>がたくさんある。

e. 2階建<ruby>にかいだ</ruby>てだ。

f. 商 店街<ruby>しょうてんがい</ruby>が近<ruby>ちか</ruby>い。

g. 門<ruby>もん</ruby>がある。

h. 家賃<ruby>やちん</ruby>が安<ruby>やす</ruby>い。

i. まわりが安全<ruby>あんぜん</ruby>(*safe*) だ。

j. プールがある。

k. 駅<ruby>えき</ruby>に近<ruby>ちか</ruby>い。

l. 駐車場<ruby>ちゅうしゃじょう</ruby>がある。

Now Read It!

Ms. Ishiguro, a member of the aerobics class that Hitomi Machida attends, has recently moved into a new house. She has invited her classmates to visit her new house, and Hitomi has written a notice to the members about the upcoming visit.

青川カルチャーセンターのエアロビクス・クラスのみなさんへ

私たちのクラスの石黒さんが、今月8日に大田区田園調布に新しく家を建て、引っ越しました。新しい家は二階建て、3LDKで、広い庭があります。東横線の田園調布駅のそばの、静かな住宅街の中にあります。近くには、スーパーもあって、とても便利です。また、15分ほど歩くと、谷井神社があって、散歩にもいいところです。

今月23日、土曜日にクラスのみなさんを招いて、新しい家を見せてくださるそうです。ご主人が庭でバーベキューをしてくださるそうです。バーベキューは午前11時から始まります。

石黒さんの家は田園調布駅から歩いて10分です。まず、田園調布駅で降りて、北口に出ます。北口の前の道をまっすぐ行くと、川があります。橋を渡ると、前に公園があります。公園の前の道を右に曲がります。しばらく行くと、右側に学校があります。学校の横の道を入り、二つ目の角を左に曲がります。角から3軒目の左側が石黒さんの家です。住所は大田区田園調布3-8-19です。門のある青い屋根の家です。石黒さんの家の地図は先週火曜日のクラスでみなさん渡しましたが、まだもらっていない人は、私に連絡してください。

みんなで石黒さんにお祝いの品をさしあげたいと思います。なにかいい考えのある人は、木曜日までに私に知らせてください。

町田ひとみ

大田区田園調布 *Den'enchoobu, an upscale neighborhood in Tokyo's Oota ward.*

お祝の品 *congratulatory present*

After You Finish Reading

1. Answer these questions in English.

    a. When did the Ishiguros move into their new house?

    b. How many stories does the house have?

    c. What else is in the neighborhood?

    d. Is the neighborhood quiet or noisy?

    e. Where is the Tanii shrine?

    f. When are the club members invited to visit the Ishiguros?

    g. What color is the roof?

百二十二

122

At Home

2. Write a short note in Japanese to Hitomi Machida in which you suggest what to buy as a gift for Ms. Ishiguro. Mention why you think the recommended item would be good.

Writing 1

Write a short note to your friends inviting them to your house. Your invitation should include the following information.

1. You are inviting them to your house next Sunday.
2. The reason is that you moved into a new house last week and would like to show it to them.
3. Give directions to your house.
4. Tell them not to bring anything.

Reading 2　高原の別荘

Before You Read

Which item in each group doesn't belong? Why?

1. 秋、春、夏、冬、北
2. 暑い、涼しい、遠い、寒い、暖かい
3. 二時間、一週間、三ヶ月間、日本間、十分間
4. 寝室、教室、リビングルーム、キッチン、浴室
5. 窓、天井、壁、床、庭
6. 冷蔵庫、オーブン、ガスレンジ、ガレージ、トースター
7. 勉強、買い物、洗濯、掃除、料理
8. 車、電車、バス、タクシー、飛行機

If you had a summer home, where would you like it to be? What kind of summer home would you like to have? Discuss in class.

Now Read It!

Useful Vocabulary:　高原 *plateau,* 別荘 *vacation home,* 考える *to think; to ponder,* 貸し別荘 *vacation rental,* さらに *furthermore,* 空気 *air,* 全部 *in total,* どの...も *each,* 利用（する）*make use of,* もちろん *of course,* 美しい *beautiful,* 付く *to be attached,* 大丈夫（な）*all right, no problem,* 村 *village,* 料金 *charge; fee,* 只今 *right now,* 発売中 *on sale,* ...以上 *more than...,* たずねる *to inquire,* こむ *to be crowded,* すぐ *immediately; soon*

今年の夏は高原の別荘で過ごしてみませんか。

夏休みが取れたら、涼しいところでゆっくり休みたいなあ！そう考えているあなた、山川高原の貸し別荘はいかがですか。

東京駅から電車で３時間半、山川駅で降りて、さらに、バスで１時間行くと、青い空、きれいな空気、緑の山があなたを待っています。

山川高原の別荘は全部で２５軒。どの別荘にも寝室が３つ、リビングルーム、キッチン、浴室の広い別荘です。会社のグループで、ご家族で、また友だちとご利用ください。もちろん、お一人でも利用できます。リビングルームの大きい窓からは美しい山中湖が見えます。寝室にはベランダが付いていて、ベランダからは山川高原が見えます。モダンなデザインのキッチンには、冷蔵庫、レンジが付いていますから、料理もできます。スーパーは、バス

で１５分の山川村に３軒ありますから、お買い物も簡単です。別荘には洗濯機も付いていますから、洗濯も大丈夫です。

別荘の料金は一泊１万９千円です。只今、東京から山川までの電車、バスの切符、別荘の料金をパックにした旅行クーポンを発売中です。６月中にこのクーポンを買う

と、便利な旅行バッグをさしあげます。クーポンはお近くの旅行代理店でどうぞ。

６０歳以上の方には、シルバーディスカウントがあります。くわしいことは旅行代理店でおたずねください。７月、８月はとてもこみます。今すぐご予約ください。

After You Finish Reading

Using the advertisement, fill in the missing information in these English brochure excerpts.

How about spending this summer in a vacation rental in Yamakawa?

It takes about (   ) to get to the summer houses from Tokyo by (   )

and (   ).

(   ), (   ), and (   ) await you!

Each spacious house includes these rooms: (   ).

The houses afford a view of (   ) and (   ).

You can do your grocery shopping at (   ).

Now on sale is a travel coupon that includes (   ).

If you buy the coupon in June, you will receive (   ).

Write a short letter in Japanese to one of your Japanese friends to ask if he or she would like to share a vacation rental in the Yamakawa Highlands this summer. In your letter, write about some of the features of the summer house, where it is located, the rental charge, and when you would like to go there.

Writing 2

Your employer has assigned you to work at the company's Tokyo office for one year. You want to rent out your house while you are gone. Write a short paragraph describing each room and the special features of your house to attract prospective renters.

[例]　にぎやかな町の便利な家に住んでみませんか。
キッチンはモダンなデザインで、いろいろな電気製品があります。
居間は、...

Language Functions and Situations

Looking for a House

久保：あのう、このへんで家を探しているんですが...
不動産屋：ああ、このへんにはいい家がたくさんありますよ。
　　　　どんな家をお探しですか。
久保：5人家族ですので、大きい家がいいんですが...
不動産屋：じゃ、部屋はいくつぐらいがいいですか。

KUBO: Uh, I'm looking for a house in this neighborhood but...(could you help me?).　REALTOR: Oh, yes. There are many good houses around here. What kind of house are you looking for?　KUBO: There are five people in my family, so a big house would be good.　REALTOR: How many rooms do you want? (Lit., *About how many rooms is good?*)

久保：　そうですね。ダイニング・キッチン、居間、それに寝室が3つ
　　　　ほしいですね。車があるので、ガレージもほしいですね。

不動産屋：　ああ、いい家がありますよ。これがその写真です。

久保：　いい家ですね。

不動産屋：　ええ、小さいですが、裏庭があります。

久保：　駅に近いですか。

不動産屋：　ええ、中野駅から歩いて15分です。バス停もすぐそばに
　　　　あります。

久保：　じゃあ買い物も便利ですね。

不動産屋：　ええ、近くに商店街がありますから...

久保：　学校はそばにありますか。

不動産屋：　はい、小学校と中学校までは歩いて10分です。

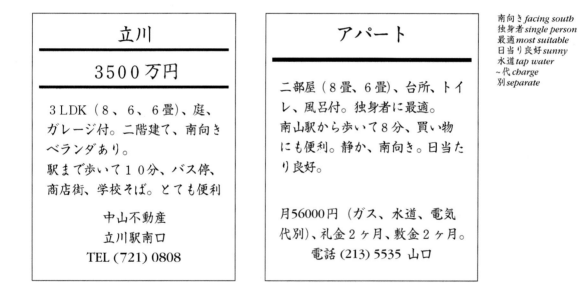

立川

3500万円

3LDK（8、6、6畳）、庭、
ガレージ付。二階建て、南向き
ベランダあり。
駅まで歩いて10分、バス停、
商店街、学校そば。とても便利

中山不動産
立川駅南口
TEL (721) 0808

アパート

二部屋（8畳、6畳）、台所、トイ
レ、風呂付。独身者に最適。
南山駅から歩いて8分、買い物
にも便利。静か、南向き。日当た
り良好。

月56000円（ガス、水道、電気
代別）、礼金2ヶ月、敷金2ヶ月。
電話 (213) 5535 山口

南向き *facing south*
独身者 *single person*
最適 *most suitable*
日当り良好 *sunny*
水道 *tap water*
~代 *charge*
別 *separate*

KUBO: Let me see. I would like an eat-in kitchen, a living room, and three bedrooms. I have a car, so I want a garage, too.　REALTOR: Oh, I have a good house. Here is a photo of it.　KUBO: What a nice house.　REALTOR: Yes. It's small, but there is a backyard.　KUBO: Is it near a station?　REALTOR: Yes, it's a fifteen-minute walk from Nakano Station. There is also a bus stop very close by.　KUBO: Is it convenient for shopping?　REALTOR: Yes. There is a shopping area nearby, so…　KUBO: Are there schools nearby?　REALTOR: Yes. It is a ten-minute walk to an elementary school and a junior high school.

CULTURE NOTE • Renting an Apartment in Japan

To rent an apartment in Japan, you must have a lot of cash on hand. In addition to the first month's rent, you must pay the landlord a deposit (敷金 [しききん]) in the amount of two or three months' rent and so-called key money (礼金 [れいきん]) equal to two or three months' rent. Some of this money goes to the realtor who helped you find the apartment. Therefore, to move into an apartment where the monthly rent is 50,000 yen, you need at least 250,000 yen, 200,000 of which (the deposit and key money) you will never see again. This is tremendously unfair to renters, and makes all renters think twice before moving to another apartment, but it is an established custom in Japan that seems unlikely to change as long as the demand for apartments continues to exceed the supply. Foreigners who plan to stay in Japan for a year or less may be better off in a so-called **gaijin** house or an apartment hotel. The rents for these are much higher than the rents for apartments of comparable quality, but at least the tenant need not come up with several months' rent all at once.

Inviting People to Your Home

加藤： 来週の日曜日、うちへ来ませんか。

山下： かまいませんか。

加藤： ええ、どうぞ。11時ごろ来てください。

山下： じゃあ、喜んで。

加藤： きたない家ですが。...これ、うちの地図です。

山下： どうもありがとうございます。じゃ、楽しみにしています。

加藤： こちらこそ。

山下： ごめんください。

加藤： はい、どなたですか。

山下： 山下です。

加藤： ああ、山下さん。いらっしゃい。お待ちしていました。どうぞお上がりください。

山下： 失礼します。

加藤： どうぞこちらへ。

KATO: Won't you come to our house next Sunday?   YAMASHITA: Is it all right? (Lit., *Don't you mind?*)
KATO: No. Please come about 11:00.   YAMASHITA: OK, with pleasure.   KATO: It's a dirty house, but...Here is a map to our house.   YAMASHITA: Thank you very much. I'm looking forward to it.
KATO: I am too. (Lit., *I'm the one [who's looking forward to it]*.)

YAMASHITA: Hello! (Lit., *Excuse me.*)   KATO: Who is it?   YAMASHITA: Yamashita.   KATO: Oh, Mr. Yamashita. Welcome. I was waiting for you. Please come in.   YAMASHITA: Excuse me.   KATO: Please (come) this way.

山下：お邪魔します。

加藤：どうぞお座りください。

山下：あのう、これ、つまらないものですが、どうぞ...

加藤：いやあ、そんな...

山下：本当にたいしたものじゃありませんが、...

加藤：こんなことをされては困ります。

山下：いいえ、どうぞ...

加藤：そうですか。じゃあ、恐れ入ります。

Role Play

Work in pairs. You have just moved into a new house. Invite your partner to your
house. Receive your guest, and show him or her the house. Your guest
compliments you on the house and other things.

Offering Food to a Guest

加藤：あのう、何もありませんが、ごはんでもいかがですか。

山下：どうぞご心配なく。

加藤：いいえ、お口に合うかどうかわかりませんが、遠慮しないでください。

山下：そうですか。では、いただきます。

加藤：もう少しいかがですか。

山下：いいえ、もう結構です。たいへんおいしかったです。
　　　ごちそうさまでした。

Leave-Taking

山下：あっ、もうこんな時間ですか。そろそろ失礼します。

加藤：まだ、いいじゃありませんか。

山下：いいえ、もう遅いですから。今日はどうもありがとうございました。

加藤：そうですか。じゃ、また、いらっしゃってください。

山下：では、失礼します。さようなら。

加藤：お気をつけて。

YAMASHITA: Excuse me. (Lit., *I'll inconvenience you.*)　KATO: Please take a seat.　YAMASHITA: Well, this is
a trifling thing, but please...(accept it).　KATO: No, that kind of thing...(won't do).　YAMASHITA: It's
really not anything significant, but...　KATO: It's upsetting if you do this sort of thing.　YAMASHITA: Oh,
no. Please...　KATO: Really? Thank you very much for your kindness.

KATO: Well, we don't have anything (to offer), but how about lunch?　YAMASHITA: Please don't worry
about me.　KATO: Oh, no. I don't know if you will like it, but please, don't hold back.
YAMASHITA: Really? Then, thank you, I will have some...　KATO: How about a little more?
YAMASHITA: No, thank you. It was really delicious. Thank you very much.

YAMASHITA: Oh, is it already this late (lit., *this time*)? I must leave. (Lit., *I will excuse myself soon.*)
KATO: Why don't you stay? (Lit., *It's still OK, isn't it?*)　YAMASHITA: No, it's already late. Thank you very
much for (inviting me) today.　KATO: I see. Please come again.　YAMASHITA: Excuse me. Good-bye.
KATO: Please take care.

Role Play

Work in pairs. The host will offer the visitor a meal. After the meal is over, the visitor will leave.

Review

Go over the dialogues in this section, and study what set phrases are used in the following situations.

1. inviting people to your house
2. greeting guests at the door, arriving at someone's house
3. asking a visitor to take a seat
4. giving and receiving a gift
5. offering and accepting a meal
6. leave-taking
7. taking one's leave, seeing a guest off

Note that you apologize both for entering the house and taking leave of your host. Also note Kato's ritualized refusal of Yamashita's present, the way both Kato and Yamashita belittle the things belonging to them, Yamashita's initial refusal of the food, and Kato's insistence that Yamashita stay longer.

Listening Comprehension

1. A real estate agent is showing a house to Ms. Swan. Listen to the agent's explanation, and write down the features of each part of the house.
2. Mr. and Ms. Yoshioka are talking about what they will give their acquaintances as year-end gifts. While listening to their conversation, write down what they received from other people this summer and what they will give to them this winter.

Vocabulary

Housing

いま	居間	living room
おてあらい	お手洗い	rest room; toilet
かいだん	階段	stairway; steps
きゃくま、おうせつま	客間／応接間	sitting room for entertaining guests; Western-style room for entertaining guests

げんかん	玄関	entry hall; foyer
けんちくか	建築家	architect
じゅうたく	住宅	residence; housing
しんしつ	寝室	bedroom
すむ	住む	to live; to reside
せんめんじょ	洗面所	washstand (area with sink for washing one's face and hands)
だいく	大工	carpenter
ダイニング・キッチン		eat-in kitchen (lit., *dining kitchen*)
たてる	建てる	to build
だんち	団地	public housing development; apartment complex
てんじょう	天井	ceiling
と	戸	door
トイレ		toilet; rest room
(に)かいだて	(二)階建て	(two-)story
にほんま／わしつ	日本間／和室	Japanese-style room
にわ	庭	garden; yard
へや	部屋	room
...ま	...間	counter for rooms
マンション		condominium
もん	門	gate
やね	屋根	roof
ゆか	床	floor
ようま／ようしつ	洋間／洋室	Western-style room
よくしつ	浴室	bathing room (room with bathtub/shower)

Loanwords: ガラス、ドア

Review: アパート、家、椅子、絵、～階、カーテン、壁、キッチン、近所、～軒、公園、狭い、台所、机、テーブル、庭、広い

Furnishings and Appliances

エアコン		air conditioner
かがみ	鏡	mirror
かぐ	家具	furniture
クーラー		air conditioner (cooler)
すいはんき	炊飯器	rice cooker
スタンド		floor lamp, desk lamp
ストーブ		space heater
せんたくき	洗濯機	washing machine
せんぷうき	扇風機	electric fan
そうじき	掃除機	vacuum cleaner
たんす／タンス		chest of drawers
でんき	電気	electric light, electricity
でんきせいひん	電気製品	electric appliance

でんしレンジ	電子レンジ	microwave oven
ほんだな	本棚	bookshelf
るすばんでんわ	留守番電話	answering machine
れいぞうこ	冷蔵庫	refrigerator

Review: ステレオ、テレビ、電話、時計、ラジオ

Household Chores

アイロンをかける		to iron
かじ	家事	housework; household chores
かたづける	片付ける	to straighten (something) up; to clear (something) off
せんたく	洗濯	(to do) laundry
せんたくもの	洗濯物	laundry (things to be laundered)
そうじ (する)	掃除 (する)	housecleaning (to clean)
なおす	直す	to mend; repair
にわいじり (する)	庭いじり (する)	gardening (to do gardening)
ぬいもの (をする)	縫い物 (をする)	(to do) sewing
はく	掃く	to sweep
ほす	干す	to air-dry (something); to air (something) out
みがく	磨く	to polish

Review: 洗う

Verbs

いれる	入れる	to turn on (a switch)
うごかす	動かす	to move (something)
おく	置く	to put
かす	貸す	to lend; to rent out
かりる	借りる	to borrow; to rent (from)
きる	切る	to turn off (a switch)
けす	消す	to turn off (a light)
さがす	探す	to look for
つける	付ける	to turn on (a light)
てつだう	手伝う	to help; to assist
はこぶ	運ぶ	to transport; to carry (a large object)

Review: 開ける

Adjectives

Review: 静か (な)、不便 (な)、便利 (な)

Vocabulary

あげる	to give (*to a second or third person*)
いただく	to receive (*from a superior*)
くれる	to give (*to speaker or in-group member*)
さしあげる	to give (*to a superior or outsider*)
しか...ない	only; not except for
...ずつ	each..., per...
...ため (に)	for the purpose of; for the sake of
~たり、~たり	(do) this and that
...ちゅう ...中	during; in the middle
~ておく	to do for future use
~てもいい	it is all right if you...
...ところ	point in time
~ないでください	please don't...
ばかり	only
...ほうがいい	it's better to...
もらう	to receive (*from an equal or inferior*)
やる	to give (*to a social inferior*)

Kanji

Learn these **kanji:**

新 開 公 園 住 階 広 直 戸 古 門 室
伝 洗 建 友 貸 借 置 静 庭 便 利 不

チェックリスト

Use this checklist to confirm that you can now

- ☐ Talk about houses, furnishings, and appliances
- ☐ Talk about household chores
- ☐ Express a purpose
- ☐ Talk about giving and receiving
- ☐ Express permission
- ☐ Offer advice
- ☐ Scan directions to houses
- ☐ Scan real estate ads
- ☐ Talk with real estate agents
- ☐ Invite people to your house

Review Chapter 2

アクティビティー　1

どこでしますか。(*Where do you do it?*)

Indicate a room or a part of your house or apartment where you do each of the following activities. Also mention any furniture or other things you use for the activity.

[例]　勉強する →
　　　勉強する時は、私の部屋でします。机といすと本とノートとペンを使います。

1. テレビを見る
2. 昼寝する
3. 靴を脱ぐ
4. お風呂に入る
5. 朝ごはんを食べる
6. 服を着る
7. リラックスする
8. 寝る

アクティビティー　2

関連づけ (*Association*)

For each of the words given, find two additional words that are somehow related. Then explain exactly how the three words are related.

[例]　寝室 → (ベッド、ふとん) 寝るときに使います。or
　　　　　　(居間、台所) 部屋の名前です。

1. 不動産屋
2. 庭
3. 冷蔵庫
4. 掃除

アクティビティー　3

贈り物 (*Gifts*)

You are very creative when choosing gifts for your friends. Work in pairs. Discuss what you will buy for Christmas for each person listed. Why? How much do you expect to spend on each gift?

1. 国広一郎、60歳の男の人、サラリーマン、音楽が好き
2. 沢井武夫、18歳の男の人、大学生、趣味はウインター・スポーツ
3. 金井由美、7歳の女の子、本を読むのが好き、甘いのもが好き
4. 星野国俊、38歳の男の人、学校の先生、グルメ
5. 花山鈴子、43歳の女の人、先月新しい家を買った

アクティビティー　4

私の夢の家 (*My dream house*)

Work with a partner. One of you is planning your dream house, and the other is an architect. Describe your preferences (for example, you want a large window in the living room, three bathrooms, and a stereo in the bathroom). Tell where you would like certain furniture and appliances. The architect should make suggestions and draw a house plan according to your instructions.

Show your house plan to another pair of students, and explain it to them. Ask for their opinions and suggestions.

3

第
三
章

車
と
交
通

くるま

こう

つう

Automobiles and Transportation

駅のターミナル

えき

Objectives

In this lesson, you are going to

- Talk about cars, driving, and public transportation systems

- Learn the difference between transitive and intransitive verbs and how they are used in Japanese

- Learn to express an attempt

- Learn to express a just completed action

- Learn to scan a driving manual and a driving guide for travelers

- Learn to write the directions to your home or campus

- Learn to ask for and give instructions

- Examine the public transportation system in Japan

Vocabulary and Grammar 3A

Vocabulary and Oral Activities

Cars and Driving

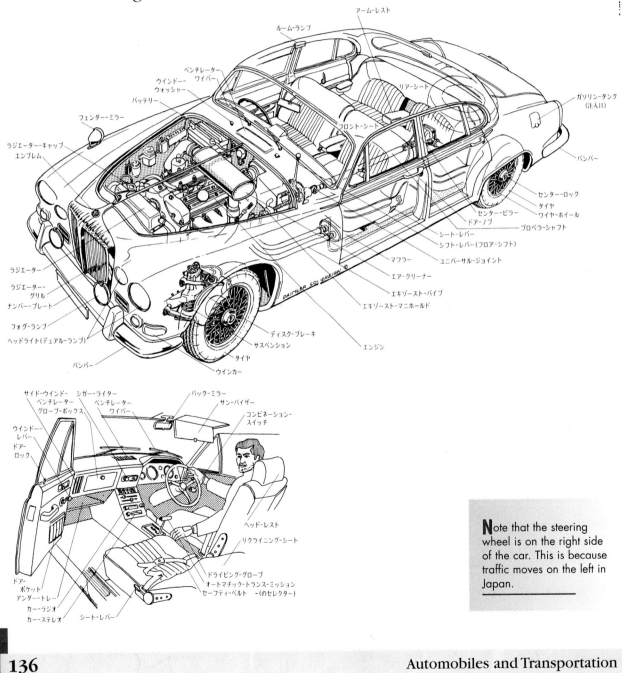

アームレスト
ルームランプ
ベンチレーター
ウインドー
ワイパー
ウォッシャー
バッテリー
フェンダーミラー
ラジエーターキャップ
エンブレム
リアーシート
フロントシート
ガソリンタンク
(注入II)
バンパー
センターロック
タイヤ
センターピラー
ワイヤーホイール
ドアーノブ
プロペラーシャフト
シートレバー
シフトレバー(フロアーシフト)
ユニバーサルジョイント
マフラー
エアークリーナー
エキゾーストパイプ
エキゾーストマニホールド
エンジン
ラジエーター
ラジエーターグリル
ナンバープレート
フォグランプ
ヘッドライト(デュアルランプ)
バンパー
ディスクブレーキ
サスペンション
タイヤ
ウインカー

サイドウインド
ベンチレーター
グローブボックス
シガーライター
ベンチレーター
ワイパー
バックミラー
サンバイザー
コンビネーション
スイッチ
ウインドー
レバー
ドアー
ロック
ヘッドレスト
リクライニングシート
ドアー
ポケット
アンダートレー
カーラジオ
カーステレオ
シートレバー
ドライビンググローブ
オートマチックトランスミッション
セーフティーベルト　(のセレクター)

> **N**ote that the steering wheel is on the right side of the car. This is because traffic moves on the left in Japan.

Vocabulary: Cars

自動車	じどうしゃ	automobile, car
道路	どうろ	street, road
交通	こうつう	traffic
(交通)信号	(こうつう)しんごう	traffic light
運転免許(証)	うんてんめんきょ(しょう)	driver's license
運転手	うんてんしゅ	driver
ガソリン		gasoline
アクセル		accelerator
ブレーキ		brake
タイヤ		tire
パンク(する)		flat tire (to get a flat tire)
クラクション		horn
チェンジレバー		gear shift lever
ハンドル		steering wheel
エンジン		engine
ラジエーター		radiator
バッテリー		battery
ワイパー		(windshield) wiper
アンテナ		antenna
ナンバープレート		license plate
カーステレオ		car stereo system
チェックする		to check

Review: 車、道、運転(する)、ドライブ(する)、ガソリン・スタンド、駐車場、走る、乗る

※ **アクティビティー　1**

何ですか。(*What is it?*)

Match each word in the first column with the appropriate definition in the second column.

Useful Vocabulary: 動かす *to set in motion; to move (something),*
交差点 *intersection,* 穴があく *a hole develops*

1. ガソリン　　a. 雨や雪が降っている時に使います。
2. ワイパー　　b. 自動車を止める所です。
3. 信号　　　　c. 車の行く方向をコントロールするために使います。
4. ハンドル　　d. カーステレオを聞く時に使います。
5. アクセル　　e. 車を動かすために、タンクに入れます。

Review ...ため
(Chapter 2,
Grammar 10) and ...時
(Chapter 7,
Grammar 40,
in Book 1).

6.　アンテナ　　　　f.　車のスピードをコントロールする時に使います。

7.　パンク　　　　　g.　交差点にある赤、黄色、青のライトです。

8.　駐車場　　　　　h.　タイヤに穴があくことです。

Vocabulary Library

Actions Involved in Driving

ハンドル（を握る／を切る）	ハンドルをにぎる／きる	(to take the) wheel／(to turn the) wheel
踏む	ふむ	to step on; to pedal
スピードを出す	スピードをだす	to increase speed
ブレーキをかける		to apply the brakes
エンジンをかける		to start the engine
タイヤをかえる		to change a tire
シートベルト		seat belt
締める	しめる	to attach; to buckle up
外す	はずす	to release; to undo
クラクションを鳴らす	クラクションをならす	to sound a (automobile) horn

アクティビティー　2

あなたのカーライフ (*Your driving experience*)

Answer these questions.

Useful Word: 安全（な）*safe, safety*

1.　あなたは運転免許を持っていますか。何歳の時に取りましたか。

2.　あなたは車を持っていますか。どんな車ですか。新しいですか。
　　大きいですか。アメリカ製の車ですか。

3.　あなたは運転が好きですか。

4.　運転する時、いつもシートベルトを締めますか。

5.　運転している時、カーステレオを聞きますか。

6.　運転している時、クラクションをよく鳴らしますか。

7.　安全運転をしていますか。

8.　スピードをよく出しますか。

Grammar and Practice Activities

17. How to Do Something: ～方^{かた}

どうちて

ブラウン：このお肉^{にく}、おいしいですね。

山口：どうもありがとう。

ブラウン：作^{つく}るのはむずかしいんですか。

山口：いいえ、とても簡単^{かんたん}よ。

ブラウン：じゃあ、今度^{こんど}、作^{つく}り方^{かた}を教^{おし}えてください。

町田：林さん、どうしたの？

林：新^{あたら}しいカーステレオを買ったんだけど、使^{つか}い方^{かた}がわからなくて...

町田：取^とり扱^{あつか}い説明書^{せつめいしょ}を読んでみたらどう。

林：そうだね。

しっていますか。

The conjunctive form of a verb followed by ～方^{かた} makes a phrase meaning *how to...*

Conjunctive form of verbs + 方^{かた}

---

how to (do something); the way of (doing something)

方 is a noun meaning *method* or *way* in this context, so when you add 方 to a verb, that verb becomes a noun. For this reason, を is replaced by の.

手紙^{てがみ}を書く *to write a letter*

手紙^{てがみ}の書^かき方^{かた} *how to write a letter*

Here are some sample sentences with verb + ～方.

カワムラさんは、箸^{はし}の使^{つか}い方^{かた}が上手ですね。

Mr. Kawamura, you are good at using chopsticks (lit., *the way of using chopsticks is skillful*).

For the formation of the conjunctive form of verbs, refer to Book 1, Chapter 3, **Grammar 12**.

BROWN: This meat (dish) is delicious.   YAMAGUCHI: Thank you very much.   BROWN: Is it difficult to prepare?   YAMAGUCHI: No, it's very simple.   BROWN: Then please teach me how to prepare it sometime.

MACHIDA: What's the matter, Mr. Hayashi?   HAYASHI: I bought a new stereo system for my car but I don't know how to use it.   MACHIDA: How about reading the instruction manual?   HAYASHI: Oh, right.

Vocabulary and Grammar 3A

139

百三十九

この漢字の読み方は何ですか。
*What is the reading of this **kanji**?* (Lit., *What is the way of reading this **kanji**?*)

あの人の話し方はちょっと変わっている。
The person's way of speaking is a bit unusual.

アクティビティー　3

着物の着方を知りたい時、どうしますか。(*What do you do when you want to know how to put on a kimono?*)

Answer the questions following the example. Choose whichever of the suggested alternatives you would be more likely to follow.

[例]　着物の着方を知りたい時、どうしますか。
　　　着物の本を読む
　　　日本語の先生に聞く
　　　→ 着物の着方を知りたい時は、着物の本を読みます。

1. ビデオの使い方を知りたい時、どうしますか。
   マニュアルを見る
   友だちに聞く
2. マージャンの仕方を知りたい時、どうしますか。
   日本人の友だちに聞く
   マージャンの本を読む
3. 漢字の読み方を知りたい時、どうしますか。
   先生に聞く
   辞書を引く
4. すきやきの作り方を知りたい時、どうしますか。
   料理の本を読む
   日本の友だちに手紙を書いて、聞く

Now see if you can answer giving multiple options using the 〜たり . . . 〜たり construction.

アクティビティー　4

この漢字、書けますか。(*Can you write this kanji?*)

Change the verbs in the parentheses to the appropriate form.

1. この漢字の (書く) 方がわからないんです。
2. 正しい (correct) タイプの (する) 方を教えてください。
3. あの先生は (教える) 方が上手ですね。
4. あの人の (歩く) 方はおもしろい。
5. 上手な写真の (撮る) 方を教えてあげましょう。
6. このワープロの (使う) 方、わかりますか。
7. 箸の (持つ) 方は、これでいいですか。
8. あの人はコーヒーの (入れる) 方にうるさい。(*That person is fussy about how to make coffee.*)

アクティビティー　5

車の運転マニュアル (*Driving manual*)

When do you use the following items? Use 〜方 in your answers.

1. 車の運転のマニュアル
2. 漢字の辞書
3. 日本語の辞書
4. 料理の本
5. コンピュータのマニュアル

❋ アクティビティー　6

ダイアログ：駐車の仕方を教えてくれませんか。(*Won't you teach me how to park a car?*)

ブラウン：日本で車を運転するのはむずかしいでしょうね。
高田：ええ、道が狭いですからねえ。
ブラウン：今度、狭い道での駐車の仕方を教えてくれませんか。
高田：ええ、いいですよ。

Practice the preceding dialogue by changing the underlined part to the following.

1. 狭い道での運転の仕方
2. 運転免許の取り方
3. オートバイ (*motorcycle*) の乗り方

BROWN: I guess driving a car in Japan is difficult, right?　TAKADA: Yes, that's because the streets are narrow.　BROWN: Won't you teach me how to park a car on a narrow street sometime? TAKADA: Yes, OK.

Vocabulary and Grammar 3A

141

百四十一

CULTURE NOTE • Driving in Japan

Owning and driving a car in Japan is not a simple matter. To obtain a driver's license (運転免許証 [うんてんめんきょしょう]), you have to go to driving school (自動車学校 [じどうしゃがっこう]), which is demanding in time and money. After taking a test that covers traffic regulations and basic mechanics, you get a provisional license that lets you practice driving on roads with an instructor until you have passed the road test. Once you have your license, you must attach a "beginning driver" sticker to your car for one year.

In many cases, becoming a licensed driver can cost hundreds of dollars. Furthermore, to register your car, you must bring it to a government-run checking station. This is done after three years for a new car and yearly thereafter, and it is quite costly.

In large cities such as Tokyo, you are not allowed to own a car unless you have off-street parking at home. Because of this parking problem, many people don't drive at all even though they have a driver's license. These people are called ペーパードライバー.

On weekends, the freeways (高速道路 [こうそくどうろ]) leading to popular leisure destinations are so crowded that using the trains and buses is faster and more convenient.

Vocabulary Library

くるま　ぶぶん
車の部分: **Parts of a Car**

バックミラー	rearview mirror
フロントガラス	windshield
ボンネット	hood
ハンドブレーキ、サイドブレーキ	parking brake
ウィンカー	turn signal
スピードメーター	speedometer

Loanwords: リクライニングシート、カーラジオ、クラッチ、ヘッドライト、フェンダー、マフラー、バンパー、トランク、ダッシュボード、グラブコンパートメント

わせいえいご
和製英語

English-speaking learners of Japanese sometimes believe mistakenly that they can just **katakana**-ize any English word and arrive at the Japanese equivalent. Although this tactic works in many cases, you need to be aware that the Japanese have made up their own words and phrases from English, resulting in words that do not exist in any English-speaking country. These words are called 和製英語, "made-in-Japan English." Examples of 和製英語 are パンティ・ストッキング for *panty hose,* クーラー for *air conditioner,* ガソリン・スタンド for *gas station,* ワイシャツ for *dress shirt,* コンセント for *electric outlet,* マスコミ for *mass communication,* カンニング for *cheating (on an exam),* and ナイター for *nighttime baseball game.* Some other examples of 和製英語 related to automobiles are ハンドル for *steering wheel,* ノークラッチ for *automatic transmission,* and ドアミラー for *sideview mirror.* Note that many English words entered Japanese from British English: for instance, ボンネット (bonnet) for *hood (of a car)* and ジャンパー (jumper) for *windbreaker jacket.*

婿なかな

✳ ## アクティビティー　7

くるま
車のマニュアル：窓の開け方は何ページですか。(*Manual: On what page are the instructions for how to open the windows?*)

Consult the owner's manual shown here, and ask your partner where to find information on the following aspects of driving a car.

[例]　s1: 窓の開け方は何ページですか。
　　　s2: ８ページです。

1. 車をコントロールする
2. ボンネットを開ける
3. タイヤをかえる
4. ワイパーを動かす

5. 車を止める
6. アンテナを出す
7. ガソリンを入れる
8. ライトをつける

18. Transitive and Intransitive Verbs

カワムラ：この部屋、ちょっと暗いね。
　町田：ええ。電気をつけてくれる？
カワムラ：うん。あれ、つかないよ。
　町田：スイッチがこわれたかしら。
カワムラ：電球がきれたのかもしれないね。

KAWAMURA: This room is a bit dark, isn't it?　MACHIDA: Yes. Would you turn on the light?
KAWAMURA: OK. (Hey!) It doesn't turn on!　MACHIDA: I wonder if the switch is broken.
KAWAMURA: The lightbulb may have burned out.

ダイハツ・シャレード・デラックス1998年型(ねんがた)
運転(うんてん) マニュアル　目次(もくじ)

かしら...

かしら is an informal sentence-final phrase that female speakers use when wondering about something. This phrase is attached to the informal ending of predicates, nouns, or pronouns.

> ギブソンさんはもうデパートへ行ったかしら。
> *I wonder if Ms. Gibson has already gone to the department store.*
> チンさんは病気かしら。
> *I wonder if Ms. Chin is sick.*

In the same context, male speakers use かな or かなあ.

> ギブソンさんはもうデパートへ行ったかなあ。
> チンさんは病気かな。

Verbs that semantically require a direct object marked by the particle を are called *transitive verbs* (他動詞[たどうし] in Japanese). Transitive verbs represent a situation in which the subject's (doer's) action affects the direct object or the subject acts on the direct object. Verbs that require a subject but no direct object are called *intransitive verbs* (自動詞[じどうし] in Japanese). Intransitive verbs express a situation in which the subject undergoes or performs an action on its own.

In English, the same verb usually functions as either a transitive or an intransitive, depending on the context. In fact, modern English has only three pairs of verbs with transitive and intransitive forms that differ: *rise* and *raise* (*The curtain is rising; They are raising the curtain*); *lie* and *lay* (*I will lie down on the bed; I will lay the child down on the bed*); and *fall* and *fell* (*The tree is falling; They are felling the tree*). In most cases, however, the transitive and intransitive are the same:

1. *They changed the plans.* (transitive)
   The plans changed. (intransitive)
2. *I am walking my dog.* (transitive)
   My dog is walking. (intransitive)

In Japanese there are dozens of transitive and intransitive verb pairs that share the same root but have different endings. The table shows some commonly used pairs of transitive and intransitive verbs.

TRANSITIVE VERBS		INTRANSITIVE VERBS	
上げる	to raise	上がる	to rise; to go up
開ける	to open (something)	開く	to open (by itself)
集める	to gather (things, people) together; to collect	集まる	to gather together; to congregate
出す	to put out; to take out	出る	to come/go out; to appear
始める	to begin (something)	始まる	to begin
入れる	to put in; to insert; to include	入る	to enter; to be included; to fit inside
返す／帰す	to return; to give back	返る／帰る	to return (home)
間違える	to make a mistake (about something)	間違う	to be in error
見つける	to find	見つかる	to be found
直す	to fix	直る	to get better
残す	to leave behind	残る	to be left; to remain
落とす	to drop (something)	落ちる	to fall (from a height)
終わる／終える	to end (something)	終わる	to (come to an) end
下げる	to lower (something)	下がる	to go down; to dangle
閉める	to close (something)	閉まる	to close
起こす	to wake (someone) up	起きる	to wake up
かける	to hang (something) on; to lay (something) on (something else)	かかる	to hang (on a vertical surface); to lean; to take (*time, money, etc.*)
付ける／つける	to attach; to turn (something) on	付く／つく	to stick; to become attached; to go on
消す	to extinguish; to put out	消える	to be extinguished; to go off; to disappear
並べる	to line (things) up	並ぶ	to get in line

Automobiles and Transportation

TRANSITIVE VERBS		INTRANSITIVE VERBS	
止める	to stop (something)	止まる	to come to a stop
動かす	to set in motion; to move (something)	動く	to move; to be in motion
乗せる	to put on a vehicle; to give a ride to	乗る	to board a vehicle; to ride
寝かす	to put to bed	寝る	to go to bed; to sleep
なくす	to lose	なくなる	to get lost; to disappear
こわす	to break (something)	こわれる	to become broken
立てる／建てる	to erect; to build	立つ／建つ	to stand; to be built
通す	to send through; to allow to pass through	通る	to pass through; to go along (a road)
回す	to turn (something); to send around	回る	to turn around; to go around
切る	to cut	切れる	to be cut
切らす	to run out of; to use up	切れる	to be used up
変える／かえる	to change (something)	変わる／かわる	to (undergo) change

ブラウンさんは部屋の電気を消しました。
Ms. Brown turned off the light in the room. (transitive)
急に電気が消えました。
Suddenly the lights went off. (intransitive)
どこに車を止めましょうか。
Where shall we stop (park) the car? (transitive)
家の前に赤い車が止まりました。
A red car stopped in front of the house. (intransitive)
それでは、ミーティングを始めます。
Now we will start the meeting. (transitive)
授業 (*class session*) は毎日8時に始まります。
Class starts at eight o'clock every day. (intransitive)

The noun or pronoun that is the object of Japanese transitive verb is not always expressed explicitly, so the lack of an expressed direct object does not necessarily mean that the verb in question is intransitive.

このへんに止めますか。
Shall we stop (the car) around here? (transitive)

In the following cases, the verbs are intransitive, although the particle を is used.

あの道を通って、公園へ行った。
Going along that street, we went to the park. (intransitive)

3時に家を出ましょう。
Let's leave home at three o'clock. (intransitive)

アクティビティー　8

ホテルの前に人が集まっています。(*People are gathered in front of the hotel.*)

Is the underlined verb transitive (T) or intransitive (I)?

1. ホテルの前に人が集まっていますよ。
2. すみませんが、窓を閉めてください。
3. 3時に家を出ましょう。
4. 14日までに本を図書館に返さなければなりません。
5. パーティーは12時に終わりました。
6. 答えを間違えました。
7. このお金、なくさないでね。
8. 冬は天気がよく変わる。
9. 公園の中を通って、大学へ行った。
10. 父がドアを直しました。

アクティビティー　9

ドアが閉まった。(*The door closed.*)

Change the sentences containing transitive verbs to sentences with intransitive verbs, and vice versa. Remember to make all the appropriate changes in particles, and be sure that you understand how the two sentences differ in meaning.

[例]　窓が開きました。→　窓を開けました。
　　　ドアを閉めた。→　ドアが閉まった。

百四十八

148

Automobiles and Transportation

1. 鍵(*lock*)がかかりました。
2. 犬を外に出しました。
3. 髪の色が変わりましたね。
4. 子供をベッドに寝かせた。
5. 昨日、かばんがなくなりました。
6. 車を直しましたか。

アクティビティー　10

ドアが開いた。(*The door opened.*)

Choose from the pair of transitive and intransitive verbs in the first column to fill in the blanks in the second column with the appropriate verb in the plain, past form.

[例]　(開く、開ける)

　　　ドアが（　　　）。→　（開いた）

　　　ギブソンさんがドアを（　　　）。→　（開けた）

1. (起きる、起こす)
   a. 6時になったので、カワムラさんを（　　　）。
   b. 今朝、7時半に（　　　）。

2. (落ちる、落とす)
   a. 風でりんごが木から（　　　）。
   b. カワムラさんは棒(*stick*)を使って、木からりんごを（　　　）。

3. (入る、入れる)
   a. 授業(*class session*)が始まる前に、教室に（　　　）。
   b. タンクにガソリンを（　　　）。

4. (こわれる、こわす)
   a. このラジオを（　　　）のはだれですか。
   b. 昨日、時計が（　　　）。

5. (上がる、上げる)
   a. 答えがわかったので、手を（　　　）。
   b. 先月、ガソリンの値段が1リットル40円（　　　）。

6. (出る、出す)
   a. 高田さんは暑いので、外に（　　　）。
   b. 高田さんは窓から顔を（　　　）。

7. (消える、消す)
   a. 風が吹いて、火(*fire*)が（　　　）。
   b. 寝る前に、火を（　　　）。

8. (動く、動かす)
   a. 地震(*earthquake*)で、家が少し（　　　）。
   b. このソファーをここへ（　　　）。

ダイアログ：乗せてあげましょう。 (*I will give you a ride in my car.*)

町田：林さん、ねえ、ねえ、見て！

林：わあ、これが町田さんの新しい車なの？カッコいいなあ。

町田：乗ってみたい？

林：うん、うん。

町田：じゃ、乗せてあげるわ。

＊ アクティビティー 12

全自動です。 (*It's fully automatic.*)

You are a car salesperson. The cars that you sell perform many functions automatically for drivers. Explain them to a potential buyer, basing your explanation on the diagram of the dashboard below.

Useful Verb: 押す *to push*

[例]　シートを前に動かしたいんですが、...
　　　3番のボタンを押すと、動きますよ。

1. 窓を開けたいんですが...
　　　（　　）番のボタンを押すと、（　　）ますよ。

2. ドアを閉めたいんですが...
　　　（　　）番のボタンを押すと、（　　）ますよ。

3. エアコンを入れたいんですが...
　　　（　　）番のボタンを押すと、（　　）ますよ。

4. テープを止めたいんですが...
　　　（　　）番のボタンを押すと、（　　）ますよ。

5. 音楽を変えたいんですが...
　　　（　　）番のボタンを押すと、（　　）ますよ。

6. シートを上げたいんですが...
　　　（　　）番のボタンを押すと、（　　）ますよ。

MACHIDA: Hey, Mr. Hayashi, look!　HAYASHI: Wow, is this your new car? It looks great.　MACHIDA: Would you like to go for a ride in it?　HAYASHI: Yes, yes.　MACHIDA: Then I'll give you a ride.

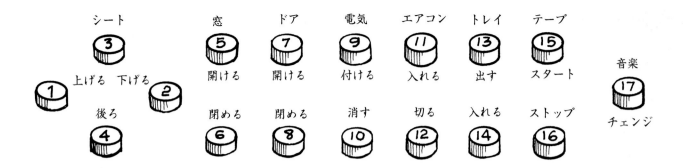

シート 上げる 下げる 後ろ

窓 開ける 閉める

ドア 開ける 閉める

電気 付ける 消す

エアコン 入れる 切る

トレイ 出す 入れる

テープ スタート ストップ

音楽 チェンジ

19. Expressing Results and States of Being: ～てある and ～ている

> 山口： ブラウンさんはまだですか。
> カワムラ： ええ。もうすぐ来ると思いますが...
> 山口： 寒いから、ヒーターを入れておいた方がいいですよ。
> カワムラ： ええ、もう入れてありますよ。
>
> ギブソン： 道路地図、買った？
> 林： うん、もう買ってあるよ。車のチェックもしてあるし、いつでも出られるよ。
> ギブソン： ホテルの予約はしてある？
> 林： ううん。今は部屋がたくさん空いているから、予約はしなくても大丈夫だよ。

19.1 The te-form of a transitive verb plus ある indicates that something is in a state of having already been done with some purpose or for some reason. It can indicate that something is (or is not) ready. The agent of the action is commonly omitted, because he or she is unknown, unimportant, or obvious from the context.

Review the use of もう and まだ in Book 1, Chapter 5.

YAMAGUCHI: Isn't Ms. Brown (here) yet?   KAWAMURA: No, but I think that she'll be here soon.
YAMAGUCHI: It's cold, so you'd better turn on the heater (ahead of time).   KAWAMURA: It has already been turned on.
GIBSON: Have you already bought a road map?   HAYASHI: Yes, it's been bought. The car's been checked, too, so we can leave anytime.   GIBSON: Have hotel reservations already been made?   HAYASHI: No, we don't have to make reservations, because there are a lot of rooms available now.

> Te-form of transitive verb + ある（あります）

Something has been done; someone has done something.

ラジエーターはもう直してあります。
The radiator has already been repaired.

テーブルの上に箸が出してある。
Chopsticks have been put out on the table.

ガレージの前に車が止めてあるので、私の車が出せません。
A car has been parked in front of the garage, so I cannot move my car out.

車はまだチェックしてない。
The car has not yet been checked.

> The plain negative form of ある *(to exist)* is ない.

In this construction, the direct object can be marked by either が or を.

カーエアコンがつけてあります。
カーエアコンをつけてあります。
The car air conditioner has been turned on.

19.2 For most of the transitive-intransitive pairs, the te-form of the intransitive verb plus いる means that something is in a state brought about by an unidentified individual or by a natural force.

> Te-form of intransitive verb + いる（います）

Something occurred, and the resulting state remains.

ヘッドライトがついていますよ。
Your headlights are on.

前の車のトランクが開いている。
The trunk of the car in front of us is open.

カーティスさんの車が止まっています。
Mr. Curtis's car has stopped.

何が入っていますか。
What's inside? What's included?

As explained in Chapter 5 of Book 1, the te-form of the verb plus いる can also express an action in progress.

あっ、ギブソンさんが昼ごはんを食べていますよ。
Oh, Ms. Gibson is eating lunch.

How do you know which interpretation is correct in a given sentence? The answer lies in the nature of the verb. Verbs such as 食べる, 走る, 見る, 聞く, 書く, 読む, and 作る denote actions that can be continued indefinitely. When you see one of these so-called continuous (継続的［けいぞくてき］) verbs in the construction of the te-form plus いる, you can be sure that it describes an ongoing action, much like the English present progressive (*is eating; is running*) form. Most transitive verbs are continuous.

The so-called punctual (瞬間的［しゅんかんてき］) verbs describe either/or situations. From the Japanese point of view, a door that is not completely closed is open, a light that is not completely on is off, and a car that is not completely stopped is moving. When you see one of these punctual verbs in the construction of the te-form plus いる, you can be sure that it describes a state resulting from an action. Almost all the intransitive verbs that have transitive partners are punctual verbs, and there is no short, simple way to describe the transition from one such state to another in Japanese. Thus 閉まっている always means *is closed* and cannot mean *is closing*. A few other common verbs, such as 行く, 来る, 死ぬ, and 結婚する, are also considered punctual, as you learned in Chapter 5, Book 1.

アクティビティー　13

電気が消してある。(*The light has been shut off.*)

Match the sentences with the drawings that they best describe.

1. 電気が消してある。
2. カワムラさんが電気をつけている。
3. 電気がついている。
4. 窓が閉めてある。
5. ブラウンさんが窓を閉めている。
6. 窓が開いている。
7. ビールが出してある。
8. 三村さんがビールを出している。
9. ビールが冷蔵庫に入っている。

A.

B.

C.

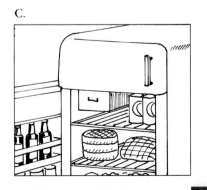

D.

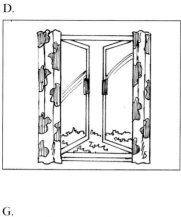

E.

F.

G.

H.

I.

アクティビティー　14

部屋の窓が... (*The window in the room is...*)

Refer to this drawing in order to complete each sentence, using the
te-form of the verbs given plus あります or います.

1. 部屋の窓が (閉める)
2. 机の上に本が (出る)
3. カーテンが (開く)
4. 壁に絵が (かかる)
5. 机の上に花が (置く)
6. 机の引き出し (*drawer*) が (閉まる)
7. 机の下にペンが (落ちる)
8. 電気が (つく)
9. 本が (開ける)

※ アクティビティー 15

車のドアが開いています。(*The car door is open.*)

A suspicious car is parked in front of your house, as shown in the drawing. Call the police, and explain the condition of the car.

[例] 車のドアが開いています。

Vocabulary and Grammar 3B

Vocabulary and Oral Activities

Car Maintenance and Repairs

Vocabulary: Car Troubles and Repair

故障(する)	こしょう(する)	breakdown (to have a mechanical breakdown; to become out of order)
修理(する)	しゅうり(する)	repair (to repair)
修理工	しゅうりこう	mechanic
直す	なおす	to fix; to repair
部品、パーツ	ぶひん	part (*of a mechanical object*)
オイル		motor oil
交通事故	こうつうじこ	traffic accident
事故を起こす	じこをおこす	to cause an accident
事故にあう	じこにあう	to get involved in an accident
衝突(する)	しょうとつ(する)	collision (to collide)

Loanwords: サービス・ステーション、メンテナンス、チェックする

❋ アクティビティー 16

インタビュー (*Interview*)

Walk around the classroom, and find people who fit the following statements.
You may not ask the same person two questions in a row. Ask for the signature
of each person whose situation is described by the statement.

1. 車がよく故障します。
2. 毎日、運転する前に、車を点検します。
3. 車を自分で修理できます。
4. 自分でオイルをチェックしたことがありません。
5. 車の修理に一年に500ドル以上使います。
6. 車のワイパーはこわれていて、動きません。
7. 去年、交通事故にあいました。
8. 車はいつもきれいです。

Grammar and Practice Activities

20. Expressing an Attempt

大_{おおの}野：三村君_{みむらくん}、宿題_{しゅくだい}はしましたか。

三_{みむら}村：いいえ。 しようとしたんですが、ちょっとむずかしいところが
あって...

大野：まだ、していないんですか。

三村：ええ、まだなんです。(because)
　　　　plain　express
　　　　form　reason

町_{まちだ}田：三村_{みむら}さん、このビデオのプログラムの仕方_{しかた}、知_しってる？

三_{みむら}村：^{masc.}うん、一度_{いちど}したことがあるよ。

町田：今、しようとしているんだけど、なかなかうまくいかないのよ。

三村：取_とり扱_{あつか}い説明書_{せつめいしょ}は読_よんだ？

町田：ええ。でも、よくわからないのよ。

20.1 The following construction means *to attempt to; to try to; to be about to....*

> Plain, volitional form of the verb + とする／とします

歌_{うた}を歌_{うた}おうとしましたが、声_{こえ}が出_でませんでした。
I tried to sing a song, but nothing came out (lit., *the voice didn't come out*).
窓_{まど}を開_あけようとしたが、開_あかなかった。
I tried to open the window, but it wouldn't open.

> To review the volitional form of verbs, refer to Chapter 6, **Grammar 37**, in Book 1.

20.2 You have already learned that the te-form of the verb plus みる can sometimes be translated as *try*, so you may be wondering what is different about this new construction. Actually, the two constructions are quite different, and the fact that both of them allow the English translation of *try* is just a coincidence.

OONO: Mr. Mimura, did you do your homework?　MIMURA: No. I tried to do it, but there's a part I just don't get, so (lit., *there's a little difficult place*)...　OONO: So you haven't done it yet?　MIMURA: No, not yet.

MACHIDA: Mr. Mimura, do you know how to program this VCR?　MIMURA: Yes, I've programmed it once before.　MACHIDA: I've been trying to program it, but it's not going well.　MIMURA: Have you read the manual?　MACHIDA: Yes, but I still don't get it.

The te-form + みる construction really means *to do something to see what will happen or what it is like*. Thus, we get sentences like

納豆(*fermented beans*) を食べてみました。
*I tried eating **nattoo** (to see what it was like).*
ドアを開けてみました。
I opened the door (to see what would happen).

In contrast, the plain, volitional + とする construction often implies that although the desire was present or some effort was made, the action was ultimately impossible or futile, especially when the construction is used in the past tense. In the present progressive tense, its only connotation is that the subject is attempting to do something.

納豆を食べようとしたけれど、まずくて、食べられなかった。
*I tried to eat the **nattoo**, but it tasted bad and I couldn't eat it.*
ドアを開けようとしたけど、鍵がかかっていた。
I tried to open the door, but it was locked.
私の母はインターネットを始めようとしています。
My mother is trying to learn how to use the internet.

The plain, volitional form of the verb + とする construction has an additional use, which is to describe interrupted actions, particularly when the construction appears in its 〜たら form or before 時 or ところ. These are similar to the English *just as I was about to....*

家を出ようとしたら、ブラウンさんが来た。
Just as I was about to leave the house, Ms. Brown came.
お風呂に入ろうとしたところ、電話がなりました。
Just as I was about to get into the bath, the telephone rang.

アクティビティー 17

ドライブに行こうとしたけど... (*I tried to go for a drive, but...*)

Complete the sentences in the first column by choosing the best option from the second column.

1. _____ が、ガソリンがなかった。
2. _____ が、雨が降ってきた。
3. _____ が、鍵がかかっていた。
4. _____ が、電池 (*battery*) がなかった。
5. _____ が、カワムラさんが「食べるな」と言った。

a. ウォークマンを聞こうとした
b. ピクニックに出かけようとした
c. ドレスを着て、どこかへ出かけようとしていた
d. ドライブに行こうとした
e. 彼女を映画に誘おう (*invite*) としている

6. 高田さんは山本さんが好きで、　　f. おとといた作ったすしを食べよう
　　　　　　　。　　　　　　　　　　　　　とした
7. 村山さんのアパートへ行くと、　　g. ドアを開けようとした
　　　　　　　。

アクティビティー　18

エンジンがかかりますか。(*Does the engine start?*)

Change the verbs in parentheses to the plain, volitional form.

1. エンジンを (かける) としたが、かからなかった。
2. 山本さんと (話す) としましたが、忙しくて、話す時間が
　 ありませんでした。
3. ホットケーキを (作る) としたが、焦がして (焦がす *to scorch*)
　 しまった。
4. そこで本を (読む) としましたが、子供がうるさくて読めません
　 でした。
5. 散歩へ (行く) としたら、高田さんが来ました。
6. 林さんに (会う) としましたが、どこにいるかわかりませんでした。
7. その近所でアパートを (借りる) としましたが、高くて、やめました。
8. その学生は来年から日本の大学で (勉強する) としています。

アクティビティー　19

窓は開きますか。(*Does the window open?*)

Complete the following sentences by changing the verbs in the parentheses to
〜ようとする／した or 〜てみる／みた.

1. 窓を (開ける) が、どうしても開かなかった。
2. 窓を (開ける) が、外には誰もいなかった。
3. 日本語で手紙を (書く) が、時間がかかりました。
4. 日本語で手紙を (書く) が、時間がありませんでした。
5. 来週、あの新しいレストランへ (行く)。

6. このケーキ、とてもおいしいですよ。ちょっと（食べる）ください。

7. 日本語で（話す）が、ことば *(words)* が口から出て来なかったんです。

8. 日本語で（話す）が、誰^{だれ}もわかってくれなかったんです。

アクティビティー　20

チンさんはバスに乗^のろうとしている。(*Ms. Chin is about to get on the bus.*)

Describe what each person or object is trying to do or is about to do by using
～ようとしている.

[例]　チンさんがバスに乗^のろうとしている。

1. カワムラさんは...
2. ブラウンさんは...
3. 町田さんは...

4. 車^{くるま}は...
5. 林^{はやし}さんは...
6. 三村^{みむら}さんは...

Automobiles and Transportation

ダイアログ：窓を開けようとしたんですが、...（*I tried to open the window, but...*）

　町田：すみません。ちょっと見てもらいたいんですが...

修理工：どうしましたか。

　町田：<u>窓を開けよう</u>としたんですが、<u>開かない</u>んです。

修理工：ちょっと見てみましょう。

Now practice this dialogue, substituting the following words for the underlined parts of the dialogue. Use the proper verb forms.

1. 窓を閉める、閉まる
2. ワイパーを使う、動く
3. ヘッドライトをつける、つく
4. シートを前に出す、出る
5. ライトを消す、消える
6. ハンドルを回す（*to turn*）、回る

21. Expressing a Just-Completed Action: The Ta-Form of the Verb ＋ ばかり／ところだ

おくさま

　山口：カワムラさん、ケーキ、買ってきたんですけど、食べませんか。　　*ガ*　*v. polite*

カワムラ：残念だな。今、夕ごはんを食べたばかりなんですよ。

　山口：そうですか。でも、ほら、小さなケーキだから、食べられますよ。　*look*

カワムラ：そうですね。じゃあ、いただきます。

　町田：あの方はどなた？

　チン：私の友達のリーさん。

　町田：中国人の方？

　チン：ええ、昨日ペキンから着いたばかりな<del>の</del>んです・*Female*

MACHIDA: Excuse me, but I'd like to have you look (at my car).　MECHANIC: What's wrong?
MACHIDA: I tried to open the window, but it doesn't open.　MECHANIC: Let's take a look at it.

YAMAGUCHI: Mr. Kawamura, I just bought some cakes (lit., *bought cakes and came back*). Won't you have some?　KAWAMURA: Oh, too bad. I just ate dinner.　YAMAGUCHI: I see, but look, they're small cakes, so I'm sure you can eat one.　KAWAMURA: Do you think so? Then, I'll have some.

MACHIDA: Who is that person?　CHIN: My friend, Ms. Lee.　MACHIDA: Is she Chinese?　CHIN: Yes, she just arrived from Beijing yesterday.

21.1 The following construction is used when only a little time has passed since something happened.

Ta-form of verb +	ばかりだ（です） ところだ（です）

Something has just happened; someone has just done something.

ばかり is a particle meaning *only* or *nothing but what is stated* (refer to Chapter 2), whereas ところ is a noun meaning *place*, and by extension, *point in time*.

車くるまにガソリンを入れたところです。
I have just put gas in my car.

先週せんしゅう、車くるまのチェックをしたばかりです。
I just had my car checked last week.

このワープロは買ったばかりで、まだ使つかい方かたがよくわかりません。
I just bought this word processor, so I don't know how to use it yet.

21.2 The ta-form with ばかり and the ta-form with ところ differ slightly in nuance. Here are two contrasting sentences:

ニューヨークから帰かえってきたところです。
I have just returned from New York.

ニューヨークから帰かえってきたばかりです。
I have just returned from New York.

The first sentence implies that the speaker has returned from New York a very short time ago, perhaps even only a few minutes ago, but almost certainly within the same day. The second sentence implies that the speaker returned a relatively short time ago, but the definition of "a relatively short time" varies according to the context. For example, if you were talking about current conditions in New York and you had come back from a trip there ten days before, you could introduce your remarks by saying:

十日前とうかまえにニューヨークから帰かえってきたばかりなんですが...
I just returned from New York ten days ago, and...

The same sentence with ところ would be ungrammatical, because ten days is too long to be considered a point in time.

アクティビティー 22

その漢字かんじ、習ならったばかりです。(*I just learned that **kanji**.*)

Match each statement in the first column with the person who most likely said it in the second column.

1. マドンナとのインタビューを
   終えたばかりです。

2. デパートを5軒回って、今帰ってき
   たばかりです。

3. ビルと話したばかりです。

4. パリへは先月行ってきたばかり
   です。来月はウィーンへ行く
   つもりです。

5. その漢字、習ったばかりです。

6. ラビオリを食べたばかりで、
   おなかがいっぱいです。

7. 「ルーツ」を読んだばかりです。

a. バーバラ・ウォーターズ

b. 日本語を習っている学生

c. 買い物が好きな人

d. 旅行が好きな人

e. イタリアりょうりが好きな人

f. アレックス・ヘイリーの本が
   好きな人

g. ヒラリー・クリントン

アクティビティー　23

新しいスポーツカーを買ったから、帰ってきたところだから。(*I bought a new sports car and so I just got home.*)

Complete these sentences, following the example.

[例]　昼ごはんを食べたところだから、...　→
　　　昼ごはんを食べたところだから、おなかがいっぱいです。

1. 運動したところだから...

2. アメリカから来たところだから、...

3. 旅行から帰ってきたところだから、...

4. 新しいスポーツカーを買ったところだから、...

5. コーヒーを飲んだところだから...

アクティビティー　24

10キロ走ったばかりなので...　(*I've just run ten kilometers...*)

Complete these sentences, following the example.

[例]　...なので、疲れています。→
　　　10キロ走ったばかりなので、疲れています。
　　　...なので、ブラウンさんはすぐ出てくるでしょう。→
　　　映画が終わったところなので、ブラウンさんはすぐ出てくるでしょう。

1. ...なので、おなかがすいています。
2. ...なので、部屋がとてもきれいです。
3. ...なので、まだドレスを着ています。
4. ...なので、まだちょっと寒いです。
5. ...なので、今は何も食べられません。
6. ...なので、まだ上手に作れません。

✷ アクティビティー 25

ダイアログ：バッテリーをチェックしたばかりなんですが、(*I have just checked the battery.*)

町田：エンジンをかけようとしたんですが、かからないんですよ。どこが悪いかわからないんです。

三村：バッテリーかもしれませんね。

町田：でも、バッテリーは、二日前にチェックしたばかりなんですが...

三村：うん、じゃ、違うな。ガソリンは入れてありますか。

Work in pairs. Continue this dialogue with your partner, with the person playing the role of Mimura suggesting other reasons for the car's not starting and the person playing Machida explaining why that isn't the case.

✷ アクティビティー 26

中古車を売ります。(*I'm going to sell my old car.*)

You'd like to sell your old car, but it has the problems in the following list. What do you need to do to make it more attractive to a potential buyer?

[例]   —フロントガラスがきたない。→
       洗っておきます。

Useful Verb: ...にペンキを塗る *to paint...*

> **R**eview the use of the te-form of verbs + おく in Chapter 2, **Grammar 16**.

1. バッテリーがあがっている (*the battery is dead*)。
2. ラジエーターがこわれている。
3. タイヤがパンクしている。
4. ドアがちょっとさびている (*is rusted*)。

MACHIDA: I tried to start the engine, but it won't start. I don't know what's wrong.   MIMURA: It could be the battery.   MACHIDA: But I just checked the battery two days ago.   MIMURA: Hm, then it's not that. Is there gas in the tank? (Lit., *Has gas been put in?*)

5. ワイパーが動かない。

6. ライトが切れている。

7. スペアタイヤがない。

8. バックミラーがない。

Now your car looks new. A prospective buyer is making complimentary remarks and asking questions about it, and you explain what you have done with the car.

[例]　―フロントガラスがピカピカですね。→
　　　昨日洗ったばかりです。

1. バッテリーは新しいんですか。

2. ラジエターは大丈夫ですか。

3. タイヤは大丈夫ですか。

4. ワイパーは動きますか。

5. スペアタイヤはありますか。

6. ライトはつきますか。

✻ アクティビティー　27

どんな車ですか。(*What kind of car is it?*)

You have advertised your car, and a prospective buyer has called you. Answer his or her questions, which appear after the descriptive advertisement. If the necessary information is not included in the advertisement, make up your own answers.

1993年マツダ・ファミリア87万円

4ドア、5人乗り、白

5万キロ

サンルーフ、カーステレオ、カーエアコン付

リクライニング・シート

エンジン、水冷4気筒SOHC/1800cc、1997年オーバーホール

4速、オートマチック

ハイオク・ガソリン使用、タンク70リットル

燃費 6.8 km/リットル、とても経済的

タイヤ、新しいタイヤに替えたばかり

---

1. 日本車ですか。

2. 何色ですか。

3. いくらですか。

4. 何人乗りですか。

5. エンジンは新しいですか。

6. 経済的な (*economical*) 車ですか。

7. 運転しやすい (*easy to drive*) ですか。

8. 乗り心地がいい (*comfortable to ride in*) ですか。

9. 何年型の車ですか。

10. トランクは広いですか。

Ask a classmate these same questions about his or her car or about his or her family's car.

Vocabulary and Grammar 3C

Vocabulary and Oral Activities

Transportation and Traffic in the City

Vocabulary: Vehicles (1)

交通機関	こうつうきかん	means of transportation
オートバイ		motorcycle
モペット		moped
トラック		truck
スポーツカー		sports car
救急車	きゅうきゅうしゃ	ambulance
消防車	しょうぼうしゃ	fire engine
パトカー		patrol car; police car
モノレール		monorail

Review: バス、タクシー、自転車、電車、地下鉄、停留所、乗る

❋ アクティビティー 28

バスをよく使いますか。(*Do you often use a bus?*)

Discuss your use of public transportation by discussing the following issues.

1. あなたの住んでいる町にはどんな交通機関がありますか。

2. あなたはバスをよく使いますか。

Automobiles and Transportation

3. バスのいい点は何だと思いますか。悪い点は何だと思いますか。
4. どんな時にタクシーを使いますか。
5. このへんのタクシーは高いと思いますか。
6. 車が多いと、どのような問題がありますか。
7. 地下鉄に乗ったことはありますか。
8. モノレールに乗ったことはありますか。

✳ アクティビティー 29

ダイアログ：このバスは江戸博物館へ行きますか。(*Does this bus go to the Edo Museum?*)

ブラウン：すみません。このバスは<u>江戸博物館</u>へ行きますか。
運転手：いいえ。<u>江戸博物館</u>へ行くのは<u>5番</u>のバスです。
ブラウン：ここで乗れますか。
運転手：いいえ、<u>3番</u>乗り場に行ってください。
ブラウン：ありがとうございます。

Practice the preceding dialogue by changing the first two underlined parts according to the following information.

1. 東京タワー (Number 7 bus, Stop Number 4)
2. 早稲田大学 (Number 1 bus, Stop Number 1)

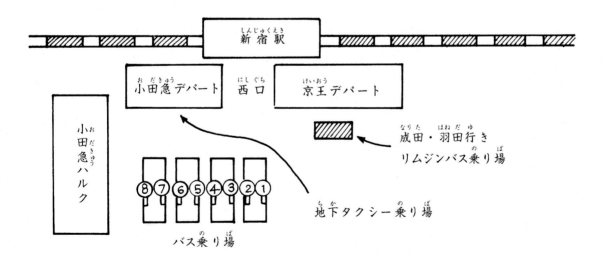

BROWN: Excuse me. Does this bus go to the <u>Edo Museum</u>?   DRIVER: No, the bus that goes to the <u>Edo Museum</u> is the <u>Number 5 bus</u>.   BROWN: Can I get on it here?   DRIVER: No, go to <u>Stop Number 3</u>. BROWN: Thank you.

Vocabulary Library

Transit

ワンマンバス		bus without a conductor
回数券	かいすうけん	coupon ticket; strip of tickets
定期券	ていきけん	monthly commuter pass
改札口	かいさつぐち	turnstile gate at a transit station

Loanwords: トロリーバス、トレーラー、トラクター、セダン、クーペ、ハッチバック、リムジン、ジープ、バン、ミニバン

Review: 切符(きっぷ)

CULTURE NOTE • Public Transportation

Few Japanese commute to work or school by car. Instead, most people rely on a highly developed, carefully coordinated, well-maintained, virtually crime-free network of buses, JR trains, private railroads, and, in the largest cities, subways.

During the morning and evening rush hours, the trains and subways run as often as every three minutes, and even then they can be packed so tightly that the passengers are unable to move. The system is uncomfortable enough that commuters have dubbed

文化ノート

百六十八

it 通勤地獄 (つうきんじごく), "commuting hell," a takeoff on 受験地獄 (じゅけんじごく), the "entrance examination hell" that high school students endure. Still, the passengers almost always arrive at work or school on time and don't have to worry about getting stuck in traffic.

To save time, most commuters buy either monthly passes (定期券 [ていきけん]) or strips of tickets (回数券 [かいすうけん]), allowing them to pass right through the turnstile (改札口 [かいさつぐち]) without stopping at the ticket machine. For less frequent commuters there are the so-called オレンジ・カード, prepaid cards that allow people to buy tickets at the machines without having to have money on hand.

Fortunately, rush hour is only a small portion of the day, and people who ride the trains and subways during the middle of the day, when they run every eight or ten minutes, can usually find a place to sit.

Bus systems are well developed in almost every part of Japan. In addition to 市内バス (しないバス), which run within cities and towns, there are the 長距離バス (ちょうきょりバス), which run between cities. If you need to go to the airport, you may find that a リムジンバス is your most economical option.

You can pick up taxis at taxi stands (タクシー乗り場 [タクシーのりば]) in front of stations, or at hotels. Large numbers of taxis constantly cruise the through streets of major cities, so if you are not near a station or hotel, you can simply go to the nearest busy street and summon a passing cab by raising your hand.

Grammar and Practice Activities

22. Without Doing: 〜ないで

カワムラ： もう8時5分？大変だ。寝坊しちゃった。
山口： 朝ごはんはテーブルの上よ。
カワムラ： 今日は朝ごはんを食べないで、学校へ行きます。
山口： 朝ごはんを食べないと、体に悪いわよ。
横井： みなさん、これを読んでみてください。
カーティス： 辞書を使ってもいいですか。
横井： 辞書は引かないで、読んでください。

22.1 The negative form (the ない form) of verbs ＋ で, the negative te-form of the verb is used to make an adverbial clause meaning *without doing...*

KAWAMURA: Is it already 8:05? Oh, no! I overslept.   YAMAGUCHI: Your breakfast is on the table.
KAWAMURA: I'll go to school without eating breakfast today.   YAMAGUCHI: If you don't eat breakfast, it's bad for your health (lit., *body*), you know.

YOKOI: Everybody, please try reading this now.   CURTIS: May I use a dictionary?   YOKOI: Please read it without looking things up in a dictionary.

昨日の夜はぜんぜん寝ないで、宿題をしていました。
Last night I did homework without sleeping at all.

靴を脱がないで、家の中に入ったんですか。
You went into a house without taking off your shoes?

This form is also used for negative commands, as you learned in Chapter 2.

22.2 The 〜ないで form can be replaced with the negative te-form, 〜なくて, when the subsequent clause expresses emotions, judgments, or reasons. In fact, the alternative with 〜なくて is probably more common in these cases.

三村さんと話さなくて、いいですか。
Is it all right not to talk to Mr. Mimura?

人があまり来なくて、さびしいパーティーだった。
Not very many people came, and it was a forlorn party.

22.3 In Chapter 2 (and in Book 1) you studied the te-form of verbs + おく, which means *do something as a preparation for a future occasion*. The negative of this construction, 〜ないで + おく, means *leave something undone for the time being* or *for a specific reason*.

お父さんのためにそのステーキを食べないでおきました。
I left that steak uneaten for my father (so that he could eat it).

来月旅行にお金を使うので、今月はあまり使わないでおいた。
Because I'm going to spend money on a trip next month, I didn't spend so much money this month.

言語ノート

体に悪いわよ

The sentence-final particle わ, not to be confused with は, the topic particle, indicates mild emphasis and is used mostly by female speakers in the Tokyo-Yokohama area. Male speakers in certain other parts of Japan also use it, but in the Tokyo-Yokohama region, it has a definitely feminine flavor. It most commonly appears in informal sentences, where it is one of the features distinguishing the feminine style from the masculine.

大変だ。(masculine)
大変だわ。(feminine) } *It's awful.*

できないよ。(masculine)
できないわよ。(feminine) } *I can't.*

The distinctions between masculine and feminine speech are less strict than they used to be, but it is still more acceptable for a female to use slightly masculine speech than for a male to use feminine speech.

Automobiles and Transportation

The Conjunctive Form of the Verb as a Coordinating Structure

The conjunctive form of verbs (see Chapter 3, Book 1) can be used to connect two clauses.

スイッチを入れ、ライトがつくかどうか確かめます。
I'll put on the switch, and check whether or not the light goes on.

一番目の角を左に曲がり、まっすぐ行きます。
Turn left at the first corner, and go straight.

Like the te-form of the verb, the conjunctive form is used to express sequential and contrasted actions.

電気を消し、部屋を出た。(sequential actions)
電気を消して、部屋を出た。
I turned off the light and left the room.

私は京都へ行き、村山さんは大阪へ行きました。
(contrastive actions)
私は京都へ行って、村山さんは大阪へ行きました。
I went to Kyoto, while Ms. Murayama went to Osaka.

The conjunctive form sounds more formal than the te-form, and it is more common in writing and formal or scripted speech than in everyday conversation. You will often see it in written instructions.

> The conjunctive form of verbs is the form to which ます (nonpast, polite affirmative ending) is attached.

アクティビティー 30

本を見ないで答えてください。(*Please answer without looking at the book.*)

Rewrite these sentences following the example.

[例] 本を(見る)、答えてください。→
本を見ないで、答えてください。

1. となりの人に(聞く)、答えてください。
2. めがねを(かける)、運転した。
3. 顔を(洗う)、学校へいきました。
4. ノートに何も(書く)、聞いていてください。

5. 席に（座る）、立っていた。
6. 電気を（つける）、勉強していました。
7. 傘を（持つ）、家を出ました。
8. そのセーターを（買う）、帰ってきました。

アクティビティー　31

ノートを見ないで「おんがく」を漢字で書けますか。(*Can you write the kanji for "ongaku" without looking at your notebook?*)

Answer these questions.

1. ノートを見ないで、「おんがく」という漢字が書けますか。
2. 三日間何も食べないで、我慢 (*endurance*) できますか。
3. 誰にも聞かないで、「さんぜんよんひゃくごじゅうはち」が漢字で書けますか。
4. 辞書を引かないで、「高田さんは去年、マダガスカルに旅行しました」の意味がわかりますか。
5. クラスに出ないで、家でテレビを見ていたことがありますか。
6. 一晩中寝ないで、勉強したことがありますか。

アクティビティー　32

山口さんは紙も見ないで、スピーチをしました。(*Mr. Yamaguchi gave a speech without looking at his notes.*)

Complete each sentence by choosing the appropriate expression from the given list of vocabulary and changing it to the ～ないで form.

[例]　山口さんは ＿＿＿＿ スピーチをしました。すごいですね。（紙を見る）→
山口さんは紙も見ないで、スピーチをしました。すごいですね。

Vocabulary:　お風呂に入る、さようならを言う、ライトをつける、エアコンを入れる、ごはんを食べる

1. カワムラさんは ＿＿＿＿、勉強していますよ。大丈夫ですか。
2. 三村さんは ＿＿＿＿、帰りました。失礼な人ですね。
3. あの車は ＿＿＿＿、走っています。危いですね。
4. 一週間も＿＿＿＿、きたないですね。
5. こんなに暑いのに、＿＿＿＿、何しているのですか。

ダイアログ：あそこで曲がらないで、まっすぐ行ってください。(*Please just go straight without turning there.*)

タクシーの中で

運転手：3丁目1番地はこのへんですかね。

町田：ええと、ここはまだ2丁目ね。

運転手：<u>あそこで曲がりますか。</u>

町田：いいえ、<u>あそこで曲がらないで</u>、もう少しまっすぐ行ってください。

Practice the preceding dialogue, changing the underlined parts to the following words.

1. ここで止める　　2. あそこでUターンする　　3. あの道に入る

Vocabulary and Oral Activities

Vocabulary: Traffic (1)

歩道	ほどう	sidewalk
歩行者	ほこうしゃ	pedestrian
横断歩道	おうだんほどう	pedestrian crossing
車道	しゃどう	road
高速道路	こうそくどうろ	freeway
違反する	いはんする	to violate rules
警察に捕まる	けいさつにつかまる	to be caught by the police
時速	じそく	speed per hour (時速60 km = 60 kilometers per hour)
制限速度	せいげんそくど	speed limit
駐車禁止	ちゅうしゃきんし	No Parking
近道	ちかみち	shortcut
回り道	まわりみち	detour
工事中	こうじちゅう	under construction
道に迷う	みちにまよう	to lose one's way
道路地図	どうろちず	road map
交通渋滞	こうつうじゅうたい	traffic jam

In a taxi　　DRIVER: Is No. 1, 3-choome (the third district) around here?　　MACHIDA: Hmm, this is still 2-choome.　　DRIVER: Do I <u>turn there</u>?　　MACHIDA: Please just go straight a little more, <u>without turning there</u>.

✳ ## アクティビティー　34

交通標識 *(Traffic signs)*

<small>こうつうひょうしき</small>

What do you think these signs mean? Some of them may be obvious to you, while others will require some guesswork. Match each sign with the sentence that most closely describes its meaning. For unfamiliar terms, see the Vocabulary Library on the next page.

Review 〜はいけません、なさい in Chapter 1.

1. 通ることができません。
2. 自転車は通ることができません。
3. Uターンしてはいけません。
4. 追い越しをしてはいけません。
5. 午前8時から午後8時までは1時間駐車をしてもいいです。
6. ここはバスだけが通ることができます。
7. クラクションを鳴らしなさい。(鳴らす *to sound*)
8. 真っすぐ行きなさい。
9. 人は通れません。
10. 一度止まりなさい。

a.   b.   c.   d.

e.   f.   g.   h.

i.   j.

Vocabulary Library

Traffic (2)

一方通行	いっぽうつうこう	one-way traffic
追い越し (する) ／追い越す	おいこし (する) ／おいこす	passing; (to pass)
Uターン (する)	ユーターン (する)	(to make a) U-turn
Uターン禁止	ユーターンきんし	No U-turn
左側通行	ひだりがわつうこう	driving on the left
ノロノロ運転	ノロノロうんてん	sluggish traffic
酔っぱらい運転 (する)	よっぱらいうんてん (する)	drunk driving (to drive drunk)

Loanwords: ガードレール、インターチェンジ、カーブ、サービスエリア、センターライン、バイパス

❋ アクティビティー 35

何と言いますか。(*What do you say?*)

What would you say to these people? Give a warning by using 〜ないでください。

[例] ―車道を歩いている人→
　　　車道を歩かないでください。

1. あなたの家のガレージの前に車を止めている人
2. クラクションをうるさく鳴らしている人
3. 一方通行の道に入ってきた人
4. センターラインを越えて (越える *to go over; to go beyond*) 運転している人
5. 狭い道で追い越しをしようとしている人
6. Uターン禁止の道でUターンしようとしている人
7. 自転車しか入れない道を運転している人
8. お酒を飲んで運転している人

❋ アクティビティー 36

運転の準備 (*Preparation for a drive*)

What would you do to prepare for the following driving situations? Discuss in class.

1. コロラドに車で行って、スキーをしようと思う時
2. 夏の暑い時に運転する場合 (*case*)

3. 雨の日に運転する時
4. 長い距離を運転する時
5. 初めての場所 (*place*) を運転する時
6. 雪が降っている時に、運転する場合
7. 交通渋滞の時に、運転する場合
8. 夜、運転する時

Language Skills

Reading and Writing

Reading 1   安全運転

Before You Read

Which of the following factors is most important for you when you buy a car?

値段が安い   カッコいい

安全   長持ちする (*durable*)

経済的 (*economical*)

Now Read It!

安全な運転の仕方

1. 運転の前

   運転前には、次の点をチェックしましょう。

   a. 運転席でのチェック

      ブレーキペダル、ハンドブレーキ、ガソリンの量、バックミラー、
      サイドミラー

   b. エンジンルームのチェック
      ブレーキのリザーブタンク、ラジエーターのリザーブタンク、
      エンジンオイルの量、ファンベルト

次の *following* / 点 *point*

運転席 *driver's seat*

量 *amount*

c. 車のまわりのチェック

エンジンスイッチを入れ、ウインカー、ブレーキライトがつくかどうか点検しましょう。タイヤのみぞの深さが十分かどうか点検しましょう。定期点検をしたばかりでも、これらの点をいつも点検することが大切です。発車する前には、車の前後に人がいないかどうか、車の下に子供がいないかどうか確かめましょう。

みぞ *(tire) tread*／深さ *depth*
十分 *sufficient*
定期点検 *regular checkup*

発車する *to start a car*

確かめる *to make sure*

2. 車に乗る時

車に乗る時は、後ろから来る車にも注意して、乗りましょう。シートは倒さないで、深く腰かけましょう。シートベルトは必ず締めてください。子供を助手席に乗せるのは危険です。幼児用シートか後部座席に乗せましょう。

注意する *to watch for; to be cautious; to take care*
倒す *knock over; set back*
腰かける *to sit down; to take a seat*
助手席 *passenger seat*／幼児 *infant*
後部座席 *rear seat*

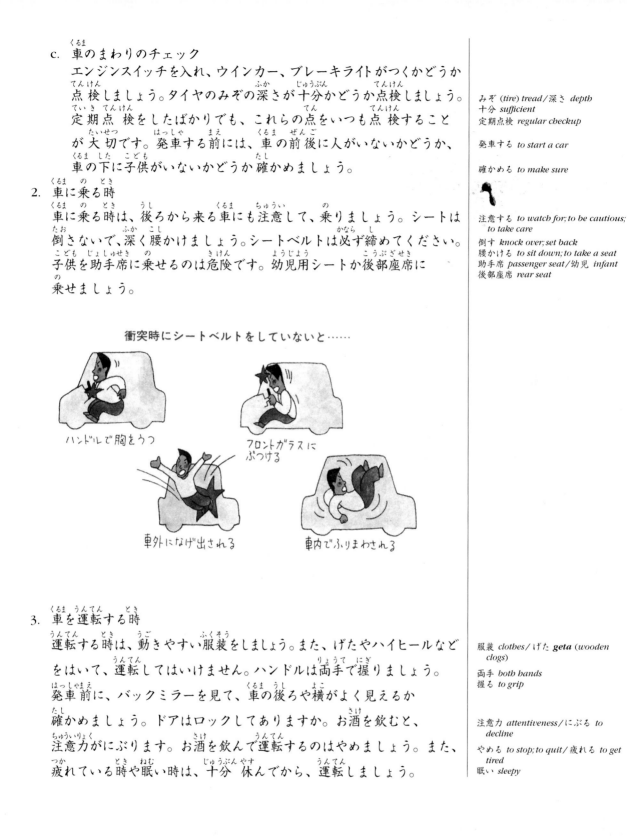

衝突時にシートベルトをしていないと……

ハンドルで胸をうつ

フロントガラスにぶつける

車外になげ出される

車内でふりまわされる

3. 車を運転する時

運転する時は、動きやすい服装をしましょう。また、げたやハイヒールなどをはいて、運転してはいけません。ハンドルは両手で握りましょう。発車前に、バックミラーを見て、車の後ろや横がよく見えるか確かめましょう。ドアはロックしてありますか。お酒を飲むと、注意力がにぶります。お酒を飲んで運転するのはやめましょう。また、疲れている時や眠い時は、十分休んでから、運転しましょう。

服装 *clothes*／げた **geta** *(wooden clogs)*

両手 *both hands*
握る *to grip*

注意力 *attentiveness*／にぶる *to decline*

やめる *to stop; to quit*／疲れる *to get tired*
眠い *sleepy*

After You Finish Reading

The previous paragraph mentions things you should watch for (1) before driving, (2) while getting in the car, and (3) while you are driving. In which part do you think the following sentences should be added?

1. ハンドルは10時10分の位置に握ります。
2. シートレバーでシートの前後の位置を変えます。
3. 車を出す前に、バックミラーで車の後ろやまわりの安全をチェックしましょう。
4. フロントガラスはきれいにしておきましょう。
5. ワイパーが古くなっていませんか。
6. 一緒に車に乗っている人もシートベルトを締めなくてはいけません。
7. 雨の日は、道路がすべりやすいです。運転には特に注意しましょう。
8. 長時間休まないで、運転するのは危険です。

Following are steps in changing a flat tire, but they are out of sequence. Arrange them in the correct order. Can you tell which verbs are transitive and which are intransitive by looking at how they are used in the sentences?

ホイルナットをつけます。

エンジンを止め、エマージェンシーライトをつけます。

ハブキャップをとりつけます。

ハブキャップをつけます。

車から降ります。

ホイルナットを締めます。

ジャッキで車を下げます。

ジャッキで車を上げます。

道路のはじに車を止めます。

トランクからジャッキ、スペアタイヤを出します。

ホイルナットを緩めます。

サイドブレーキをかけます。

パンクしたタイヤを取り、スペアタイヤをつけます。

Writing 1

You would like to sell your car. Write a short advertisement. Make it as attractive as possible to prospective buyers.

Reading 2　上手なドライブの仕方

(かたがない)
it can't be helped
There's no way to do it.

Before You Read

1. When you go for a long-distance drive, what do you take along? What do you do before leaving? Discuss in Japanese with your classmates.
2. List three good points and three bad points for travel by car and travel by air. Compare your answers with those of your classmates.

Now Read It!

上手なドライブの仕方

■　道路交通情報センター

ドライブする時に一番気になるのは交通渋滞ですね。交通渋滞にあうと、せっかくのドライブのプランも台無し。ドライブの前に道路情報を聞いておきましょう。道路交通情報センターに電話すると、日本中の主な道路の情報、渋滞の情報、交通事故の情報を教えてくれます。東京の電話番号は3581-7611です。

giving
くださる

■　JAFの旅行サービス

目的の場所までどのようなコースで行けばいいか、ドライブ・コースを教えてくれるのはJAFの旅行サービスです。ドライブ・プラン、ドライブ・コースの相談にのってくれますし、旅館やホテルの予約もしてくれます。また、車の故障、交通事故、パンクの時には24時間いつでもエマージェンシー・サービスをしてくれます。JAFの電話番号は3436-2811です。

plain form before と
(=with a reason)
Also
=> anytime
いつも=always

■　レンタカー

どこか遠くへ出かけたい。でも、長時間の運転は疲れるし、途中の交通渋滞はいや。こんな方は、往復はJRを使い、観光地ではレンタカーを借りてはいかがでしょうか。レンタカーは運転免許がある人なら誰でも借りられます。料金もそんなに高くありません。例えば、スターレットが6時間6,900円、カリーナSEが6時間11,000円です。予約はトヨタレンタ予約センター3264-0120に。また、JRの往復料金とレンタカーの料金を一緒にしたトレン太くんもあります。

somewhere とお
This person かた
conjuncture
suggestion
= anyone

■　フェリーボート

九州をマイカーでドライブしたい方には、フェリーが一番。九州まではフェリーでゆっくりと行き、九州に着いたら、マイカーで自由にドライブできます。東京から九州まではオーシャンフェリーで、料金は往復大人が3280円、車は52000円です。予約は3567-0971まで。

せっかく is an adverb that adds the nuance of _having gone to all the trouble_ or _having waited this long_. It is usually followed by a suggestion of what to do because of this situation.

気になる _to be worried about; to be nervous about_
せっかく _long-awaited; going to all the trouble_ / 台無し _totally spoiled_
主（な）_main; major; chief_

情報 _information_

目的 _purpose; objective_ / 行けばいい _It would be good to go_
相談 _consultation_

疲れる _to get tired_ / 途中 _on the way_
いや（な）_disgusting; disagreeable_
往復 _round trip_

運転免許がある人なら _If it is a person with a driver's license_
料金 _fee_ / 例えば _for example_

自由に _freely_

こんなに差がある会員と非会員

■高速での事故車けん引(10km)

会員	会員証を提示すれば けん引料のみ (5kmまで無料)	合計 2,500円
非会員	基本料 (基本時間) 特別料金 作業 けん引料 (10km)	合計 16,250円

■キー閉じ込み

会員	会員証を提示すれば	無料
非会員	基本料 5,500円 (夜間料金) 作業料 2,200円	合計 7,700円

夜間走行中に車をぶつけてライト部分を破損したので、JAFのサービスカーで10kmけん引してもらった。

ドライブインで、鍵をつけたままドアロックしてしまいました。

『JAFに入っておけばよかったのに!』と困らないために

―――年中無休・24時間安心のJAF今すぐ入会を―――

●ご入会は簡単です

この振込用紙に住所＊氏名をご記入の上、最寄りの郵便局＊表記の銀行(本社＊支店)へご持参下さい。

振込先銀行名及び口座名

第一勧業銀行 (日比谷支店)　東京相和銀行 (虎ノ門支店)
さくら銀行 (東京営業部)　住友銀行 (日比谷支店)
富士銀行 (三田支店)　大和銀行 (神谷町支店)
三菱銀行 (本店)　東海銀行 (三田支店)
あさひ銀行 (本店営業部)　東京都民銀行 (本店)
三和銀行 (虎ノ門支店)　横浜銀行 (東京支店)
八千代銀行 (本店)

手数料不要

社団法人 日本自動車連盟・普通預金

After You Finish Reading

Fill in the table in English, basing your answers on the information in the brochure.

PLACE	FOR WHAT PURPOSES? ON WHAT OCCASIONS?	TELEPHONE NUMBER
		3581-7611
JAF		
		3264-0120
Ocean Ferry		

The following people each have different travel plans. What telephone number should each person call?

1. 林さんと九州に旅行したいんですが、東京から九州までの長い距離を運転するのは疲れますね。

2. 東京から新潟、金沢へドライブしますが、どんなコースがいいんですか。

3. ドライブの途中なんですが、パンクしてしまいました。タイヤの替え方がわからないんです。   替える *to change*

4. これから車で千葉へ行くんですが、途中、事故はありませんか。

5. 引っ越しするので、トラックが必要です。

6. ガールフレンドと横浜へドライブしたいんですが、車がありません。

Writing 2

Write out the directions for driving from the campus to your home by car. Then exchange directions with a classmate, and see if you can understand each other's directions. If you have a map, try to follow your partner's directions on it.

Language Functions and Situations

Asking for and Giving Instructions

自動車学校で

町田：どうやってバックするんですか。

先生：まず、後ろを見て、車の後ろの安全を確かめます。

町田：こうですか。

先生：はい。それから、クラッチを踏み、シフトレバーをRに入れます。

町田：はい、入れました。

先生：クラッチをはなしながら、アクセルをゆっくり踏みます。後ろを見ながら、ゆっくりバックします。   はなす *to release*

町田：こうですか。

先生：そうそう。ハンドルをしっかり握って...

MACHIDA: How do I back up?   TEACHER: First, you look back and make sure that it's safe in back.
MACHIDA: Like this?   TEACHER: Yes. Then press down the clutch and shift into reverse.   MACHIDA: All right, I've done it.   TEACHER: While releasing the clutch, press down slowly on the accelerator. While looking to the rear, you back up slowly.   MACHIDA: Like this?   TEACHER: Grip the steering wheel firmly.

Asking for and Giving Instructions

どのようにエンジンをかけますか。
How do I start the engine?

どうやってエンジンオイルを替えますか。
How do I change the engine oil?

ガソリンの入れ方を教えてください。
Please show me how to put gas in.

次にどうしますか。
What do I do next?

今度はどうしますか。
What shall I do the next time?

Asking What Something Is For

これは何[のため]に使いますか。
What are we going to use this for?

これは何のためにあるんですか。
What is this for?

Checking If You Are on the Right Track

これでいいですか。
Is it all right like this?

こうですか。
Do you mean like this?

Giving Instructions

まず、キーをイグニションに入れます。
First, insert the key into the ignition switch.

次に、キーを回します。
Next, turn the key.

こういうふうにします。
Do it like this.

Role Play

Work in pairs. Practice giving each other instructions on how to perform tasks you know how to do.

Cheering Up and Encouraging Others

町田：運転免許の試験、ダメだったの。

カワムラ：そう。残念だったね。

町田：もう、免許取れないんじゃないかしら。

カワムラ：今度は大丈夫だよ。

町田：そうかしら。

カワムラ：うん、がんばって。

カワムラ：おにぎりの作り方はこれでいいですか。

山口：ええ、だんだん上手になってきましたね。

カワムラ：この次はどうするんですか。

山口：こうやって海苔をまくのよ。

カワムラ：こうですか。

山口：ええ、その調子、その調子。

言語ノート

Encouraging Words

がんばって（ください）。	*Good luck.*
	Try your best.
	Hang in there.
今度は大丈夫ですよ。	*You'll do OK next time.*
元気を出して（ください）。	*Keep your spirits up.*
気を落とさないで（ください）。	*Don't be discouraged.*
しっかりやってください。	*Do a good job!*
しっかりして（ください）。	*Pull yourself together.*

Giving Assurance

はい、それでいいですね。	*Yes, it's fine like this.*
なかなか上手ですね。	*You're rather good.*

MACHIDA: I failed the driving test again.　KAWAMURA: Really? That's too bad.　MACHIDA: I bet I'll never be able to get a driver's license.　KAWAMURA: Next time will be all right.　MACHIDA: I wonder.　KAWAMURA: Yes, hang in there.

KAWAMURA: Is this way of making rice balls OK?　YAMAGUCHI: Yes, you have gradually improved.　KAWAMURA: What do I do next?　YAMAGUCHI: Wrap them in seaweed like this.　KAWAMURA: Like this?　YAMAGUCHI: Yes, that's the way to go.

もう一回やってみましょう。	Let's try again.
だんだん上手になってきましたね。	You've gotten better each time.
その調子、その調子。	That's the way to go.

Role Play

Work in pairs. The first student is in one of the following unpleasant situations and explains it to his or her partner. The second student then offers sympathy and encouragement.

1. 日本語の試験で0点を取りました。
2. 交通事故を起こしました。
3. お金をなくしました。
4. 漢字が上手に書けません。
5. 友達のコンピュータをこわしてしまいました。

Listening Comprehension

1. Ms. Gibson is trying to buy a used car. She has called three people who have cars for sale. Listen to their phone conversations, and list in English the features of Hoshi's, Kurokawa's, and Kaneko's cars and their asking prices.
2. Mr. Kawamura has witnessed a car accident. Listen as he describes the accident to a policeman. Then draw a diagram of the accident on the following map.

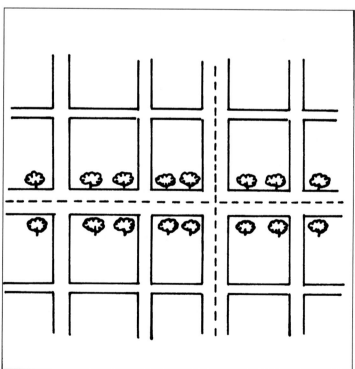

Vocabulary

Automobiles

うんてんしゅ	運転手	driver
うんてんめんきょ (しょう)	運転免許 (証)	driver's license
オートバイ		motorcycle
ガソリン		gasoline
きゅうきゅうしゃ	救急車	ambulance
こしょう (する)	故障 (する)	breakdown (to have a mechanical breakdown; to become out of order)
しゅうり (する)	修理 (する)	repair (to repair)
しゅうりこうメカニック	修理工	auto mechanic
しょうぼうしゃ	消防車	fire engine
タイヤ		tire
チェック (する)		(to) check
なおす	直す	to fix; to repair
ナンバープレート		license plate
バックミラー		rearview mirror
パトカー		patrol car
パンク (する)		(to get a) flat tire
ハンドル		steering wheel
ぶひん、パーツ	部品／パーツ	part (*of a mechanical object*)
ブレーキをかける		to apply the brakes
フロントガラス		windshield

Loanwords: アンテナ、エンジン、オイル、サービス・ステーション、スポーツカー、トラック、トランク、バッテリー、バンパー、ヘッドライト、メンテナンス、モノレール、モペット、ラジエーター、ワイパー、シートベルト

Review: 運転 (する)、ガソリン・スタンド、車、自転車、タクシー、地下鉄、電車、駐車場、停留所、ドライブ (する)、乗る、バス、走る、切符

Traffic

いはん (する)	違反 (する)	violation (to violate rules)
おうだんほどう	横断歩道	pedestrian crossing
こうさてん	交差点	intersection

こうじちゅう	工事中	under construction
こうそくどうろ	高速道路	freeway
こうつう	交通	traffic
こうつうきかん	交通機関	means of transportation
こうつうじこ	交通事故	traffic accident
こうつうじゅうたい	交通渋滞	traffic jam
(こうつう)しんごう	(交通)信号	traffic light
じこにあう	事故にあう	to get involved in an accident
しょうとつ(する)	衝突(する)	collision (to collide)
じそく	時速	speed per hour
つかまる	捕まる	to be caught
とおる	通る	to pass through; to go along
とまる	止まる	to come to a stop
ほこうしゃ	歩行者	pedestrian
ほどう	歩道	sidewalk
まよう	迷う	to get lost
まわりみち	回り道	detour

Review: 道、道路、信号
_{みち　どうろ　しんごう}

Verbs: The transitive and intransitive verbs are on pp. 146–147

Other Words

～かた	～方	how to...
さいごに	最後に	lastly
さいしょに	最初に	first
つぎに	次に	next
～ないで		without . . . ing
ばかりだ		to have just done...

Kanji

Learn these kanji:

自　駐　変　号　工
路　教　故　走　速
交　窓　差　帰　違
通　閉　点　横　反
転　消　信　働

チェックリスト

Use this checklist to confirm that you can now

- ☐ Talk about cars, driving, and public transportation systems
- ☐ Understand the difference between transitive and intransitive verbs and how they are used in Japanese
- ☐ Express an attempt
- ☐ Express a just completed action
- ☐ Scan a driving manual and a driving guide for travelers
- ☐ Write the directions to your home or campus
- ☐ Ask for and give instructions
- ☐ Talk about the public transportation system in Japan

Review Chapter 3

アクティビティー 1

Match the definitions in the first column with the appropriate word in the second column.

1. 車の中のタンクに入っています。
2. ゴムでできていて、空気が入っています。
3. 車を止めるのに必要です。
4. 車を運転する時に、持っていなければなりません。
5. カーブで曲がる時に、これを回します。
6. 車に乗った時に、これを締めます。

a. 運転免許
b. ハンドル
c. タイヤ
d. ブレーキ
e. ガソリン
f. シートベルト

アクティビティー 2

運転手 (*Drivers*)

You have just obtained a driver's license. You are applying for a job that requires a driver's license. Rank the following occupations in the order of your preference. Give your reasons for your top choice.

ニューヨークのタクシー運転手　　　リムジンの運転手
観光バスの運転手　　　　　　　　　大きなトラックのドライバー
ピザのホームデリバリーの運転手　　消防車の運転手
警察館 (*policeman/policewoman*)　　レースカーの運転手
救急車の運転手　　　　　　　　　　あなたの町のタクシー運転手

アクティビティー 3

どちらの車がいいですか。(*Which car do you prefer?*)

Compare the two cars in the table and answer the questions that follow.

町田さんの車		山本さんの車
トヨタ・カローラ	名前	ニッサン・マーチ
シルバー	色	赤
2.2リットル	エンジン	1.5リットル
5人乗り	定員	4人乗り
マニュアル5速	トランスミッション	オートマチック4速
200 km/h	最高速度	140 km/h
130万円	値段	90万円

1. どちらのエンジンのほうが大きいですか。
2. どちらのほうが高かったですか。
3. どちらのほうが人をたくさん乗せることができますか。
4. どちらのほうが速いですか。
5. あなたはどちらの車が好きですか。なぜですか。

アクティビティー　4

賛成ですか。反対ですか。(*Do you agree or disagree?*)

Do you agree or disagree with the following statements? Explain why.

1. アメリカで一番高い車はロールス・ロイスである。
2. アメリカ人は大きい車が好きだ。
3. 日本の車はアメリカの車よりもガソリンを使わない。
4. アメリカ人は公共交通機関をよく使う。
5. あなたの町の交通渋滞はひどい。
6. あなたの大学に駐車場が十分 (*sufficient*) ある。

4

第四章

体_{からだ}と健康_{けんこう}

The Body and Health

毎日、公園^{こうえん}でジョギングをしています。

Objectives

In this lesson, you are going to

- Talk about body and health
- Talk about feeling and emotions
- Learn to express analogy and exemplification
- Learn about the …は…が construction
- Learn to talk about appearance
- Learn to use causative verb forms
- Learn to express expectation
- Learn to scan medical advice
- Learn to buy medications at a drug store
- Learn how to talk about your condition at a clinic

Vocabulary and Grammar 4A

Vocabulary and Oral Activities

Body Parts

Vocabulary: Body Parts (1)

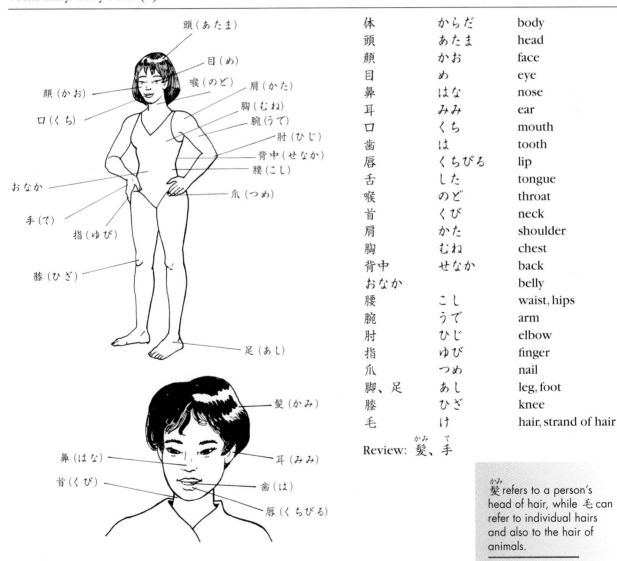

頭（あたま）
目（め）
喉（のど）
顔（かお）
口（くち）
おなか
手（て）
指（ゆび）
膝（ひざ）
肩（かた）
胸（むね）
腕（うで）
肘（ひじ）
背中（せなか）
腰（こし）
爪（つめ）
足（あし）

鼻（はな）
首（くび）
髪（かみ）
耳（みみ）
歯（は）
唇（くちびる）

体	からだ	body
頭	あたま	head
顔	かお	face
目	め	eye
鼻	はな	nose
耳	みみ	ear
口	くち	mouth
歯	は	tooth
唇	くちびる	lip
舌	した	tongue
喉	のど	throat
首	くび	neck
肩	かた	shoulder
胸	むね	chest
背中	せなか	back
おなか		belly
腰	こし	waist, hips
腕	うで	arm
肘	ひじ	elbow
指	ゆび	finger
爪	つめ	nail
脚、足	あし	leg, foot
膝	ひざ	knee
毛	け	hair, strand of hair

Review: 髪（かみ）、手（て）

髪（かみ） refers to a person's head of hair, while 毛 can refer to individual hairs and also to the hair of animals.

❋ アクティビティー 1

体のどこを使いますか。(*What part of the body would you use?*)

Tell what part of your body you would use to perform the following actions.

[例] 音楽を聞く →

音楽を聞く時は、耳を使います。

1. 歩く
2. キスをする
3. 本を読む
4. においをかぐ (*to perceive a smell*)
5. 考える (*to think*)
6. 人にさわる (*to touch*)
7. ものをかむ (*to bite*)
8. バットを握る (*to grab, to grip*)

> **R**eview 〜時. cf.
> Chapter 7,
> **Grammar 40**,
> in Book 1.

❋ アクティビティー 2

体の機能 (*The functions of the parts of the body*)

Describe when you use the following parts of the body.

[例] 口 → 口は何かを食べたり、話したりする時に使います。

1. 目	3. 鼻	5. 爪	7. 唇
2. 足	4. 手	6. 歯	

❋ アクティビティー 3

人間の体 (*Human body*)

Answer these questions.

1. 人間は目がいくつありますか。
2. 耳はいくつありますか。
3. 耳は顔のどこにありますか。
4. 鼻はいくつありますか。
5. 鼻は顔のどこにありますか。
6. 腕は何本ありますか。
7. 手に指は何本ありますか。
8. 足は何本ありますか。

> **R**eview counters
> (Appendix 4, Book 1) and
> verbs of existence
> (**Grammar 6**, Book1).

Vocabulary Library

Body Parts (2)

右利き	みぎきき	right-handed
左利き	ひだりきき	left-handed
片〜 (+ name of body part)	かた〜	one (of something that comes in pairs)
両〜 (+ name of body part)	りょう〜	both …
髭	ひげ	beard
口髭	くちひげ	moustache
頬／ほっぺた	ほお／ほっぺた	cheek
（お）へそ		navel
手首	てくび	wrist
足首	あしくび	ankle
かかと		heel
足の指	あしのゆび	toe
皮膚	ひふ	skin; skin surface
骨	ほね	bone
筋肉	きんにく	muscle
（お）尻	（お）しり	buttocks

The difference between the two words for *cheek* is that ほっぺた is more common in everyday conversation.

Grammar and Practice Activities

23. Analogy and Exemplification

> 山口：林さんのニックネームはなぜ「パンダ」なんですか。
> カワムラ：パンダのような顔をしているからです。
> 山口：そうですか。
> カワムラ：それに、パンダのように歩くからです。

YAMAGUCHI: Why is Mr. Hayashi's nickname "Panda"?　KAWAMURA: It's because he has a face like a panda.
YAMAGUCHI: I see.　KAWAMURA: In addition, he walks like a panda.

Vocabulary and Grammar 4A

193

百九十三

Contractions in Colloquial Speech

Just as many English speakers say *gonna* instead of *going to* or *shoulda* instead of *should have* when they are talking informally, Japanese speakers often use shortened or contracted forms in everyday, informal conversation. Here are some of the most common ones:

じゃ for では
学生じゃない for 学生ではない

Verb ちゃ for verb ては
食べちゃいけない for 食べてはいけない

Verb ちゃう／ちゃった for verb てしまう／てしまった
閉まっちゃう for 閉まってしまう
忘れちゃった for 忘れてしまった

Noun にゃ for noun には
日曜日にゃ for 日曜日には

～なきゃ for ～なければ
帰らなきゃならない for 帰らなければならない

You may be tempted to use these contractions in your own speech, but they will sound strange unless you are a fairly fluent speaker. However, Japanese people use these contractions all the time in their natural speech, so you need to learn to recognize them when you hear them. Later on, you will find yourself using these forms almost unconsciously. Even so, you should avoid using them in formal situations or when talking to a superior (cf. Chapter 5).

23.1 よう（な）is a na-type adjective used in the following constructions expressing likeness or exemplification.

1	N1 は N2 のようです（だ）	*N1 looks like N2.* *N1 is similar to N2.* *N1 is like N2.*
2	N1 のような N2	*N2 that looks like N1* *N2 that is like N2*
3	N1 は N2 のように V, A	*N1 does something (V) like N2.* *N1 is (adjective) like N2.*
4	V1 ように V2	*…do something (V2) like V1*
5	V ような N	*An N that seems to be V-ing / V-ed*

The Body and Health

本がたくさんあって、この家は図書館のようだ。
There are so many books that this house is like a library.
子供のようなことをしてはいけません。
You shouldn't behave like a child.
今日はまるで夏のように暑いですね。
Today is just as hot as summer.
私が発音するように発音してください。
Please pronounce (it) as I pronounce it.
町田さんが言うように、その本は面白かった。
As Ms. Machida says, that book was interesting.

まるで is an adverb meaning *just* or *completely* and is used to emphasize similarity.

The na-adjective みたい (it is always written in **hiragana**) can also be used in these contexts in colloquial speech with the same meaning. Thus, …みたい, like …よう, can express appearance and conjecture as well as likeness. The pattern is similar to that of よう, with みたい substituting for (の)よう.

(の)よう can be used in any style of speech.

本がたくさんあって、この家は図書館みたいだ。
This house looks like a library because there are many books.
私が発音するみたいに発音してください。
Please pronounce it as I pronounce it.

23.2 When you would like to describe the appearances of people and things by comparing them to something else, you can use the following constructions.

Adjective Nのような Nみたいな Vみたいな Vような	顔 スタイル 形 色 すがた かっこう …..	をしている (しています) ~~がする（します）~~

X has an (adjective) face, style, shape, color, appearance,…
X has a face, style, shape, color, appearance,… like…
X has a face, style, shape, color, appearance that looks as if it…

林さん、赤い顔をしていますね。
Mr. Hayashi, your face is red (lit., you have a red face).
その赤ちゃんの唇はいちごのような形をしていて、かわいいですね。
That baby's lips are shaped like a strawberry, and they are cute.
サンタクロースみたいなかっこうをして、どうしたんですか。
What's going on? You're dressed like Santa Claus.

外でへんな音がしていますよ。見てきてください。

I'm hearing a strange sound coming from outside. Can you go check?

ここに立つと、先生になったような気がする。

When I stand here, I feel as if I have become the teacher.

アクティビティー　4

城のような家... (*A house like a castle*)

Fill in the blanks with the appropriate word.

Suggested Words:　夏、マイケル・ジョーダン、日本人、梅雨、ピカソ、ガソリン、すきやき、りんご、コンピュータ、城 (*castle*)

1. カーティスさんはまるで（　　）のように、日本語を上手に話しますね。
2. 雨ばかり降って、（　　）のようなお天気だ。
3. チンさんは計算 (*calculation*) が速くて、（　　）のようですね。
4. あの人は、大きくてりっぱな、（　　）のような家に住んでいる。
5. あの絵は何ですか。（　　）の絵みたいですね。
6. 今日は（　　）のように暑い。
7. この（　　）のようなおかしなにおいは何ですか。
8. （　　）みたいな日本の食べ物が好きですか。
9. 彼女のほっぺたは（　　）のように赤い。
10. カワムラさんはバスケット・ボールが上手で、（　　）みたいですね。

アクティビティー　5

私がしてみせるようにしてみてください。(*Try to do it the way I'll show you.*)

Fill in the blanks with the appropriate forms of よう（だ）、ような、orように.

[例]　私もその（ような）コンピュータがほしい。

1. 先生が書く（　　）、書きなさい。
2. 今日の（　　）天気の日には、海岸へ行きたい。

The Body and Health

3. それはちょっとむずかしい（　　　）と山本さんは言いました。
4. あなたは氷(ice)の（　　　）冷たい(cold)人だ。
5. 子供の（　　　）ことを言ってはいけません。

アクティビティー　6

先生の車はトマトみたいに赤い。(*The teacher's car is red like a tomato.*)

Make up sentences using the following phrases.

[例]　雪のように
　　　→ 町田さんの手は雪のように白い。

1. 春のような
2. フランス人のように
3. 私の言うように
4. 老人 (*elderly person*) みたいに
5. コメディアンのようだ

アクティビティー　7

コーヒーのような味がする。(*It has a taste like coffee.*)

Fill in the blanks with 形, 色, かっこう, 顔, 味, におい, 音, 気, 感じ, or 気持ち.

1. あの温泉のお湯は白くて、ミルクのような（　　　）をしています。
2. 風邪をひいて、山口さんは青い（　　　）をしている。
3. 日本には富士山のような（　　　）をした山がたくさんある。
4. 冷蔵庫の中はひどい魚の（　　　）がする。
5. このハンバーガーはとてもいい（　　　）がする！
6. 今日は、何かいいことが起こるような（　　　）がします。
7. 初めて温泉に入って、どんな（　　　）がしましたか。
8. むこうから人が歩いてくる（　　　）がします。聞こえますか。

✳ アクティビティー　8

宇宙人がやって来た！（*The ET's are here!*）

1. This is a drawing of an extraterrestrial, an 宇宙人. Describe it in Japanese. Try to use the following constructions in your description.

頭はオレンジのような形をしています。

目はチューリップのような形をしています。

Useful Vocabulary

形	かたち	shape; form
丸い	まるい	round
四角い	しかくい	rectangular; square
三角の	さんかくの	triangular
菱形	ひしがた	lozenge; diamond-shaped
ハート形	ハートがた	heart-shaped

2. Work in pairs.
   a. Draw an imaginary extraterrestrial. Describe it to your partner in Japanese.
   b. Your partner will draw an illustration following your description.
   c. Compare the two illustrations.

24. Describing Attributes: The …は…が Construction

三村： チンさんはあそこの看板が見える？

チン： ええ、さくら銀行の看板？

三村： チンさんは目がいいね。

チン： あんな大きな看板が見えないの？

MIMURA: Can you see the billboard over there?　CHIN: Yes, it's a Sakura Bank billboard.　MIMURA: You have good eyesight.　CHIN: You can't see that big billboard?

～ても

The te-form of predicates plus the particle も is equivalent to *even if…* or *even though…*

野口さんに話しても、わかってくれませんよ。
Even if you talk to Mr. Noguchi, he won't understand (your situation).
あの人はハンサムでも、デートしたくありません。
Even if he is handsome, I don't want to date him.
三村さんが友だちでも、許せません。
Even though Mr. Mimura is my friend, I can't forgive him.

You will learn more about this construction in Chapter 7.

24.1 The following construction is used to describe an essential, permanent (or quasi-permanent) attribute of people and things. This attribute must be something that distinguishes that person or thing from others of its type.

N1	は	N2	が	Adjective

N1's N2 is/are (adjective).
As for N1, its/his/her N2 is (adjective).

村山さんは顔が細長い。
Ms. Murayama's face is long and narrow.
この机は脚が長くて、すわりがわるいです。
The legs of this desk are so long that it's unstable.
このステレオは音がとてもいいですね。
This stereo has a very good sound.

In these examples, N2 is a part of N1. This construction is also used when you have pain in some part of your body.

私は頭が痛い。
I have a headache.

24.2 Verbs expressing abilities that are used in this construction are わかる (*to understand; to be comprehensible*), 見える (*to be visible*), and 聞こえる (*to be audible*). Another group of verbs that take this construction are those expressing need and necessity, 要る and 必要だ.

> **W**hen you ask what part of someone's body hurts, you use どこが痛いんですか. Note that you use どこ, not 何.

Vocabulary and Grammar 4A

Similarly, おなかがすく (*to get hungry*), 吐き気がする (*to feel nauseated*), 目まいがする (*to feel dizzy*), and other health-related constructions follow this pattern.

24.3 This …は…が construction is also used with adjectives expressing emotions such as 怖い (*fearful; frightening*), うらやましい (*envious*), 恥ずかしい (*embarrassed; ashamed*), and so on.

> 私は三村さんがうらやましいですね。
> *I am envious of Mr. Mimura.*

When talking about a third person's emotions, you should use forms such as 怖がる, うらやましがる, 恥ずかしがる, and so on. The idea is that you can't know another person's thoughts or emotions directly, so making direct statements about someone else's feelings is inappropriate. These 〜がる forms have the meaning of *acts frightened, acts envious, acts frustrated, acts embarrassed,* and so on.

> ブラウンさんは、暗い所をとても怖がる。
> *Ms. Brown is very much afraid of dark places.*

Incidentally, many of these emotional adjectives can describe either the person who is feeling the emotion or the object of the emotion:

> 恥ずかしいことをしてしまいました。
> *I ended up doing something embarrassing.*
> こんなことをしてしまって、恥ずかしいです。
> *I'm embarrassed to have ended up doing something like this.*

24.4 Finally, the …は…が construction is also used in sentences that single out an individual member of a set of similar items.

> すしは、まぐろが一番だ。
> *As for sushi, tuna is best.*
> 山は、富士山が一番有名だ。
> *As far as mountains are concerned, Mount Fuji is the most famous.*

❇ ## アクティビティー　9

ダイアログ：町田さんは指が長いですね。(*Ms. Machida, you have long fingers, don't you!*)

カワムラ： 町田さんは<ruby>指<rt>ゆび</rt></ruby>が<ruby>長<rt>なが</rt></ruby>いね。

町田： そうですか。<ruby>気<rt>き</rt></ruby>がつかなかったわ。

カワムラ： <ruby>御家族<rt>ごかぞく</rt></ruby>の<ruby>皆<rt>みな</rt></ruby>さんは？

町田： うん、そう言えば、<ruby>家族<rt>かぞく</rt></ruby>のみんなも<ruby>指<rt>ゆび</rt></ruby>が長いわね。

カワムラ： <ruby>遺伝<rt>いでん</rt></ruby>だね。

Practice the dialogue by changing the underlined parts to the following.

1. <ruby>足<rt>あし</rt></ruby>が大きい
2. <ruby>耳<rt>みみ</rt></ruby>たぶ (*earlobe*) が大きい
3. <ruby>鼻<rt>はな</rt></ruby>すじが<ruby>通<rt>とお</rt></ruby>っている (*to have a high-bridged nose*)
4. <ruby>歯並<rt>はなら</rt></ruby>びがいい (*to have evenly spaced teeth*)
5. <ruby>手首<rt>てくび</rt></ruby>が<ruby>細<rt>ほそ</rt></ruby>い (*thin in circumference*)

アクティビティー　10

きりんとイルカ (*Giraffes and dolphins*)

Following the example, make up ...は...が sentences. You may have to change the order of the words.

[例] <ruby>鼻<rt>はな</rt></ruby>、<ruby>象<rt>ぞう</rt></ruby> (*elephant*)、<ruby>長<rt>なが</rt></ruby>い → 象は鼻が長い。
<ruby>着物<rt>きもの</rt></ruby>、たいへん、<ruby>着<rt>き</rt></ruby>る → 着物は着るのがたいへんだ。

1. きりん (*giraffe*)、<ruby>首<rt>くび</rt></ruby>、<ruby>長<rt>なが</rt></ruby>い
2. <ruby>歌<rt>うた</rt></ruby>、バーバラ・ストライサンド、<ruby>上手<rt>じょうず</rt></ruby>
3. <ruby>足<rt>あし</rt></ruby>、<ruby>速<rt>はや</rt></ruby>い、チータ
4. <ruby>亀<rt>かめ</rt></ruby> (*tortoise*)、<ruby>歩<rt>ある</rt></ruby>く、のろい (*slow*)
5. イルカ (*dolphin*)、いい、<ruby>頭<rt>あたま</rt></ruby>
6. <ruby>有名<rt>ゆうめい</rt></ruby>、シカゴ、ピザ
7. <ruby>村山<rt>むらやま</rt></ruby>さん、やさしい、<ruby>心<rt>こころ</rt></ruby> (*heart*)
8. 高い、<ruby>声<rt>こえ</rt></ruby>、チンさん

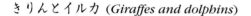

KAWAMURA: Ms. Machida, you have long fingers, don't you?　MACHIDA: Really? I hadn't noticed.
KAWAMURA: How about the members of your family?　MACHIDA: Well, now that you mention it, they have long fingers, too.　KAWAMURA: It's hereditary then, isn't it?

アクティビティー　11

何が怖いですか。(*What is frightening?*)

Answer these questions in Japanese.

1. あなたはこの世 (*in this world*) で何が一番怖いですか。
2. あなたの町は何が有名ですか。
3. 日本語の教科書はどれが一番いいですか。(*It's obvious!*)
4. あなたはコンパクトな車の中で、どれが一番好きですか。
5. あなたは１キロ先 (*one kilometer ahead*) が見えますか。
6. 日本語は何がむずかしいですか。何がやさしいですか。

✳ アクティビティー　12

誰でしょうか。(*Who might it be?*)

Work in pairs. One member of the pair chooses a third classmate but does not reveal that person's identity. The second member of the pair tries to guess the third student's identity by asking questions, using a "Twenty Questions" format. Concentrate on questions about the person's physical appearance.

Sample questions:
その学生は髪が長いですか。
その学生は髪が何色ですか。

Vocabulary and Grammar 4B

Vocabulary and Oral Activities

Feeling and Emotions

Vocabulary: A Variety of Emotions

気持ち	きもち	feeling; mood; atmosphere
感じる	かんじる	to feel (an emotion)
心	こころ	mind; feeling; "heart"

嬉しい	うれしい	happy; delighted
喜ぶ	よろこぶ	to be delighted
楽しい	たのしい	enjoyable, fun
笑う	わらう	to laugh; to smile
悲しい	かなしい	sad
悲しむ	かなしむ	to be sad
寂しい	さびしい	lonely
苦しい	くるしい	oppressively painful
怖い	こわい	frightening; afraid
怖がる	こわがる	to be frightened
恥ずかしい	はずかしい	shameful; embarrassed
泣く	なく	to cry; to weep
怒る	おこる	to get angry
怒っている	おこっている	to be angry
驚く	おどろく	to be surprised
心配（する）	しんぱい（する）	worry (to be worried)
安心（する）	あんしん（する）	peace of mind (to be relieved)
がっかりする		to be disappointed
びっくりする		to be surprised
困る	こまる	to have difficulty; to be troubled
イライラする		to be irritated

Adjectives describing emotional states, such as 嬉しい and 悲しい, can be used only when talking about your own emotions or when asking another person about his or her own emotions. See **Grammar 25 and 26** for details.

※ アクティビティー 13

どんな気持ちですか。(*How do you feel?*)

1. How do you feel on these occasions?
   a. ペットが死んだ時
   b. 日本語のクラスで Aを取った時
   c. 誰もあなたに話しかけて (*speak to*) くれない時
   d. お金をなくした時
   e. 人前でころんだ (*trip and fall*) 時
   f. 隣の人がうるさい時

2. Give examples of two occasions on which you might feel these emotions.
   a. どんな時うれしいですか。
   b. どんな時悲しいですか。
   c. どんな時寂しいですか。
   d. どんな時楽しいですか。
   e. どんな時苦しいですか。
   f. どんな時怒りますか。
   g. どんな時恥ずかしいですか。

Grammar and Practice Activities

25. Talking about Appearance: …よう, 〜そう, …らしい, and …みたい

高田：ブラウンさん、今日は元気そうだね。

ブラウン：うん、昨日飲んだ薬はよく効くみたい。もう、頭痛もないし、咳も出ないし…

高田：でも、まだ、休んでいた方がいいよ。

ブラウン：ええ、今年の風邪はしつこいようね。

ギブソン：ブラウンさん、風邪をひいていたらしいわよ。

町田：えっ、本当？

ギブソン：ええ、高田さんから聞いたの。もうだいぶよくなったみたいだけど。

町田：みんな風邪をひいているみたいね。横井先生も、今日は休講するらしいわ。

25.1 In addition to similarity and likeness (see **Grammar 23**), the na-type adjectives …よう and みたい are used to express appearance and likelihood.

Noun	の／だった	
Na-adjective	Root + な／だった	ようだ／ようです
I-adjective	Plain form	みたい／みたいです
Verb	Plain form	

It seems that; it looks like; it appears that

TAKADA: Ms. Brown, you look healthy today.   BROWN: Yes, the medicine I took yesterday seems to work well. I no longer have a headache, and I'm not coughing anymore.   TAKADA: But you should still be taking it easy.   BROWN: Yes, the flu this year seems to hang on for a long time.

GIBSON: It seems that Ms. Brown has come down with the flu.   MACHIDA: Oh, really?   GIBSON: Yes, I heard it from Mr. Takada. Apparently she has gotten a lot better.   MACHIDA: It looks as if everyone has the flu. I hear that Professor Yokoi is going to cancel her classes today, too.

This construction is usually used to express statements based on the speaker's firsthand, reliable information (mostly visual information) or his or her reasonable knowledge.

昨日の試験はやさしかったようです。みんな30分で終わりましたから。

Yesterday's exam seems to have been easy. Everyone completed it in thirty minutes.

This construction is also used to state something indirectly or without committing oneself.

私の言ったことが正しかったようですね。

It appears that what I said was right.

25.2 〜そう, which conjugates like a na-adjective, expresses how someone or something appears to the speaker. In this case, the statement is limited to directly observable things or actions. However, it is not used with adjectives that are always visual, like colors or shapes. It also expresses the speaker's guess or conjecture and, when attached to verbs, it carries the connotation of *looks as if it is about to...* Note that nouns and pronouns cannot be used in front of 〜そう.

Na-adjective	Root	
I-adjective	Root	〜そうだ／そうです
Verb	Conjunctive form	

It seems; it looks; it looks like; it appears; it feels like

> The conjunctive form is equivalent to the stem of the ます form.

このあたりは便利そうですね。

This neighborhood looks convenient.

時計をもらって、林さんはうれしそうだった。

Receiving a watch, Mr. Hayashi looked happy.

チンさんは今にも倒れそうだった。

Ms. Chin looked as if she were about to collapse at any moment.

> Note that the adjective いい + そう results in よさそう, looks good. The 〜そう form of ない is なさそう, it looks as if there/it isn't...

The negative counterpart of this construction is formed in the following way.

Noun / Na-adjective	1. Root ＋ 〜そうではない 2. Root ＋ では ＋ なさそうだ
I-adjective	1. Root ＋ 〜そうではない 2. Root of the negative form ＋ なさそうだ
Verb	Root ＋ 〜そうにない／そうもない

> なさそうだ is the combination of the negative ない + そうだ. The negative of いい + そうだ results in よくなさそうだ.

三村さんはまったく恥ずかしそうではない。
Mr. Mimura doesn't look embarrassed at all.

三村さんはまったく恥ずかしくなさそうだ。
Mr. Mimura looks completely unembarrassed.

あのお客さんは帰りそうにない。

あのお客さんは帰りそうもない。
That guest doesn't look as if he's about to leave.

The adverbial form of this construction, 〜そうに, means *in a manner that looks as if...* For example:

患者は苦しそうに歩いている。
The patient is walking as if in great pain.

25.3 …らしい, which conjugates like an i-adjective, is used in the following construction to express what appears true to the speaker based on information that he or she obtained indirectly, for instance, by reading or hearing it.

Noun	Noun/noun + だった	
Na-adjective	Root/root + だった	+ らしい (です)
I-adjective	Plain form	
Verb	Plain form	

I hear that; the word is that; I understand that; it says that

三村さんは先週病気だったらしいです。
I understand that Mr. Mimura was sick last week.

台風が来るらしいですよ。
It says that a typhoon is coming.

> Note that 病気 is a noun, not an adjective.

A negative conjecture is expressed by 〜ない／なかった + らしい.

その話は本当じゃないらしい。
My understanding is that that story is not true.

…らしい, preceded by a noun, can express the idea that the subject possesses those qualities considered essential and natural for his or her role or status. For example, if you say 町田さんは女らしいです, the sentence can mean either, *My understanding is that Ms. Machida is a woman,* or, *Ms. Machida is womanly;* that is, she has those qualities that Japanese culture considers essential for women. Both 女らしい and 男らしい are common expressions in Japanese, because the culture has traditionally had very definite ideas about how men and women should act.

> These ambiguous meanings are formally distinguished in the corresponding negative sentences. 町田さんは女らしくない人だ。*Ms. Machida is not womanly.* 町田さんは女ではないらしい。*It seems that Ms. Machida is not a woman.*

山口さんはすごく日本人らしい日本人です。

Mr. Yamaguchi is an extremely Japanese Japanese person. (In other words, he fits the common image of a Japanese person.)

それはあなたらしくない。

That's not like you. (In other words, the person being addressed is acting out of character.)

25.4 The following sentences illustrate the differences between でしょう, らしい, 〜そう, and よう.

三村さんは忙しいでしょう。

Mr. Mimura is probably busy.

三村さんは忙しいらしいです。

I heard that Mr. Mimura is busy.

三村さんは忙しそうです。

Mr. Mimura looks busy.

三村さんは忙しいようです。(or 忙しいみたいです。)

It seems that Mr. Mimura is busy (because I heard that he has many things to do).

アクティビティー　14

どう思いますか。(*What do you think?*)

Do you agree with the following statements? Base your decision on the scene depicted in the drawing.

[例]　この家は日本人の家のようではないですね。→
　　　はい、私もそう思います。
　　　玄関がありませんから。

[例]　この家は日本人の家のようですね。→
　　　いいえ、違うと思います。
　　　玄関がありませんから。

1. この家には食べ物はないようですね。

2. 子供は本を読むのが好きなようですね。

3. お父さんは仕事を探しているようですね。

4. お母さんは病気のようですね。

5. 外は風が強いようですね。

アクティビティー　15

やさしそうな練習 (*An easy-looking exercise*)

Rewrite these sentences by changing the underlined part to ～そう(だ).

[例]　おもしろい映画ですね。→ おもしろそうな映画ですね。

　　雪が降ります。→ 雪が降りそうです。

1.　あのコートは高いですね。
2.　山本さんはいい人ですね。
3.　林さんは泣きます。
4.　あなたのおじいさんは健康ですね。
5.　この宿題は時間がかかります。
6.　カフェテリアには学生がたくさんいます。

アクティビティー　16

雨が降りそう／降るそうです。(*It looks as if it's going to rain／it's supposed to rain.*)

Fill in the blanks with the correct form of the given words. Be sure to distinguish between the ～そうだ indicating appearance and the …そうだ indicating hearsay.

1.　(元気)
　　a.　山口さんのおばあさんはもう93歳ですが、写真ではとても（　　　）そうです。
　　b.　さとみさんが言っていましたが、山口さんのおばあさんはとても（　　　）そうです。

2.　(いい)
　　a.　カワムラさんに会いましたが、顔色がとてもよくて、調子が（　　　）そうでした。
　　b.　カワムラさんに会ったギブソンさんによると、顔色はとても（　　　）そうです。

3.　(行きたい)
　　a.　チンさんははっきりとは言いませんでしたが、私たちと一緒に（　　　）そうでした。
　　b.　チンさんは私たちと一緒に（　　　）そうです。何度もそう言っていました。

4. （出かける）

    a. 窓からブラウンさんが見えますが、間もなく（　　　）そうです。

    b. さっき、ブラウンさんが電話してきましたが、間もなく
      （　　　）そうです。

5. （ない）

    a. 先生は何も言わなかったので、試験は（　　　）そうです。

    b. 三村さんによると、来週は試験が（　　　）そうです。

アクティビティー　17

この練習は楽しそうです。(*This exercise looks fun.*)

Match each statement in the first column with the most logical response in the second column.

1. おいしそうなケーキですね。	a. 急ぎましょう。
2. 暇そうですね。	b. ちょっと手伝ってもらえますか。
3. 眠たそうですね。	c. スーツケース、私が持ちましょうか。
4. 重そうですね。	
5. パーティーに遅れそうですよ。	d. さあ、聞きに行きましょう。
6. 話が始まりそうですよ。	e. 食べてもいいですか。
	f. 夕べ、何時に寝たんですか。

アクティビティー　18

マリアさんは中国語もできるらしいです。(*I gather that Maria can speak Chinese, too.*)

Respond to these statements by using the words given in the parentheses and …らしいです。Don't forget to state your source of information or the basis for your conjecture.

[例]　フランス語の試験はいつですか。（来週）→

    来週あるらしいです。カーティスさんがそう言っていました。
    ブラウンさんはどこかへ行くんですか。（泳ぐ）→
    ええ、泳ぎに行くらしいです。水着を持っていましたから。

1. ギブソンさんはお休みですか。（病気）

2. カワムラさん、苦しそうですね。どうしたんでしょう。（風邪をひく）

3. 佐野さんはどんな仕事をしていたんですか。（英語の先生）

Vocabulary and Grammar 4B

二百九

209

4. このおさしみ、変な味がしますね。（ちょっと古い）

5. カワムラさんはもう起きたんですか。（ジョギング）

6. 山本さんはいくつぐらいですか。（22, 3歳）

* ### アクティビティー 19

どんな顔をしていますか。(*What kind of face is it?*)

What emotions do you think each of the following faces expresses? Match each
description with the appropriate drawing.

1. 何かを怖がっているような顔
2. 驚いているような顔
3. リラックスしているような顔

4. 悲しそうな顔
5. 怒っているような顔
6. うれしそうな顔

A.

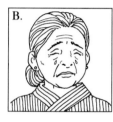
B.

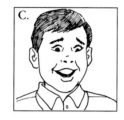
C.

D.

E.

F.

Vocabulary and Grammar 4C

Vocabulary and Oral Activities

Health and Illness

Vocabulary: Sickness and Injuries (1)

病気になる	びょうきになる	to get sick
治る	なおる	to recover
怪我（をする）	けが（をする）	injury (to get injured)
風邪（をひく）	かぜ（をひく）	(to catch) a cold or the flu
痛い	いたい	painful
頭痛（がする）	ずつう（がする）	(to have a) headache
頭が痛い	あたまがいたい	one's head hurts

腹痛	ふくつう	stomachache
体温	たいおん	body temperature
熱(がある)	ねつ(がある)	(to have a) fever
下痢(をする)	げり(をする)	(to have) diarrhea
吐き気(がする)	はきけ(がする)	nausea (to be nauseated)
咳(をする)	せき(をする)	(to) cough
医者／医師	いしゃ／いし	medical doctor
看護婦	かんごふ	nurse
入院する	にゅういんする	to be hospitalized
退院する	たいいんする	to get out of the hospital
手術(をする)	しゅじゅつ(をする)	(to perform) surgery
注射(をする)	ちゅうしゃ(をする)	(to give an) injection
レントゲンを撮る	レントゲンをとる	(to take) X rays
受ける	うける	to undergo (*surgery, X rays, an injection*)
薬(を飲む)	くすり(をのむ)	(to take) medicine
アスピリン		aspirin
薬屋／薬局	くすりや／やっきょく	pharmacy

Review: 救急車、健康、病院、病気、休む

✳ アクティビティー 20

毎日ジョギングをしているようです。(*She seems to be jogging every day.*)

One of your friends, Ms. Nakayama, seems to be exceptionally healthy. Answer the following questions about her habits and lifestyle by using ようです.

[例] 中山さんは何か運動をしていますか。
—はい、毎日ジョギングをしているようです。

1. タバコを吸いますか。
2. 野菜や果物が好きですか。
3. お酒を飲みますか。
4. 夜遅くまで仕事をしますか。
5. 中山さんは食欲がありますか。
6. 朝ごはんに何を食べますか。

✳ アクティビティー 21

体にいいですか。悪いですか。(*Is it good or bad for your body?*)

Tell whether or not the following are good for your body and health.

1. 毎日運動をすること
2. 野菜をたくさん食べること
3. タバコを一日20本吸うこと
4. 週末でも休まないで、一日12時間働くこと
5. 毎日お酒をたくさん飲むこと
6. 朝ごはんを食べないこと
7. 暗いところで本を読むこと
8. 一週間シャワーを浴びないこと

Vocabulary and Grammar 4C

211

CULTURE NOTE • Attitudes Toward Alcohol, Tobacco, and Drugs

Visitors to Japan cannot help noticing that drinking plays a prominent role in society. First they notice that beer and other alcoholic drinks are sold even in sidewalk vending machines. If they ride the trains or walk through entertainment districts late at night, they see people in various stages of inebriation.

Drinking is a major part of men's socializing, partly because drinking provides a way for the harried, overworked サラリーマン to unwind and to overcome inhibitions as he interacts with others. Also, Japanese society is extremely tolerant of anything that a drunk person does. The one exception to the overall tolerance for drinking is drunken driving, 酔っ払い (よっぱらい) 運転, which is severely punished.

If you go to Japan as a student or on business, you will most likely be asked to go out drinking with friends or colleagues. If you prefer not to drink, you can go along to be sociable and order a soft drink.

You never pour your own drink. Instead, people pour for one another and try to make sure that no one's glass or **sake** cup is ever empty. If you have had enough, a polite but unmistakable way to refuse further drinks is to leave a full glass untouched.

Like drinking, smoking receives little disapproval in Japan. Until recently, the Japanese government made almost no efforts to discourage smoking or to accommodate nonsmokers. There are few nonsmoking areas anywhere, and restaurants with nonsmoking sections are rare.

While Japanese society tolerates and even encourages smoking and drinking, illegal drugs are absolutely forbidden. If you are caught using or even possessing marijuana in Japan, you will be arrested and tried by a criminal justice system in which the accused has few rights. The worst-case scenario is five years in a Japanese prison, as a number of foreign drug users have learned from bitter experience.

✳ **アクティビティー　22**

お酒をたくさん飲んでいたらしいです。(*It seems that he drank a lot.*)

One of your friends has been hospitalized with multiple health problems. Evidently, he did a lot of things that are bad for one's health. Explain your understanding of what he did or failed to do using …らしいです。

[例]　運動をしなかったらしいです。

✳ **アクティビティー　23**

どうしますか。(*What are you going to do?*)

Match the health problems in the first column with the possible solutions in the second column.

1. 頭が痛いです。
2. 下痢をしています。
3. アスピリンがほしいです。

a. 薬屋へ行きます。
b. 風邪薬を飲みます。
c. 救急車を呼びます。

4. 大怪我をしました。
   (おおけが)

5. 風邪をひきました。
   (かぜ)

d. アスピリンを飲みます。

e. トイレへ行きます。

＊ アクティビティー 24

ダイアログ：病院で (At a hospital)
(びょういん)

医者：どうしましたか。
(いしゃ)

林：おなかが痛いんです。
(はやし) (いた)

医者：いつからですか。

林：昨日からです。
(きのう)

医者：熱はありますか。
(ねつ)

林：いいえ、ありません。

Practice the dialogue by substituting the following phrases for the underlined portions.

1. 頭が痛い、おととい、少しあります
   (あたま)(いた)
2. 咳が出る、先週、37度くらいあります
   (せき)(で)(せんしゅう)
3. 下痢をしているんです、月曜日、ちょっとあります
   (げり)
4. 吐き気がする、先週、昨日は38度ありました
   (は)(け)(しゅうまつ)(ど)

Vocabulary Library

Sickness and Injuries (2)

患者	かんじゃ	patient
診察 (する)	しんさつ (する)	medical examination (to perform a medical examination)
体温計	たいおんけい	clinical thermometer
カルテ		patient's chart
血液型	けつえきがた	blood type
ビールス／ウイルス		virus
もどす／はく		to vomit
整形手術	せいけいしゅじゅつ	cosmetic surgery
錠剤	じょうざい	pill
シロップ		syrup; liquid medicine
食前	しょくぜん	before meals
食後	しょくご	after meals
(お)見舞い (に行く)	(お)みまい (にいく)	(to pay) a visit to a sick person

DOCTOR: What's wrong?　HAYASHI: I have a stomachache.　DOCTOR: Since when?　HAYASHI: Since yesterday.　DOCTOR: Do you have a fever?　HAYASHI: No, I don't.

頭が痛そうですね。(*He looks as if he has a headache.*)

Match each statement in the first column with the most appropriate response in the second column.

1. 田中さんは頭が痛そうですね。　　a. いいえ、やさしいですよ。

2. 苦しそうですね。　　　　　　　　b. ええ、50万円もらったそうです。

3. 外は寒そうですね。　　　　　　　c. ええ、雪が降っています。

4. 本田さんはうれしそうですね。　　d. 風邪をひいたそうです。

5. 金井さんは悲しそうですね。　　　e. ガールフレンドにふられた (*was dumped*) そうです。

6. 日本語のテストはむずかしそうですね。　f. ええ、咳が止まらないんです。

Grammar and Practice Activities

26. Causatives

町田：チンさんにお酒を飲ませたんですか。

林：ええ。

町田：ダメですよ。チンさんは顔が真っ赤ですよ。

林：え？チンさんはお酒が飲めないんですか。

カワムラ：郵便局に小包が届いたそうです。

山口：そうですか。大助に取りに行かせましょう。

カワムラ：僕に行かせてください。

山口：そうですか。じゃ、お願いします。

MACHIDA: Did you give Ms. Chin liquor? (Lit., *Did you have Ms. Chin drink liquor?*)　HAYASHI: Yes.
MACHIDA: That's no good. Her face is really red.　HAYASHI: Do you mean that she can't drink?

KAWAMURA: They said that a package has arrived at the post office.　YAMAGUCHI: I see. I'll have Daisuke pick it up.　KAWAMURA: Please let me go.　YAMAGUCHI: Really? Then can you go?

Many East Asians have a metabolic condition that, among other things, causes their faces to turn bright red when they drink alcohol.

26.1 The following sentences are called *causative sentences* because they refer to making or allowing another person to do something.

> *I made him go to school.*
> *His father let him do whatever he wanted to do.*

In Japanese, sentences like these are built around the following causative verb forms.

	RULES	EXAMPLES
Class 1 verbs	Root + a-column **hiragana** corresponding to the dictionary ending + せる	書く → 書かせる
Class 2 verbs	Root + させる	食べる → 食べさせる
Class 3 verbs	Irregular	来る → 来させる

When the dictionary form ends in う, わ is inserted between the root and せる (e.g., 買う, 買わせる).

Note that all causative forms conjugate like Class 2 verbs.

26.2 The causative construction takes different particles depending on whether the verb is an intransitive verb or a transitive verb.

N1 が (は)	N2 に／を	Causative form of intransitive verbs

N1 makes N2 do / N1 lets N2 do

N1 が (は)	N2 に	N3 を	Causative form of transitive verbs

N1 makes N2 do N3 / N1 lets N2 do N3

For the distinction between intransitive and transitive verbs, refer to Chapter 3.

1a. 山口さんはさとみさんを外へ行かせた。
   Ms. Yamaguchi made Satomi go out.

1b. 山口さんはさとみさんに外へ行かせた。
   Ms. Yamaguchi let/allowed Satomi to go out.

In the first sentence (1a), where the particle を is used, Ms. Yamaguchi forced Satomi to go out against her will. This is usually called the *coercive causative*. The second sentence (1b), where に is used, means that Satomi wanted to go out, and Ms. Yamaguchi permitted her to do so. Thus, when the verb is intransitive, the meaning of the sentence differs, depending on whether you use を or に. On the other hand, only one type of causative sentence can be made from a sentence with a verb that is transitive.

2a. 山口さんはさとみさんにシチューを作らせた。
Ms. Yamaguchi made Satomi make stew.
Ms. Yamaguchi let Satomi make stew.

This sentence is ambiguous. You must figure out from the context whether or not Satomi wanted to cook.

In causative sentences, N1 must usually be higher in status or age than N2.

先生は二日おきに学生に宿題を出させた。
The teacher made the students turn in homework every other day.

Expressing the Frequency of Actions and Events

A time word plus おきに is used to express the frequency of actions and events, meaning *every...*

この薬は三時間おきに二錠飲んでください。
Please take this medicine, two pills every three hours.
カワムラさんは一週間おきに病院へ行く。
Mr. Kawamura goes to the clinic every other week.

In certain limited, impersonal contexts, N2 can be higher than N1.

親にそんなことをさせる子供がいますか！
Is there a child who makes the parents do such a thing?

When talking about having an equal or superior do something, the te-form of the verb plus もらう or いただく is more appropriate.

横井先生に読んでいただきましょう。
Let's have Professor Yokoi read it.

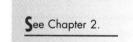

See Chapter 2.

Study the following examples to get a better idea of the use of the causative.

こんなくだらないことで、私を来させたのですか。
Did you make me come for this trivial thing?
母は娘に着物を着させた。
The mother made her daughter wear a kimono.
The mother let her daughter wear a kimono.
大助さんはだれも自分の部屋に入らせない。
Daisuke doesn't allow anyone to enter his room.

The Body and Health

自分 (self, own)

自分 is a reflexive pronoun—that is, it refers back to another noun—corresponding to the English *myself, yourself, themselves,* and so on. It usually refers to the subject, almost always a human, and allows you to avoid repeating the same noun in the sentence.

林さんは毎晩、自分で夕ごはんを作ります。
Mr. Hayashi cooks dinner by himself every night.

チンさんは自分のしたことを恥ずかしく思っている。
Ms. Chin is embarrassed about what she did.

26.3 The te-form of causative verb forms + ください is used to ask a superior for his or her permission to do something or to offer to do something for such a person.

先生、私に黒板を消させてください。
Professor, please let me clean the blackboard.

When you would like to ask someone not to make you do something, use the negative te-form of causative verbs + ください.

太りますから、あまりたくさん食べさせないでください。
I'll get fat, so please don't make me eat so much.

Asking for and granting permission also can be expressed by using verbs of giving and receiving. For example,

山口さんは僕に掃除機を使わせてくれました。
Ms. Yamaguchi let me use the vacuum cleaner.

アクティビティー 26

山口さんはどこへ行かせましたか。(*Where did Ms. Yamaguchi make you go?*)

Change these sentences to corresponding causative sentences, framing them as if Mr. or Ms. Yamaguchi is making or letting various people do things.

[例] 私は公園まで歩きました。→
山口さんは私を公園まで歩かせました。
山口さんは私に公園まで歩かせました。
私は歌を歌った。→
山口さんは私に歌を歌わせた。

1. 私はシーツを洗った。
2. 町田さんはアパートに帰った。
3. カワムラさんは日本語を勉強した。
4. 林さんは医者に行きました。
5. 犬は公園を走りました。
6. 山本さんはそこに8時に来た。
7. 村山さんは着物を着た。
8. 私は1時まで待ちました。

アクティビティー 27

私に何か言わせてください。 *(Please let me say something.)*

Match the sentences in the first column with those in the second column to make
logical statements.

Useful Vocabulary: 絶対 (に) *absolutely,* しあわせ *happy,* やめる *to quit,*
おごる *to treat someone (to dinner, etc.)*

1. うちの電話がこわれたんです。
2. 家内が病気なんです。
3. 娘さんを絶対しあわせに
   します。
4. 簡単にできると思います。
5. もうこんな仕事はきらいです。
6. 山本さんに話があるんです。
7. 父からお金をたくさんもらった
   んです。
8. あなた一人で話さないで
   ください。

a. ここは私におごらせて
   ください。
b. 私にやらせてください。
c. おたくのを使わせてください。
d. 早く帰らせていただきたいん
   ですが。
e. 私にも何か言わせてください。
f. やめさせてください。
g. 結婚させてください。
h. 会わせてください。

アクティビティー 28

私にさせてください。 *(Please let me do it.)*

What would you say if someone said the following? Answer using a causative plus
ください。We'll assume that because of your personality, you are generous and
tend to say "yes" to anything.

[例] 　誰かこのトラックを運転できる人はいませんか。→
　　　はい、私に運転させてください。

1. 田中さんが駅で待っているんだけど、誰か迎えに行ってくれませんか。
2. 今日の昼ごはんは私が払いましょう。あっ、財布 (wallet) を忘れた (forgot)。
3. このかばん、ちょっと重いですね。私には持てませんよ。
4. 私が長谷川さんと話すの？あの人と話すのは苦手だな。
5. この車、ちょっと汚いね。
6. このドア、重くて、開きませんね。
7. ああ、おなかがすいた。何か食べる物はありませんか。
8. これを1時までに300部コピーしなくてはならないんです。
　　だれか手伝ってくれませんか。

✹ アクティビティー　29

毎日運動させます。(*I would make him/her exercise every day.*)

If you were a parent of a ten-year-old child, what would you make him or her do to stay healthy? Choose the five items from the following list that you think are most important for parents to insist on.

　　一日三度食事をさせる。
　　野菜と果物をたくさん食べさせる。
　　毎日牛乳を飲ませる。
　　毎日運動をさせる。
　　甘いものは食べさせない。
　　早寝・早起きの習慣 (*habit, custom*) をつけさせる。
　　テレビはあまり見させない。
　　インスタント食品やファーストフードは食べさせない。
　　あまり勉強させない。
　　毎日シャワーを浴びさせる。

✳ アクティビティー　30

右手を上げなさい。(*Raise your right arm [hand].*)

Work in groups of three. Student 1 gives Student 2 a simple command, which Student 2 follows. Then Student 3 describes what Student 1 ordered Student 2 to do.

[例]　学生A：左足を上げなさい。

　　　学生B：(左足を上げる)

　　　学生C：AさんはBさんに左足を上げさせました。

Useful Vocabulary: Body Actions (Of Course, You Can Also Use the Verbs Introduced in Previous Chapters.)

掛ける	かける	to hang (something) up
踊る	おどる	to dance
蹴る	ける	to kick
触る	さわる	to touch; X にさわる to touch X
叩く	たたく	to hit with the hand, to knock
つかむ		to grab, hold, catch
閉じる	とじる	to close (*eyes, books*)
跳ぶ	とぶ	to jump
伸ばす	のばす	to extend or stretch (something)
振る	ふる	to shake (something)
曲げる	まげる	to bend (something)
真似る／真似をする	まねる／まねをする	to imitate
向く	むく	to face toward; X を向く face toward X
戻す	もどす	to return something to its previous place
渡す	わたす	to hand over

✳ アクティビティー　31

日本語のクラスで先生は学生に何をさせますか。(*What does the instructor make the students do in Japanese class?*)

Discuss these questions in class.

1. 日本語のクラスで先生は学生に何をさせますか。
2. あなたが子供の時、両親はあなたに何をさせましたか。
3. もし、あなたがとなりの人に何でも命令 (*command*) できたら、何をさせたいですか。
4. 子供にさせてはいけないことは何ですか。

The Body and Health

27. Constructions Using Interrogatives

山本：村山さん、ブラウンさん、どこへ行ったか知っていますか。

村山：いいえ、でも、さっき宮井クリニックがどこにあるか聞いてきたわ。

山本：宮井クリニック？それ、どんな病院。

村山：あら、宮井クリニックがどんな病院か知らないの？有名な整形美容の病院よ。

３時10分前、３時10分過ぎ

In Japanese, as in English, it is possible to express times that are not on the hour or half-hour in terms like *2:50* or *3:10,* and this is what you will usually see on schedules or hear in formal announcements. In everyday conversation, however, English-speakers often say things like *ten minutes to three* or *ten after three.* The same is true of Japanese. To express minutes before the hour, you say x時x分前, as in the following examples.

8時15分前	*quarter to eight*
11時20分前	*twenty minutes to eleven*

To express minutes after the hour, you say x時x分過ぎ.

8時15分過ぎ	*quarter after eight*
11時20分過ぎ	*twenty minutes after eleven*

27.1 When you would like to ask for specific information or clarification about someone or something that has been mentioned, the following construction is commonly used. This pattern is particularly useful for asking for definitions of words that you don't understand.

YAMAMOTO: Mr. Murayama, do you know where Ms. Brown went?   MURAYAMA: No, but a little while ago she came asking me where the Miyai Clinic is.   YAMAMOTO: Miyai Clinic? What kind of clinic is that? MURAYAMA: Oh, you don't know what kind of clinic the Miyai Clinic is? It's a famous cosmetic surgery clinic.

| X | というのは
っていうのは
とは
って | Interrogatives
Interrogative expressions | ([の]こと)ですか |

「キリキリ痛（いた）む」とはどういうことですか。
What does キリキリ痛む mean?
大野（おおの）っていうのは誰（だれ）？
Who is Oono? (Who is this Oono person?)

とは is a shortened form of というのは. っていうのは and って are the colloquial counterparts of というのは and とは, respectively.

27.2 An embedded question is a question placed inside another question or a statement.

> *Do you know where Mr. Hayashi is from?*
> *I will tell you what it is.*

In these two examples, the questions, "Where is Mr. Hayashi from?" and, "What is it?" are embedded in the main clauses, "Do you know..." and, "I will tell you...." In effect, the first example is two questions. The main clause asks whether the listener knows certain information, while the embedded question asks where Mr. Hayashi is. The second example is an answer inside a statement. In Japanese, this type of sentence typically takes the following construction.

EMBEDDED QUESTION	MAIN CLAUSE
Plain form of predicates + か	Plain or polite form

昨日ここに来たのは誰（だれ）（だった）か覚（おぼ）えていますか。
Do you remember who the person who came here yesterday was?
どの薬（くすり）が一番良（よ）かったか教（おし）えてください。
Please tell me which medicine was best.
山本さんは何時に来るかわかりますか。
Do you know what time Ms. Yamamoto will come?

アクティビティー　32

アナハイムというのはどんな所（ところ）ですか。(*What's this place Anaheim like?*)

What do you think are the questions that would yield the following answers?
Make up questions by using …というのは + どんなところ／人／もの + ですか.

[例] ディズニーランドがあって、観光客が多いところです。→
アナハイムというのはどんな所ですか。

1. アメリカの副大統領 (*vice president*) です。

2. 有名なコンピュータの会社です。

3. 7月4日です。

4. 風がとても強い所です。

5. 牛肉を使った日本の料理です。

6. 日本人が年の終わりにあげるおくりものです。

アクティビティー 33

結婚しました。 (*They got married.*)

Following is the announcement of the wedding of Heather Gibson's sister, as published in a Canadian newspaper. Before she returned to Japan, Ms. Gibson sent this clipping to her landlady, who doesn't read English very well. Pretend that you are another English-speaking tenant of the same apartment building, and answer the landlady's questions in Japanese, based on the information contained in the clipping.

WEDDINGS _____

Jean Elizabeth Gibson Marries Brian Alexander Wilson

Edmonton– Jean Elizabeth Gibson exchanged wedding vows with Brian Alexander Wilson in a candlelight ceremony at Northland United Church on June 12, with the Rev. John Williams officiating.

The bride, the oldest daughter of John and Marianne Gibson of Edmonton, was born in Vancouver. A graduate of the University of British Columbia, she is a computer programer with Northern Telecom.

The groom, the only son of William and Molly Wilson, graduated from the University of Toronto and teaches English at Queen Elizabeth High School in Calgary.

The bride's younger sister Heather, who is currently studying in Japan, came home to serve as maid of honor. Other bridesmaids included Ann Marie Parrish and Lori Simms. The bride's attendants wore pale blue, floor-length dresses and carried mixed bouquets of early summer flowers.

The best man was Jason Howard, the groom's college roommate, and Scott Carey and Gregory Callahan served as ushers.

A reception was held at the Edmonton Hilton Hotel. After a two-week honeymoon in Acapulco, Mexico, the couple will make their home in Calgary.

[例] ギブソンさんのお姉さんはどこの出身かわかりますか。→
はい、わかります。バンクーバーです。
ヘザー・ギブソンさんはいつ日本へ戻る (return) かわかりますか。→
いいえ、わかりません。

1. ギブソンさんのお姉さんはどんなお仕事をしているかわかりますか。
2. お姉さんの御主人はどんなお仕事をしているかわかりますか。
3. お二人はいつ結婚したかわかりますか。
4. お二人はどこで結婚式をあげたかわかりますか。
5. 御主人のルームメートがどんな服を着たかわかりますか。
6. 新婚旅行 (honeymoon) にどこに行ったかわかりますか。
7. 何というホテルに泊まったかわかりますか。
8. お二人はどこに住んでいるかわかりますか。

アクティビティー 34

だれから聞いたか忘れました。 (*I've forgotten who I heard it from.*)

Make up embedded question sentences by embedding the first question in the second sentence.

[例] チンさんはどこに行きましたか。林さんから聞きました。→
林さんから、チンさんがどこに行ったか聞きました。

1. カワムラさんはどんなワープロを買いましたか。わかりますか。
2. 大学病院はどこにありますか。教えてください。
3. 山口さんは何時に帰りますか。忘れてしまいました。
4. 東京からそこまで電車で何時間かかりますか。時刻表 (*timetable*)
を調べておいてください。

5. パーティーに何人の人が出ますか。三村さんに先に (ahead) 電話で知らせてください。

6. カーティスさんに何をあげますか。チンさんと相談して (discuss, confer) おいてください。

7. どんな食べ物がきらいですか。はっきり言ってください。

8. ブラウンさんはなぜクラスに来ませんでしたか。聞くのを忘れました。

28. Expressing Expectation: ...はず

林：ブラウンさん、遅いね。今日も休みかな。
カワムラ：ブラウンさん、今日は来るはずだよ。
林：本当？風邪、よくなったのかな。
カワムラ：うん、今朝、電話でそう言っていたよ。

The following construction is used to express the speaker's expectation that something was, is, or will be true. Note that the speaker expresses his or her expectation based on reliable information or strong evidence.

Noun	Noun + の／だった	
Na-adjective	Root + な／だった	はずだ／はずです
I-adjective	Plain form	
Verb	Plain form	

I expect that; it is expected that; I am sure that; ought to; no wonder; is supposed to; I assume that

佐野さんはサラリーマンだったはずだ。
Mr. Sano is supposed to have been a salaried worker.
その近辺は住宅地だから、静かなはずだ。
That neighborhood is a residential area, so it ought to be quiet.
その薬はドイツ製だから、高いはずだ。
Because that medicine is manufactured in Germany, it's natural that it's expensive.

N̶ote that this construction cannot be used to express what the speaker expects to do or intends to do, although it can be used to express what someone else is expected to do. It can also express someone else's expectation of what the speaker was expected to do. To express one's own intentions or expectations about one's own actions, つもり (see Chapter 6, Book 1) is used.

HAYASHI: Ms. Brown is late, isn't she? I wonder if she'll take today off, too.　KAWAMURA: I expect her to come today.　HAYASHI: Really? Did she get over her cold?　KAWAMURA: Yes, she told me so on the phone this morning.

Note that this construction can be used when the speaker has found the reason for something.

手術は成功したから、また目が見えるはずだ。

The surgery was successful, so he must be able to see again.

はず, which is a noun, can be modified by such demonstrative pronouns as その, あんな and the like can be used to modify another noun (in this case, connected by の), but it cannot be used independently.

ギブソンさんは来ますか。
Is Ms. Gibson coming?
ええ、そのはずです。
Yes, I expect so.
今夜食べるはずのおさしみはどこですか。
Where is the sashimi that we are supposed to eat tonight?

There are two ways to make this construction negative.

| Plain negative sentence | ＋はずだ／はずです |
| Plain sentence | ＋はずがない／はずはない |

Of the two, the second alternative is the stronger, carrying the connotation of, *There's no reason to suppose that... or, It's out of the question that....*

高田さんは入院しないはずだ。

We can expect that Mr. Takada won't be hospitalized.

高田さんが入院するはずはない。

There's no reason to suppose that Mr. Takada will be hospitalized.

✳ アクティビティー　35

ダイアログ：一回に何錠飲むかわかりますか。(*Do you know how many pills to take each time?*)

カワムラ：この薬、何の薬かわかりますか。
山口：ええ、風邪薬ですよ。
カワムラ：一回に何錠飲むかわかりますか。
山口：さあ。説明書が箱の中にあるはずですよ。

The counter for pills is 〜錠, and it is also the counter for doses of powdered and liquid medicine.

KAWAMURA: Do you know what this medicine is for?　YAMAGUCHI: Yes, it's cold medicine.
KAWAMURA: Do you know how many pills to take each time?　YAMAGUCHI: I don't know. There should be an instruction sheet inside the box.

The Body and Health

アクティビティー 36

わからないはずがありません。(*There's no reason that you shouldn't understand.*)

Match the clause in the first column with a sentence in the second column that it supports.

1. もう12月19日だから、
2. カワムラさんの靴はまだある から、
3. ハンスさんは10年間日本語を 勉強していたから、
4. ブラウンさんはここに何度も 来ているから、
5. 今日は日曜日だから、
6. クラスは3時間前に終わった から、
7. 山口さんのおばあさんは明治生 まれだから、
8. バーゲンセールの時に買った から、

a. もう80歳以上のはずです。
b. とても安かったはずです。
c. 銀行は閉まっているはずです。
d. 迷う (*get lost*) はずが ありません。
e. 学校は冬休みに入るはずです。
f. まだ学校に行っていないはず です。
g. 漢字が読めるはずです。
h. 学生はもう家に帰ったはず です。

アクティビティー 37

私たちはできるはずです。(*We're supposed to be able to do this.*)

Fill in the blanks to complete the following sentences.

[例] （　　　　）から、父は遅く帰るはずです。→
今日は残業があるから、父は遅く帰るはずです。

1. （　　　　）から、とてもうるさいはずです。
2. （　　　　）から、もう着いているはずです。
3. （　　　　）から、そんなことできるはずがありません。
4. （　　　　）から、とてもお金持ちのはずです。
5. （　　　　）から、病気になるはずがありません。
6. （　　　　）から、今日は家にいるはずです。
7. （　　　　）から、あの人は知っているはずです。

8. (　　　) から、あの人は日本が好きなはずです。

9. (　　　) から、とても面白いはずです。

10. (　　　) から、食べたことがないはずです。

アクティビティー　38

Answer the following questions by using …はずです, …だろうと思います, or …かもしれません, depending on the degree of certainty in your mind.

[例]　カワムラさんは今夜、うちにいるでしょうか。→
　　　今夜はカワムラさんの好きなテレビの番組があるので、うちにいる
　　　はずです。
　　　or
　　　カワムラさんは夜、あまり外に出かけないので、いるだろうと
　　　思います。or さあ、よくわかりませんが、いるかもしれません。

1. あなたのお父さんは今、どこにいますか。
2. お母さんは今週、電話してくると思いますか。
3. あなたは日本語のクラスでAが取れると思いますか。
4. 近所のデパートで、来週、バーゲンセールがありますか。
5. 御両親はお元気ですか。
6. 御両親は誕生日に何をくれると思いますか。

✱ アクティビティー　39

とても健康なはずです。(*One can suppose that he is very healthy.*)

Look at the illustrations to provide an explanation for each of the following.

[例]　ブラウンさんは＿＿＿ から、今日は休むはずです。→
　　　ブラウンさんは病気だから、今日は休むはずです。

1. カワムラさんは＿＿＿ から、とても健康なはずです。
2. 林さんは＿＿＿ から、最近少しやせたはずです。
3. 町田さんは＿＿＿ から今日はジョギングをしないはずです。
4. 山口さんは＿＿＿ から、お酒をやめているはずです。
5. カーティスさんは＿＿＿ から、とても疲れているはずです。

Language Skills

Reading and Writing

Reading 1　健康相談
けんこうそうだん

Before You Read

1. In the following magazine article, a professor of medicine answers a question from a reader. Imagine that you have the opportunity to consult a famous medical expert about some health problem. Write a brief question in Japanese, and compare your question with those of your classmates. What seem to be the most common concerns of you and your classmates?

2. Which of the following do you try to do in order to maintain or improve your health? Discuss.

   a. 毎日運動をする
   うんどう

   b. できるだけ (*as much as possible*) 車を使わないで、歩く

    c. 偏食 (*unbalanced diet*) をしない

    d. 野菜、果物をたくさん食べる

    e. 1日8時間寝る

    f. お酒、コーヒーを飲まない

    g. たばこを吸わない

3. What else do you do to maintain or improve your health?

Now Read It!

健康相談

質問

小学生5年生の息子は身長146cm、体重53kgで、ちょっと太り過ぎです。先日、学校の定期検診で、血中コレステロールが230ミリグラムもあることがわかりました。コレステロールを減らすためには、どのようなことをさせるといいでしょうか。

    東京都港区
    野間まり子 (35歳、主婦)

お答え

(東京大学医学部教授 佐藤清先生)

    日本人の食事は健康にいいので、20年前までは日本ではコレステロールはあまり問題になりませんでした。ところが、最近は日本人の食生活も欧米型になり、コレステロールが多過ぎる人も増えてきました。最近は、野間さんの息子さんのように、子供のコレステロールも問題になっています。では、コレステロールを減らすためには、また、増やさないためには、どうしたらいいでしょうか。

    太り過ぎの子供は血中コレステロールが高いようですから、太り過ぎに気をつけましょう。そのためには、偏食させないことが大切です。また、最近の子供はハンバーグ・ステーキのような肉料理が好きで、野菜を食べさせるのは大変なようですが、野菜、果物、海草などを食べさせてください。

    それから、毎日運動させましょう。ジョギングや縄跳びのような運動を毎日させ、体をフルに動かすようにさせてください。体を使う家の手伝いもさせましょう。これだけでも、コレステロールがかなり下がるようです。

身長 (body) height / 体重 (body) weight / 太り過ぎ overweight
定期検診 regular health checkup
血中 in the blood
減らす to decrease (something)

医学部教授 professor at a medical school

食生活 customary diet
欧米型 European and American style
増える to increase; to become greater

増やす to increase (something)

気をつける to watch for; to take care / 偏食 eating between meals
間食 = snacks
海草 seaweed

縄跳び jumping rope

ストレスもコレステロールを上げる原因らしいことがわかってきました。
最近の子供は受験のため、学校のほかに、塾へ行ったり、土曜日、日曜日も
勉強しているようですが、子供の健康のためにも、時々ゆっくり休ませて
あげましょう。
　このように食生活などお母さんやまわりの人の協力が一番大切なよう
です。

原因 *cause*

受験 *preparing for and taking school and university entrance examinations* / ...のほかに *in addition to...* / 塾 *cram school*

協力 *assistance; cooperation* / 大切 (な) *important*

After You Finish Reading

First let's understand the most essential points in this article.

1. What is the gist of Mrs. Noma's question?
2. Professor Satoo lists four things Mrs. Noma should take care of. What are they? (Hint: He uses causative sentences.)
3. Professor Satoo's response consists of five paragraphs. What is the main topic of each paragraph?
4. Professor Satoo uses よう and らしい several times in his answer. What are the underlying meanings expressed by these forms?

Writing 1

You are writing a regular health column in a local paper in Japan. You have received the following question from one of your readers.

> うちの18歳の娘の健康が心配で、質問します。娘は大学受験のため、
> 毎日夜遅くまで勉強しています。朝はごはんも食べないで、学校へ
> 行きます。昼ごはんにハンバーガーやピザを食べているようです。
> 学校から帰ってくると、夕食を10分ぐらいで終えて、すぐ勉強
> します。夜食には甘いケーキやインスタント・ラーメンばかり食べ
> ています。最近、顔色が悪く、とても疲れているようです。どうし
> たらいいでしょうか。

Respond to this letter. Make several suggestions, following the example.

[例]　朝ごはんは毎日食べさせましょう。
　　　甘いケーキは食べさせないでください。

Try to include introductory and closing comments as Professor Satoo did.

Reading 2 あなたも指圧してみませんか。

Before You Read

Review the body parts listed and illustrated at the beginning of the Vocabulary and Oral Activities section. In recent years, Japanese finger-pressure therapy (指圧) has become popular in the West. The following passage explains how to do it at home. While reading the passage, find what part of your body you should apply finger pressure to in order to treat your problems and the ones listed here.

目の疲れ *fatigue*, 肩のこり *stiffness*, 腰の痛み *pain*, 頭痛 *headache*, イライラ *irritability; nervousness*, 食欲不振 *lack of appetite*, 不眠症 *insomnia*, 脚のだるさ *tiredness; languidness*

Do you have any health problems or any aches and pains? Indicate the places where you have problems. Do any of your problems appear in the preceding list?

The following words and **kanji** for which definitions are given should be enough to allow you to guess the meanings, and sometimes even the pronunciations, of the undefined words. See how many you can figure out.

両親 (*parents*)　両手 (　　　)　両足 (　　　)　両目 (　　　)

重い (*heavy, serious*)　病気 (　　　)　重病 (　　　)　重体 (　　　)

健康 (*health*)　体 (　　　)　健康体 (　　　)

方法 (*method*)　健康法 (　　　)

調子 (*condition*)　体調 (　　　)

部屋中 (*throughout the room*)　体中 (　　　)

部分 (*part*)　頭 (*head*)　後頭部 (　　　)

左側 (*left side*)　右側 (*right side*)　外側 (　　　)　内側 (　　　)

満足 (*satisfaction*)　不満 (*dissatisfaction*)

規則的 (*regular*)　不規則な (　　　)

飽きる (*to get bored*)　飽きやすい (　　　)

This is the toughest one! (Or maybe it's easy for you.)

二日 (*second day*)　酔い (*drunkenness*)　二日酔い (　　　)

Now Read It!

体がだるくて、疲れが取れない。集中力がなくて、飽きやすい。長時間デスクワークをすると、頭痛がして、肩がこってしまう。いつもコンピュータを使うので、目が疲れてしまう。こんな方はいませんか。

集中力 *concentration*

こる *to become stiff*

ちょっとした疲れや痛みも、放っておくと、治りにくくなります。また、これが重病の原因にもなってしまい、たいへん危険です。毎日、ツボを指圧して、あなたも健康体を維持しませんか。ツボを探すのはむずかしそうですが、実はとても簡単です。自宅や学校やオフィスで簡単にできるし、すぐに疲れや痛みがとれるので便利です。

東洋医学では、健康体を維持するためのエネルギーが体中に流れていると言います。このエネルギーがスムーズに流れなくなると、疲れや痛みが出て、そして、病気になります。エネルギーがスムーズに流れていない部分のツボを指で押すと、エネルギーの流れがスムーズになります。

では、日ごろのちょっとした疲れ、痛み、ストレスを治すツボを紹介しましょう。

- 目の疲れ
  両目の外側を押すと、目がスッキリします。
- 首、腕、肩のこりと痛み
  後頭部、首のつけ根、首の横を押します。
- 腰の痛み
  腰を押すだけでなく、足の裏も押します。
- 頭痛
  頭のてっぺん、額、首の後ろを押します。
- 二日酔い
  おへその回りをゆっくりと押します。
- 気分のイライラ
  手首の小指側、耳たぶ、足の裏を押します。
- 下痢
  おへそより15cm下の部分と腰を押します。
- 不眠症
  背中を上から下にゆっくりと押していきます。足の親指のつけ根、頭のてっぺんも押します。

指圧は、いつでも簡単にできます。薬を使いませんから、副作用もありません。どこでも簡単にできて、時間がかからないので、忙しくて不規則な生活を送っている現代人には、とても便利な健康法です。あなたも自分のツボを覚えておいて、ベストな体調を維持しましょう。

Glossary (margin):

ちょっとした *simple, easy* / 放っておく *to leave as is; to not deal with*
危険 (な) *dangerous*
維持 (する) *maintenance (to maintain)* / ツボ **tsubo,** *pressure point*
実は *actually; to tell the truth*

流れる *to flow*

日ごろ *daily*

スッキリする *to feel refreshed*

つけ根 *base; root*

...だけでなく *not only ...* / 足の裏 *sole of the foot*

てっぺん *top of the head* / 額 *forehead*

耳たぶ *earlobe*

副作用 *side effect*

不規則 *irregular; unstable* / 現代人 *people of the modern age*

After You Finish Reading

1. Read the first three paragraphs quickly, and give the gist of each paragraph in English.
2. Read the paragraphs in which the writer explains how to do **shiatsu.** Using your own body or a partner's, indicate where you should press in the various circumstances described.
3. What does the writer want to say most in the last paragraph?

Writing 2

What do you do to maintain your health? Write a short passage on this topic.

Language Functions and Situations

At a Pharmacy

カワムラ： すみません。風邪薬はありますか。
薬屋： どんな症状ですか。
カワムラ： 頭痛がして、のどが痛いんです。
薬屋： 熱はありますか。
カワムラ： ええ、7度3分くらいあります。
薬屋： せきは出ますか。
カワムラ： いいえ。
薬屋： では、この薬がいいでしょう。
カワムラ： そうですか。おいくらですか。
薬屋： 50錠入りが1500円、25錠入りが800円です。
カワムラ： 50錠入りをください。
薬屋： 1日3回食後に3錠ずつお飲みください。暖かくして、ゆっくり休んだ方がいいですよ。
カワムラ： ええ、明日は学校を休むつもりです。
薬屋： お大事に。

KAWAMURA: Do you have cold medicine?　PHARMACIST: What are your symptoms?　KAWAMURA: I have a headache, and my throat hurts.　PHARMACIST: Do you have a fever?　KAWAMURA: Yes. It is about 37.3 degrees.　PHARMACIST: Are you coughing?　KAWAMURA: No.　PHARMACIST: Then I recommend this medicine.　KAWAMURA: I see. How much is it?　PHARMACIST: ¥1,500 for fifty pills and ¥800 for twenty-five pills.　KAWAMURA: Please give me the one with fifty pills.　PHARMACIST: Take three pills three times a day after meals. It would be a good idea for you to keep yourself warm and rest. KAWAMURA: Yes, I'm planning to take time off from school tomorrow.　PHARMACIST: Take care.

Dialogue Practice

Make up dialogues that start with the following phrases. Be as creative as possible.

1. すみません。頭痛の薬をください。
2. すみません。腹痛の薬をください。
3. すみません。咳止め (*cough suppressant*) のシロップをください。

Role Play

Work in pairs. Practice buying medicine at a pharmacy in the following situations.

1. Your child has a cold. You prefer liquid medicine to pills.
2. You feel fatigued and have a slight headache.
3. You accidentally ate some spoiled food. You have diarrhea.
4. You have a bad cough.

文化ノート

CULTURE NOTE • Health Care in Japan

The kind of situation portrayed in the preceding dialogue is typical of one aspect of health care in Japan. That is, people tend to go to a pharmacist first for everyday ailments, and they consult a physician only if the pharmacist suggests it or the pharmacist's treatment doesn't work. Many people also like to use traditional Chinese medicine (漢方薬 [かんぽうやく]) for minor medical problems.

Most doctors work from their own neighborhood clinics, called either 病院 (びょういん) or 医院 (いいん), and they may even have a few beds on the premises for seriously ill patients. (There are also large institutions called 病院, which are more like what Westerners think of when they hear the term *hospital*.)

Almost all Japanese have health insurance, either through their employers or through a government insurance program. If you ever live in Japan, you would be well advised to enroll in some kind of health insurance, because the medical fees charged to uninsured people are as high as or higher than those charged in the United States.

言語ノート

Explaining Your Symptoms

(Please refer also to the vocabulary boxes throughout the chapter)

心臓病 (にかかる)	しんぞうびょう (にかかる)	(to develop) heart disease
肺病 (にかかる)	はいびょう (にかかる)	(to catch) pneumonia
癌 (ができる)	がん (ができる)	(to develop) cancer
寒気 (がする)	さむけ (がする)	(to have) chills

Language Skills

くらくらする		to feel dizzy
気分が悪い	きぶんがわるい	to feel out of sorts
鼻水が出る	はなみずがでる	to have a runny nose
鼻がつまる	はながつまる	to have a stuffy nose
胸やけ（がする）	むねやけ（がする）	(to have) heartburn
胸が苦しい	むねがくるしい	to have chest pains
息切れする	いきぎれする	to be short of breath
腕に怪我をする	うでにけがをする	to injure one's arm
…がかゆい		…is itchy
…の骨を折る	…のほねをおる	to break one's…bone
…をねんざする		to sprain…
…にやけどする		to get a burn on…
…から血が出る	…からちがでる	to bleed from…
肉離れを起こす	にくばなれをおこす	to pull a muscle
…にあざができる		to bruise…
傷	きず	wound, scar
関節	かんせつ	joints
かぶれる		to get a rash

At a Clinic

先生：どうぞ、そこへかけてください。

チン：はい。

先生：どうしましたか。

チン：食欲がなくて、夜眠れないんです。

先生：どこか痛みはありますか。

チン：いいえ。

先生：疲れやすいですか。

チン：ええ。

先生：いつごろからそのような症状ですか。

チン：先週くらいからです。

先生：何か心配事はありますか。

チン：いいえ、特に。

先生：そうですか。じゃあ精密検査をしてみましょう。

DOCTOR: Please take a seat there.   CHIN: Yes.   DOCTOR: What's wrong?   CHIN: I don't have any appetite, and I can't sleep at night.   DOCTOR: Do you have any pain?   CHIN: No.   DOCTOR: Do you tire easily?   CHIN: Yes.   DOCTOR: Since when have you been feeling this way?   CHIN: Since last week. DOCTOR: Is there anything that you're worried about?   CHIN: Not in particular.   DOCTOR: I see. Well, let's give you a thorough checkup.

At a Clinic or Hospital

前にも起こりましたか。
Has this happened before?

これまでに大きな病気をしたことがありますか。
Have you ever been seriously ill before now?

深呼吸をしてください。
Please take a deep breath.

先生、具合はどうでしょうか。
Doctor, how is he/she?

アレルギーはありますか。
Are you allergic to anything?

入浴はしないでください。
Please don't take any tub baths.

ちょっと様子を見てみましょう。
Let's observe your condition for a while.

面会は何時からですか。
What time do visiting hours start?

御見舞に来てくれて、どうもありがとう。
Thank you for coming to visit me while I'm sick.

何かほしいものはありませんか。
Is there anything you want (me to get for you)?

Role Play

Work in pairs.

1. One of you has a bad respiratory infection, and the other is a physician. Role play a visit to the doctor's office.
2. One of you has been hospitalized. The other student visits you in the hospital.

Listening Comprehension

1. Ms. Adachi, who has been living in an apartment in a suburb of Tokyo, has been missing for the past two weeks. Even before disappearing, she mostly kept to herself and had little contact with her neighbors. The police had to interview three neighbors to get sufficient information about her. Listen to their descriptions of Ms. Adachi's physical features and personal characteristics, and jot down what each neighbor says. Then write up as complete a description as you can.

2. It's 7:30 A.M. now. Ms. Yoshimura, a nurse who is just coming off duty, is reporting to the head nurse, Ms. Koyama, about the patients she treated in the emergency room during the night. Listen to their conversation, and summarize the condition of each patient in English.

Vocabulary

Body, Body Parts

あし	脚、足	leg, foot	け	毛	hair, strand of hair
あたま	頭	head	こし	腰	waist, hips
うで	腕	arm	した	舌	tongue
おなか		belly	せなか	背中	back
かお	顔	face	つめ	爪	(finger or toe) nail
かた	肩	shoulder	のど	喉	throat
からだ	体	body	は	歯	tooth
くち	口	mouth	はな	鼻	nose
くちびる	唇	lip	ひざ	膝	knee
くび	首	neck	ひじ	肘	elbow
みみ	耳	ear	め	目	eye
むね	胸	chest	ゆび	指	finger

Review: 髪、手

Feeling, Emotion

あんしん（する）	安心（する）	peace of mind (to be relieved)
イライラする		to be irritated
うれしい	嬉しい	happy; delighted
おこる	怒る	to get angry
おどろく	驚く	to be surprised
かなしい	悲しい	sad
がっかりする		to be disappointed
きぶん	気分	feeling; state of physical well-being
きもち	気持ち	feeling; mood; atmosphere
くるしい	苦しい	oppressively painful
こまる	困る	to have difficulty; to be troubled
こわい	怖い	frightening; afraid

こわがる	怖がる	to be frightened
さびしい	寂しい	lonely
しんぱい（する）	心配（する）	worry (to be worried)
たのしい	楽しい	enjoyable; fun
なく	泣く	to cry; to weep
はずかしい	恥ずかしい	shameful; embarrassed
びっくりする		to be surprised
よろこぶ	喜ぶ	to be delighted
わらう	笑う	to laugh; to smile

Sickness and Injuries

いしゃ／いし	医者／医師	medical doctor
いたい	痛い	painful
うける	受ける	to undergo (*surgery, treatment, etc.*)
かぜ（をひく）	風邪（をひく）	(to catch) a cold or the flu
かんごふ	看護婦	nurse
くすり（をのむ）	薬（を飲む）	(to take) medicine
けが（をする）	怪我（をする）	injury (to get injured)
げり（をする）	下痢（をする）	(to have) diarrhea
しゅじゅつ	手術	surgery
ずつう	頭痛	headache
せき（をする）	咳（をする）	(to) cough
たいいん（する）	退院（する）	(to get) out of the hospital
たいおん	体温	body temperature
ちゅうしゃ	注射	injection
にゅういんする	入院する	hospitalization (to be hospitalized)
ねつ	熱	fever
はきけ（がする）	吐き気（がする）	nausea, to be nauseated
びょうきになる	病気になる	to get sick
ふくつう（がする）	腹痛（がする）	(to have a) stomachache
レントゲンをとる	レントゲンを撮る	to take X rays

Loanword: アスピリン

Review: 救急車、健康、病院、病気、休む、薬屋、薬局、直る

Body Actions

かける	掛ける	to hang (something) up	とぶ	跳ぶ	to jump
おどる	踊る	to dance	ならぶ	並ぶ	to get in line
ける	蹴る	to kick	のばす	伸ばす	to extend or stretch (something)
さわる	触る	to touch; X にさわる to touch X			
たたく	叩く	to hit with the hand, to knock	ふる	振る	to shake (something)
ちかづく	近づく	to draw close	まねる	真似る	to imitate
つかむ		to grab, hold, catch	わたす	渡す	to hand over

Shape

かたち	形	shape
かっこう	格好	appearance
さんかくの	三角の	triangular
しかくい	四角い	rectangular; square
まるい	丸い	round

Grammar

〜させる	*causative ending*		みたい(な)	like…
〜せる	*causative ending*		…よう(な)	like, appearance
〜そう(な)	looking like; looking as if		まるで	just like
〜ても	even if		…らしい	it seems that…, the word is that…
…はず	expectation			

Kanji

Learn these **kanji:**

体	首	角	死	薬
頭	指	持	元	局
顔	足	立	病	
鼻	毛	心	院	
耳	形	配	痛	
歯	丸	苦	熱	

チェックリスト

Use this checklist to confirm that you can now

- ☐ Talk about body and health
- ☐ Talk about feeling and emotions
- ☐ Express analogy and exemplification
- ☐ Use the … は …が construction
- ☐ Talk about appearance
- ☐ Use causative verb forms
- ☐ Express expectation
- ☐ Scan medical advice
- ☐ Buy medications at a drug store
- ☐ Talk about your condition at a clinic

Review Chapter 4

アクティビティー　1

見て！強盗だ！ (*Look! Robbers!*)

You witnessed a robbery while shopping at a local 7-Eleven. A policeman is asking you questions about the two robbers. Describe the robbers.

1. 強盗 (robber) は何歳くらいでしたか。
2. 身長はどれくらいでしたか。
3. 体重はどれくらいでしたか。やせていましたか。太っていましたか。
4. 目と髪は何色でしたか。髪は長かったですか。
5. どんな服を着ていましたか。
6. どんな顔をしていましたか。どんな声でしたか。

アクティビティー　2

健康について話しましょう。(*Let's talk about your health.*)

What do the following words remind you of? Think of all the related words you can, and then talk about your experience connected with these words.

1. ビタミン
2. 風邪
3. 食欲
4. リラックス
5. 病院
6. 感情
7. レントゲン
8. 東洋医学 (*Eastern medicine*)

アクティビティー　3

何をさせますか。(*What do you make someone do?*)

What should you make someone do for his or her own benefit in the following situations?

[例]　タバコを一日二箱吸う人
→ タバコをやめさせる。タバコを一日一箱に減らさせる。

1. 一日中コーヒーを飲んでいる人
2. 寒い時でも、Tシャツしか着ない人
3. 目が悪いのに、めがねもかけないで、車を運転する人
4. いつも怒っている人
5. ファストフードばかり食べている人
6. 暗いところで本を読んでいる人

アクティビティー　4

風邪を引いたようです。(*He seems to have caught a cold.*)

Answer the following questions according to the example.

[例]　カワムラさん、今日クラスを休んでいますね。
　　　→ ええ、風邪をひいたようです。

1. チンさん、何も食べませんね。
2. 林さん、とても怒っているようですね。
3. カーティスさん、悲しそうですね。
4. 三村さん、手が痛そうですね。
5. 大野先生、胸が苦しそうですね。

アクティビティー　5

健康的な生活を送っていますか。(*Do you lead a healthy life?*)

1. Make a note of your habits regarding food and drink (be specific), salt intake, sleep, exercise, smoking and alcohol, dress, skin care, physical and dental checkups, and so forth. Do you think you are leading a healthy life? How about your classmates? Do they appear to be leading a healthy life, based on their habits?
2. Write a short passage on your attitude toward health, following the example.

[例]　私はとても不健康な生活を送っています。野菜や果物はあまり
　　　食べません。甘いものをたくさん食べています。特にアイスクリーム
　　　が大好きです。...

5 Life and Careers

職場で：クォリティー・コントロールのディスカッション
しょくば

Objectives

In this lesson, you are going to

- Talk about life events and experiences
- Talk about careers and occupations
- Learn to express respect
- Learn to use passives
- Learn to scan a description of someone's work
- Learn to scan a short biography
- Learn how to use the services of a job placement center
- Learn how to participate in a job interview
- Write a résumé

Vocabulary and Grammar 5A

Vocabulary and Oral Activities

From Cradle to Grave

Vocabulary: Life

人生	じんせい	life; human life
生まれる	うまれる	to be born
誕生日	たんじょうび	birthday
赤ちゃん／赤ん坊	あかちゃん／あかんぼう	baby
幼稚園	ようちえん	kindergarten
保育園	ほいくえん	day care center
小学校	しょうがっこう	elementary school (*grades 1-6*)
中学校	ちゅうがっこう	middle school, junior high school (*grades 7-9*)
高校	こうこう	high school (*grades 10-12*) (*abbreviation of* 高等学校)
生徒	せいと	elementary, middle school, or high school student; pupil
短大	たんだい	two-year college (*abbreviation of* 短期大学)
教育（する）	きょういく（する）	education (to educate)
入学（する）	にゅうがく（する）	school entrance (to enter a school)
卒業（する）	そつぎょう（する）	graduation (to graduate)
若い	わかい	young (*in one's teens or twenties*)
未成年	みせいねん	underage person; minor
就職（する）	しゅうしょく（する）	getting a job (to get a job)
独身	どくしん	single; unmarried
結婚（する）	けっこん（する）	marriage (to get married)
Xと結婚する		to marry X
離婚（する）	りこん（する）	divorce (to get divorced)
中年	ちゅうねん	middle age

赤ちゃん and 赤ん坊 both mean *baby*, but the first one has a slight honorific connotation, so you would always refer to someone else's baby as 赤ちゃん.

Unlike two-year colleges in North America, Japanese 短期大学 are almost exclusively for young women and offer training in what are traditionally regarded as feminine occupations, such as clerical work, nursery school teaching, and home economics.

退職（する）	たいしょく（する）	retirement (to retire)
老人	ろうじん	elderly person
年をとる	としをとる	to grow older
死	し	death

Review: 子供、男の子、女の子、大学、大学院、学校、死ぬ

❋ アクティビティー　1

人の一生 (A person's life)

Tell when the following things happen to people in general.

[例]　高校に入学する → 15歳で高校に入学します。
　　　高校を卒業する → 18歳で高校を卒業します。

1. 生まれる
2. 高校を卒業する
3. 幼稚園に入園する
4. 大学に入学する
5. 中年になる
6. 結婚する
7. 就職する
8. 退職する
9. 死ぬ

> **R**eview how to express one's age. See Book 1, Chapter 1, Personal Information.

文化ノート

CULTURE NOTE • The Japanese Educational System (1): Elementary School

Although kindergartens, 幼稚園 (ようちえん), are not part of the system of compulsory education, and they charge tuition, most preschool children attend either public or private kindergartens from age three through five.

Compulsory schooling begins with elementary school, 小学校 (しょうがっこう), which includes grades one through six. The main task during these first six years of schooling is to give children a grounding in the Japanese writing system. They also receive thorough instruction in other subjects, not only mathematics and science but also music and art. Despite the demanding curriculum, the school day contains opportunities for hands-on learning, group activities, and recreation.

There are some significant differences between the day-to-day operations of a Japanese school and those of a North American school. For example, the Japanese school year begins in April, with a six-week summer vacation beginning in mid-July, two weeks or so around the New Year's holiday, and a month-long spring vacation in March. Furthermore, school is in session for half a day three out of four Saturdays per month. Another difference is that the students themselves clean the school and school grounds, and although paid staff prepare lunch, students do the actual serving.

Vocabulary and Grammar 5A

二百四十五

小学校の音楽の
時間です。

✳ アクティビティー　2

8歳の時 (*When you were 8 years old,...*)

Answer these questions.

あなたは8歳の時、

1. どこに住んでいましたか。
2. どの学校に通っていましたか。
3. どんなことをするのが好きでしたか。
4. スポーツはしましたか。どんなスポーツをしましたか。
5. 夏休みには何をしましたか。
6. 大きくなったら何になりたいと思っていましたか。

あなたが高校生の時

1. どこに住んでいましたか。
2. どんなクラスが好きでしたか。どんなクラスが嫌いでしたか。
3. 放課後 (*after class*)、何をしましたか。
4. たくさん勉強しましたか。

5. デートはよくしましたか。

6. 夏休みには何をしましたか。

7. 将来何になりたい／何をしたいと思っていましたか。

✳ アクティビティー 3

卒業した後 (*After graduation*)

Answer these questions.

1. いつ卒業するつもりですか。

2. 卒業した後、大学院へ行くつもりですか。

3. 卒業した後、就職するつもりですか。どんな仕事をしたいですか。

4. どこで仕事を探したいですか。

5. 今結婚していますか。独身ですか。

6. もしまだ独身だったら、いつか結婚したいですか。何歳で？

7. 退職した後、何をしたいですか。

Vocabulary Library

More on Life

生年月日	せいねんがっぴ	date of birth
年齢	ねんれい	age; age group
産む	うむ	to give birth
妊娠（する）	にんしん（する）	pregnancy (to get pregnant)
恋愛	れんあい	romantic love
愛する	あいする	to love
見合い結婚	みあいけっこん	arranged marriage
プロポーズ（する）		marriage proposal (to propose marriage)
婚約（する）	こんやく（する）	engagement (to get engaged)
婚約者	こんやくしゃ	fiance/fiancee
恋人	こいびと	boyfriend/girlfriend
結婚式	けっこんしき	wedding
新婚旅行	しんこんりょこう	honeymoon
（お）葬式	（お）そうしき	funeral
（お）墓	（お）はか	grave

✳ ## アクティビティー 4

あなたの略歴 (りゃくれき) (*Your brief personal history*)

1. Write a brief life history in outline form, and explain it in Japanese.
2. Work in pairs. Ask your partner these questions.

   a. 生年月日 (せいねんがっぴ) はいつですか。
   b. どこで生 (う) まれましたか。
   c. 幼稚園 (ようちえん) へ行きましたか。
   d. どこの高校 (こうこう) を卒業 (そつぎょう) しましたか。
   e. この大学に入 (はい) る前に、ほかの大学へ行きましたか。
   f. 独身 (どくしん) ですか。今、恋愛 (れんあい) していますか。
   g. 婚約 (こんやく) していますか。結婚 (けっこん) していますか。

言語ノート

Greetings on Special Occasions

North Americans like to say something original to express congratulations or sympathy, but Japanese people are content to use the same greetings as everyone else, so don't hesitate to use these phrases on appropriate occasions.

御入学 (ごにゅうがく) (御出産 (ごしゅっさん)、御卒業 (ごそつぎょう)、御就職 (ごしゅうしょく)、御結婚 (ごけっこん))
おめでとうございます。

Congratulations on entering school (childbirth, graduation, getting a job, your marriage).

お誕生日 (たんじょうび) おめでとうございます。

Happy birthday.

お喜 (よろこ) び申 (もう) し上げます。

I am very happy for you.

ご愁傷 (しゅうしょう) さまです。

My sympathy (at your bereavement).

If you need to congratulate someone and aren't sure of the proper phrase, just say おめでとうございます。

Grammar and Practice Activities

29. Describing a Change in State: ...ようになる

ブラウン：佐野さんはお酒はお飲みにならないんですか。

佐野：ええ、昔はたくさん飲んだんですが、全然飲まないように
なってから、ずいぶんたちます。

ブラウン：どうしてお酒をおやめになったんですか。

佐野：お酒を飲むと、おなかのこのあたりが痛くなるようになったん
です。

ブラウン：肝臓のあたりですね。

The verbal counterpart to the construction of an adjective + なる is as follows.

The dictionary form of a verb The negative form of a verb	+ ようになる（ようになります）

get to be; get so that; become able to; reach the state of

This construction is often translated into English as *start to.* However, the verb + ようになる does not denote a situation in which someone starts doing something on a single occasion. Instead it refers to the beginning of a new ability or habit or to a natural development. Here are some examples of the "habit formation" use.

毎日ウエート・トレーニングをするようになりました。
I started doing weight training every day.
コーラをやめて、フレッシュジュースを飲むようになった。
I gave up cola and started drinking fresh juice.

The "ability" use requires either a potential verb or a verb such as わかる or できる that contains the notion of being able to do something.

料理ができるようになりました。
I became able to cook.
ニュース放送 (*broadcast*) がわかるようになって、よかった。
It's good that I have become able to understand the news broadcasts.

BROWN: Mr. Sano, you don't drink?　SANO: No. I used to drink a lot, but not at all now. It's been a long time since I quit.　BROWN: Why did you quit drinking?　SANO: Whenever I drank, this area of my stomach started hurting.　BROWN: That's around your liver, isn't it?

✳ アクティビティー 5

ダイアログ：来週には歩けるようになると思います。(*I think that she'll be able to start walking next week.*)

カワムラ： おばあさんの具合はいかがですか。

山口： ええ、だいぶ良くなりました。昨日からおかゆが食べられるようになりました。

カワムラ： それはよかったですね。

山口： 来週には歩けるようになると思います。

Practice the dialogue by replacing the underlined part with the following.

1. ジュースが飲める

2. ベッドで起き上がれる (*sit up in bed*)

3. ことばが話せる

4. ごはんが食べられる

わかる and 知る

While わかる means *to figure out the content of something* or *to be clear* or *to be understandable*, 知る means *to find out something* or *to become acquainted with something* or *someone*.

　　スペイン語がわかりますか。
　　Do you understand Spanish?
　　スペイン語を知っていますか。
　　Do you know Spanish?

知る, with its basic meaning of *to find out* or *to become acquainted*, is translated as *know* when it appears in its -ている form (lit., *is in the state of having found out* or *having become acquainted*). This is why you use 知っている for knowing people and being familiar with places and ideas.

　　—カワムラさんの住所を知っていますか。
　　Do you know Mr. Kawamura's address?

KAWAMURA: How is your grandmother's condition?　YAMAGUCHI: It's improved a lot. She was able to start eating **okayu** yesterday.　KAWAMURA: That's great.　YAMAGUCHI: I think that she'll be able to start walking next week.

Okayu is a rice porridge commonly fed to sick people.

Life and Careers

—いいえ、知(し)りません。でも、調(しら)べれば、わかりますよ。
No, I don't. But I'll know (lit., *it will be clear*) *if I check it.*

Both わかりません and 知りません can be used for *I don't know*, but the nuance is quite different. 知りません can imply *I don't know and have no reason to,* so it can sound a bit rude if the question is one that you could be expected to know the answer to. That is why, when you ask a store clerk a question about the merchandise, he or she answers with わかりませんね instead of 知りません.(The ね makes it clear that the meaning is *I don't know,* not *I don't understand you.*)

In fact, saying 知らない directly to another person's face is a way of saying *I disapprove of what you are doing and want nothing to do with you.* Furthermore, since 知る refers to finding out something that you didn't have any reason to know, it sounds odd to use 知りません in reference to something concerning yourself, such as your own future plans or your own wants.

However, 知りません is a perfectly acceptable response when you don't know a person, are unfamiliar with a place or idea, or have no expertise in a certain subject area.

アクティビティー 6

よく眠(ねむ)れるようになった。(*I've become able to sleep very well.*)

Match the sentence beginnings in the first column with the endings in the second column.

1. 毎日、日本語のテープを
   聞いていたので、

2. 病気(びょうき)が治(なお)ったので、

3. 12月になって、

4. 近くに図書館(としょかん)ができたので、

5. ガールフレンドができて、

6. 車を買ってから、

7. コーヒーを飲むのをやめて
   から、

8. あの二人はけんか (*quarrel*)
   をしてから、

a. 全然口(ぜんぜんくち)をきかないようになった。

b. よく本を借(か)りるように
   なりました。

c. 授業(じゅぎょう) (*class session*) に出(で)られる
   ようになりました。

d. いろいろな所(ところ)にドライブに行く
   ようになった。

e. きちんと髪(かみ)をとかす (*comb*)
   ようになりました。

f. 毎日、雪(ゆき)が降(ふ)るようになった。

g. 夜(よる)、よく眠(ねむ)れるようになった。

h. 日本語がわかるようになった。

アクティビティー　7

クラスに早く行くようになった。(*I began going to class early.*)

Complete the following sentences by using ...ようになる.

[例] 学校のそばのアパートに移ってから、→
学校のそばのアパートに移ってから、学校に早く行くようになった。

1. 毎日、日本語の新聞を読んでいるので、
2. 春になって、
3. 試験が近づいてきて、
4. 大学を卒業してから、
5. 日本に来てから、
6. 毎日、プールへ行ったので、
7. 一生懸命 (*with all one's might*) 練習すると、
8. もっと部屋を暖かくすると、

言語ノート

Adjective + する

You have already learned how to use the adjective + なる construction (Chapter 5, **Grammar 31**, Book 1) to mean that something becomes large, expensive, beautiful, or whatever. Adjective + する refers to causing something to become large, expensive, beautiful, or whatever. As with the adjective + なる construction, i-adjectives go into their -く form, and na-adjectives and nouns go into their に form:

長くする　　　　　　　　　*to make long*
便利にする　　　　　　　　*to make convenient*
グリーンにする　　　　　　*to make green*

These constructions are sometimes ambiguous, and only the context can clear up the meaning.

きれいにしましょう。
Let's make it beautiful. Or, Let's do it beautifully.
はやくしましょう。
Let's make it so that it's fast. Or, Let's do it quickly.

二百五十二

252

Life and Careers

However, not every adjective + なる construction has a corresponding adjective + する construction. For example, you often hear things like 食べたくなる (*get to want to eat*), but *食べたくする is not used.

✳ **アクティビティー 8**

子供が話すようになるのは、いつごろですか。(*When do children start talking?*)

Answer these questions, either by yourself or working in pairs.

1. 子供が話すようになるのは、何歳ぐらいですか。
2. 赤ん坊が歩くようになるのは、いつごろですか。
3. 文字 (*written symbols*) が書けるようになるのは、何歳ぐらいですか。
4. 若い人が異性 (*opposite sex*) を意識する (*to be conscious of*) ようになるのはいつごろですか。
5. この大学で勉強しようと思うようになったのは、いつごろですか。
6. 今勉強していることを専攻しようと思うようになったのはいつごろですか。
7. ひらがなが書けるようになるまで、どれくらいかかりましたか。
8. 日本語で簡単な手紙を書けるようになったのは、いつごろですか。

文化ノート

CULTURE NOTE • The Japanese Educational System (2): Secondary Education

After completing elementary school, children proceed to the last three years of compulsory education, junior high school (中学校 [ちゅうがっこう]). Students now have different teachers for different subjects, but instead of moving from classroom to classroom, they stay in one room, and the teachers, who have desks in a central office area, come to them.

During these years, with the prospect of high school entrance exams, studying takes on increased importance. Public high schools are inexpensive, but there are not enough places for everyone to attend, so competition is fierce, especially for those high schools known to send many graduates to prestigious universities. Students also may opt for a private high school or choose to spend a year as a 浪人 (ろうにん) preparing for a second try at a public high school.

At the senior high school level, 高等学校 (こうとうがっこう) or 高校 (こうこう), competition intensifies as university-bound students prepare for the entrance exams for the university of their choice. Besides keeping up with their regular homework, many students attend cram schools and devote endless hours to studying old entrance exams.

As if the long hours of studying were not enough, senior high school students face other constraints. There are almost no electives in the curriculum. Almost all junior and senior high schools require uniforms and also specify acceptable hairstyles, shoes, socks, coats, sweaters, and accessories. Rules of

修 学旅行で：ハイ、チーズ！

behavior are strict, covering behavior not only within the school but outside it as well.

Vocabulary and Grammar 5B

Vocabulary and Oral Activities

Careers and Occupations

Vocabulary: Occupations (1)

職業	しょくぎょう	occupation
会社員	かいしゃいん	company employee
公務員	こうむいん	government employee; civil servant
工員	こういん	factory worker
店員	てんいん	store clerk
事務員	じむいん	office clerk
セールスマン		(outside) salesperson
受付	うけつけ	receptionist

秘書	ひしょ	secretary
銀行員	ぎんこういん	bank employee
技師	ぎし	engineer
教師	きょうし	schoolteacher
コック		cook
調理師	ちょうりし	cafeteria cook
弁護士	べんごし	lawyer
新聞記者	しんぶんきしゃ	journalist
電話交換手	でんわこうかんしゅ	telephone operator
建築家	けんちくか	architect
歌手	かしゅ	singer
俳優	はいゆう	actor
女優	じょゆう	actress
美容師	びようし	women's hairdresser
理容師	りようし	barber

> 教師 is the neutral term for *teacher,* whereas 先生 is honorific. For this reason, teachers in Japan introduce themselves by saying 教師です rather than *先生です, which would sound as if they were showing respect to themselves.

Review: 医者、ウエーター、ウエートレス、運転手、会社、銀行、仕事、スチュワーデス、先生、歯医者、パイロット、働く、大工、看護婦、タイピスト

✹ アクティビティー　9

誰の仕事ですか。(*Whose job is it?*)

Tell who does these things.

[例]　事務所でタイプを打ちます。→ タイピストの仕事です。

1. 料理を作ります。
2. 飛行機の中で飲み物を出します。
3. タクシーを運転します。
4. 家を建てます。
5. 髪にパーマをかけます。
6. 工場でもの (*things*) を作ります。
7. お金を貸します。

Vocabulary Library

Occupations (2)

裁判官	さいばんかん	judge
科学者	かがくしゃ	scientist
教授	きょうじゅ	college professor

軍人	ぐんじん	military personnel
警察官	けいさつかん	police officer
消防士	しょうぼうし	firefighter
郵便配達員	ゆうびんはいたついん	mail carrier
駅員	えきいん	station employee
芸術家	げいじゅつか	artist
音楽家	おんがくか	musician
写真家	しゃしんか	photographer
会計士	かいけいし	accountant
通訳	つうやく	interpreter
翻訳者	ほんやくしゃ	translator
作家	さっか	author
スポーツ選手	スポーツせんしゅ	athlete
保母	ほぼ	daycare worker
家政婦	かせいふ	housekeeper; cleaning help
農民	のうみん	farmer
神父	しんぷ	Catholic priest
牧師	ぼくし	Protestant minister
僧侶	そうりょ	Buddhist priest or monk (also お坊さん)
神主	かんぬし	Shinto priest
主婦	しゅふ	housewife
外交官	がいこうかん	diplomat
政治家	せいじか	politician
葬儀屋	そうぎや	funeral director
自由業	じゆうぎょう	self-employed

Loanwords: カーレーサー、デザイナー、テストドライバー、バーテンダー、ファッションモデル、レポーター、コンサルタント、コピーライター、コーチ、ピアニスト、バレリーナ、テレビ・キャスター、アナウンサー

✳ アクティビティー　10

連想 (*Associations*)

With what professions and jobs do you associate the words or phrases in the numbered list? From the list of occupations, choose all the jobs that fit each description.

俳優	大工	警察官
主婦 (主夫)	弁護士	政治家
建築家	バーテンダー	僧侶
銀行員	パイロット	大統領 (*president*)
コック	ヘアースタイリスト	

Life and Careers

1. ライセンスが必要である。
2. 責任 (*responsibility*) が大きい。
3. お金がもうかる。(*is earned*)
4. 名誉 (*prestige*) のある仕事である。
5. 8時から4時までの仕事である。

6. つまらない仕事である。
7. 前は男しかしなかったが、今は女もする。
8. 前は女しかしなかったが、今は男もする。

言語ノート

Describing an Effort: …ようにする

The dictionary or negative form of a verb + ようにする is used to express the idea of making an effort or carrying out actions to make sure that something will happen. Often the most appropriate English equivalent is *be sure to*, especially in commands or requests. Unlike a verb + ようになる, a verb + ようにする may be used in talking about one-time events.

寝る前にストーブなどを消すようにしてください。
Before you go to bed, be sure to turn off the space heater and so on.

大切な会議ですから、遅れないようにしてください。
Because it's an important meeting, make an effort not to be late.

同僚達と仲良く (*congenially*) 仕事をするようにしています。
I'm making sure that I work with my colleagues in a congenial manner.

✳ アクティビティー 11

ダイアログ：フランス語の映画をたくさん見るようにしているわ。(*I'm trying to watch a lot of French movies.*)

カワムラ： 町田さんは卒業したら、どんな仕事をしたいの。

町田： うーん、フランス語の通訳の仕事をしたいわ。

カワムラ： それで、フランス語のクラスを取っているんだね。

町田： ええ、それにフランス語の映画をたくさん見るようにしているの。

KAWAMURA: Ms. Machida, what kind of job would you like to do after graduation?   MACHIDA: Well, I'd like to work as a French interpreter.   KAWAMURA: That's why you're taking <u>French</u> classes.   MACHIDA: Yes. In addition, I'm trying to watch a lot of French movies.

Vocabulary and Grammar 5B

Practice the dialogue by replacing the first and second underlined parts with the following. Make up the third underlined part on your own.

1. 弁護士になる
   法学

2. 建築デザインの仕事をする
   建築学

✳ アクティビティー 12

責任感 (*Sense of responsibility*)

What do you think is the most important responsibility for people who have the following occupations? Discuss in class.

1. 政治家
2. 弁護士
3. 看護婦
4. 家政婦
5. 秘書
6. 店員
7. タクシーの運転手
8. 医者
9. 日本語の先生

Grammar and Practice Activities

30. Expressing Respect (1): Honorific Forms

高田：これは先生がお書きになったんですか。

先生：いやあ、うちの家内が書いたんだ。

高田：奥様、字がお上手ですね。

先生：子供の時に、習字を習っていたそうだよ。

カワムラ：ただいま。

山口：あっ、カワムラさん、横井先生がお待ちですよ。

カワムラ：もっと早く帰るつもりだったんだけど、電車が遅れて
しまって... お待たせして、申し訳ないな。

山口：客間で待っていらっしゃるわ。

TAKADA: Did you write this, Professor? PROFESSOR: No, my wife wrote it. TAKADA: Your wife has very good handwriting. PROFESSOR: She says that she studied calligraphy when she was a child.

KAWAMURA: I'm home. YAMAGUCHI: Oh, Mr. Kawamura. Professor Yokoi is waiting for you.
KAWAMURA: I intended to come back earlier, but the train was late. I'm so sorry to have kept her waiting.
YAMAGUCHI: She's waiting in the parlor.

敬語 (けいご)

The Japanese language has significant built-in indicators of respect to the listener or a third party. The Japanese word for this system of respectful language is 敬語, but we use the English term *honorifics* in this textbook.

The system of 敬語 has many facets. First, we need to make a distinction between politeness and honorifics. The term *polite form* is the usual English translation of 丁寧語（ていねいご）or 丁重語（ていちょうご）, and it refers to the use of the -ます forms of verbs and the copula です as opposed to plain verbs and the copula だ. It may indicate only that the two speakers don't know each other well, although it plays an important part in the system of honorifics as well.

Because the decision whether or not to use -ます／です forms depends on your relationship to the listener, it is possible to speak honorifically in plain form. For example, you could talk to a close friend or family member in the plain form about your instructor, using honorifics. On the other hand, you could talk to a stranger in the polite form about some impersonal topic, with no honorifics necessary.

30.1 When you talk about actions or events related to someone superior to you, those actions or events are usually expressed by an honorific form of the verb. There are three ways to make a verb honorific. The most common and regular is お + conjunctive form of the verb + になる（になります）.

> To review the conjunctive form of the verb, refer to Book 1, **Grammar 12**. お is a prefix that expresses politeness.

VERB CLASSES	DICTIONARY FORM	HONORIFIC FORM
Class 1	書く	お書きになる
Class 2	考（かんが）える	お考（かんが）えになる

Caution: Some commonly used verbs, including 見る, 着（き）る, いる, ある, 来（く）る, and する, do not allow you to form their honorifics in this way. These irregular forms are found in **Grammar 30.2**.

横井（よこい）先生は黒板（こくばん）に本の名前をお書きになりました。
Professor Yokoi wrote the name of the book on the chalkboard.
今日の午後、社長（しゃちょう）が皆（みな）さんにお話しになります。
This afternoon, the (company) president will speak to you all.

Vocabulary and Grammar 5B

259

Who Is Superior to You?

It is all very well to say that you use honorifics to people superior to you, but how do you decide who is superior to you? Actually, both personal and contextual factors affect this decision. Unlike the case in the military, a person who is a "general" in one situation in civilian life may be a "private" in another situation.

Personal factors include, for instance, *position within an organization.* Lower-ranking employees use 敬語 (けいご) to their superiors, with the people in each position using 敬語 to those who rank above them in the organization hierarchy. *Age* is another important factor: younger people use 敬語 in speaking to older people. *Length of experience* is another personal factor. Even when two people are at the same rank in the same occupation, the one with the longer experience is usually considered superior to the one with less experience. This is also true among university students, who speak politely to their **senpai,** 先輩, the members of the classes ahead of them and the alumni of their school. A *benefactor-recipient relation* can also influence the use of honorifics. Those who receive a benefit usually use honorifics to those who provide the benefit. This is why shop clerks use honorifics in speaking to their customers.

Another important personal factor is the *degree of familiarity in the relationship.* All other things being equal, you will become less formal as you become better acquainted. The *gender of the speaker and addressee* is also a factor. Female speakers tend to speak more politely and formally than male speakers.

Finally, it is customary to use honorifics *when you don't know the identity of the person you are talking to.* This usage is heard most often in telephone conversations, when the person who answers the phone starts out speaking in honorific language, because he or she does not want to risk being offensive in case it is a high-ranking person on the other end of the line.

30.2 There are a number of irregular honorific forms of verbs, as shown in the table. These are very commonly used, so you should memorize them.

DICTIONARY FORMS / NONHONORIFIC	IRREGULAR HONORIFIC FORMS
見る	ご覧 (らん) になる
行く／いる／来る	いらっしゃる おいでになる

Life and Careers

DICTIONARY FORMS/NONHONORIFIC	IRREGULAR HONORIFIC FORMS
言う	おっしゃる
食べる／飲む	召し上がる
する	なさる
着る	お召しになる
くれる	くださる
死ぬ	お亡くなりになる
知っている	ご存じだ

社長、この書類はご覧になりましたか。
President, did you take a look at this document?
社長は今日はまだ何も召し上がっていない。
The (company) president has not eaten anything yet today.
横井先生、もうご存じでしょうが、明日チンさんが中国に帰ります。
Professor Yokoi, you probably know this already, but Ms. Chin is going back to China tomorrow.

いらっしゃる and おいでになる can be used as the honorific form of 行く、いる, and 来る. You have to figure out the meaning based on the context.

横井先生も成田空港までいらっしゃるそうです。
I heard that Professor Yokoi, too, will go to Narita Airport.
横井先生は今研究室にいらっしゃいますか。
Is Professor Yokoi in her office now?

いらっしゃる, くださる, なさる, and おっしゃる conjugate like class 1 verbs, as just indicated. They are irregular, however, in the conjugation of the so-called ます form and the imperative form.

DICTIONARY FORM	POLITE, NONPAST AFFIRMATIVE	IMPERATIVE
いらっしゃる	いらっしゃいます	いらっしゃい
くださる	くださいます	ください
なさる	なさいます	なさい
おっしゃる	おっしゃいます	おっしゃい

You have already studied the use of ください Chapter 5, Book 1 and なさい Chapter 1, Book 2 in requests and commands.

Vocabulary and Grammar 5B

261

30.3 The honorific form of the progressive form of verbs (see Chapter 5, Book 1) is commonly expressed by the te-form of verbs + いらっしゃる (いらっしゃいます).

　　　社長は今電話をかけていらっしゃいます。
The (company) president is now making a phone call.

With certain verbs, お + conjunctive form of a verb + だ (です) also expresses an action in progress.

DICTIONARY FORM	HONORIFIC FORM
書く	お書きだ

　　　社長、田中さんが応接室でお待ちです。
President, Mr. Tanaka is waiting for you at the reception room.

30.4 The honorific forms of adjectives are formed by adding the polite prefix お.

　　　社長はいつもお忙しいので、昼ごはんを召し上がらない。
Because the president is always busy, he doesn't eat lunch.
　　　佐野さんの御主人はいつもお元気です。
Mr. Sano is always healthy.
　　　部長はゴルフがお上手でいらっしゃいますね。
Manager, you're good at golf, aren't you?

30.5 The polite prefix お, when attached to nouns, expresses politeness, respect, or humbleness, or simply gives the sentence a refined and elegant feel, depending on the context.

　　　先生がお手紙をくださいました。
My professor wrote a letter to me (respectful).
　　　お昼御飯にしましょう。
Let's have lunch (polite, elegant).

Japanese-origin words usually take this お prefix, whereas Chinese-origin words take another polite prefix, 御. This rule applies to na-adjectives as well. Thus Japanese-origin na-adjectives take お, whereas Chinese-origin na-adjectives take 御. But some of the most common Chinese-origin nouns and na-adjectives take お instead of 御.

　　　お勉強、お電話、お買い物、お天気、お時間、お料理
　　　お洋服 *clothes*, お歳暮 *year-end gift*, お返事 *reply*, お上手、お元気、
　　　お葬式 *funeral*

Note that this formation of honorific i-adjectives is not possible with all i-adjectives. For example, 面白い, つまらない, 遠い, 大きい, and so forth don't take the polite prefix お.

お is the polite prefix. ていらしゃる sounds more polite than だ, but it is used only in reference to people.

Some na-adjectives do not take the polite prefix お, such as those of foreign origin like ハンサム or those with negative meanings like 下手, 不器用 (*clumsy*), or けち (*stingy; ungenerous*).

These words are fully assimilated to Japanese and are considered to be Japanese-origin words. That's why お is attached.

Some words are always used with the polite prefix お or 御. In these words, the prefix is considered a part of the original words, and they are not used without the prefix. These include the following.

御飯 *rice meal,* おなか *belly,* おかず *side dish,* お守り *good luck charm,*
おみくじ *a kind of fortune telling,* お転婆 *tomboy*

30.6 In Book 1, you learned that the copula です is a polite form of だ. An even more polite form is でございます. When used in reference to a person, でございます is humble. (The corresponding honorific form for human subjects is でいらっしゃいます.) Compare:

私は林でございます。 *I am Hayashi.*

加藤先生でいらっしゃいますか。 *Is it you, Professor Katoo?*

When used in reference to something nonhuman, でございます simply gives the whole sentence an extra feeling of politeness and formality. (でいらっしゃいます is not used in reference to nonhuman subjects at all.)

30.7 Even the title さん has a more polite form, 様. When referring to a high-ranking person's relatives, you can say お母様, お嬢様, お父様, or 奥様. Employees of high-class stores, restaurants, and hotels may address their customers as お客様.

✳ アクティビティー 13

ダイアログ：部長がお話しになりますか。(*Manager, will you speak to him?*)

高田： 部長、田中さんがお見えになりましたが、部長がお話しになりますか。

部長： 僕はこれから会議に行かなくちゃならないから、君がかわりに話してくれないかな。

高田： はい、かしこまりました。

部長： うん、よろしく頼んだよ。

Practice the dialogue by replacing the underlined parts with the appropriate form of the following verbs.

1. 会う   2. 話を聞く   3. 一緒に昼ごはんを食べる

TAKADA: Manager, Mr. Tanaka has arrived (lit., *has become visible*). Will you <u>talk</u> with him?
MANAGER: I have to go to a meeting now, so will you <u>talk</u> to him for me?   TAKADA: Yes. I will.
MANAGER: All right, please take care of it for me.

アクティビティー 14

これからお出かけになりますか。(*Are you going out now?*)

In the following sentences, identify the honorific expressions.

1. 先生は毎日、何時にお出かけになりますか。
2. 社長 (*company president*) はどちらの御出身でいらっしゃいますか。
3. もうお帰りですか。もう少し、お待ちになりませんか。
4. 先生が今度お書きになった御本はアメリカの大学についてのものでございますね。
5. 先生がアメリカにいらっしゃってから、何年になりますか。
6. 先生、何を御覧になっているんですか。
7. もうご存じかもしれませんが、山下さんがお亡くなりになったそうです。
8. 社長のお嬢様は、おしとやか (*gentle, refined*) でいらっしゃいますね。

アクティビティー 15

山田先生がおっしゃいました。(*Mr. Yamada said so.*)

Change the underlined parts into their honorific forms.

先生、元気ですか。私は元気です。こちらは毎日暑い日が続いています。そちらはどうですか。

　　先生がアメリカへ行ってから、3ヶ月になります。そちらの生活にもう慣れたことと思います。毎日、研究に忙しいことと思います。新しい本を書いているのでしょうか。先生が書く本はいつも面白くて、全部読んでいます。今も先生がアメリカへ発つ前に出した本を読んでいます。先生のすばらしい考えに感服しています。奥様はどう過ごしていますか。先日、奥様が病気だと、山田先生が言っていました。心配しています。今日はこのへんで失礼します。

慣れる *to get used to* / 研究 *research*

出す (*in this context*) *to publish*

考え *idea* / 感服する *to be struck with admiration*

心配 *worry*

失礼する (*in this context*) *to excuse oneself*

アクティビティー 16

わたしとショパン (*Chopin and me*)

You have been asked to introduce a famous pianist at a banquet, and you show your proposed speech to a Japanese friend, who tells you that the speech is grammatically correct but lacks the proper honorifics. Rewrite this speech so that all the honorifics are in place.

本田先生は1945年6月30日に大阪で生まれました。子供のころから、ピアノを習い、6歳の時にはコンサートでショパンの曲を弾いたそうです。学校で得意な学科は、やはり音楽だったそうです。

ショパン Chopin (name of a composer) / 曲 a piece of music; a tune
やはり after all

　1963年に東京音楽大学に入学しました。大学では、三島花子先生のもとで、ピアノを勉強しました。1967年に大学を卒業すると、すぐヨーロッパに渡りました。1971年にモスクワのチャイコフスキーコンクールで2位になり、1972年のパリ・ピアノコンクールでは優勝しました。1973年にはヨーロッパから帰り、東京、大阪など日本各地でコンサートを開きました。

コンクール a competition

優勝する to win a championship

　現在は東京とパリに家を持ち、一年の半分は日本、残りの半分はパリに住んでいます。日本とヨーロッパにたくさんの生徒を持ち、ピアノを教えています。

現在 at present / 半分 half
残り the rest; remainder

　先生は昨日、ヨーロッパから帰ったばかりです。旅行で疲れている中をわざわざ来てくれました。

わざわざ going to all the trouble

　今日は「私とショパン」というタイトルで話してくれます。話の後、ショパンの曲も弾いてくれるそうです。

Vocabulary and Grammar 5C

Vocabulary and Oral Activities

In the Workplace

Vocabulary: Looking for a Job (1)

求人広告	きゅうじんこうこく	help-wanted advertisement
パートタイム		part-time job; part-timer
探す	さがす	to look for
募集（する）	ぼしゅう（する）	recruitment; announcement of an opening (to recruit)
雇う	やとう	to hire
応募する	おうぼする	to apply for a job; to respond to an advertisement
履歴書	りれきしょ	résumé
面接（する）	めんせつ（する）	job interview (to interview)
推薦状	すいせんじょう	letter of recommendation

Review: アルバイト

しごと　さが
仕事を探しています。(*I am looking for a job.*)

1. What do you do when you look for a job? Rank these activities in the
order you would do them.

りれきしょ　　　　　めんせつ
履歴書を持って、面接に行く

しんぶん　きゅうじんこうこく
新聞の求人広告を見る

かいしゃ　　　　　　　　　　めんせつ　にちじ　き
会社に電話をかけて、面接の日時を決める

じんじぶ　　　　　めんせつ
人事部の人と面接をする

りれきしょ　ようし
履歴書の用紙 (*résumé paper*) を買う

しんぶん
新聞を買う

りれきしょ
履歴書を書く

Vocabulary Library

Looking for a Job (2)

失業 (する)	しつぎょう (する)	unemployment (to become unemployed)
応募用紙	おうぼようし	application form
記入 (する)	きにゅう (する)	filling in forms (to fill in forms)
経験 (する)	けいけん (する)	experience (to experience)
学歴	がくれき	educational history
職歴	しょくれき	employment history
給料	きゅうりょう	salary
通勤 (する)	つうきん (する)	commuting to work (to commute)
残業 (する)	ざんぎょう (する)	overtime (to work overtime)

2. Referring to the personnel ads, tell what information is included in them.

▆▆▆▆▆▆ 募集（男子）▆▆▆▆▆▆
30歳迄月30万コンピュ
セールス ーターソフト経験不要
東京ソフト(03)5429-9012

▆▆▆▆ 募集（女子）▆▆▆▆	
店員	年齢経験不問パート可 時給900円月曜休日 食付山川とんかつ店 青山(03)3123-5678

Note that many abbreviations are used in these ads to include a lot of information in a limited space.

CULTURE NOTE • 社会人

North American students often joke about entering "the real world" after college or becoming "real people" as opposed to students, but in Japan the division between people who are still in school and people who are out in the working world is no joking matter; it is very real.

University students are granted a great deal of leeway in their behavior. If they want to dress like the members of their favorite alternative music group, devote their time to video games or shopping, or be less than fastidious in their use of language, no one minds.

This situation changes abruptly when they take their first full-time job. Now they are 社会人, "society persons," and they are expected to act like adults.

They have to dress conservatively, act responsibly, and subordinate their personal inclinations to the good of their employers and families. They may live with their parents until marriage, but the parents are less tolerant of youthful irresponsibility than before and keep reminding them that they are 社会人 and must behave as such.

Ever since Japanese youth began imitating the fashions and attitudes of the West after World War II, observers have been predicting that "this new generation" will not accept the old rules of behavior. Yet, over the years, a succession of greasers, beatniks, hippies, disco dancers, and punk rockers have traded in their boutique clothes for business suits and quietly turned into 社会人.

Grammar and Practice Activities

31. Expressing Respect (2): Humble Forms

しゃちょう
社長：電話帳、ある？
ひしょ
秘書：電話番号をお調べになるんですか。
社長：うん。田中さんの自宅の電話番号を...
秘書：じゃあ、私がお調べいたします。

31.1 Humble expressions, or 謙譲語 (けんじょうご), express the lower status of the speaker or his or her in-group member and express respect toward a superior or out-group person. As with the honorific forms, there are both regular and irregular ways to express this linguistic function. This regular form is お + conjunctive form of a verb + する (します)／いたす (いたします).

> お is the polite prefix. いたす is considered more polite than する.

DICTIONARY FORM	HUMBLE FORM (1)	HUMBLE FORM (2)
書く	お書きする	お書きいたす
借りる	お借りする	お借りいたす

In these formations, the subject's action generally must affect a superior in some way, usually, but not always, implying that the subject does something for the superior person's sake.

> しゃちょう　　　　　　てがみ
> 社長、私がお手紙をお書きいたします。
> *President, I will write a letter for you.*
> しゃちょう　　　たかだ
> 社長、高田さんをお呼びいたします。
> *President, I will summon Mr. Takada for you.*

31.2 Some important and commonly used verbs have irregular humble forms, as shown in the table.

COMPANY PRESIDENT: Do you have a telephone directory?　SECRETARY: Are you going to look for a telephone number?　PRESIDENT: Yes. I would like to check Mr. Tanaka's home phone number.
SECRETARY: Then I will check it for you.

NONHUMBLE FORM	IRREGULAR HUMBLE FORM
いる	おる
する	いたす
行く／来る	参る
言う	申す／申し上げる
借りる	拝借する
会う	お目にかかる
見る	拝見する
飲む／食べる／もらう	いただく
あげる	差し上げる
知っている	存じている
聞く／たずねる (to inquire)	伺う
見せる	お目にかける
思う	存じる
たずねる (to visit)	伺う／お邪魔する

私は大学で日本語を勉強しております。
I am studying Japanese at a university.
先生の誕生パーティーには私も参るつもりです。
I am planning to go to your birthday party, Professor.
どこかで一度お目にかかったことがあると存じます。
I think that I have met you once somewhere.
ちょっと申し上げたいことがあるのですが...
There's something I want to say...
はい、存じております。
Yes, I know.

31.3 In the case of nominal verbs, the humble form is formed with お or 御 + noun plus する (します)／いたす (いたします).

The selection of お and 御 follows the rules discussed in **Grammar 30**.

社長、会議の結果は私が御報告いたします。
President, I will inform everyone of the results of the conference.
出口まで御案内いたします。
I'll guide you to the exit.

31.4 You can also express humbleness with expressions related to giving and receiving, particularly in cases when a superior or an out-group member clearly received a favor from you, or when you have early received a favor from a superior or out-group person, in which case you use ＋ いただく.

Vocabulary and Grammar 5C

わたし　　　　　　　　　　　　　じょう
私がお嬢さんからのお手紙を読んで差し上げましょう。
　　　　　　　　　　　　　　　　　　　　　　　　　　　　　さ　あ

I will read the letter from your daughter for you.

せんせい　　　　　　　ことば　　かんじ
先生にその言葉を漢字で書いていただきました。

*I had my instructor write that word in **kanji** for me.*

言
語
ノ
ー
ト

Honorifics and In-group versus Out-group Distinctions

One characteristic of honorifics in Japanese is the consideration of in-group and out-group. Depending on the situation, you may refer to the same person with either honorific or humble forms.

In the following case, we have two 社員 of roughly equal rank talking to each other about their superior.

しゃいん　ひらい　　　　　　たなかかちょう　　　　　　　　　　　　　　ごしゅっせき
社員（平井）：田中課長が明日のパーティに御出席になるか
　　　　　　　　　　　　　　　　　　　　　　　　　　　　　し
　　　　　　　どうか知っていますか。
しゃいん　もりやま　　　　　　　　　　　ごしゅっせき
社員（森山）：ええ、御出席になるとおっしゃっていました。

As employees of the same company, and therefore members of the same in-group, they use honorific language (尊敬語 [そんけいご]) when talking *about* Mr. Tanaka, even if he is not present, because he is superior to both of them in the company hierarchy.

Next let's consider the case in which Moriyama receives a call from someone outside the company, let's say, Ms. Koshino of Company B.

しゃいん　もりやま　　　　　　　　　　　　　そうむか
社員（森山）：もしもし、総務課です。
こしの　　　　　たなかかちょう　　　ねが
越野：田中課長をお願いします。
しゃいん　もりやま　　　　　　　　　　　　　　　　せき
社員（森山）：田中はただいま、席をはずしておりますが、…

Note that Moriyama is not using 尊敬語 to talk about his superior's action while talking to Ms. Koshino, an out-group person. In the third line, Moriyama doesn't attach an honorific title to Tanaka, not even -さん. Also, Moriyama uses the humble form （おります） to talk about his superior's action. This illustrates one of the important rules of Japanese honorifics. You should not use 尊敬語 to talk about your in-group person while talking to an out-group person, even when the in-group person is your superior.

STAFF MEMBER (HIRAI): Do you know if Mr. Tanaka will attend tomorrow's party?
STAFF MEMBER (MORIYAMA): Yes, he said that he would attend.

STAFF MEMBER (MORIYAMA): Hello, this is the general affairs department.　KOSHINO: Section Chief Tanaka, please.　STAFF MEMBER (MORIYAMA): Tanaka has stepped out for a minute. (Lit., *He's away from his seat right now.*)

二百七十

270

Life and Careers

✳ アクティビティー 18

ダイアログ：コーヒーをお入れします。(*I will make coffee for you.*)

部長：高田君、疲れたね。ちょっと休もうか。

高田：はい、今、コーヒーをお入れします。
部長：それはありがたいね。
高田：インスタントですが、よろしいでしょうか。
部長：ああ。
高田：砂糖とミルクはお入れしましょうか。
部長：ああ、砂糖をちょっと。

アクティビティー 19

お目にかかりたい。(*He'd like to see you.*)

In the following sentences, identify the humble expressions.

1. すみません。高田さんにお目にかかりたいのですが...

2. このケーキ、いただいてもよろしいですか。

3. コンタクトレンズ、私がお探しいたします。

4. 明日お返ししますから、この辞書を拝借してもよろしいでしょうか。

5. ちょっとおたずねしますが、図書館はどちらでしょうか。

6. お客さまにお知らせいたします。ただいま4階の文房具売場で万年筆をお買い上げの方に、ボールペンを差し上げております。

7. 皆様の切符を拝見させていただきます。

アクティビティー 20

どういたしましょうか。(*What shall I do?*)

Rewrite these sentences using humble expressions.

[例]　それは先生から聞きました。→ それは先生から伺いました。

1. 先生、私がします。

2. 明日は、七時に来る。

MANAGER: Mr. Takada, we're tired, aren't we? Shall we take a little rest?　TAKADA: Yes. I will make coffee for you.　MANAGER: I appreciate that.　TAKADA: It's instant. Is that all right with you?　MANAGER: Yes.
TAKADA: Shall I add sugar and milk for you?　MANAGER: Yes, a little sugar.

3. 私から奥様に言いましょう。

4. これは先生からもらった辞書です。

5. 山田社長は三年前から知っています。

6. 先生のお名前はいつも新聞で見ています。

7. ペンをちょっと借りたいのですが、…

8. あの本は私が社長にあげました。

アクティビティー 21

おわかりになりますか。(*Do you understand?*)

Change the underlined parts to honorific or humble expressions, whichever is appropriate to the situation.

先生、元気ですか。私も元気です。

　先生が来月 京都に来るのを、妻も私も楽しみにしています。その日は妻が駅まで迎えに行きます。何時の新幹線で着くか、手紙でお知らせください。京都ではどうぞ我が家に泊まってください。私が市内を案内していろいろなところを見てもらおうと思っています。また、めずらしい京都の料理も食べてもらおうと妻と話しています。それから、私の妹も先生にぜひ会いたいと言っています。先日先生の本を読み、感銘し、先生にいろいろと聞きたいそうです。どうかよろしくお願いします。先生に会うのは5年ぶりで、いろいろ話すことがありそうです。手紙を待っています。

我が家 *our house* / 市内 *within the city*

ぜひ *by all means*

感銘する *to be impressed, to be struck with admiration*
願う *to request* / 5年ぶり *It's been five years since...*

Companies and Offices

The Company and Its Workers

商社	しょうしゃ	trading company
社長	しゃちょう	president of a company
重役	じゅうやく	executive
部長	ぶちょう	department head
課長	かちょう	section chief
係長	かかりちょう	subsection chief
OL	オーエル	female clerical worker (*from* オフィス・レディー)
同僚	どうりょう	colleague
上司	じょうし	superior; supervisor

Employees of Japanese companies customarily address their own superiors not by name + さん, but by name + job title or else just by job title. Thus the subordinates of a 課長 named Yamada would call him or her 山田課長 or just 課長 not 山田さん.

部下	ぶか	subordinate
先輩	せんぱい	someone who started working for your employer, attending your school, or being involved in an organization or activity before you did
後輩	こうはい	the opposite of 先輩; someone who has been employed, enrolled, or involved for less time than you have
職場	しょくば	workplace
株式会社	かぶしきがいしゃ	incorporated company; corporation
企業	きぎょう	enterprise; company
本店	ほんてん	main store; bank headquarters
支店	してん	branch store; bank branch office
事務所	じむしょ	office
工場	こうじょう	factory

Loanwords: ビジネスマン、キャリアウーマン

Review: 会社（かいしゃ）、会社員（かいしゃいん）、銀行（ぎんこう）、銀行員（ぎんこういん）

Office Equipment

タイプを打つ	タイプをうつ	to type
OA	オーエー	office automation
電卓	でんたく	electric calculator
そろばん		abacus
セロテープ		cellophane tape
ホッチキス		stapler
書類	しょるい	documents; papers
情報	じょうほう	information

Loanwords: タイプライター、テレックス、ファイル、キャビネット、プリンター、プログラマー、ロッカー、ワープロ (= ワードプロセッサー)、ファックス (= ファクシミリ)、コピーマシン

Company Activities

会議	かいぎ	meeting
出勤する	しゅっきんする	to come to work; to show up at work
首になる	くびになる	to be fired
首にする	くびにする	to fire
遅刻 (する)	ちこく (する)	lateness (to be late)
早退 (する)	そうたい (する)	leaving early (to leave early)
組合	くみあい	union
スト (ライキ)		strike

お水をお持ちしましょうか。(*Shall I bring water for you?*)

People in service occupations use a lot of humble language on the job. Here are the neutral forms of some language that service personnel might use in the course of a day. What are the humble forms?

[例]　ウエーター、ウエートレス：

   a. お水を持って来ましょうか。→ お水を持ってまいりましょうか。

   b. お皿を下げましょうか (*Shall I clear the dishes?*) →
　　　お皿をお下げしましょうか。

1. 洋服屋の店員
   a. 試着室 (*fitting room*) へ案内しましょうか。
   b. 包みましょうか。(*Shall I wrap it?*)

2. ホテルのベルボーイ
   a. 荷物を運びます。
   b. カーテンを開けます。

3. 空港のカウンターの人
   a. 出発 (*departure*) のゲートを教えます。
   b. 荷物を預かります。(*I'll take charge of the luggage.*)

4. スチュワーデス、スチュワード：
   a. この飛行機の安全設備 (*safety feature*) を説明します。
   b. ブランケットを持ってきましょうか。

32. Passives

チン：林さん、どうしたんですか、その腕？
林：昨日、自転車に乗っていたら、車にぶつけられたんです。
チン：本当ですか。大丈夫ですか。
林：ええ、たいしたことないんです。

CHIN: Mr. Hayashi, what happened to your arm?　HAYASHI: I was hit by a car while riding my bike yesterday.　CHIN: Really? Are you all right?　HAYASHI: Yes, it's no big deal.

カーティス：　三村君、眠そうだね。

三村：　うん、昨日、となりの赤ん坊に一晩中泣かれて、4時まで
　　　　眠れなかったんだ。

カーティス：　大変だったね。

三村：　それだけじゃないんだ。やっと眠れたと思ったら、5時に
　　　　電話で起こされてしまって、それも間違い電話だったんだ。

カーティス：　さんざんだったね。

32.1 In both English and Japanese it is possible to restate a situation so that what would normally be the direct object becomes the subject. This kind of a restatement is called the *passive*.

For example, if one of your cousins were a writer, you could hold up one of his or her books and brag, "My cousin wrote this book." In the same situation, however, you could also say, "This book was written by my cousin."

The second sentence, in which the usual direct object has become the subject, is a *passive* sentence. The first sentence, with the subject and direct object in their usual roles, is an *active* sentence.

32.2 The passive is formed as shown in the table.

CLASS 1	CLASS 2	CLASS 3
Root + the a-column **hiragana** corresponding to the dictionary ending + れる	Root + られる	Irregular
書く → 書かれる 買う → 買われる	食べる → 食べられる 見る → 見られる	する → される 来る → 来られる

u-column → a-column

　く → か
　す → さ
　つ → た
　ぬ → な
　む → ま
　る → ら
　ぶ → ば
　う → わ

Note that when the dictionary ending is う, it changes to わ in the passive form, just as in the negative form. The passive form conjugates like a Class 2 verb.

Many verbs that have passive forms in English do not have passive forms in Japanese. For example, there is no passive form for わかる or 要る.

CURTIS: Mr. Mimura, you look sleepy.　MIMURA: Yeah, I had the baby next door crying all night, and I couldn't get to sleep until four.　CURTIS: That's terrible.　MIMURA: That's not all. Just when I thought I could finally get to sleep, I was awakened by a phone call at five. And it was the wrong number! CURTIS: That was really harsh.

32.3 The normal sentence pattern is

N1 は／が N2	に から	Passive verb form

N1 was V-ed by N2.

Here N2 is the agent or causer of an action, while N1 is the patient or recipient of the action.

> 林さんはその男になぐられました。
> *Mr. Hayashi was beaten by that man.*
> このウィルス (*virus*) は山中 博士によって発見 (*discover*) されました。
> *This virus was discovered by Dr. Yamanaka.*

When the agent is clear from the context or when the agent's identity is unknown or of no particular interest, it does not have to be expressed.

> この家は17世紀に建てられました。
> *This house was built in the seventeenth century.*

It is likely that no one knows anymore exactly who built the house.

You cannot assume, however, that all English passives will correspond exactly to Japanese passives or vice versa. For example, Japanese uses the passive less than English, particularly if the *agent* is being mentioned directly. The second sample sentence above, for instance, could be restated as

> このウイルスは山中博士が発見しました。
> Lit., *This virus, Dr. Yamanaka discovered it.*

particularly in normal conversation, as opposed to formal writing. Another example of the active used where English would have the passive is

> その事故で二人の人が死亡しました。
> *Two people were killed in the accident.* (Lit., *By means of that accident, two people perished.*)

32.4 A type of passive that is common in Japanese is the *adversative passive* or *indirect passive*. The implication of this type of sentence is that something happened and the subject was adversely affected by it or was upset about it. Note that the subject doesn't have any control over the action. The direct object of the active counterpart remains the direct object in this construction.

> 私はどろぼうにステレオを取られました。
> (Lit., *I was taken the stereo by a thief.*) *I had my stereo taken by a thief.*
> 母に日記 (*diary*) を読まれました。
> (Lit., *I was read [my] diary by my mother.*) *I had my diary read by my mother.*

If you said 殺されました *were killed* instead of 死亡しました *perished*, it would sound as if the accident killed them on purpose.

32.5 An English passive can be formed only on a transitive verb, that is, a verb with a direct object. A Japanese passive can be formed on an intransitive verb such as 来る or 死ぬ. And the resulting passive sentences are adversative passives.

しつこい (*annoyingly persistent*) セールスマンにうちへ来られました。
(Lit., *I was come to the house by an annoyingly persistent salesman.*)
I had an annoyingly persistent salesman come to the house.
小さい時に両親に死なれました。
(Lit., *I was died by my parents when I was small.*) *I suffered the death of my parents when I was small.*

Remember to use this construction only when you want to express your displeasure at what has happened. When you are pleased with another person's action or have benefited from it, you need to use a favor construction.

アクティビティー　23

ダイアログ：ウエーターに水をかけられました。(*I had water spilled on me by a waiter.*)

沢田：高田さん、そのズボン、びしょ濡れ。どうしたの。
高田：喫茶店で、ウエーターに水をかけられたんです。
沢田：まあ。
高田：まわりの人に笑われるし、さんざんでした。

アクティビティー　24

どんなものが作られていますか。(*What kind of things are made?*)

Answer the following questions in Japanese.

1. あなたの大学は何年前に誰によって建てられましたか。
2. あなたの町ではどんな新聞がよく読まれていますか。
3. あなたの国ではどんな歌がよく歌われていますか。
4. あなたの州 (*state*) ではどんなものが作られていますか。
5. あなたの町ではどのテレビ局 (*television station*) のニュースがよく見られていますか。

SAWADA: Mr. Takada, those pants are soaking wet. What happened?　TAKADA: At the coffee shop I had water spilled on me by a waiter.　SAWADA: Oh my!　TAKADA: I got laughed at by the people around me. It was tough!

アクティビティー 25

いつ書かれましたか。(*When was it written?*)

Rewrite the following sentences in the passive form.

1. ジェームス・クラベルが「しょうぐん」を書きました。
2. たくさんの人が「しょうぐん」を読んだ。
3. テロリストは村の人を殺した。
4. カワムラさんは三村さんを呼んだ。
5. 日本人がゴッホ (*Van Gogh*) のその絵を買いました。
6. 日本人もこの歌をよく歌います。
7. 日本でもこの番組を放送 (*broadcast*) しています。

アクティビティー 26

雨に降られました。(*It snowed on me.*)

Take the active sentence at the beginning of each mini-dialogue, change it to the passive, and insert it at the proper point in the dialogue.

1. (子供が一晩中泣いた)
   - A: 眠そうですね。目も赤いですよ。
   - B: ええ、昨日、全然眠れなかったんです。
   - A: どうしたんですか。
   - B: ＿＿＿＿ んです。

2. (雨が降った)
   - A: 先週のピクニック、どうでしたか。
   - B: ＿＿＿＿ て、さんざん (*terrible*) でした。
   - A: それは大変でしたね。

3. (みんなが笑った)
   - A: 真っ赤な顔して、どうしたんですか。
   - B: ＿＿＿＿ んです。
   - A: どうしてですか。
   - B: バナナの皮ですべって、ころんだんです。

4. (誰も話を聞かない)
   - A: ねえねえ、いい話があるの。
   - B: ええ、何？
   - A: ここじゃダメ。＿＿＿＿ ところに行きましょう。
   - B: そんないい話なの？

✳ アクティビティー 27

だれが言いましたか。(*Who said that?*)

Match the statements in the first column about experiences on the job with the appropriate person in the second column.

1. 時々、犬にかまれたり、
   追いかけられたりします。

2. 病気の人がいれば、夜でも病院
   に呼ばれます。

3. お客さんに笑ってもらうのが、私
   の仕事です。

4. 注文を間違えて、お客さんに
   叱られました。

5. みんなによく道を聞かれます。

6. 単位を落とした (*lost points*) 学生
   に泣かれて、困りました。

7. 玄関のところで、よく
   断られます。

a. セールスマン   *かむ to bite*

b. 交番のおまわりさん   追いかける *to chase*

c. 郵便配達員

d. コメディアン

e. ウエートレス

f. お医者さん

g. 先生

叱る *to scold*

断る *to refuse*

Language Skills

Reading and Writing

Reading 1　私の選んだ仕事

選ぶ *to choose, select*

Before You Read

The first column is a list of jobs or professions. The second column is a list of types of schooling or training required. The third column is a list of reasons for choosing a job. Match each job in the first column with the training required for it and the reason a person might choose it.

Language Skills

279

二百七十九

職業 (しょくぎょう)	学歴・訓練 (がくれき・くんれん)	理由 (りゆう)
1. 弁護士 (べんごし)	a. 大学の教育学部 (きょういくがくぶ)	A. スターに なりたかった
2. コンピューター ・エンジニア	b. デザイン学校 (がっこう)	B. みんなにおいしい 料理 (りょうり) を食べて もらいたい
3. 学校の先生	c. 料理学校 (りょうりがっこう)	C. 弱い (よわ) 人を助けたい (たす)
4. ロック歌手 (かしゅ)	d. 大学の法学部 (ほうがくぶ)	D. 機械 (きかい) (machines) が好きだった
5. コック	e. ギターと歌の練習 (うた・れんしゅう)	E. 海 (うみ) が大好きだ
6. ダイバー	f. 水泳とダイビング (すいえい) の練習 (れんしゅう)	F. 人に教える (おし) ことが 好きだ
7. ファッション・ デザイナー	g. 大学の工学部 (こうがくぶ)	G. ドレスをデザイン するのが好き だった

Now Read It!

Ms. Machida, who is scheduled to graduate this year and is looking for her first job, found the following article in a magazine for job searchers. In the article, two women explain why they chose their current jobs.

いろいろな分野 (ぶんや) で御活躍 (ごかつやく) なさっている女性 (じょせい) に、御自分 (ごじぶん) の仕事 (しごと) についてお話ししていただきました。

留学 (りゅうがく) カウンセラー
佐藤 (さとう) まどかさん (25歳 (さい))

短大 (たんだい) を卒業 (そつぎょう) した後 (あと)、英語 (えいご) を勉強するためにボストンに二年間留学 (りゅうがく) しました。日本からたくさんの学生が来ていました。ボストンから帰 (かえ) ってきて、今の会社 (かいしゃ) に就職 (しゅうしょく) し、留学 (りゅうがく) カウンセラーの仕事 (しごと) を始 (はじ) めました。自分 (じぶん) の経験 (けいけん) が生 (い) かせる仕事 (しごと) なので、この仕事を選 (えら) びました。留学 (りゅうがく) を希望 (きぼう) する女子学生 (じょしがくせい)、OLの方 (かた) がたくさんカウンセリングを受けにいらっしゃいます。その方々 (かたがた) に会 (あ) って、どんなことを勉強したいかなど希望 (きぼう) を伺 (うかが) い、アドバイスして差 (さ) し上 (あ) げます。遠 (とお) くの方 (かた) からの御質問 (ごしつもん) には、手紙 (てがみ) や電話でお答 (こた) えしています。留学 (りゅうがく) の期間 (きかん) や目的 (もくてき) は違 (ちが) いますが、皆 (みな) さん、大きな夢 (ゆめ) をお持 (も) ちになっているようです。皆 (みな) さんが夢 (ゆめ) を実現 (じつげん) するようお手伝 (てつだ) いできると思 (おも) うと、うれしいですね。

分野 *field of endeavor* / 活躍する *to play an active role, to be prominent*

経験 *experience*

生かす *to put to use* / 希望する *to desire; to hope for*

期間 *period; length of time* / 目的 *goal; objective* / 夢 *dream*
実現する *to realize; to bring to reality*

弁護士
青山洋子さん (43歳)

私は父が弁護士でしたので、子供の時から、父のように弁護士になりたいと思っていました。それで、大学も法学部へ行きました。大学を卒業して、会社のOLをしながら、司法試験の勉強をしました。夜、アパートに帰ってから、朝2時くらいまで勉強しました。OLになって、4年後に司法試験にパスしました。しばらく東京の弁護士事務所で仕事をしました。主に、離婚問題を扱いました。夫に愛人のできた主婦や、夫に捨てられた主婦などのケースをたくさん扱いました。女性の地位を高めなければいけないと考え始めたのはこのころからです。去年、独立して自分の事務所を持ちました。セクハラ・ホットラインを作り、セクハラに悩んでいるOLの皆さんの相談にのっています。私もOLをしていたのでOLの方々の気持ちがよくわかります。去年、アメリカへ行ってきましたが、セクハラについては日本はアメリカに10年以上遅れていると思いました。セクハラをなくして、女性の働きやすい社会を作るのが私の夢です。

司法試験 bar exam

弁護士事務所 law office / 主に mainly
離婚 divorce / 問題 issue; case
愛人 lover / …を扱う to deal with…

地位 position, status / 高める to raise
独立する to become independent; to start one's own business
…に悩む to suffer from…

社会 society

After You Finish Reading

Based on the preceding passage, create and complete a table in English with the following headings.

NAME	OCCUPATION	THE REASON THAT SHE CHOSE THIS OCCUPATION

Writing 1

1. Interview someone who has a job. Ask the person why he or she chose that job. Write down the results of your interview in Japanese.

2. What is your career goal? In Japanese, write down what job you would like to do in the future and why you would like to do it.

Reading 2 佐久間社長の生い立ち

生い立ち *life history; life's path*

Before You Read

Work together as a class. Interview your instructor to find out the following. Do not forget to use honorifics in referring to him or her and his or her family members.

1. Where was he or she born?
2. What kind of work did his or her parents do?
3. What university or college did he or she graduate from?
4. Did he or she study hard as a child?
5. What food does he or she like? What food does he or she dislike?
6. What means of transportation does he or she use to come to school?
7. Does he or she see movies often?
8. How long has he or she been living in this country? (If your instructor was born in this country, ask how long he or she has been living in your community or how long he or she lived in Japan.)

Make up your own questions, too, if you like, but remember to use honorifics.

Now Read It!

The other day Mr. Takada attended a birthday party for Mr. Katsuo Sakuma, president of Sakuma Industries, Inc., 佐久間産業 (さくまさんぎょう), with which Mr. Takada's company has business relations. Following is a brief biography of Mr. Sakuma that Mr. Takada found in the party program.

佐久間社長は昭和5年 (1930年) 4月15日、山口県下関市でお生まれになりました。佐久間社長のお父様は大きな呉服屋をなさっており、下関でとても有名だったということでございます。佐久間社長も幼年時代は何の不自由もなく、非常に恵まれた環境でお育ちになったそうです。しかし、佐久間社長が12歳の時に、お父様が事業に失敗なさり、家と財産をすべてなくされたそうです。そのため、社長は小学校を御卒業なさるとすぐ、大阪の薬問屋に見習いとして送られたそうです。そこでは、朝は4時にお起きに

呉服屋 *store selling traditional Japanese-style clothing and accessories*

不自由 *disadvantage* / 恵まれる *to be blessed with* / 環境 *circumstances; environment* / 育つ *to grow up* 事業 *enterprise; business* / 失敗する *to fail* / 財産 *property; assets* / 全て *all; the whole thing* / 問屋 *wholesaler* / 見習い *apprentice*

Life and Careers

なり、店の掃除をなさり、朝御飯の後から、重い荷物をお背負いになり、
薬を売って夕方の5時までお歩きになったそうです。お給料は全部、下関の
御両親と妹さんにお送りになっていたそうです。戦争のため、薬問屋も
つぶれ、戦後は靴みがき、大工、掃除夫、ゴミ屋、食堂の店員など、
いろいろなお仕事をなさいました。その間に、お金をお貯めになり、
昭和30年、25歳の時に東京にお出になり、秋葉原で小さな電気屋をお開き
になりました。ご自分で本をお読みになり、電気について勉強なさったそう
です。昭和33年にポータブル・ラジオを御発明になり、これが
「佐久間ラジオ」として有名になりました。昭和35年に工場をお作りになり、
ラジオの大量生産をお始めになりました。ポータブル・ラジオはアメリカ、
カナダ、ヨーロッパに輸出され、大ヒットしました。その後、佐久間産業は
年々大きくなり、現在はラジオのほか、コンピュータ、テレビ、
CDプレーヤー、ステレオなどを生産しています。佐久間産業が今日のように
世界的な会社になったのも、佐久間社長の御努力の結果です。佐久間社長は
昭和31年に友子夫人と御結婚なさいました。お二人の間には息子さんお二人、
お嬢さんがお一人いらっしゃいます。佐久間社長は65歳になられた今日も、
毎日朝7時に会社にお出になり、夜6時までお働きになるのを日課となさって
います。佐久間社長には今後もますます御健康で、御活躍いただきたいと
存じます。

荷物 load (to carry) / 背負う to carry on one's back

戦争 war

つぶれる to go under; to be crushed / 戦後 after the war / 靴みがき bootblack; shoe polishing business / 掃除夫 sweeper / ごみ屋 garbage collector
貯める to save up

発明する to invent

...として as...; in the capacity of...

大量生産 mass production

輸出する to export

生産する to produce

世界的な worldwide / 努力 effort / 結果 result
夫人 an honorific title for the wife of a prominent man

日課 daily schedule

After You Finish Reading

Answer these questions in English.

1. Referring to this text, describe Mr. Sakuma's childhood.
2. Explain what happened to Mr. Sakuma at these times.
   a. when he was 12 years old
   b. after he graduated from elementary school
   c. after the war
   d. when he was 27 years old
   e. in **Showa** 30
   f. in **Showa** 33
   g. in **Showa** 35
3. Describe the current situation of Sakuma Industries, Inc.
4. Describe Mr. Sakuma's family.
5. Describe is Mr. Sakuma's daily routine.

List all the honorific and humble expressions used in the text. Then list all the passive forms of verbs used in the text.

Writing 2

Write a short life history of someone you greatly respect. He or she could be a historical figure, celebrity, or someone close to you. Use honorific forms.

Language Functions and Situations

At a Job Placement Center: Looking for a Job

ブラウン：すみません。アルバイトを探しているんですが、…

係員：それでは、まず、この求職票に記入してください。最初、ここにお名前を書いてください。

ブラウン：はい、ふりがなは必要ありませんね。

係員：ええ、カタカナのお名前ですから。ここに学生番号を書いてください。後は、学部、学年、生年月日と本籍と現住所と電話番号も書いてください。

ブラウン：本籍というのはアメリカの両親の住所でいいんですか。

係員：ええ、そうですね。あとは、今までどのような仕事をしたことがあるかということと、仕事の希望を書いてください。

ブラウン：はい、わかりました。

ブラウン：あのう、全部、記入しました。これでよろしいでしょうか。

係員：はい、結構です。英語を教えるアルバイトを探しているんですね。

ブラウン：ええ。

A person's 本籍 is the municipality where his or her family has their family registry (戸籍) and it may not be the same as the actual residence. Children are usually inscribed in their father's family registry at the local government office, and this process makes them Japanese citizens.

BROWN: Excuse me. I'm looking for a part-time job.   CLERK: Then first please fill out this job application form. Please write your name here.   BROWN: Yes. I don't need to write **hiragana,** do I?   CLERK: No, because it's a name written in **katakana.** Please write down your student number here. Then please write your department, year in school, birth date, legal residence, current address, and telephone number.   BROWN: For legal residence, is my parents' address in America all right?   CLERK: Yes, that's OK. Then please write what job experience you have and what type of job you are looking for. BROWN: All right.   BROWN: Excuse me. I've finished filling in this form. Is this OK?   CLERK: Yes, this is fine. You're looking for an English teaching job, aren't you?   BROWN: Yes.

係員：　ええと、それでは、これはどうですか。渋谷にあるフェニックス
　　　　英語学校というところなんですが。時給3800円で、月・水・金の
　　　　6時から9時までですね。

ブラウン：もう少し時給が高い仕事はありませんか。

係員：　そうですね。時給4000円というのがありますが、土、日の仕事
　　　　ですよ。

ブラウン：それじゃ、ダメですね。

係員：　それでは、これがフェニックス英語学校の電話番号ですから、
　　　　沢井さんという方に電話してください。

ブラウン：はい、わかりました。いろいろありがとうございました。

係員：　どういたしまして。

沢井：　はい、フェニックス英語学校です。

ブラウン：沢井さんをお願いします。

沢井：　私が沢井ですが、…

ブラウン：私、東京大学のリンダ・ブラウンと申します。大学の学生
　　　　センターでそちらの英会話の教師のアルバイトを紹介して
　　　　もらったんですが…

沢井：　ああ、そうですか。では、一度お目にかかって、お話しをしたい
　　　　ので、こちらに来ていただけますか。

ブラウン：はい。いつお伺いしたらいいでしょうか。

沢井：　今日の午後はいかがですか。

ブラウン：授業が3時に終わりますから、4時にはそちらに行けると思います
　　　　が…

沢井：　じゃ、4時にこちらへ来ていただけますか。

ブラウン：はい、わかりました。よろしくお願いします。

CLERK: Let me see. Then how about this job? It's at Phoenix English Language School in Shibuya. The hourly wage is 3,800 yen. You teach from six to nine P.M. on Mondays, Wednesdays, and Fridays. BROWN: Isn't there a job that pays a little bit more? CLERK: There is a job that pays 4,000 yen per hour, but you have to work on Saturdays and Sundays. BROWN: That's not good. CLERK: Then this is the phone number of Phoenix English Language School. Please call Mr. Sawai. BROWN: I see. Thank you very much for your help. CLERK: You're welcome.

SAWAI: Hello. This is Phoenix English Language School. BROWN: May I speak to Mr. Sawai? SAWAI: Speaking. BROWN: I am Linda Brown of the University of Tokyo. I was referred to you by the Student Center about the part-time position teaching English conversation. SAWAI: Oh, I see. Well, I'd like to meet with you, so can you come here? BROWN: Yes. When may I stop by? SAWAI: How about this afternoon? BROWN: My class is over at three, so I think I can arrive at your place by four. SAWAI: Then please come here at four. BROWN: All right.

Activity

Fill in the following job search sheet with your own personal information.

求職票	**受付け日** _____
	受付け番号 _____

氏名	ふりがな
生年月日 大正・昭和・平成　　　　年　　　　月　　　　日	
年齢	満　　　　　　　　歳
本籍	
現住所	郵便番号　〒
電話番号	
学歴	中学・高校・短大・大学　　卒業・中退・ その他（　　　　　　　）　　　在学中
職歴	
家族	あり・なし　　　　　　　人
希望する仕事	
希望する給料	
希望する勤務地	
希望する勤務時間	

Role Play

Work in pairs. One student is looking for a part-time job. Visit the Students' Job Placement Office, where the other student is working as a clerk. Conduct this activity based on these ads from one of Tokyo's English-language newspapers.

English Teacher Wanted. Established, reputable school in Nihonbashi. Applicant must be native speaker with excellent oral and writing skills. ¥4000/hour. Call (03) 3987-6543.

Soccer coach / Cross-country coach / American football coach for international school. Must have university-level playing experience. 3-5 pm Mon thru Fri. ¥3000/hour. Call (03) 5123-4567.

Waiter / Waitress (experienced only) for coffee shop of large hotel. Must be fluent in Japanese and English. Third language (French, German, Chinese) desirable. Evening hours. ¥2000/hour. Call (03) 3012-3456.

Foreign models (male and female) for promotion by new discount store. Experience preferred. Possibility of continuing contract. ¥5000/hour. Call (03) 3210-9876.

Job Interview: At One of Maiko Sushi's Chain Stores

コンコン。(ドアをノックする音)

人事部長：どうぞお入りください。

コリン：失礼致します。はじめまして。私、ジェニファー・コリンと申します。

PERSONNEL MANAGER: Please come in.   COLLIN: Excuse me. How do you do? I am Jennifer Collin.

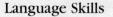

人事部長：はじめまして。人事部長の川上義広と申します。履歴書を拝見
　　　　　しましたが、いくつか質問させていただきます。

　コリン：はい。

人事部長：これまでどんな仕事をした経験がありますか。

　コリン：マクドナルドでアルバイトをしたことがあります。

人事部長：どれくらいですか。

　コリン：ええと、大学1年から3年までですから、ほぼ3年です。

人事部長：どんなお仕事でしたか。

　コリン：初めはハンバーガーを作る仕事でしたが、後で
　　　　　アシスタント・マネージャーになりました。

人事部長：大学の専攻は経営学ですか。

　コリン：はい、そうです。マーケティングが専門でした。

人事部長：日本語がとてもお上手ですが、...

　コリン：いいえ、まだまだです。

人事部長：日本語はどれくらい勉強なさいましたか。

　コリン：アメリカの大学で3年間、勉強しました。その後、日本に来て、
　　　　　2年になります。

人事部長：我が社で働いてみたいとお考えになったのはなぜですか。

　コリン：おすしのテークアウトのようなファーストフード産業に興味が
　　　　　あるからです。

人事部長：今日はわざわざ来ていただき、ありがとうございました。

　コリン：こちらこそ、どうもありがとうございました。

人事部長：結果は後ほど、電話でお知らせ致します。

　コリン：どうぞよろしくお願い申し上げます。

PERSONNEL MANAGER: How do you do? I am Yoshihiro Kawakami, personnel manager. I've seen your résumé, but let me ask you some questions.　　COLLIN: All right.　　PERSONNEL MANAGER: What job experience do you have?　　COLLIN: I worked part-time at McDonald's.　　PERSONNEL MANAGER: How long?　　COLLIN: Well, I worked from my freshman to junior years, so it's almost three years.　　PERSONNEL MANAGER: What kind of job was it?　　COLLIN: In the beginning, I made hamburgers. Later I became an assistant manager.　　PERSONNEL MANAGER: Was your major business management?　　COLLIN: Yes, that's right. My specialty was marketing.　　PERSONNEL MANAGER: You are very good at Japanese.　　COLLIN: Oh, no. Still a lot of room to improve.　　PERSONNEL MANAGER: How long have you studied Japanese?　　COLLIN: I studied it for three years at a university in America. Then I came to Japan and have been here for two years.　　PERSONNEL MANAGER: Why do you want to work for our company?　　COLLIN: I am interested in fast-food industries like take-out **sushi**.　　PERSONNEL MANAGER: Thank you very much for coming today.　　COLLIN: It is I who should thank you very much for your time.　　PERSONNEL MANAGER: I will notify you of our decision by phone later.　　COLLIN: Thank you for your consideration.

● 履歴書の記入例

履歴書　昭和51年 6月 1日現在

ふりがな 氏名	やまもと　けんじ 山本 健二　㊞	※男・女

写真をはる位置
写真をはる必要が
ある場合
1.縦　36 ～ 40 ㎜
横　24 ～ 30 ㎜
2.本人単身胸から上
3.裏面にのりづけ

※明治 大正 昭和	29年 5月 10日生 （満 22才）	本籍	愛知	都 道 府県

ふりがな　とうきょうとちゅうおうく　あかしちょう
現住所 〒104- 　東京都中央区明石町2番1号

電話	局番（　03　） 542-9511　方呼出

ふりがな　あいちけんなごやしひがしくひがしさくら
連絡先（現住所以外に連絡を希望する場合のみ記入） 〒461- 愛知県名古屋市東区東桜1丁目9番26号　山本茂雄方

電話	局番（　052　） 951-6711　方呼出

年	月	学歴・職歴（各別にまとめて書く）
		学　歴
昭和42	3	名古屋市立平和小学校卒業
昭和45	3	東京都立第一中学校卒業
昭和45	4	東京都立第三高等学校入学
昭和48	3	東京都立第三高等学校卒業
昭和48	4	城北大学経済学部入学
昭和52	3	城北大学経済学部経済学科卒業見込
		職　歴
		なし
		以上

記入注意　1. 鉛筆以外の黒又は青の筆記具で記入　　　3. ※印のところは○でかこむ
　　　　　2. 数字はアラビア数字で、文字はくずさず正確に書く

年	月	免許・資格
昭和49	8	普通自動車一種免許
昭和50	10	情報処理技術者認定二種合格

得意な学科	健康状態
語学（英・独）	良好

趣味 音楽鑑賞	志望の動機 1.貴社の将来性 2.貴社の業務及び社風が自己 の性格に最適
スポーツ 野球	

本人希望記入欄（特に給料・職種・勤務時間・勤務地・その他についての希望などがあれば記入）
職　種：営業部門
勤務地：東京、名古屋

家族氏名	性別	年令	家族氏名	性別	年令
山本茂雄	男	51			
雅子	女	47			
一郎	男	24			
恵美	女	19			

通勤時間 約 時間 50分	扶養家族数 （配偶者を除く） 0 人	配偶者 ※有・無	配偶者の扶養義務 ※有・無

保護者（本人が未成年者の場合のみ記入）
ふりがな
氏名　　　　住所 〒　　- 　　電話 市外局番（　）　（　）　方呼出

コクヨ

Discussion

Discuss the questions you would ask applicants if you were a personnel manager and the questions you would ask a personnel director if you were a job applicant during an interview. Make a list in Japanese.

Role Play

Work in pairs. One student is applying for a job at a company where the other student is personnel manager. Practice conducting a job interview using the résumé you have written. Refer to the questions you listed earlier. Before conducting the interview, decide what type of business the company is doing and what type of position the job interview is for.

Language Skills

289

二百八十九

Practicing Japanese Outside of Class

The few hours you spend in class each week are not enough time for practicing Japanese. But once you have done your homework and listened to your tapes until you have them practically memorized, how else can you practice your Japanese outside of class?

1. Practice "talking to yourself" in Japanese as you walk across campus, wait for a bus, and so on. Try keeping a diary in Japanese.
2. Hold a conversation hour—perhaps on a regular basis—with other students of Japanese or with your classmates and a few native speakers.
3. See Japanese-language movies when they are shown on campus or in local movie theaters. The foreign film section of your local video rental store may have subtitled copies of some of the most famous Japanese movies, and if there are a lot of Japanese people in your community, there is probably at least one store that rents nonsubtitled videos of current movies and television programs.
4. Check local bookstores, libraries, and record stores for Japanese-language magazines and music. Comic books and children's books are especially good for beginners. If your local Japanese import store sells educational enrichment workbooks for children, you can challenge yourself with the **kanji** quizzes and other puzzles contained in them.
5. Practice speaking Japanese with a native speaker—either a permanent resident or a Japanese student. (Be patient and persistent, because the Japanese person may not be prepared to hear you speaking Japanese and may also be very determined to speak English as much as possible.) Every bit of practice will enhance your ability to speak Japanese.

Listening Comprehension

1. Ms. Shigeko Takagi, personnel manager of Nihon Export Company, is interviewing Ms. Momoyo Sakamoto, who is applying for a position at the company. Summarize Ms. Sakamoto's career objectives, educational background, job history, special skills, and anything else that seems significant.
2. Mr. Komiyama and Ms. Hanamiya are talking about their jobs. Record their answers to the following questions.
    a. What are their current jobs?
    b. What companies are they working for?

c. Why are they working at those jobs?

d. What is one good aspect of their jobs?

e. What is one bad aspect of their jobs?

f. Do they want to change their jobs?

Vocabulary

Life

あかちゃん	赤ちゃん	baby
うまれる	生まれる	to be born
きょういく	教育	education
けっこん (する)	結婚 (する)	marriage (to get married)
こうこう	高校	high school
こうはい	後輩	a person who started at a job, school, or activity after you did
し	死	death
しゅうしょく (する)	就職 (する)	looking for a job (to look for a job)
しょうがっこう	小学校	elementary school
じんせい	人生	life; human life
せんぱい	先輩	a person who started at a job, school, or activity before you did
そつぎょう (する)	卒業 (する)	graduation (to graduate)
たいしょく (する)	退職 (する)	retirement (to retire)
たんきだいがく	短期大学	two-year college (abbreviation: 短大)
ちゅうがっこう	中学校	middle school; junior high school
ちゅうねん	中年	middle age
としをとる	年をとる	to grow older
どくしん	独身	single; unmarried
にゅうがく (する)	入学 (する)	entering a school (to enter school)
ほいくえん	保育園	day care center
みせいねん	未成年	a minor; an underage person
ようちえん	幼稚園	kindergarten
りこん (する)	離婚 (する)	divorce (to get divorced)
ろうじん	老人	elderly person
りゅうがく (する)	留学 (する)	study abroad (to study abroad)
わかい	若い	young

Review: 男の子、女の子、学校、子供、死ぬ、大学、大学院

Occupations

うけつけ	受付け	receptionist
かいしゃいん	会社員	company employee
かしゅ	歌手	singer
きょうし	教師	schoolteacher
ぎし	技師	engineer
ぎんこういん	銀行員	bank employee
けんちくか	建築家	architect
こういん	工員	factory worker
こうむいん	公務員	government employee; civil servant
コック		cook
しょくぎょう	職業	occupation
じょゆう	女優	actress
しんぶんきしゃ	新聞記者	journalist
じむいん	事務員	office clerk
セールスマン		(outside) salesperson
ちょうりし	調理師	(cafeteria) cook
でんわこうかんしゅ	電話交換手	telephone operator
はいゆう	俳優	actor
ひしょ	秘書	secretary
びようし	美容師	women's hairdresser
べんごし	弁護士	lawyer
りようし	理容師	men's hairdresser; barber
レジ		cashier

Review: 医者、ウェーター、ウェートレス、運転手、銀行、仕事、スチュワーデス、先生、歯医者、パイロット、働く、大工、店員

Loanwords: タイピスト、ヘアードレッサー、メカニック

Companies

おうぼ(する)	応募(する)	application for a job; response to an advertisement (to apply for a job, to respond to an ad)
オーエル	OL	female clerical worker
かかりちょう	係長	subsection chief
かちょう	課長	section chief
きゅうじんこうこく	求人広告	help-wanted advertisement
ししゃ	支社	company branch office
しゃちょう	社長	president (of a company)
しょうしゃ	商社	trading company
しょくば	職場	workplace
じゅうやく	重役	executive
じょうし	上司	superior; supervisor
どうりょう	同僚	colleague
ぶか	部下	subordinate

ぶちょう	部長	department head
ぼしゅう（する）	募集（する）	recruitment of employees (to recruit employees)
めんせつ（する）	面接（する）	job interview (to interview for a job)
やとう	雇う	to hire
りれきしょ	履歴書	résumé

Review: アルバイト、会社

Loanword: パートタイム

Grammar

お…いたす	regular humble form of verb
お…する	regular humble form of verb
お…だ	honorific form of progressive construction
お…になる	regular honorific form of verb
おいでになる	to come; to go (*honorific*)
…ようにする	to be sure to…
…ようになる	to reach the point of… -ing
〜られる	passive ending for Class 2 verbs
〜れる	passive ending for Class 1 verbs

Kanji

Learn these **kanji:**

校	職	愛	式	者	知
卒	退	恋	研	師	存
業	育	初	究	銀	申
仕	若	結	御	亡	召
就	老	婚	医	忙	様

チェックリスト

Use this checklist to confirm that you can now

- ☐ Talk about life events and experiences
- ☐ Talk about careers and occupations
- ☐ Express respect
- ☐ Use passives
- ☐ Scan a description of someone's work
- ☐ Scan a short biography
- ☐ Use the services of a job placement center
- ☐ Participate in a job interview
- ☐ Write a résumé

Vocabulary

Review Chapter 5

アクティビティー　1

職業紹介所 (*Employment agency*)

As an employment agent, what job would you recommend for each of the
people who have made the following statements? Before recommending a job,
what questions would you ask them?

1. 旅行が大好きで、これまでにもいろいろな国に行ったことがあります。
   フランス語とドイツ語が話せるので、ヨーロッパへ行くことが多い
   です。面白い場所やショッピングにいい場所を探すのが大好きです。

2. 子供の時から、いろいろなことを習うのが好きでしたし、大人に
   なってからは、人にものを教えるのが好きです。特に子供に音楽を
   教えたり、子供とゲームをしたりしていると、時間がたつのを
   忘れますね。

3. 今までいろいろなことをしてきましたが、すぐ飽きて (*get tired of*)
   しまいます。何か面白い仕事を探しています。自分で何かを考えたり、
   作ったりするのが好きです。

4. 家族ともっと一緒に過ごしたいので、土曜日、日曜日もきちんと
   休めて、出張があまりなくて、残業 (*overtime*) のない仕事がいいですね。
   夏休みもたくさん取れる仕事はありませんかね。

アクティビティー　2

人生 (*A person's life*)

Work in pairs. One student thinks of a famous person and gives hints describing
events in the person's life, traits, and major achievements. The second student
tries to guess who it is.

アクティビティー　3

どんな仕事が向いていますか。(*What occupation suits you?*)

Answer the following questions. Then let a classmate analyze the results in order
to recommend a suitable occupation for you. Do you like the recommendation?
Why or why not?

	とても好きだ	まあまあ好きだ	あまり好きではない	きらいだ
1. 手を使う	☐	☐	☐	☐
2. 外で仕事をする	☐	☐	☐	☐
3. 機械を使う	☐	☐	☐	☐
4. コンピュータを使う	☐	☐	☐	☐
5. 外国語を使う	☐	☐	☐	☐
6. 人とよく話す	☐	☐	☐	☐
7. 一人で仕事をする	☐	☐	☐	☐
8. 料理をする	☐	☐	☐	☐
9. 子供と一緒にいる	☐	☐	☐	☐
10. 計算をする	☐	☐	☐	☐

アクティビティー　4

賛成ですか。反対ですか。(*Do you agree or disagree?*)

Decide whether you agree or disagree with the following statements. Then
compare your opinions with those of your classmates and discuss in class.

1. 男は外で仕事をし、女はうちで家事をしている方がいい。
2. 夫婦は子供は二人以上いらない。
3. 結婚するより、恋人と一緒に住んだ方がいい。
4. 夫婦げんかするより、離婚した方がいい。
5. 両親が年をとったら、子供と一緒に住んだ方がいい。
6. 未成年は結婚しない方がいい。

Communication and Media

日本人はテレビを見るのが大好きです。

Objectives

In this lesson, you are going to

- Talk about telecommunication
- Talk about postal service
- Talk about media, entertainment, and journalism
- Learn how to use the ば conditionals
- Learn more about expressing respect
- Learn to express causative-passives
- Learn to express concession
- Learn how to write a letter
- Learn how to make a phone call
- Learn to communicate at the post office

Vocabulary and Grammar 6A

Vocabulary and Oral Activities

Telecommunications

Vocabulary: Telephone

電話が鳴る	でんわがなる	the phone rings
電話を切る	でんわをきる	to hang up the phone
内線	ないせん	extension
問い合わせる	といあわせる	to inquire
電話ボックス	でんわボックス	telephone booth
通話料	つうわりょう	telephone charge
長距離電話	ちょうきょりでんわ	long-distance call
国際電話	こくさいでんわ	international call
コレクトコール		collect call
ダイヤル(する)		dial (to dial)
プッシュホン		push-button telephone
留守番電話	るすばんでんわ	telephone answering machine
ファックス		facsimile; fax machine
話し中	はなしちゅう	(the line is) busy
ポケベル		pager, beeper
間違い電話	まちがいでんわ	wrong number
いたずら電話	いたずらでんわ	annoying call; crank call
伝言	でんごん	telephone message

Review: 電話、(に)電話(を)する、(に)電話をかける、電話番号、電話帳

CULTURE NOTE • 公衆電話 (*Public Telephones*)

Although the disparity is rapidly closing, especially with the recent proliferation of cellular or mobile phones (携帯電話 [けいたいでんわ]) and pagers, as a national average Japanese households are less likely to have a private home telephone than North American households are. Thus you still see more public telephones in a Japanese community than in a North American community of the same size, but it is reported that the number has begun to fall.

All telephone calls, both local and long distance, are priced by the minute, and until the early 1980s, people needed to have a good supply of ten-yen and hundred-yen coins on hand before making a call from a phone booth. It's not surprising, therefore, that pre-paid debit cards, or テレホン・カード, became popular in Japan long before they were available in North America. Companies issue commemorative telephone cards for special occasions or the release of new products, and some people simply buy and collect the most colorful cards without ever using them to make calls.

公衆電話で：これからお伺いしてよろしいでしょうか。

✻ アクティビティー　1

何ですか。誰ですか。(*What is it? Who is it?*)

Match the definitions in the first column with the appropriate words in the second column.

1. 外国に電話すること
2. 電話番号を知りたい時に見る本
3. 電話を受け取る (*receive*) 人がお金を払う通話 (*conversation*)
4. 家にいない時にメッセージを取って (*take*) おいてくれる機械
5. ダイヤルのかわりに (*in place of*) ボタンが付いている電話
6. 町の中にある誰でも使える電話

a. 国際電話
b. 公衆電話
c. コレクトコール
d. 電話帳
e. プッシュホン
f. 留守番電話

Communication and Media

よく長電話^{ながでんわ}しますか。(*Do you often make lengthy phone calls?*)

Answer these questions.

1. よく長電話^{ながでんわ}しますか。誰^{だれ}と話しますか。
2. 何分以上^{なにじょう}の電話が長電話^{ながでんわ}だと思いますか。
3. よく国際電話^{こくさい}をかけますか。どの国^{くに}にかけますか。
4. 電話帳^{ちょう}をよく使いますか。それとも、交換手^{こうかんしゅ}に聞きますか。番号案内^{ばんごうあんない}は何番ですか。
5. 火事^{かじ}(*fire*) の時の電話番号^{ばんごう}は何番ですか。
6. 留守番電話^{るすばん}を持^もっていますか。
7. あなたの町の市外局番^{しがい}(*area code*) は何番ですか。
8. いたずら電話をされたことがありますか。

Telephone and Telegram

受話器を取る	じゅわきをとる	to pick up the receiver
かけ直す	かけなおす	to call back
テレホン・カード		prepaid telephone card
携帯電話	けいたいでんわ	cellular phone
通話	つうわ	telephone conversation
電報(を打つ)	でんぽう(をうつ)	telegram (to send a telegram)

Grammar and Practice Activities

33. ば-Conditionals

カワムラ： 長野^{ながの}の明日のお天気^{てんき}を知^しりたいんですが、...

山口^{やまぐち}： 新聞^{しんぶん}のお天気欄^{てんきらん}を見^みれば、書いてありますよ。

カワムラ： ああ、そうでしたね。長野^{ながの}までの道路情報^{どうろじょうほう}も新聞^{しんぶん}に書いてありますか。

山口^{やまぐち}： いいえ、それは (3264)1331番に電話すれば、教^{おし}えてくれますよ。

KAWAMURA: I'd like to know tomorrow's weather for Nagano.　YAMAGUCHI: If you look at the weather section of the newspaper, it's written there.　KAWAMURA: Oh, that's right. Does the paper report the condition of the road to Nagano?　YAMAGUCHI: If you dial (3264) 1331, they'll give you the information.

林：　このへんは便利そうだね。

ブラウン：　ええ、その角を右に曲がれば、すぐスーパーだし、左へ
曲がればコイン・ランドリーもあるし…

林：　いい所に住んでるね。

ブラウン：　大学にもう少し近ければ、もっといいんだけど。

33.1 You have already learned two constructions, 〜たら and …と, that can correspond to the English *if*. The third and last one is 〜ば, which can attach to either verbs or adjectives. Its uses overlap somewhat with those of both 〜たら and …と, but in some ways it is more restricted than either of the other forms.

33.2 The ば conditional is formed as shown in the table.

RULE	EXAMPLES
Class 1 verbs: root + the e-column of hiragana + 〜ば	洗えば、書けば、読めば、わかれば、待てば、呼べば
Class 2 verbs: root + 〜れば	見れば、食べれば、起きれば
Class 3 verbs: change 〜る to 〜れば	すれば、来れば
Copula and na-adjectives: change だ or です to なら (ば) or であれば	きれいなら、学生なら、便利なら きれいであれば、学生であれば、便利であれば
I-adjectives and negative endings: root + the e-column of hiragana + 〜ば	安ければ、むずかしければ、いかなければ 高くなければ

33.3 The 〜ば conditional states a hypothetical condition that is necessary for the resultant clause to come about. The condition has to be something that has not yet occurred and perhaps may not occur but is still necessary for a certain result. Compare the following examples, all of which can be translated as, *If it snows, we can go skiing.*

1. 雪が降ったらスキーに行けます。
2. 雪が降るとスキーに行けます。
3. 雪が降ればスキーに行けます。

HAYASHI: This neighborhood looks convenient.　BROWN: Yes, if you turn right at that corner, there's a supermarket right there. If you turn left, there's a laundromat.　HAYASHI: You live in a good place. BROWN: It would be better if it were a little closer to the university.

Example 1 means something like, *If or when it snows, we can go skiing.*
Example 2 carries the connotation of, *When(ever) it snows, we can go skiing.*
However, Example 3 means something like, *If and only if it snows, we can go skiing.* It answers the underlying question, *Under what condition will we be able to go skiing?*

33.4 You have already seen the negative form, 〜なければ, in Chapter 1,
Grammar 8, in the form of the construction 〜なければなりません. However,
〜なければ used by itself carries the connotation of the English word *unless,* as
in the following sample sentences.

> あの本を読まなければわかりません。
> *If you don't read* (or *unless you read*) *that book, you won't understand.*
> ちゃんと練習しなければ危ないですよ。
> *If you don't practice* (or *unless you practice*) *properly, it's dangerous.*

33.5 Normally, the resultant clause cannot be a command, request, invitation,
wish, or expression of intention. If you want to say something like, *If I go to
Kyoto, I think I want to stay in a traditional inn,* you need to use the 〜たら
form:

> もし京都に行ったら、旅館に泊まりたいと思います。

The exception is when the conditional clause is built around an adjective or a
nonaction verb.

> 安ければ買いましょう。
> *If it is cheap, let's buy it.*
> 時間があればシーツなども洗ってください。
> *If you have time, please wash the sheet, etc., too.*

33.6 The construction 〜ばいいです can be used to give advice about some
future situation. The meaning is something like, *All you have to do is…* This is
similar to the 〜たらいいです construction, but it is usually not used to give
advice about a current situation.

> 店員に聞けばいいです。
> *All you have to do is ask a store employee.*
> 砂糖を入れればいいです。
> *All you have to do is add sugar.*

33.7 You can also express wishes and hopes using the construction 〜ばいい
ですが／けど／のに. You are literally saying that it would be good if only a
certain thing would happen, but the が, けど, or のに at the end indicates that
this desired thing has, in fact, not happened.

> 車があればいいのに！
> *I wish I had a car!*

Vocabulary and Grammar 6A

カワムラさんがダンス・パーティーに誘ってくれればいいんだけど…
I wish Mr. Kawamura would invite me to the dance.

満点が取れればいいんですが…
I wish I could get a perfect score.

33.8 An idiomatic use of the 〜ば form is in a construction comparable to the English *the more…the…* For example:

古ければ古いほどおもしろいです。
The older it is, the more interesting it is.
まじめならまじめなほど上手になります。
The more serious they are, the more skillful they become.
これは使えば使うほど気に入ります。
The more you use this, the more you will like it.

33.9 The irregular 〜ば form of the copula, なら, is used in a variant of the conditional construction. The pattern is verb/adjective/noun + なら. In this construction, you are taking the current situation or something that another person has said as the basis for your conjecture. It is comparable to the English, *If, as you say,…* or, *If it is true that …*

鈴木さんが来ないなら、私は帰ります。
If (as you say) Ms. Suzuki isn't coming, I'll go home.
コンピュータが故障しているなら、タイプライターを使いましょう。
If (it is true that) the computer is broken, let's use the typewriter.

This construction is similar in meaning to …のだったら.

33.10 Contrary-to-fact wishes, in which you wish that something had happened, even though it in fact did not happen, are expressed with either the 〜ば or the 〜たら form followed by よかった. The addition of …のですが or のに at the end implies that the speaker is scolding or criticizing another person for having failed to do something.

予約すればよかった。
I wish I had made a reservation.
もっと練習したらよかったのに！
I wish you had practiced more!
行かなければよかった。
I wish I hadn't gone.
何か言ったらよかったのに！
I wish you had said something!

33.11 In the case of contrary-to-fact conditionals, that is, sentences in which you say that if X had happened, then Y would have happened or would happen, but in fact, neither X nor Y happened, the first clause goes into the 〜たら or 〜ば form, and the second clause goes into the past tense + のですが construction. Like the contrary-to-fact wishes, this construction makes little sense when translated literally into English, so just learn it as a pattern and don't try to analyze it.

前もって (*beforehand*) こういうことを知っていれば、彼とは結婚しなかったんですが...
If I had known these things beforehand, I wouldn't have married him.
もし警察 (*police*) が早く来ていたら、皆助かったのですが...
If the police had come quickly, everyone would have been rescued.

✳ アクティビティー 3

ダイアログ：図書館に電話すれば、教えてくれるわよ。(*If you call the library, they'll tell you.*)

カワムラ： <u>東京の人口</u>が知りたいんですが、どうすればいいでしょうか。

山口： <u>図書館</u>に電話すれば、教えてくれるわよ。

カワムラ： <u>図書館</u>の電話番号はわかりますか。

山口： 電話帳を見れば、わかるわ。私が調べてあげるわ。

Practice the dialogue, substituting the items in the first column for the first underlined section and the items in the second column for the items in the second and third underlined sections.

1. 国際電話料金   KDD
2. 映画の時間   映画館
3. 明日のお天気   天気案内 (*weather information*)
4. 田中さんの住所 (*address*)   田中さんの会社

> KDD is the largest international phone company in Japan. KDD is an abbreviation of Kokusai Denshin Denwa Gaisha (International Telegraph and Telephone Company). The largest domestic telephone company in Japan is NTT, Nippon Telephone and Telegraph Company.

アクティビティー 4

もう少し安ければ... (*If it were a little cheaper...*)

Complete these sentences with a logical conclusion to the condition.

[例] ビデオを持っていれば、→
ビデオを持っていれば古い映画が見られます。

KAWAMURA: I'd like to know the population of Tokyo. What should I do?   YAMAGUCHI: If you call the library, they'll tell you.   KAWAMURA: Do you know the library's phone number?   YAMAGUCHI: If you look in the directory, you can find out. I'll look it up for you.

Vocabulary and Grammar 6A

303
三百三

1. コンピュータを使えば、
2. 今日の新聞を読めば
3. あの人が数学の先生であれば、
4. アパートがもう少し駅に近ければ、
5. 明日、天気が良ければ、
6. 病気でなければ、
7. もう少し安ければ、
8. もっと勉強しなければ、

アクティビティー　5

バスで行けば早いですよ。(*It'll be fast if you go by bus.*)

Complete the following dialogues by using the ば-conditional form of an appropriate predicate. Choose from among the predicates listed.

[例]　A: 日本に一週間しかいなかったんですか。
　　　B: ええ、もっと時間が＿＿＿、もっといたんですが。 → あれば

Choices:　見る、暇がある、高い、タクシーで行く、安い、来ている、飲む、なる

1. A: 桜 (*cherry blossoms*) はまだ咲きません (*bloom*) か。
   B: ええ、まだです。もう少し暖かく＿＿＿、咲くでしょう。
2. A: 次の電車は何時でしょうか。
   B: あそこの時刻表を＿＿＿、わかりますよ。
3. A: 頭が痛いんですが、
   B: この薬を＿＿＿、頭痛も直りますよ。
4. A: ケーキ、まだありますか。
   B: もう少し早く＿＿＿、あったんですが...
5. A: 前に人がいっぱいいて、パレードが全然見えませんね。
   B: ええ、もう少し背が＿＿＿、見えるんですが...
6. A: これから「ニンジャ5」を見に行くんですよ。
   B: ＿＿＿、私も来週行きますから、場所を教えてください。

アクティビティー　6

ねむいですか。コーヒーを飲めばいいですよ。(*Are you sleepy? You should drink some coffee.*)

Make suggestions to the following people by using ～ばいいですよ。

[例]　頭が痛いんですが、... → この薬を飲めばいいですよ。

1. 日本語の会話が上手になりたいんですが、…
2. おいしい日本料理を食べたいんですが、…
3. この町のことをもっと知りたいんですが、どうすればいいですか。
4. アメリカの歴史について知りたいんですが、どうすればいいですか。
5. この本を明日までにワシントンに送りたいんですが、どうすればいいですか。
6. ドライブしたいんですが、車がないんです。
7. 旅行中なんですが、トラベラーズチェックを落としてしまったんです。
8. 明日試験なんですが、全然勉強していないんです。どうすればいいですか。

✳ アクティビティー 7

どうすればいいですか。(*What should I do?*)

Give instructions in response to the questions, forming your answers along the
lines of the example.

[例] この書類を早く日本に送りたいんですが、どうすればいいですか。
（ファックスを使う）→
ファックスを使えばいいですよ。

1. 電車の中に忘れ物をしたんですが、どうすればいいですか。
（駅に電話してみる）（駅に行ってみる）

2. いたずら電話で困っているんですが、どうすればいいですか。
（電話局 [*telephone company*] に電話する）（電話番号を変える）

3. 家にいない時に、電話がたくさんかかってくるんですが、どうすればいいですか。
（留守番電話を買う）（ポケベルを使う）

Now come up with your own solutions for these problems.

4. 娘が長電話をして困っているんですが、どうすればいいですか。

5. 日本語が上手になりたいんですが、どうすればいいですか。

6. 日本の大学で勉強したいので、日本の大学について調べたいんですが、どうすればいいですか。

7. 日本に一年間住みたいんですが、お金がありません。どうすればいいですか。

Now work in pairs. Each of you makes up three questions concerning a problem or puzzling situation, using the form ...どうすればいいですか.Then answer each other's questions.

34. Wanting to Have Something Done: 〜てほしい

カワムラ： 大助さん、ちょっとこの日本語の宿題を見てもらいたいんですが...

大助： ああ、いいよ。日本語ならおやすい御用だ。

カワムラ： 特に漢字が正しく書けているか調べてほしいんです。

大助： わあ、カワムラさん、上手な日本語を書きますね。

鈴木： 係長、この書類に判を押していただきたいのですが。

村山： はい、ここですね。

鈴木： それから、今日はちょっと早く帰らせていただきたいのですが...

村山： どうしたんですか。

The following constructions can be used when stating that you would like to have someone do something for you.

(A は)	(B に)	Te-form of the verb	ほしい／ほしいです もらいたい／もらいたいです いただきたい／ いただきたいです

For the usage of ほしい, refer to Chapter 6 of Book 1.

A wants to have something done (by B).

林さんに話してほしいんですか。
Do you want me to talk with Mr. Hayashi?
ちょっとテレビをつけてほしいんだけど...
I want you to turn on the TV.
郵便局へ行ってきてもらいたいんですが...
I would like you to go to the post office.

When A and B are obvious from the context, you don't have to express them.

KAWAMURA: Daisuke, I want you to take a look at this Japanese homework.　DAISUKE: Yes, of course. If it's Japanese, it's no problem.　KAWAMURA: I especially want you to check if the **kanji** are written correctly.　DAISUKE: Wow, Mr. Kawamura, you write good Japanese.

SUZUKI: Section Chief, I want you to put your seal to this paper.　MURAYAMA: Yes, here it is.
SUZUKI: Also, I want you to let me leave a little early today.　MURAYAMA: What's going on?

Communication and Media

The combination of the te-form of the verb and ほしい or もらいたい is used when A's social status is equal or superior to B's. When B's social status is superior to A's, いただきたい must be used.

もらいたい is the たい form of もらう. See Chapter 6 of Book 1 and Chapter 1 of Book 2.

私たちは先生に参加していただきたいんですが、...
We would like you to attend, please, Professor.

When A is the third person, the te-form of the verb + もらいたがっている or いただきたがっている is usually used. Alternatively, you may be able to use もらいたいそうだ or いただきたいそうだ.

いただく is the humble form of もらう. いただきたい is the たい form of いただく. See Chapter 6 of Book 1 and Chapter 1 of Book 2.

カーティスさんは林さんにこの葉書を読んでもらいたがっています。
Mr. Curtis would like Mr. Hayashi to read this postcard.
学生たちは横井先生にもテレビに出ていただきたいそうです。
The students would like Professor Yokoi to appear on TV.

When asking someone not to do something, you can use either ～ないでほしい (です) or ～てほしくない (です).

仕事中は私用電話をしないでほしいですね。
I want you not to make private calls during working hours.
家族がいることを忘れてほしくないです。
I don't want you to forget that you have a family.

✳ アクティビティー　8

ダイアログ：早く連絡してほしいそうよ。(*He says he wants you to contact him quickly.*)

カワムラ：　ただいま。

山口：　ああ、カワムラさん。おかえりなさい。林さんからお電話が
あって、早く連絡してほしいそうよ。

カワムラ：　本当？何だろう。

山口：　わかんないわ。でも、何だか急いでいたみたい。

Practice the dialogue, replacing the underlined part with the following phrases.

1. 駅前の喫茶店に来る

2. 町田さんの家に電話する

わかんない is a contraction of わからない.

JOHN KAWAMURA: I'm back.　　YAMAGUCHI: Welcome back, Mr. Kawamura. There was a call from Mr. Hayashi, and he said he wanted you to contact him quickly.　　KAWAMURA: Really? I wonder what it's about.　　YAMAGUCHI: I don't know, but somehow he sounded in a hurry.

3. すぐにブラウンさんに会う
4. 横井先生のお宅の電話番号を教える

アクティビティー 9

今どこにいますか。(*Where are we right now?*)

Where do you think you would hear the following statements? Match the statements in the first column with the appropriate places in the second column.

1. そのお塩、取ってほしいんだけど...
2. これを30部、コピーしてもらいたいんだけど...
3. クラスに遅刻 (*tardiness*) しないでほしいね。
4. そこを右に曲がってほしいんですが...
5. ちょっと静かにしてほしいんですが... みんな本を読んでいるんですから。
6. このトースター、直してほしいんですが...

a. 図書館
b. タクシーの中
c. 電気屋
d. 会社のオフィス
e. 学校
f. 台所

アクティビティー 10

父に早く帰ってほしい。(*I want Father to get back soon.*)

Complete the following dialogue by using an appropriate verb ＋ 〜てほしい or 〜ていただきたい.

1. A: 林さん、この椅子を ＿＿＿＿。
   B: ええ、いいですよ。どこへ動かしましょうか。

2. A: 先生、この作文を ＿＿＿＿。
   B: どれどれ。ああ、なかなかよく書けていますね。

3. A: 部長、ここに ＿＿＿＿。
   B: ああ、いいよ。ペンはあるかね。

4. A: ブラウンさん、町田さんに ＿＿＿＿。
   B: はい、わかりました。横井先生、町田さんの電話番号はお持ちですか。

5. A: 高田さん、ちょっと郵便局へ＿＿＿＿。
   B: あのう、すみませんけど、今、ちょっと手が放せないんですが。
6. A: 部長、午後の会議に＿＿＿＿。
   B: 悪いけど、午後はちょっと。

アクティビティー　11

教えていただきたいんです。(*I'd like you to teach me.*)

How would you make a request in the following situations? Answer using
〜てほしい, 〜てもらいたい, 〜ていただきたい, and so on.

1. Ask your friend not to call you after 10 P.M.
2. Ask your professor to teach you how to use a computer.
3. Ask your friend not to move from where he or she is now.
4. Ask your subordinate to come to the office at 7:00 A.M. tomorrow.
5. Ask a stranger on the street to tell you the way to the post office.

アクティビティー　12

何をしてほしいですか。何をしてもらいたいですか。(*What do you want him or her to do?*)

What do you say in the following situations? Express your requests following the example.

Useful Vocabulary: くずす *to change; to break*, 千円札を百円玉にくずす
to break a 1,000-yen note into 100-yen coins.

[例] 公衆電話で長電話している人がいます。10人以上の人が順番 (*turn*)
を待っています。→
「長電話 (*long phone conversations*) は、やめてほしいです。」or
「長電話しないでほしいです。」

1. 日本語の先生がまた宿題を出そうとしています。他の授業
   (*class session*) の宿題がたくさんあります。
2. 公衆電話から電話しようとしましたが、こまかいお金がありません。
3. おなかがとてもすきました。何か食べるものを買いにいきたいんです
   が、仕事が忙しくて行けません。友達が買い物に行ってくると言って
   います。

4. あなたは真面目な学生です。日本語の授業ではいつも日本語を話す
   ようにしています。でも、あなたの隣の人はいつも英語で話します。

5. また、今日もいたずら電話がかかってきました。

6. またです。あなたの隣の人はいつもあなたのペンを使います。使う
   だけでなく、いつも持っていってしまいます。

…だけで[は]なく

…だけで[は]なく—the は is optional—means *not only… (but also)*.
Nouns, pronouns, and the plain form of adjectives and verbs may be
used before it. The clause following it often contains も *also*.

カワムラさんはハンサムなだけでなく、とても親切だ。
Mr. Kawamura is not only handsome, he's very kind.
見ているだけでなく、食べてみてください。
Don't just look at it; try eating it.

In ordinary colloquial speech, じゃなくて is often used instead of
で[は]なく.

アメリカだけじゃなくてカナダへも行きたいです。
I would like to go not just to America but also to Canada.

Vocabulary and Grammar 6B

Vocabulary and Oral Activities

Post Office

Vocabulary: Mail and Postal Service (1)

郵便	ゆうびん	mail
郵便を出す	ゆうびんをだす	to mail
Xを郵便で送る	Xをゆうびんでおくる	to send X by mail
郵便ポスト	ゆうびんポスト	mailbox (*for depositing items to be mailed*)

封筒	ふうとう	envelope
便箋	びんせん	stationery
葉書	はがき	postal card
切手を貼る	きってをはる	to put a stamp on
小包	こづつみ	package
郵便番号	ゆうびんばんごう	postal code (*comparable to the ZIP code in the United States*)
受け取る	うけとる	to receive
はんこ		seal
返事(を書く)	へんじ(をかく)	(to write a) reply
配達(する)	はいたつ(する)	delivery (to deliver)
船便	ふなびん	surface mail
航空便	こうくうびん	airmail
速達	そくたつ	express mail
書留	かきとめ	registered mail
現金書留	げんきんかきとめ	cash registered mail
宛て名	あてな	recipient's address
宅配便	たくはいびん	door-to-door package delivery

Review: 絵葉書、(を)送る、切手、住所、手紙、郵便局

✳ **アクティビティー 13**

手紙を出します。(*I'm going to mail a letter.*)

You would like to write and mail a letter. Number the following actions in the order that they would normally occur. Three are already numbered for you.

__9__ 封筒の重さを計ってもらう

____ 郵便局に行く

____ 手紙を書く

____ 封筒に封をする (*to seal*)

____ 便箋を折る (*to fold*)

____ 必要な切手を買う

__1__ 文房具屋に行って、便箋と封筒を買う

____ 切手を封筒に貼る

____ 封筒に宛て名を書く

____ 封筒を郵便ポストに入れる

__5__ 便箋を封筒に入れる

手紙にしますか。電話にしますか。(*Do you do it by mail or by phone?*)

Answer these questions.

1. よく手紙を書きますか。誰に書きますか。
2. よく郵便が来ますか。どんな郵便が来ますか。
3. どんな時に小包を出しますか。
4. 近所に郵便局はありますか。どんな時に郵便局に行きますか。
5. 両親にお金を送ってほしい時、手紙を書きますか。電話をかけますか。
6. 郵便が電話よりいい点は何ですか。
7. 電話が郵便よりいい点は何ですか。
8. あなたの国の切手にはどんな絵がかかれていますか。

言語ノート

...することがある

In Chapter 6 of *Yookoso!*, Book 1, you learned to use the ta-form of the verb + ことがある construction to express the idea that you have had the experience of doing something. Using the nonpast, plain form of predicates gives you a construction meaning that you do the action occasionally. Here are some examples:

> ファースト・フードを食べることがある。
> *I occasionally eat fast food.*
> あの先生でもきびしいことがある。
> *Even that professor is strict from time to time.*

If you substitute も for が, you are admitting that you do the action but implying that this happens only rarely. This construction is usually followed by an explanation or contradiction.

> ファースト・フードを食べることもありますけれども、
>   たいていは自分で料理します。
> *There are occasions when I eat fast food, but usually I do my
>   own cooking.*

In place of こと, you may use とき (*time*) or 場合 (*case*). The use of 場合 makes the resulting sentence sound formal.

> 家では、ラジオを聞いているときもあります。
> *I occasionally listen to the radio at home.*

部長が会議に出席する場合もある。

There are occasions when the department head attends meetings.

When the negative form appears before こと, forms such as these are used.

週末は全然勉強しないことがある。

I occasionally don't study at all on weekends.

あの先生の試験はむずかしくないことがない。

There's never a time when that professor's tests aren't difficult. (Or, That professor's tests are always difficult.)

The question form of this construction means, *Does it ever happen that...?*

横井先生はクラスを休講になさることがありますか。

Does Professor Yokoi ever cancel her class?

カワムラさんから電話が来ることがある？

Do you ever get phone calls from Mr. Kawamura?

✳ アクティビティー 15

ダイアログ：現金書留で現金を送ることはありますか。(*Are there occasions when you send cash by registered mail?*)

ブラウン：山本さんは<u>現金書留で現金を送る</u>ことはありますか。

山本：<u>一年に二・三回ぐらい送ることがあります</u>。

ブラウン：めんどうですか。

山本：いいえ、簡単ですよ。

ブラウン：じゃあ、今度<u>送り方</u>を教えてくださいね。

Practice the dialogue, replacing the first underlined part with a selection from the first column and the second underlined part with a selection from the second column. Change the last underlined part appropriately.

1. 宅配便でものを送る　　　時々送ることがあります
2. 郵便為替でお金を送る　　あまり送ったことがありません
3. テレホンカードを使う　　いつも使っています
4. 記念切手を買う　　　　　一年に四・五回買うことがあります
5. 電報を打つ　　　　　　　最近は少なくなりました

BROWN: Ms. Yamamoto, are there occasions when you send cash by registered mail?　YAMAMOTO: <u>Two or three times a year.</u>　BROWN: Is it difficult to send cash by registered mail?　YAMAMOTO: No, it's easy. BROWN: Next time, please tell me <u>how to send it</u>.

Vocabulary and Grammar 6B

CULTURE NOTE • Special Services at the Post Office

The Japanese postal system offers a service not found in most countries: guaranteed registered mailing of cash (現金書留 [げんきんかきとめ]). However, even though Japan has an enviably low crime rate, people don't just stick the cash into any old envelope and drop it into the nearest mailbox. Instead, they go to the post office, fill out forms, and put the money into a special envelope like the one shown here before handing it to the postal clerk.

Another service offered by the post office is the postal savings account (郵便貯金 [ゆうびんちょきん]). Before the spread of automatic teller machines, this kind of account offered the advantage of allowing customers to deposit and withdraw money at any post office in the country.

The postal system carries off an impressive feat at New Year's. When people check their mail on New Year's Day, they find all the New Year's cards (年賀状 [ねんがじょう]) that their friends and associates have sent them, bundled and lying in their mailbox. In other words, the post office saves up and sorts all New Year's cards mailed by a certain date so that they may be delivered on the same day throughout the country.

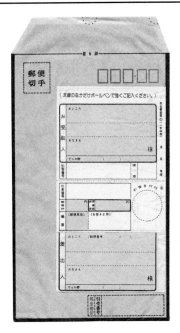

Vocabulary Library

Mail and Postal Service (2)

郵便局員	ゆうびんきょくいん	post office clerk
往復葉書	おうふくはがき	return postal card (*with a prepaid detachable portion for the recipient's reply*)
年賀状	ねんがじょう	New Year's card
差出人	さしだしにん	sender

Loanword: エアメール

Grammar and Practice Activities

35. Expressing Respect (3): Honorifics

近藤：部長は今日はいらっしゃらないんですか。

高田：ええ、出張で今朝、金沢へ行かれました。

近藤：いつお帰りになりますか。

高田：今夜は金沢に泊まられて、明日の夜、東京に帰られます。会社には月曜日から出られると思います。

The passive form of the verb can also be used as an honorific. These honorific forms look exactly the same as the passives you studied in Chapter 5, but no passive meaning is implied.

Class 1	Root + the a-column of hiragana + れる	書く 読む 買う	書かれる 読まれる 買われる
Class 2	Root + られる	食べる	食べられる
Class 3	Irregular	する 来る	される 来られる

先生は黒板にご自分のお名前を書かれた。
The professor wrote his/her own name on the board.
社長はもうこのレポートを読まれましたか。
President, did you already read this report?

The degree of politeness expressed by this form is not as high as in the お + verb + になる form and in the special honorific forms introduced in Chapter 5. The ～られる form of a Class 2 verb is ambiguous in that it can express an honorific meaning, a passive meaning, or a potential meaning. The following sentence illustrates the ambiguity.

KONDOO: Isn't the department head in today?　TAKADA: No, he went to Kanazawa on business this morning.　KONDOO: When will he return?　TAKADA: He'll stay overnight in Kanazawa and return to Tokyo tomorrow night. He'll be back in the office as of Monday.

横井先生はてんぷらを食べられました。
Professor Yokoi ate tempura (honorific).
Professor Yokoi had (her) tempura eaten (by someone else)
    (indirect/adversative passive).
Professor Yokoi could eat tempura (potential).

In cases like these, you have to figure out the correct meaning from the context.

アクティビティー 16

先生、お帰りになりますか。(*Are you going home, Professor?*)

Rewrite the following sentences in their corresponding お + verb + になる or special honorific forms.

[例]　山口さん、先に帰られて、結構ですよ。→
　　　山口さん、先にお帰りになって、結構ですよ。

1. 社長は何時にパリを発たれますか。
2. 先生、今日の新聞を読まれましたか。
3. 横井先生はそのことをもう聞かれているそうですよ。
4. 部長も会議室に来られるようです。
5. 先生もパーティーに行かれないんですか。
6. 社長のお嬢さんが先週、結婚された。
7. 1時のニュースをラジオで聞かれましたか。
8. 社長、奥様にはどのようにして会われたんですか。

アクティビティー 17

いつ聞かれましたか。(*When did you hear it?*)

Rewrite the following sentences using れる／られる honorific forms.

[例]　町田さんに電話しましたか。→ 町田さんに電話されましたか。

1. 山口さんは私の横に座った。
2. 明日の会議に出ますか。
3. 何時の新幹線に乗りますか。
4. カワムラさんと会いますか。

5. もうあのニュースは聞きましたか。
6. ちょっとこのへんを歩きませんか。
7. これでいいと思いますか。
8. 社長はこのペンを使った。

✳ アクティビティー 18

クラスメートと先生にインタビューしましょう。(*Let's interview our classmates and instructor.*)

Work in pairs. Ask these questions of your partner and write down his or her answers.

1. 一週間に何通ぐらい手紙を書きますか。
2. 友達からの手紙に返事を書きますか。
3. 手紙を書くのが好きですか。
4. 一日に何回電話をかけますか。
5. 留守番電話を使っていますか。
6. 誰に一番よく電話をしますか。

Next, discuss with your partner what forms would be most appropriate for asking the same questions of a superior, such as your instructor. Then ask your instructor the six questions, using the proper honorific forms and writing down the answers. Discuss in Japanese the comparison between your partner's answers and your instructor's. (Don't forget to use honorifics when discussing your instructor's answers.)

36. Causative-Passives

高田：　ブラウンさん、遅くなって、ごめん。
ブラウン：　いいえ、私もさっき来たばかりです。
高田：　部長の手伝いをさせられていて、遅くなってしまったんだ。
ブラウン：　高田さんの部長さんはいろいろなことをさせるんですね。

TAKADA: Ms. Brown, I'm sorry for being late.　BROWN: That's OK. I arrived just a couple of minutes ago, too.　TAKADA: I was made to help my department head, so I ended up being late.　BROWN: Your department head makes you do all sorts of things, doesn't he?

カワムラ： 大助さん、昨日のパーティーはどうでしたか。

山口： いやあ、みんなの前で歌を歌わせられたり、踊りを
踊らせられたりして、大変でしたよ。

カワムラ： 大助さんは歌も踊りも得意だったんじゃないんですか。

山口： とんでもない！

The passive form of the causative form, generally called the causative-passive form, is used to express the meaning *to be made to do something (by someone)*.

CLASS	THE FORMATION OF THE CAUSATIVE	EXAMPLES	
Class 1	Root + the a-column of hiragana + せられる	書く	書かせられる
Class 2	Root + させられる	食べる	食べさせられる
Class 3	Irregular	する 来る	させられる 来させられる

In this construction, the person who makes someone do something is marked by に, while the person who is made to do something by someone else is marked with は or が.

Xは／が	Yに	(Z を)	Causative-passive verb form

X is caused (forced, made) by Y to do Z.

その男に無理やり名前を書かされました。
I was forced by that man to write my name.
子供の時は、にんじんを食べさせられるのが嫌だったけど、
今はにんじんが大好きです。
When I was a child, I hated being forced to eat carrots, but now I like them.

KAWAMURA: How was the party yesterday?   YAMAGUCHI: Well, I was made to sing in front of everybody and to dance. It was terrible.   KAWAMURA: I thought you were good at both singing and dancing. YAMAGUCHI: No way!

Communication and Media

When the person who makes someone do something is clear from the context, or when it is not necessary to identify that person, Y に can be omitted in this construction.

みんなの前で話をさせられた。
I was forced to give a talk in front of everyone.

✳ アクティビティー　19

ダイアログ：年賀状の宛て名を書かせられるんです。(*I have to address the New Year's cards.*)

高田：ああ、手が痛くてたまらないや。
山本：高田さん、どうしたんですか。
高田：この季節になると、会社の年賀状の宛て名を書かせられるんです。
山本：それは大変ですね

Practice the dialogue, replacing the underlined parts with the following.

1. 足　　　会社のカレンダーを配り (*delivery*) に行かされる
2. 目　　　レポートをたくさん読まされる
3. 頭　　　パーティーでお酒をたくさん飲まされる

アクティビティー　20

いつも働かされます。(*I always have to work.*)

Following are complaints about three managers from their subordinates. Tell in English the name of each manager and the complaints against him or her.

[例]　私は田中部長にお弁当を買いに行かせられます。→ Tanaka makes subordinates buy box lunches for him.

1. 私は佐藤部長に私用の (*private*) 手紙をワープロで打たせられます。
2. 私は田中部長に遅くまで働かされます。
3. 僕は休みの日に山田部長にゴルフに一緒に行かされます。私は佐藤部長にパーティーでお酒を無理やり飲まされました。
4. 僕は山田部長に机の上の掃除をさせられました。

TAKADA: My hand hurts so much I can't stand it.　YAMAMOTO: Mr. Takada, what happened?
TAKADA: Around this time of year (lit., *around this season*), I have to address New Year's cards for the company.　YAMAMOTO: That's tough.

5. 私は佐藤部長に部長の友人の観光ガイドをさせられました。
6. 私は山田部長にいつもお茶を入れさせられます。

アクティビティー 21

歌わされた。(*They made me sing.*)

Rewrite the following sentences in the corresponding passive form.

[例] 部長はみんなにカラオケで歌わせた。→
みんなは部長にカラオケで歌わせられた。

1. あの課長はよく残業 (*overtime*) をさせます。
2. セールスマンは山口さんに事典を買わせた。
3. 母親は子供をおつかい (*errand*) に行かせました。
4. 先生は学生にそのダイアログを暗記 (*memorization*) させました。
5. 先生は日本の歴史に関する (*concerning*) 本を何冊も読ませました。
6. 警官 (*police officer*) は車のトランクを開けさせました。
7. 三村さんはチンさんにすしを食べさせました。
8. 部長は部下にお茶を入れさせました。

アクティビティー 22

部長にコピーを取らせられた。(*I was made to do the copying by the department head.*)

Following the example, complete the following causative and corresponding causative-passive sentences.

[例] (お中元を届ける)
部長は高田さんにお中元を届けさせた。
高田さんは部長にお中元を届けさせられた。

1. (テレビを修理する)
兄は弟に(　　　)。
弟は兄に(　　　)。
2. (サラダを食べる)
母親は子供に(　　　)。
子供は母親に(　　　)。
3. (ソファーに座る)
彼はカワムラさんを(　　　)。
カワムラさんは彼に(　　　)。
4. (ブラウンさんを呼ぶ)
彼はカワムラさんに(　　　)。
カワムラさんは彼に(　　　)。

したくなかったけど... (*I didn't want to do it, but...*)

Describe the situations shown in the following drawings using causative and causative-passive sentences. Assume that the subject of the passive-causative sentence is unhappy about the situation.

[例]　お母さんは子供に着物を着せました。→
　　　子供はお母さんに着物を着せられました。

1.　お母さんは子供に部屋を
　　子供はお母さんに部屋を

2.　お医者さんは山口さんにお酒を
　　山口さんはお医者さんにお酒を

3.　奥さんは御主人にダイヤの指輪を
　　御主人は奥さんにダイヤの指輪を

4.　部長は私に予算 (*budget*) を
　　私は部長に予算を
　　(予算を立てる = *draw up a budget*)

5.　兄は私に郵便局に
　　私は兄に郵便局に

Ex.

1.

2.

3.

4.

5.

仕事の不満 (*Dissatisfaction on the job*)

Everyone has some complaints about his or her job. What kinds of complaints do you think these people have? Following the example, write down these people's possible complaints using causative-passive, passive, and 〜なければならない.

[例] 外国語の先生

- 学生の下手な外国語を聞かなければならない。
- 学生の下手な作文を読まされる
- 学生の会話の相手をさせられる。
- 学生のいいわけ (*excuses*) を聞かされる

(Hey, we're just kidding!)

1. 電話交換手
2. 秘書
3. タクシーの運転手
4. 家庭の主婦

5. 日本のサラリーマン
6. Choose one occupation not mentioned.
7. What are your complaints as a student of the Japanese language?

Vocabulary and Grammar 6C

Vocabulary and Oral Activities

Media

Vocabulary: Mass Communication (1)

Newspapers

マスコミ		mass communication
ジャーナリズム		journalism
新聞をとる	しんぶんをとる	to subscribe to a newspaper
...に載る	...にのる	to appear in (*a publication*)
新聞記事	しんぶんきじ	newspaper article

| 広告（する） | こうこく（する） | advertisement (to advertise) |
| 記者 | きしゃ | reporter |

Review: インタビュー（する）、新聞、ニュース、〜部

Books, Publishing

出版（する）	しゅっぱん（する）	publishing (to publish)
週刊誌	しゅうかんし	weekly magazine
漫画	まんが	comic book; comic magazine; cartoon
事典	じてん	encyclopedia
小説	しょうせつ	novel
エッセイ		essay

Review: 教科書、〜冊、雑誌、辞書、本、本屋、料理の本

Broadcasting

放送（する）	ほうそう（する）	broadcasting (to broadcast)
NHK	エヌエイチケー	Nippon Hoosoo Kyookai 日本放送協会（*Japan's government-owned radio and television network*)
民放	みんぽう	commercial broadcasting
番組	ばんぐみ	(TV, radio) program
ホーム・ドラマ		soap opera
トーク・ショー		talk show
アニメ		animated cartoon
時代劇	じだいげき	samurai drama
連続ドラマ	れんぞくドラマ	dramatic series; miniseries
教育番組	きょういくばんぐみ	educational program
チャンネル（を変える）	チャンネル（をかえる）	(to change) channels
CM	シーエム	commercial (*from commercial message*)
スタジオ		studio
マイク		microphone
出演する	しゅつえんする	to appear (*as a performer*)
…に出る	（〜に）でる	to appear on… (*as a performer*)
司会者	しかいしゃ	MC
タレント		TV personality
アンテナ		antenna
衛星放送	えいせいほうそう	satellite broadcast

Review: カメラ、カラーテレビ、テレビ、天気予報、ドラマ、ビデオ、ラジオ

CULTURE NOTE • Television Stations and Newspapers

NHK, which has both a general-interest and an educational channel, is a semigovernmental network that does not broadcast any commercials and is supported by a monthly fee assessed on all television sets. In each local prefecture, you can usually watch two NHK stations and a few commercial stations that are affiliated with the Tokyo-based networks, but in the past decade, satellite and cable television have been reaching an increasing percentage of the population. Japanese television networks are unusual in that unlike networks in most other countries, they broadcast few American or other foreign series, and some American series that were hits everywhere else in the world have failed to interest Japanese viewers.

Japanese newspapers are divided into nationwide papers (全国紙［ぜんこくし］) such as **Asahi Shinbun** (朝日新聞), **Yomiuri Shinbun** (読売新聞), and **Mainichi Shinbun** (毎日新聞), which are available throughout the country and carry national and international news, and local papers (地方紙［ちほうし］), which are available only in a small area and concentrate on local news. In addition, four daily English-language newspapers serve the growing community of foreign residents and are widely available in the larger cities.

Communication and Media

アクティビティー 25

何ですか。(*What is it?*)

Match each of the definitions in the first column with the appropriate word from the second column.

1. 新聞記事を書く人
2. 一週間に一度出版される雑誌
3. 言葉 (*word*) の意味 (*meaning*) が
   わからない時に使うもの
4. テレビ、ラジオの番組の前後、途中の広告
5. ゲストにインタビューしたり、
   いろいろな話をしたりする番組
6. さむらいが出てくるドラマ
7. 外国語を教えたり、
   コンピュータの使い方を教えたりする番組
8. 人々に情報 (*information*) を伝える
   メディアのこと

a. 時代劇
b. CM
c. 教育番組
d. 辞書
e. 週刊誌
f. マスコミ
g. 新聞記者
h. トーク・ショー

アクティビティー 26

毎日新聞を読みますか。(*Do you read a newspaper every day?*)

Answer these questions.

1. 新聞をとっていますか。
2. 雑誌をとっていますか。どんな雑誌が好きですか。
3. 教科書以外 (*other than*) の本を読みますか。どんな本を読みますか。
4. よくテレビを見ますか。一日に何時間くらい見ますか。
5. あなたの国で一番人気のある番組は何ですか。
6. コマーシャルをどう思いますか。
7. テレビ番組で暴力 (*violence*) シーンが多すぎると思いますか。
8. 勉強しながら、ラジオを聞きますか。
9. テレビやラジオに出演したことがありますか。

Grammar and Practice Activities

37. Expressing Concession

高田：部長、橋本さんのお宅に何度電話しても、誰も出ないんですが…

部長：それはおかしいね。誰か橋本君がどこにいるか知らないのかね。

高田：それが、誰に聞いてもわからないんです。

部長：それはますますおかしいね。

言語ノート

…まま

まま is a noun expressing that a certain condition or state remains unchanged.

靴のまま、家に入らないで下さい。

Please don't enter the house with your shoes on.

寒かったので、コートを着たままでいました。

I kept wearing my coat because it was cold.

座ったまま、私の話を聞いて下さい。

Please listen to me while (still) seated.

まま also means *exactly as it is.*

見たままを書きなさい。

Write down exactly what you saw.

このままでいいですよ。

It's fine just like this.

そのままで食べてもいいです。

It's all right to eat it like that (just as it is).

> でいる is a variant of だ／です used only in reference to animate subjects and emphasizing their being in a continuous position or state.

The 〜ても and でも constructions are used to express dependent clauses meaning *even if* or *even though.*

忙しくても、新聞は毎日読む。

Even if I am busy, I read a newspaper every day.

TAKADA: Department Head, no matter how many times I call Mr. Hashimoto's house, no one answers.
DEPARTMENT HEAD: That's strange. Is there anyone who knows where Mr. Hashimoto is?　TAKADA: Well, no matter whom I ask, nobody seems to know.　DEPARTMENT HEAD: That's even more strange.

326   Communication and Media

彼<ruby>かれ</ruby>はハンサムでも、性格<ruby>せいかく</ruby>がよくないから好きじゃない。

Even though he is handsome, I don't like him because his personality is not good.

When you would like to emphasize the meaning of concession, you can add たとえ (*even granting that…*), かりに (*just supposing*), or 万が一 (*even in the unlikely event that…*). Another way to emphasize this meaning is to use a plain predicate + としても.

万<ruby>まん</ruby>が一<ruby>いち</ruby>我々<ruby>われわれ</ruby>の計画<ruby>けいかく</ruby>がうまくいかなくても、誰<ruby>だれ</ruby>にも言うな。

In the remote event that our plan doesn't go well, don't tell anyone.

かりにそれが冗談<ruby>じょうだん</ruby>だとしても、そんなことを言ってはいけない。

Even if it is a joke, don't say such a thing.

Interrogatives can be used in this clause to express ideas such as *no matter* (*what, who, when, where, how,* and so on).

誰<ruby>だれ</ruby>と話しても、みんながカワムラさんのことをほめる。

No matter whom I talk with, everyone praises Mr. Kawamura.

何を聞いても、林さんはわからないと言うだけだった。

Whatever we asked him, Mr. Hayashi just said he didn't know.

この町は、どこへ行っても清潔<ruby>せいけつ</ruby>です。

This town is clean wherever you go.

どう考<ruby>かんが</ruby>えても、その話はおかしい。

No matter how we think about it, that story is strange.

いくら練習<ruby>れんしゅう</ruby>しても、上達<ruby>じょうたつ</ruby> (improvement) しません。

No matter how much I practice, I don't improve.

The ても form of some adjectives expressing quantity or time mean *at the very…*

早くても3時まではかかります。

It will take until three o'clock at the earliest.

遅<ruby>おそ</ruby>くても朝9時までに家を出<ruby>で</ruby>なければ間<ruby>ま</ruby>に合<ruby>あ</ruby>わない。

We won't make it unless we leave home by nine in the morning at the latest.

多くても100人くらいしかパーティーに来ないだろう。

At most only one hundred people will come to the party.

This ても construction is semantically close to the use of が or けれども, meaning *but*.

手紙<ruby>てがみ</ruby>を出<ruby>だ</ruby>しても、返事<ruby>へんじ</ruby>をくれなかった。

Even though I sent him a letter, he didn't reply.

手紙<ruby>てがみ</ruby>を出<ruby>だ</ruby>したけれども、返事<ruby>へんじ</ruby>をくれなかった。

手紙<ruby>てがみ</ruby>を出<ruby>だ</ruby>したが、返事<ruby>へんじ</ruby>をくれなかった。

I sent him a letter, but he didn't reply.

Note, however, that けれども and が cannot be used with interrogatives. The ても construction can express a hypothetical situation, whereas a sentence containing が or けれども expresses only actions that have already happened or that are relatively certain to happen in the future. Compare:

手紙を出しても、返事をくれないでしょう。
Even if I send him a letter, he probably won't reply.
手紙を出してみるけれども、返事をくれないでしょう。
I'll try sending him a letter, but he probably won't reply.

アクティビティー　27

忙しくても手伝いますよ。(*Even though I'm busy, I'll help.*)
Answer the following questions.

[例]　下手でも、日本語をたくさん使うようにした方がいいですか。→
　　　はい下手でも、たくさん使った方がいいと思います。

1. 日本語の授業 (*class session*) のない日でも、日本語を勉強した方がいい
   ですか。
2. どんなに高くても、日本語のいい辞書を買いますか。
3. 勉強が忙しくても、運動はした方がいいですか。
4. どんなに給料が安くても、どんな仕事もいつもきちんとしなければ
   いけません。
5. どんなにむずかしい試験でも、最後まであきらめない
   (あきらめる means *give up*) でしますか。

アクティビティー　28

どんなにお金がかかっても... (*No matter how much money it takes...*)

Complete the following dialogues using verbs or adjectives ending in 〜ても.

[例]　A: 明日は雨が降りますよ。
　　　B: 雨が降っても、ジョギングはするつもりです。

1. A: 水はまだ冷たいかもしれませんよ。
   B: どんなに＿＿＿＿、サーフィンはできますよ。
2. A: これ、ちょっとまずいですよ。
   B: どんなに＿＿＿＿、おなかがすいているから、何でも食べますよ。
3. A: カワムラさんは今とても忙しいですよ。
   B: ＿＿＿＿、私には会ってくれますよ。

Communication and Media

4. A: 林さんと話してみたらどうですか。

   B: 林さんと ＿＿＿、わかってくれませんよ。

5. A: 大学へ行くのはお金がかかりますよ。

   B: どんなに ＿＿＿、子供は大学へ行かせたいんです。

6. A: 今日は土曜日ですよ。

   B: ＿＿＿、日本の学校では授業があるんですよ。

アクティビティー 29

今それをしなくてもいいですよ。(*It's OK if you don't do it now.*)

Complete the following sentences with a logical follow-up to the introductory phrase.

[例] 夏でも、＿＿＿。 →
     夏でも、セーターを着ているんですか。

1. どんなに天気がよくても、＿＿＿。
2. お金が全然なくても、＿＿＿。
3. どんなにがんばっても、＿＿＿。
4. どんなに彼が頼んでも、＿＿＿。
5. いくらたくさん運動しても、＿＿＿。

✳ アクティビティー 30

どんなに言っても、テレビばかり見ています。(*No matter how many times I tell him, he is always watching TV.*)

青山さんはブラウンさんの隣に住んでいます。

ブラウン：息子さん、受験で大変でしょう。

青山：どんなに勉強しろと言っても、テレビばかり見ているんですよ。

ブラウン：息子さん、勉強しなくても、頭がいいから大丈夫ですよ。

青山：そうだといいんですけど。少なくても1日4時間はテレビを
     見ているんですよ。

Mrs. Aoyama lives next door to Linda Brown. BROWN: Your son must be working hard for his entrance exams. AOYAMA: No matter how much I tell him to study, he's always watching TV. BROWN: Even if he doesn't study, he'll be OK because he's smart. AOYAMA: I hope that's the case. He watches TV at least four hours a day.

インタビュー (*Interview*)

Walk around the classroom, and ask your classmates the following questions. If their answer is はい, ask them to sign a paper saying so. Ask as many people as you can, and don't ask all the questions of just a few people.

1. どんなに忙しくても、毎日新聞を読みますか。

2. パーティーの途中 (*middle*) でも、好きな番組を見るために家に 帰りますか。

3. 一日2時間はテレビを見ますか。

4. テレビのコマーシャルは、なくてもいいと思いますか。

5. 一週間に5時間は本を読みますか。

6. 日本語のいい辞書があったら、いくら高くても買いますか。

7. 世界で何が起こっているか知らなくても、全然かまいませんか。

8. テレビやラジオがなくても、生活できますか。

Vocabulary Library

Mass Communication (2)

Newspapers

見出し	みだし	headline
社説	しゃせつ	editorial
…欄	…らん	…section
案内広告	あんないこうこく	classified ad
事件	じけん	event, incident
伝える	つたえる	to report; to convey information
発表 (する)	はっぴょう (する)	announcement (to announce)
英字新聞	えいじしんぶん	English-language newspaper

Loanwords: グラビア、ゴシップ

Books, Publishing

購読 (する)	こうどく (する)	subscription (to subscribe)
文庫本	ぶんこぼん	paperback book
参考書	さんこうしょ	reference book
印刷 (する)	いんさつ (する)	printing (to print)
ページ		page

目次	もくじ	table of contents
索引	さくいん	index
翻訳 (する)	ほんやく (する)	translation (to translate)

Broadcasting

中継 (する)	ちゅうけい (する)	(to make a) live, remote broadcast
録音 (する)	ろくおん (する)	recording (to record sound)
録画 (する)	ろくが (する)	videotaping (to videotape)

Loanwords: DJ、ディレクター、バラエティー・ショー、プロデューサー

CULTURE NOTE・漫画、アニメ

No visitor to Japan can help noticing the proliferation of comic books (漫画) for sale on the newsstands. Some have graphically violent or pornographic illustrations on the covers, so many visitors assume that all the **manga** are equally lurid, but in fact, there are **manga** for every age and interest. **Manga** are an

excellent resource for studying the Japanese language because they are the one place where spoken Japanese is written down verbatim, including slang and contractions.

Closely related to **manga** is **anime** (アニメ), cartoon animation, much of which is based on printed **manga.** Japanese **anime,** particularly the science fiction and fantasy variety, has many fans in other countries. They like the imaginative concepts, technical excellence, and bold design and coloration of the science fiction **anime,** but there are many less flamboyant series that have achieved long-standing popularity within Japan itself, including gentle domestic comedies like **Sazae-san** (サザエさん).

Expressing Certain Conviction: ...にちがいない

The ...にちがいない construction is used to express a conjecture of which the speaker is nearly certain.

カワムラさんはもう今ごろ九州に着いているにちがいない。
There is no doubt that Mr. Kawamura has already arrived in Kyushu.

新聞記者たちはその警官と話したにちがいありません。
The newspaper reporters must have talked with that policeman.

アラスカはとても寒かったにちがいありません。
It must have been very cold in Alaska.

祖父は若いころハンサムだったにちがいない。
There is no doubt that my grandfather was handsome when he was young.

The adverb きっと (*undoubtedly; certainly*) is often used with にちがいない.

明日はきっと雨が降るにちがいない。
It will rain tomorrow for sure.

チンさんはきっと手紙を書くにちがいない。
I am sure that Ms. Chin will write a letter.

The degree of probability expressed by ...にちがいない is stronger than that of だろう and かもしれない.

アクティビティー 32

ダイアログ：新聞（しんぶん）で読んだにちがいないわよ。(*No doubt they read about it in the paper.*)

ブラウンさんは佐野（さの）さんと話しています。「ロマンス」はブラウンさんのアパートの向（む）かいの喫茶店（きっさてん）です。

ブラウン：「ロマンス」、今日は人でいっぱいですね。外にも並（なら）んでいますよ。
　佐野（さの）：みんな新聞（しんぶん）で読んだにちがいないわよ。
ブラウン：どうしたんですか。
　佐野（さの）：<u>おいしいコーヒーを出（だ）すって、新聞（しんぶん）が書いた</u>のよ。

Practice the dialogue, replacing the underlined parts with the following.

1. テレビで見た
   めずらしいコーヒーがあるって、放送（ほうそう）した
2. ラジオで聞いた
   今日はコーヒーがただだって、放送（ほうそう）した
3. 雑誌（ざっし）で読んだ
   有名（ゆうめい）なタレントがたくさん来るって、雑誌（ざっし）が書いた

アクティビティー 33

賛成（さんせい）ですか。反対（はんたい）ですか。(*Do you agree or not?*)

Do you agree with the following statements? Express your opinion.

1. マスコミの力（ちから）(*power*) は大きいから、人の心（こころ）を簡単（かんたん）に変（か）えてしまうこともある。
2. 新聞（しんぶん）やテレビのニュースは、いつも正確（せいかく）で公正（こうせい）(*impartial*) だ。
3. テレビを見過（みす）ぎるのは、健康（けんこう）に良（よ）くない。
4. 2010年までには立体（りったい）(3D) テレビができているにちがいない。
5. 2010年までには新聞（しんぶん）の配達（はいたつ）はなくなって、みんなコンピュータでニュースを読むにちがいない。
6. 2010年までには、教科書（きょうかしょ）は全部（ぜんぶ）CD になっているにちがいない。

Ms. Brown is talking to Ms. Sano. "Romance" is the name of a coffee shop across the street from Ms. Brown's apartment. BROWN: "Romance" is filled with people today, isn't it? People are even lined up outside, too. SANO: No doubt they read about it in the paper. BROWN: What happened? SANO: <u>The paper reported that they serve delicious coffee.</u>

Vocabulary and Grammar 6C 333

三百三十三

CULTURE NOTE • Popular Music

The Japanese are great fans of foreign music, especially classical, jazz, and rock music, and it is also possible to find devoted listeners and performers of country-western songs, French *chansons,* and even Caribbean salsa. All these genres exist alongside Japan's own popular music, which is a hybrid of traditional and Western influences and is little known outside Japan.

Japanese folk music is sung in a tight, slightly nasal, highly ornamented vocal style, and this way of singing carries over into **enka** (演歌 [えんか]), the most "Japanese-sounding" of the styles of popular music currently being performed. These songs are most popular among working-class and rural people, so one could say that they are the counterparts of American country-western songs, even though their sound is completely different.

Young teenagers favor the bouncy, upbeat melodies sung by the so-called idol singers (アイドル歌手 [かしゅ]). These singers, whom the talent scouts choose more for their cute, perky, innocent looks than for their musical ability, are about the age of their fans when they start their careers, and almost all of them are has-beens by the age of nineteen or twenty.

Until about fifteen or twenty years ago, almost all Japanese, from small children to elderly people, listened to the idol singers, but the market is much more fragmented now. Older teenagers and university students tend to like either foreign or home-grown rock and alternative music, while people who are past university age may listen to jazz, classical music, **enka,** or the many singer-songwriters who sing ballad-style songs while accompanying themselves on the piano or guitar.

演歌歌手：私の心に
雨が降〜る〜

Language Skills

Reading and Writing

Reading 1　手紙の書き方

Before You Read

As you learned in Book 1 (Chapter 4, Reading 1), the standard way of writing letters in Japan is somewhat different from that in Western countries. This reading selection introduces some guidelines for Japanese letter writing found in a book of etiquette published in Japan.

It is customary to refer to the weather or the season in Japanese formal letters. Which month or months do you think each of the following greetings refers to? Assume that these were written by someone in Tokyo.

1. 桜の季節も間もなくとなりました。
2. 毎日、雨が続く季節となりました。
3. 毎日暑い日が続きます。
4. おいしいなしを送ってくださって、ありがとうございました。
5. ゴールデンウイークはいかがでしたか。
6. 遠くに見える山が紅葉で赤く見える季節、いかがお過ごしですか。
7. 町はクリスマスのライトでいっぱいですが。
8. 桜の季節も過ぎて、緑がますます濃くなってきました。

過ごす *to pass or spend (time)*

ますます *increasingly* / 濃い *thick; deep; intense*

Now Read It!

As Linda Brown's written Japanese improves, she has been trying to write as many letters in Japanese as possible, even though she hasn't always fully understood the rules of Japanese letter writing. Fortunately, she has found a short article about letter writing in this week's edition of 週刊毎朝.

週刊毎朝1994年1月18日家庭欄

　最近は何でも電話ですませるようになり、手紙を書くことが少なくなりました。しかし、手紙は書かれた会話。友人から手紙を受け取ると、

すませる *to get along; to manage*

うれしいものです。手紙でなければ伝えられないこともあります。直接言いにくいことも手紙では書きやすいものです。電話では言い間違いや、聞き間違いで、誤解することもあります。手紙なら、何度でも読み直しができます。

今日は上手な手紙の書き方をエチケット評論家の吉田美鈴さんにまとめていただきました。

1. まず、手紙を出す相手によって、フォーマルに書くかカジュアルに書くか決めましょう。目上の人に書く時には、あらたまったスタイルで書きます。

2. 手紙は「拝啓」のような頭語で始まり、「敬具」のような結語で終わるのが基本的な形式です。この形式をしっかり覚えましょう。

3. 形式も大切ですが、あまり形式的すぎると、つまらない手紙になってしまいます。心をこめて、素直に書きましょう。自分の言葉で簡潔に書きましょう。

4. 手紙では「です」、「ます」のような丁寧語を上手に使いましょう。

5. お祝い、お礼、お見舞い、おわびや返事はすぐ書きましょう。遅れたら、そのおわびや理由を忘れないようにしましょう。

6. 急ぐときは、葉書を使ったらいいでしょう。でも、プライベートなことを書いてはいけません。あらたまった時には、手紙のほうがいいでしょう。

7. 便箋は白かグレー、クリーム色にしましょう。目上の人にはカラフルな便箋やイラストが入った便箋を使うのは失礼です。

手紙は人と人の心をつなぐ大切な手段です。マナーを守って、あなたの心の伝わる手紙を書きましょう。

直接 *directly*

言い間違い *slip of the tongue* / 聞き間違い *error in listening*

誤解 (する) *misunderstanding (to misunderstand)*

評論家 *critic; commentator* / まとめる *to summarize; to compile*

相手 *partner or counterpart in a mutual activity*

決める *to decide* / あらたまる *to become formal*

基本的 (な) *basic* / 形式 *form* / 覚える *to learn; to memorize*

心をこめる *to be sincere; to show feeling* / 素直 (な) *gentle, mild* / 簡潔 *concise*

お祝い *congratulations* / お見舞い *checking up on someone's well-being* / おわび *apology*
理由 *reason*

失礼 (な) *impolite; rude*

つなぐ *to link* / 手段 *means; way*
守る *to keep; to maintain*

After You Finish Reading

1. As you read the rules for letter writing, you undoubtedly noticed that some of the rules are different from the rules for writing letters in English. List the differences that you noticed; then make a second list of the similarities. Are there any Japanese rules that are completely irrelevant for English?

2. You are a student at a university in Japan, and a classmate from Thailand, who has not lived in Japan as long as you have, asks you the following questions on how to write a letter in Japanese. Since the Thai student does not speak English, you have to answer in Japanese.

a. 保証人 (*visa guarantor*) に手紙を書きたいんですが、グリーンの便箋しかないんです。このグリーンの便箋を使ってもいいですか。

b. 3ヶ月前に友達から本をもらいましたが、まだ、お礼の手紙を書いていません。どうしたらいいでしょうか。

c. 字が下手なので、手紙を書くのはきらいです。何でも電話でいいでしょう。

Writing 1

You are asked by a magazine for international students to write a short article about the etiquette of making a phone call. Following the example of the preceding article, start your essay with a short introduction about telephone calls. Then give some suggestions such as these.

Useful Words: 正しく *correctly,* はっきり（と）*clearly*

- Do not call early in the morning or late at night.
- Dial directly.
- Avoid lengthy phone calls.
- Write down what you want to say on a piece of paper in advance.
- Always put a memo pad and a pen near the phone.
- Speak clearly.
- Avoid difficult words.
- Use **aizuchi** often on the phone.

Reading 2　ラジオの番組案内

Before You Read

What TV programs do you watch? Discuss in class what programs people watch in respect to each of the following genres.

ニュース番組	トーク・ショー
メロドラマ	音楽番組
コメディー	スポーツ番組
ドキュメンタリー	アニメ

Now Read It!

Linda Brown received the following announcement from FM フジ, of which she is a regular listener.

さわやかな春の季節となりましたが、みなさまいかがお過ごしでしょうか。いつもFMフジ78をお聞き下さり、まことにありがとうございます。FMフジの来月の番組案内をお届け致します。毎週日曜日朝6時から7時までお送りしております、「サンデー・モーニング・アワー」は来月はバロック音楽の特集です。月曜日から金曜日の朝6時から9時までお送りしております「おはようフジ」は4月1日から武藤洋子さんをホステスに迎え、内容も新しく、お送り致します。最新のニュースの他、高速道路情報、JR、私鉄、バスの情報、天気予報もあります。これまで毎週月曜日から金曜日の9時から11時までお送りしておりました「日本の歌」は来月から午後1時から3時に移ります。これまで通り、お楽しみください。ウイークデーの9時から11時には今度新しく「悩みごと相談室」が始まります。悩みごとがおありの方は、東京(03)3874-2301までお電話ください。一人で悩んでいないで、お気軽にお電話ください。

　　ウイークデーのお昼の一時、お好きな歌でお楽しみになりませんか。11時から1時までは「リクエスト・ミュージック・タイム」です。歌謡曲、ロック、民謡、何でもかまいません。お聞きになりたい曲がありましたら、東京(03)3874-2203までお電話下さい。ウイークデーの午後3時から4時までは4月1日から「加納太郎のズバリ聞きます」が始まります。小説、エッセイのベストセラーで有名な加納太郎氏が政治家、会社経営者、タレントの方々にインタビューします。午後4時から6時まではこれまで通り「トワイライトフジ」でお楽しみください。パーソナリティーはFMフジの小林光夫アナウンサーと友野優子アナウンサーです。二人の楽しい話と音楽で楽しい一時をお送りください。また、この番組では皆様からのお電話もお待ちしております。みんなに聞いてもらいたい、とっておきの話、面白いお話がありましたら、東京(03)3874-2301までお電話ください。そして6時から7時までは「ニュースセンター」です。国外、国内の最新のニュースをお送りします。4月15日からは毎晩7時から「プロ野球中継」が始まります。放送カードは新聞などでお知らせします。

さわやかな *fresh; refreshing*

案内 *guidance; information* / 届ける *to deliver*

特集 *special feature; special collection*

迎える *to receive (a visitor), to greet; to look forward to* / 内容 *contents*

悩みごと *worries; personal problems* / 相談室 *consultation room*
気軽に *feeling free; without hesitation*

歌謡曲 *popular song*

民謡 *traditional Japanese folk song*

ズバリ *boldly; decisively*

氏 *Mr., Ms. (formal)* / 政治家 *politician* / 会社経営者 *company manager*

とっておき *best; treasured; valuable*

Some super-polite forms are used in this announcement, including -ます forms before nouns and 〜ましたら instead of 〜たら.

中継 *live remote broadcast*

週末の新しい番組を二つ御紹介します。土曜日の午後2時から4時まで
は世界のアーチストのライブコンサートをお送りする「ワールドライブ」
です。日曜日の午後10時から11時までは新しく「サイエンス・テクノロジー
・トゥデイ」が始まります。現在、サイエンス、テクノロジーの世界で何が
起こっているかをお知らせ致します。どうぞこれからも今まで同様、FMフジ
をあなたの生活のパートナーとして、ダイヤルをお合わせください。

起こる *to happen; to take place* / 同様 *in the same way*

After You Finish Reading

Write a broadcast schedule hour by hour, from 6:00 A.M. to 10:00 P.M., and for
weekdays, Saturday, and Sunday, for FMフジ's coming new season, using the
preceding announcement as a guide.

Writing 2

Some people who have just moved to Tokyo and are unfamiliar with the local
radio stations have asked your advice about what radio programs to listen to.
Answer in Japanese, because all these people are either Japanese or newly
arrived from non-English-speaking countries. (Don't forget to mention the time
and the day of the week for each program. Use the information in the reading
selection.)

1. 僕はプロ野球の大ファンなんですよ。
2. 私は45歳の主婦です。うちの15歳の娘のことですが、夜の1時や2時
   まで外で遊んでいて困っています。
3. 私は70年代のディスコミュージックが好きなんですが、最近のラジオ
   ではあまり聞かなくなりました。聞きたい曲がいくつかあるんですよ。
4. 僕の夢は科学者になることなんだ。いろいろな科学の本を読んで、
   勉強しているんだ。
5. 私はケニーGのファンです。あのサックスの音はいいですね。
6. 私は家で仕事をしていますが、3時頃になると、眠くなります。何か
   面白い番組はありませんか。

Language Functions and Situations

Making a Phone Call

吉野：もしもし、東京ファッション営業部です。

高田：あのう、石山部長をお願いします。

吉野：おそれいりますが、どちら様でしょうか。

高田：SONYの高田と申します。

吉野：SONYの高田様ですね。少々お待ちください。

石山：お電話かわりました。石山です。

高田：SONYの高田です。先日はどうも。

石山：いいえ、こちらこそ。

高田：新しいプロジェクトの件でお話をしたいと思いまして...明日の午後、
　　　そちらにお伺いしてもよろしいでしょうか。

石山：明日の午後ですか。ええと、2時以降でしたら、大丈夫です。

高田：それでは、明日2時半にそちらにお伺いいたします。

石山：2時半ですね。では、お待ちしております。

高田：それでは、また明日。失礼します。

石山：じゃあ、失礼します。

吉野：もしもし、東京ファッション営業部です。

高田：あのう、石山部長をお願いします。

吉野：あいにく石山は今、席をはずしておりますが、...

高田：では、伝言をお願いします。

吉野：かしこまりました。どうぞ。

YOSHINO: Hello, this is the Sales Department of Tokyo Fashion.　　TAKADA: Uh, (may I talk to)
Mr. Ishiyama (lit., *Manager Ishiyama*), please?　　YOSHINO: I beg your pardon, but (may I ask) who's
calling?　　TAKADA: I am Takada of SONY.　　YOSHINO: Mr. Takada of SONY, I see. Please wait a moment.
ISHIYAMA: This is Ishiyama speaking.　　TAKADA: This is Takada of SONY speaking. Thank you very much
for the other day.

ISHIYAMA: Oh, thank *you*.　　TAKADA: I'd like to talk with you about the new project. May I visit you tomorrow afternoon?　　ISHIYAMA: Tomorrow afternoon? Let me see. If it's after two o'clock, it's OK.
TAKADA: Then I will be there at 2:30.

ISHIYAMA: I'm looking forward to your visit.　　TAKADA: Then I'll see you tomorrow. Good-bye.
ISHIYAMA: Good-bye.

YOSHINO: Hello, this is the Sales Department of Tokyo Fashion.　　TAKADA: Uh, (may I talk to) Mr. Ishiyama
(lit., *Manager Ishiyama*), please?　　YOSHINO: I'm sorry, but Ishiyama is away from his desk just now.
TAKADA: Then may I leave a message?

YOSHINO: Yes, please.

高田：私、SONY営業部の高田洋一と申します。高田は「高い低い」の高に、
　　　田んぼの「田」、洋一は太平洋の「洋」に「一番」の「一」です。

吉野：はい。

高田：今月24日午後6時から我が社の銀座ショールームで新しい
　　　ビデオカメラの発表パーティーを行ないますので、是非御出席
　　　くださるようお願いしたくて、お電話いたしました。後ほど、
　　　改めてお電話差し上げるとお伝えください。

吉野：はい。かしこまりました。

高田：じゃ、失礼いたします。

吉野：失礼いたします。

言語ノート

Talking on the Phone

Always use honorifics as you begin a call to someone else's home or business, because you don't necessarily know who the person on the other end of the line is. Once you find out whom you are talking to or once the person you want to speak to comes to the phone, you can adjust the level of your speech accordingly. If you do not identify yourself at the beginning of the call, the person at the other end of the line is certain to ask you this or something like it:

どちら様でしょうか。
May I ask who's calling?
ブラウンと申します。
My name is Brown.
失礼ですが、どちらのブラウンさんですか。
I am sorry, but which Ms. Brown?

In a business or professional situation, you should always identify yourself by your job affiliation. If you do not, you are likely to hear something like the above question. Answer with the name of your company, school, or occupation + の + your name (without any title) + です.

Remember that when talking on the phone you should always refer to an in-group member without any honorific title and with humble language.

TAKADA: I am Yooichi Takada of the Sales Department of SONY. Takada is written with the 高 of high and low and the 田 of rice paddy. Yooichi is written with the 洋 of Pacific Ocean and the 一 of No. 1. YOSHINO: Yes. TAKADA: We're going to have a party to announce our new video camera at our Ginza Exhibit Hall starting at 6 P.M. on the 24th of this month. I'm calling Mr. Ishiyama to ask him to please be sure to attend the party. Please tell him I will call him again later. YOSHINO: All right. TAKADA: Well, good-bye. YOSHINO: Good-bye.

Language Skills

三百四十一

One way to give a message is to state briefly what you want to tell the person, end with …から or ので, and follow up with そのように おっしゃってください or そのように伝えてください. For example, if you want to leave a message that you have postponed tomorrow's meeting until ten o'clock, you could say:

明日の会議のことなんですが、かってながら10時に変更 いたしましたので、そうおっしゃってください。

It's about tomorrow's meeting, and even though it's inconsiderate of us, we've changed it to ten o'clock, so please tell (him/her) that.

And remember that on the phone or off, it is polite to conclude a request with

よろしくお願いいたします。
Please take care of it for me.

Role Play

Working with a partner, practice the following situations. (For situations 1, 2, and 3, one student must prepare a message in advance for the other student to take in Japanese.)

1. Call the Yoshioka residence, and ask for Mrs. Yoshioka, who happens to be out. Leave a message for her.
2. Call Mr. Takahashi, who is the manager of the Sales Department, ABC Automobiles (ABC自動車). He has momentarily left his desk. Leave a message for him.
3. Call Professor Yokoi's residence. Unfortunately, she is not at home. Leave a message.
4. Call your friend, and ask him or her to do something with you this weekend.

言語ノート

よろしく

よろしく is used in a variety of common courtesy expressions, all of which have to do with treating the speaker or some third person well.

As you learned in Book 1, the expression どうぞよろしくお願い します is used when introducing oneself. When people join any kind of a group in Japan, they give a brief self-introduction in front of everyone, stating their name, background, hobbies and interests, and perhaps their reasons for joining the group. Then they end their presentation with どうぞよろしくお願いします.

This phrase is also the usual conclusion to a request for a favor or a request for someone to take care of something or someone. For example, if you asked your instructor for a letter of recommendation, you would conclude the conversation with どうぞよろしくお願いいたします, the most humble form of this already humble expression.

A superior asking a subordinate to take care of something would use not どうぞよろしくお願いします but よろしく頼 (たのむ) よ (male speaker) or よろしく頼むわね (female speaker).

If the two parties are somehow taking care of or doing favors for each other, as when entering into a business relationship, then the second party replies to どうぞよろしくお願いいたします with こちらこそ, an expression that indicates that the polite phrase applies equally to the first party.

When asking someone to give your regards to a third person, use the expression X-さんによろしくお伝 (つた) えください. When speaking in informal style, you may leave off the お伝えください.

At the Post Office

郵便局員：次の方。

カワムラ：すみません。この小包を九州へ送りたいんですが。

郵便局員：壊れ物は入っていますか。

カワムラ：いいえ。

郵便局員：ええと、1キロですから、800円です。

カワムラ：何日くらいで着きますか。

郵便局員：そうですね。2～3日で着くでしょう。

カワムラ：それから、この現金書留もお願いします。

郵便局員：ええと、2万円だから、370円です。

カワムラ：それから、80円切手5枚と200円切手2枚ください。

郵便局員：これだけですか。

カワムラ：はい、そうです。

郵便局員：全部で1970円です。

カワムラ：はい、2000円。

郵便局員：おつりの30円と現金書留の領収書です。ありがとうございました。

CLERK: Next please.　KAWAMURA: Excuse me. I would like to send this package to Kyushu.
CLERK: Anything fragile inside?　KAWAMURA: No.　CLERK: Well, it weighs one kilo, so it's 800 yen.
KAWAMURA: How many days does it take?　CLERK: Let me see. Two or three days.　KAWAMURA: And I would like to mail this by cash registered mail.　CLERK: Well, the amount is 20,000 yen, so the postage will be 370 yen.　KAWAMURA: May I have five 80-yen stamps and two 200-yen stamps?
CLERK: Anything else?　KAWAMURA: That's it.　CLERK: 1,970 yen altogether, please.　KAWAMURA: Out of 2,000 yen.　CLERK: Here are your change of 30 yen and the receipt for your cash registered mail. Thank you very much.

Role Play

Working in pairs, practice the following situations.

1. You are living in Japan and would like to mail a Japanese doll as a Christmas gift to your friend in the United States. Go to the post office and mail it.
2. You have decided to apply for a job at a Japanese company and have just finished writing your application. The deadline is the day after tomorrow. Mail your application by special delivery mail.
3. You would like to send money to a friend living in Hokkaido. Go to the post office and mail it.

Listening Comprehension

1. You will listen to a telephone conversation. In this call, the person with whom the caller wanted to talk was not at her desk, so he left a message. Write down the content of the message.
2. You will listen to a TV announcement in which an announcer describes some programs they will broadcast later on today. Write the schedule hour by hour from 12:00 noon to 12:00 midnight.
3. You will hear conversations between a post office clerk and five different customers. Write down what each customer sent and how much the total postage was.

Vocabulary

Telephone

こうしゅうでんわ	公衆電話	public phone
こくさいでんわ	国際電話	international call
ダイヤル (する)		dial (to dial)
ちょうきょりでんわ	長距離電話	long-distance call
でんごん	伝言	message
でんわボックス	電話ボックス	telephone booth
でんわをきる	電話を切る	to hang up the phone
ないせん	内線	extension

はなしちゅう	話し中	(the line is) busy
プッシュホン		push-button telephone
ポケベル		pager, beeper
まちがいでんわ（をする）	間違い電話（をする）	(calling) the wrong number
るすばんでんわ	留守番電話	telephone answering machine

Loanwords: ダイヤル、ファックス、コレクト・コール

Review: 電話、(に)電話をかける、電話番号、電話帳

Postal Service

あてな	宛て名	address (*of the recipient*)
げんきんかきとめ	現金書留	registered mail for sending cash
こうくうびん	航空便	airmail
こづつみ	小包	package
たくはいびん	宅配便	delivery service
そくたつ	速達	express mail
はいたつ（する）	配達（する）	delivery (to deliver)
はがき	葉書	postal card
びんせん	便箋	stationery; writing paper
ふうとう	封筒	envelope
ふなびん	船便	surface mail
へんじ（をだす）	返事（を出す）	reply (to send a reply)
ゆうびん	郵便	mail
ゆうびんばんごう	郵便番号	postal code (*similar to ZIP code*)
ゆうびんポスト	郵便ポスト	mailbox (*for sending letters*)

Review: 絵葉書、切手、住所、手紙、郵便局

Newspaper

こうこく（をだす）	広告（を出す）	advertisement (to place an advertisement)
…にのる	…に載る	to appear in; to be covered in (*a newspaper or magazine*)
しんぶんきじ	新聞記事	newspaper article
しんぶんはいたつ	新聞配達	paper delivery
とる	取る	to subscribe (*to a magazine or newspaper*)
マスコミ		mass communication

Review: 新聞、ニュース、〜部

Books, Publishing

げっかんし	月刊誌	monthly magazine
しゅうかんし	週刊誌	weekly magazine
しゅっぱん（する）	出版（する）	publishing (to publish)

しょうせつ	小説	novel
じてん	事典	encyclopedia
まんが	漫画	comic book; comic magazine; cartoon

Loanword: エッセイ

Review: 教科書、〜冊、雑誌、辞書、本、本屋、料理の本

Broadcasting

アニメ		animation
エヌエイチケー	NHK	Nippon Hoso Kyokai
シーエム	CM	commercial (*from commercial message*)
しゅつえんする	出演する	to appear as a performer
ばんぐみ	番組	(television or radio) program
ほうそう（する）	放送（する）	broadcasting (to broadcast)
マイク		microphone

Loanwords: AM、FM、アナウンサー、アンテナ、コマーシャル、コメディー、スタジオ、スポンサー、タレント、チャンネル、ドキュメンタリー、ジャーナリズム、ファックス

Review: カメラ、カラーテレビ、テレビ、天気予報、ドラマ、ビデオ、ラジオ

Verbs

といあわせる	問い合わせる	to inquire
なる	鳴る	to make a sound, to ring (*telephone or doorbell*)
はる	貼る	to paste

Review: インタビュー（する）、送る

Grammar

…ことがある	there are occasions when…
〜させられる	*verb causative-passive ending*
〜せられる	*verb causative-passive ending*
〜ていただきたい	to want someone to do… (*humble*)
〜てほしい	to want someone to do…
〜ても	even if…, even though…
〜てもらいたい	to want someone to do…
…にちがいない	there is no doubt that…
〜ば	*conditional*
〜られる	*honorific ending*
〜れる	*honorific ending*

Kanji

Learn these **kanji:**

換 取 映 宅 放
際 報 画 重 組
留 文 郵 刊 試
守 打 紙 雑 験
受 調 送 誌 忘
器 英 達 記 困

チェックリスト

Use this checklist to confirm that you can now

- ☐ Talk about telecommunications
- ☐ Talk about the postal service
- ☐ Talk about the media, entertainment, and journalism
- ☐ Use the ば conditionals
- ☐ Express respect in different ways
- ☐ Express causative-passives
- ☐ Express concession
- ☐ Write a letter
- ☐ Make a phone call
- ☐ Communicate at the post office

Review Chapter 6

アクティビティー　1

どれくらいしますか。(*How often do you do the following?*)

Indicate how often you do the following. Then compare your answers with those of your classmates. What are the strongest preferences in means of communicating and getting information?

	毎日	時々	あまりしない	全然しない
1. 友達に電話する	☐	☐	☐	☐
2. 国際電話をする	☐	☐	☐	☐
3. 小包を送る	☐	☐	☐	☐
4. 地元 (*local*) の新聞を読む	☐	☐	☐	☐
5. ABC, CBS, NBC のニュースを見る	☐	☐	☐	☐
6. ラジオのニュースを聞く	☐	☐	☐	☐

アクティビティー　2

日本が経済危機 (*Japan in economic crisis*)

Following are headlines from newspapers. Rank them from the one most interesting to you (1) to the one least interesting (10). How do your answers compare with those of your classmates?

アフリカでクーデター　　　ガソリンが値上がり (*price hike*)

ヒュー・グラントが結婚　　来週から郵便ストライキ

日本が経済危機　　　　　　ロサンゼルスでギャングが殺される

明日スーパーボール　　　　アメリカ大統領、中国へ

アクティビティー　3

The following article stresses eight points about using honorifics. Guess what each point is about, based on your reading skills and knowledge of honorifics.

敬語入門講座

ビジネスマンのための

① 敬語には次の3種類があります。
A。尊敬語
B。謙譲語
C。ていねい語

② 尊敬語は、相手や話題に上がった人を尊敬して表現する言葉です。
「鈴木さんが言った」という会話も、尊敬語にすると、「鈴木さんがおっしゃいました」

尊敬語▼召しあがる、おっしゃる、くださる など。
謙譲語▼あげる、差し上げる、いただく、いたす、参る、伺(うかが)う、申し上げる、拝見する、拝聴す、弊社など。
ていねい語▼存じます、ございます など。

③ 謙譲語は、へりくだった表現をすることで、相手を高める言葉です。

④ ていねい語は、ていねいに表現することで、相手に敬意を表する言葉です。
「わたしは課長に申し上げた」という表現になります。

⑤ 尊敬語にするのはおかしい!
動作の主体が相手なのに謙譲語をつけるのは誤り。
「電話だ」は「電話でございます」、あるいは「電話です」

⑥ 動作の主体が自分であるとき「わたしがおっしゃった」という言葉をあてはめてみて下さい。
※これだけではわかりにくいかもしれませんが例えば「書く」という言葉を
また、動作の主体が相手なのに謙譲語にするのはおかしい!
「あなたが申し上げた」は、変だと思いませんか。

⑦ 尊敬語、謙譲語、ていねい語 それぞれに専用の言葉があります。
尊敬語▼いらっしゃる、なさる、

⑧ ちょっとした公式があります。それを覚えておくと便利。
【尊敬語】「お(ご)…になる」「お(ご)…くださる」
【謙譲語】「お(ご)…する」「お(ご)…いたす」「お(ご)…申す」
尊敬語だと、「書かれる」「お書きになる」。
謙譲語だと、「お書きします」「お書きいたします」。

✲ アクティビティー　4

賛成(さんせい)ですか。反対(はんたい)ですか。(*Do you agree or not?*)

Work in pairs. Exchange opinions about TV and the news media as you talk about the following statements. Use examples to support your opinions.

1. テレビのニュース・レポーターは公平(こうへい)(*fair*)で客観的に(きゃっかんてき)(*objectively*)ニュースを伝(つた)えている。

2. 最近(さいきん)のテレビ番組(ばんぐみ)は暴力(ぼうりょく)(*violence*)やセックス・シーンが多すぎる。

3. 犯罪率(はんざいりつ)(*crime rate*)が高いのは、最近(さいきん)のテレビ番組(ばんぐみ)の影響(えいきょう)(*influence*)だ。

4. テレビのニュースは新聞(しんぶん)ほど詳(くわ)しく(*detailed*)ないから、見る必要(ひつよう)はない。

5. テレビのファミリードラマは現実(げんじつ)(*reality*)の生活(せいかつ)を反映(はんえい)(*reflect*)している。

6. テレビのコマーシャルは生活(せいかつ)の役(やく)に立(た)つ。

7

第七章　自然と文化

宮島の厳島神社

Objectives

In this lesson, you are going to

- Talk about geography, environment, and nature
- Talk about culture and customs
- Learn to express a speaker's emotional involvement
- Learn various uses of よう
- Learn to scan letters to the editor in newspapers
- Learn to scan book reviews
- Learn to present opinions clearly and logically

Nature and Culture

Vocabulary and Grammar 7A

Vocabulary and Oral Activities

Geography

Vocabulary: Geography

大陸	たいりく	continent
島	しま	island
火山	かざん	volcano
谷	たに	valley
湾	わん	bay
海岸	かいがん	beach; shore
滝	たき	waterfall
石	いし	stone
岬	みさき	cape; promontory
流れる	ながれる	to flow
湖	みずうみ	lake
池	いけ	pond
平野	へいや	plains
丘	おか	hill
森	もり	forest
林	はやし	woods
木	き	tree
面積	めんせき	area; land area

Review: 山、海、川、地図

※ アクティビティー　**1**

インタビュー (*Interview*)

Interview one of your classmates. For each question, add one related question of your own.

1. 海のそばに住んでいますか。きれいな海岸がそばにありますか。湾はありますか。

2. 今まで見た湖で、一番大きいのはどの湖ですか。

---

3. どの山脈が一番きれいだと思いますか。

4. 火山が噴火 (erupt) しているところを見たことがありますか。

5. 山や森の中でキャンプをしたことがありますか。どこでしましたか。

✳ アクティビティー　2

どこにありますか。(*Where are they?*)

John Kawamura is spending a few days on the islands of Kuroiwa and Akaiwa.
Here is a map of the islands, with only a few features labeled. Read the following
descriptions, and draw and label the geographical features described at the
correct places on the map.

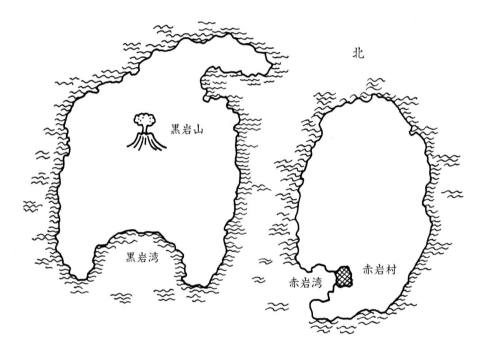

1. 黒岩山は黒岩島の真ん中にあります。高さは980mで、そんなに高く
   ありませんが、火山です。

2. 黒岩湖は黒岩山の南にあります。

3. 赤岩湖は赤岩島の北の方にあります。村から北に歩いて、30分ぐらい
   のところです。赤岩湖の南は森になっています。

4. 黒岩村は黒岩湾に面して (*facing on*) います。村の南には黒岩海岸が
   広がって (*spread out*) います。

5. 黒岩村のすぐ北には大きな林があります。この 林 は黒岩の林と
   呼ばれています。 林 の北側には広い丘が広がっています。この丘は
   黒岩の丘と呼ばれています。黒岩の丘の真ん中に黒岩沼 (*marsh*) が
   あります。

6. 赤岩湖から南に赤岩川が流れています。赤岩川は村の中を通って、
   赤岩湾に流れています。

7. 黒岩川は黒岩湖から北に流れています。黒岩川の周りは黒岩谷と
   呼ばれています。黒岩谷の真ん中に黒岩滝があります。黒岩滝は高さ
   3mの小さな滝です。

✳ アクティビティー 3

ダイアログ：午後、登ることになっています。(*It is planned that we will climb it in the afternoon.*)

カワムラ：明日の予定はどうなっていますか。

　　ガイド：朝8時に船で、黒岩島に向かうことになっています。

カワムラ：黒岩山には登らないんですか。

　　ガイド：ええ、午後、登ることになっています。

Here is Kawamura's schedule for the trip. Explain it in Japanese.

[例]　明日の夜は黒岩 山でキャンプをすることになっています。

12日午前	船で黒岩島に向かう
12日午後	黒岩山に登る
12日夜	黒岩山でキャンプをする
13日午前	黒岩滝を見る
13日午後	赤岩島に戻る
	赤岩湾で泳ぐ
13日夜	赤岩海岸でバーベキュー・パーティーをする
14日	東京に戻る

KAWAMURA: What are tomorrow's plans like?　GUIDE: We're supposed to head for Kuroiwa Island by boat at eight in the morning.　KAWAMURA: Won't we climb Mount Kuroiwa?　GUIDE: Yes, it is planned that we will climb it in the afternoon.

You are the guide for John Kawamura's tour group. For a variety of reasons, it has become necessary to change the original schedule. Write down a new schedule in the following chart, and explain why each change is necessary.

[例] 明日は台風が来るそうですから、一日中赤岩島旅館にいることに
なるでしょう。

	NEW SCHEDULE
12日	台風が来るそうですから、一日中赤岩島旅館にいることに なっています。
13日	
14日	

言語ノート

Decisions Made by Others: …ことになる

The …ことになる construction is used to express the idea that something has been decided on or happens because of circumstances beyond the speaker's control.

三村さんは4月から貿易会社で働くことになりました。
It was decided that Mr. Mimura will work for a trading company starting in April.

このアパートは家賃が高いので、間もなく引っ越すことに
なるでしょう。
Because the rent for this apartment is high, we will probably have to move out soon.

今日は天気が悪いので、ピクニックは中止することに
なった。
Because the weather is bad today, it was decided to call off the picnic.

When a decision was made at some time in the past and that decision is still in effect, になっている (なっています) is used instead of なる (なります).

明日のクラスでは、カワムラさんが平安時代の建築に
ついて発表することになっています。
Mr. Kawamura has to report on the architecture of the Heian Era in tomorrow's class.

Because of its time implications, ことになっている is sometimes used to express a custom, regularly scheduled event, rule, or expectation.

上級フランス語のクラスではフランス語しか使わないことになっています。

As a rule, we use only French in our advanced French class.

The ことになる construction is used when you don't have to specify who made a decision or you would rather not mention the decision maker specifically. In contrast, the superficially similar construction of ことにする (see Chapter 1, **Grammar 2**) requires that you state specifically who made the decision. The distinction is similar to the distinction between *We decided to leave* and *It was decided that we should leave* in English.

If you use the plain, nonpast form of the verb + ことになる even when you are the decision maker, you sound humbler than when you use ことにする。

来週から隣に引っ越してくることになりましたので、どうぞよろしくお願いいたします。

It has been decided that we will be moving in next door starting next week, so please be kind to us.

The use of a ます／です form before ので is a feature of super-polite speech.

Vocabulary Library

More on Geography

海峡	かいきょう	channel; straits
赤道	せきどう	equator
岩	いわ	rock outcropping
水平線	すいへいせん	horizon
地理	ちり	geography
世界	せかい	world
北極	ほっきょく	North Pole
南極	なんきょく	South Pole
太平洋	たいへいよう	the Pacific Ocean
大西洋	たいせいよう	the Atlantic Ocean
インド洋	インドよう	the Indian Ocean
国	くに	country, nation
州	しゅう	state (*in the U.S.*), province (*in Canada*)
地球	ちきゅう	earth
星	ほし	star
太陽	たいよう	sun
月	つき	moon
宇宙	うちゅう	outer space; the universe

Loanword: ジャングル

Grammar and Practice Activities

38. Expressing a Speaker's Emotional Involvement: ...ものだ

カワムラ：このへんは家が多いですね。

山口：10年前はこのへんは野原だったんですがね。

カワムラ：本当ですか。

山口：ええ、子供の頃はここでよく虫を取ったものですよ。

ブラウン：あら、佐野さん、かわいいお子さんですね。

佐野：長女の子供なんですよ。

ブラウン：こんにちは。

子供：...

佐野：人に会ったら、きちんと御挨拶するものですよ。

山口：さとみ、今日は学校へ行かないの。

さとみ：ええ、だって、授業がないんだもの。

山口：じゃあ、庭の掃除、手伝ってくれる？

さとみ：ダメよ。今、本を読んでいるんだもの。

山口：よく、そんなことが言えたものね。漫画を読んでいるんじゃないの？

38.1 The following construction is used to express a speaker's strong emotional involvement with an event. Depending on the exact circumstances, it can have any one of a number of English translations.

KAWAMURA: There are a lot of houses around here.   YAMAGUCHI: Ten years ago, this area was an open field, but. . .   KAWAMURA: Really?   YAMAGUCHI: Yes, when I was a child, I used to catch insects around here.

BROWN: Oh, Ms. Sano, that's a cute child.   SANO: It's my oldest daughter's child.   BROWN: Hello.   CHILD: . . .   SANO: When you meet people, you're supposed to greet them properly.

YAMAGUCHI: Satomi, aren't you going to school today?   SATOMI: Yeah, because there's no class, you see.   YAMAGUCHI: Well, will you help me clean up the yard?   SATOMI: Uh-uh. (Lit., *No good.*) Because I'm reading a book now.   YAMAGUCHI: You have a lot of nerve saying that. (Lit., *You're someone who could say that well.*) Aren't you reading a comic book?

Verb	Plain form	
I-adjective	Plain form (dictionary form/ta-form)	ものだ（ものです）
Na-adjective	Dictionary form + だ or だった	
Noun	Noun + な／だった	

should; used to; because

As explained in the Language Note that follows, the original meaning of もの is *tangible* or *visible thing*. When used as a sentence ending, もの expresses an event or a situation as if it were a tangible thing or a vivid experience. Depending on context, it expresses different types of emotions, including desire, reminiscence, excuse, admonition, command, conviction, or exclamation.

38.2 The plain past form of the verb + ものだ is used when the speaker is reminiscing about the way things used to be.

学生の時、毎日のようにパチンコをやったものです。
When I was a student, I used to play pachinko almost every day.

38.3 At other times, もの seems to add nothing more than emotional intensity to the statement.

私もその山に登ってみたいものだ。
I also want to try climbing that mountain!

38.4 This construction is also used in making generalizations, particularly when the speaker is expressing a strong impression or conviction.

友達はいいものだ。
A friend is a good thing (to have).

38.5 ものだ is also used to express what one must do or should do. The negative form, ものではない, expresses what one should not do.

大人だったら、そんなことを言うものではない。
If you are an adult, you shouldn't say such things.

In more formal speech or writing, もの can be replaced with べき. The formal negative of べきだ is べからず, which is sometimes seen on signs.

教育制度 (*educational system*) を改革 (*reform*) するべきだ。
We ought to reform the educational system.
飲むべからず。(sign on an outdoor water faucet in a park)
Do not drink.

38.6 At times, ものだ functions like から (*because*). The difference is that ものだ is used when the speaker is making an excuse or trying to justify an action or an opinion. ものだ and から are sometimes used together.

Vocabulary and Grammar 7A

357

すみませんが、今日は早く帰らせていただけませんか。
子供が病気なもので...。

I'm sorry, but today could you let me leave early? My child is sick.

38.7 The construction ものか is a protest against undesirable conditions or against what the speaker feels to be unreasonable expectations. It is not a very polite way to express one's displeasure, so it should be used with caution. It can carry the meaning of the English expression, *Do you expect me to...?*

そんな馬鹿なことがあってたまる (*put up with*) ものか。
Do you expect me to put up with that kind of nonsense?

38.8 In colloquial speech, もの is often contracted to もん.

昔は10円でいろんなものが買えたもんだ。
In the old days, you used to be able to buy a lot of things with ten yen.

言語ノート

こと and もの

こと as a noun means *phenomenon, concept, act, matter, incident*— in other words, it is often translated as the English word *thing*, but it always refers to something intangible and abstract, particularly if it is general or unspecified. For this reason, こと is often called a pseudo-noun.

そのことがあってから、三村さんは私と口をきいて
くれません。
Since that incident occurred, Mr. Mimura won't speak to me.
町田さんが面白いことを言っていましたよ。
Mr. Machida said an interesting thing.
木村先生のことを思い出しました。
I recalled (things about) Professor Kimura.

In contrast, もの refers to a concrete thing or person, not an idea or action. The following sentences illustrate the difference.

それは面白いことだ。
それは面白いものだ。

Both sentences can be translated into English as, *That's an interesting thing,* but the first one refers to an event, a situation, a piece of news, a subject of discussion, or something else intangible. The second sentence refers to a piece of artwork, a book, a new gadget, an exotic plant, or anything else that a person can see and touch.

Nature and Culture

✳ アクティビティー 4

ダイアログ：黒岩湾でよく魚をとったものです。(*I used to fish in Kuroiwa Bay*.)

ブラウン：黒岩島に新しいレジャーランドができたそうですね。

佐野：ええ、昔とすっかり変わってしまったらしいですよ。

ブラウン：佐野さんは黒岩島によく行くんですか。

佐野：いいえ、今は行かなくなりました。でも、子供のころはよく
行ったものです。黒岩湾でよく魚をとったもんですよ。

アクティビティー 5

見てみたいものですね。(*It's something I'd like to see*.)

Complete the dialogues in the first column by choosing an appropriate answer from the second column.

1. もう遅いですし、彼は来ない
   かもしれませんよ。
   帰りましょうか。

2. 山本さん、今夜どこかへ
   行きませんか。

3. 三村さんが新しい車を買った
   そうですよ。

4. カーティスさんのスピーチ、
   素晴らしかったですね。

5. 子供のころはどんなことを
   しましたか。

6. あんな人、もう大嫌いです。

a. 本当ですか。早く見てみたい
   ものですね。

b. 彼に会わないで帰るもの
   ですか。

c. そんなこと言うものでは
   ありません。

d. 明日の朝早く北海道に発つ
   もので、ちょっと…

e. アメリカ人で、よくあれだけ
   日本語を話せるものですね。

f. よく海や川で泳いだものです。

BROWN: I heard that there's a new resort development (lit., *leisure land*) in the Kuroiwa Islands.
SANO: Yes, it seems that the islands have really changed drastically since the old days.   BROWN: Do you go to Kuroiwa Island often?   SANO: No, I've stopped going, but when I was a child, I went there often. I used to fish in Kuroiwa Bay.

アクティビティー　6

あの人、よく食べたものだ。(*That man—he certainly ate a lot!*)

Complete the following dialogues by using … ものだ.

[例]　どうして遅(おく)れたんですか。
　　　目覚(めざ)し時計(どけい)が鳴(な)らなかったものですから。

1. あの海岸(かいがん)へ行ったことがありますか。

2. あんな馬鹿(ばか)なことをしてすみません。

3. ブラウンさん、日本語がすっかり上手(じょうず)になりましたね。

4. あの家、大きくていいですね。

5. あの人、プレゼントをもらっても何も言いませんね。

言語ノート

Both... and

English speakers sometimes have trouble with the concepts of *also* or *both... and* in Japanese. English grammar allows the speaker to place these elements freely in the sentence, but Japanese handles the concept of *is also* or *is both... and* by splitting だ／です into its original components of で and ある／あります and putting a も in between. Adjectives go into their く form followed by もある／あります。

　　　「朝日(あさひ)」はビールの名前(なまえ)ですか。
　　　ええ、それに新聞(しんぶん)の名前でもありますよ。(grammatical)
　　　*ええ、新聞の名前もです。(ungrammatical)
　　　Is Asahi the name of a beer?
　　　Yes, it's also the name of a newspaper.

アクティビティー　7

開発(かいはつ)！開発！開発！(*Development! Development! Development!*)

Shortly after John Kawamura's visit, a billionaire bought the Kuroiwa and Akaiwa Islands and developed them into a resort. The chart shows what has become of various areas of the islands. The drawings show some of the things people used to do in these places before the recreational facilities were built. Complete the chart in Japanese.

THEN	NOW	WHAT DID PEOPLE USED TO DO THERE?
あかいわ おか 赤岩の丘	じょう ゴルフ場	やさい くだもの 野菜や果物を作ったものです。
あかいわわん 赤岩湾	マリンランド	
くろいわやま 黒岩山	じょう の ば ハングライダー場、ボート乗り場	
あかいわ もり 赤岩の森	べっそう 別荘 (vacation homes) とテニス・コート	
くろいわむら しょうがっこう 黒岩村の小学校	ほんぶ レジャーランドの本部 (main office)	

Vocabulary and Grammar 7B

Vocabulary and Oral Activities

Nature and Environment

Vocabulary: Animals, Birds, and Insects

動物	どうぶつ	animal
動物園	どうぶつえん	zoo
飼う	かう	to raise or keep an animal
かわいがる		to treat with affection; to make a pet of
餌	えさ	animal food; bait
犬	いぬ	dog
猫	ねこ	cat
猿	さる	monkey
鼠	ねずみ	mouse; rat
馬	うま	horse
牛	うし	cow; cattle
豚	ぶた	pig
羊	ひつじ	sheep
熊	くま	bear
象	ぞう	elephant
虎	とら	tiger
鹿	しか	deer
鯨	くじら	whale
鳥	とり	bird
翼	つばさ	wing
ニワトリ		chicken
あひる		duck
七面鳥	しちめんちょう	turkey
蛙	かえる	frog
蛇	へび	snake
虫	むし	insect
蜜蜂	みつばち	bee
蚊	か	mosquito
蝿	はえ	housefly

The terms 七面鳥 and ニワトリ refer to live birds only. When cooked Western style, the meat is referred to as ターキー and チキン. When cooked Japanese or Chinese style, chicken meat is referred to simply as 鳥, or トリ肉.

The Japanese regard the buzzing and humming of the cicadas as one of the most significant signs of summer.

ゴキブリ		cockroach
蝉	せみ	cicada
蝶	ちょう	butterfly

Loanwords: ペット、ゴリラ、チンパンジー、オランウータン、スカンク、ペリカン、パンダ、ライオン、カナリア

✺ アクティビティー　8

何ですか。(*What is it?*)

What animal or insect does each of the following statements describe?

1. アフリカやインドにいる鼻の長い動物です。
2. サンクスギビングに食べる鳥です。
3. この虫にさされる (*be stung*) と、とてもかゆい (*itchy*) です。
4. 花の蜜 (*honey; nectar*) を集める虫です。
5. この動物から取る液体 (*liquid*) を飲んだり、それでアイスクリームやヨーグルトを作ります。
6. 一番大きい哺乳動物 (*mammal*) です。
7. 車が発明 (*invent*) される前に、人はこの動物に乗って旅行しました。

Now make up several "guess what" questions about animals, and try them out on your classmates.

✺ アクティビティー　9

どんな動物が好きですか。(*What animal do you like?*)

Discuss in class.

1. どんな動物が好きですか。何か動物を飼っていますか。
2. 猫と犬とどちらが好きですか。どうしてですか。
3. 人間 (*humans*) が肉を食べる動物にはどんなものがありますか。
4. 人間を食べたり殺したり (*kill*) する動物には、どんなものがありますか。
5. 人間に役に立つ (*useful*) 動物にはどんなものがありますか。
6. 動物園で人気のある (*popular*) 動物は何ですか。
7. 足の速い動物にはどんなものがありますか。飛ぶのが速い鳥にはどんなものがありますか。

Vocabulary Library

The Environment

環境	かんきょう	environment
公害	こうがい	public nuisance; pollution
汚染（する）	おせん（する）	pollution (to pollute)
保護	ほご	protection; preservation
破壊	はかい	destruction; damage
自然	しぜん	nature
産業	さんぎょう	industry
節約（する）	せつやく（する）	saving; economizing (to save, economize)
ごみ		garbage; trash
資源	しげん	resources
もったいない		wasteful

Loanwords: アスベスト、オゾン、フロン・ガス、グリーン・ハウス・エフェクト、スモッグ、リサイクルする

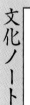

CULTURE NOTE • 公害 (*Pollution*)

From the early 1960s to the mid-1970s, the Japanese economy grew rapidly, but during this period unregulated development of heavy manufacturing industries brought about several serious incidents of mass poisoning from toxic waste. The most notorious occurred at Minamata in Kyushu, where many residents suffered brain damage and other consequences after eating fish contaminated with mercury-laden wastes from a local factory. Air pollution, water pollution, sinkholes caused by overuse of underground water, and noise pollution from traffic and construction became widespread. Increasing urbanization of the country led to the destruction of fields, hills, and forests to build housing and infrastructure.

Thanks to the advancement of environmental protection technology and strict enforcement of environmental protection laws, the situation is improving. For example, households are required to separate their burnable and nonburnable refuse in order to facilitate recycling. Taxis now run on propane instead of gasoline, leading to a decrease in auto emissions, and the government encourages building train and subway lines out into the suburbs so that residents are not dependent on cars. People who visited Tokyo twenty-five years ago used to tell of air pollution so bad that it gave them sore throats, but pollution of that severity is rare these days.

Grammar and Practice Activities

39. Various Uses of よう

町田：おつまみがもっといるわね。

ブラウン：さっきウェーターにもっと持ってくるように頼んだわ。

町田：あらあら、林さん、あんまり食べていないわね。

ブラウン：もっと食べるようにすすめたら。

山口：大助、急ぎなさい。遅れますよ。

大助：寝坊しないように目覚まし時計をセットしたのになあ。

山口：富田さんの家はどこか知っているの？

大助：うん。迷わないように地図で調べておいたよ。

> おつまみ are small portions of things like **yakitori,** salads, peanuts, tofu with shaved ginger and soy sauce, dried cuttlefish, eggplant roasted with miso sauce, and similar snacks, served along with alcoholic beverages. They have to be ordered individually.

39.1 In the following construction, ... ように is used to report the content of a request, a suggestion, or advice.

Clause ending in the plain, nonpast form of a verb	ように	Verbs expressing a command, request, suggestion, advice, etc.

to tell/ask/suggest that someone do...

三村さんに図書館の前で待つように言われた。
I was told by Mr. Mimura to wait in front of the library.
部屋の中でタバコを吸わないように、あの人たちに頼みましょう。
Let's ask those people not to smoke in the room.

As seen in these examples, the person to whom a command or request is given is marked by the indirect object marker に. This construction is called an indirect

> に after 三村さん in the second example is the marker of an agent in a passive sentence.

MACHIDA: We need more snack foods, don't we?　BROWN: I just told the waiter to bring some more.
MACHIDA: Oh, look, Mr. Hayashi hasn't eaten very much, has he?　BROWN: How about suggesting that he eat more?

YAMAGUCHI: Daisuke, hurry up. We'll be late.　DAISUKE: And here I set the alarm clock so as not to oversleep!　YAMAGUCHI: Do you know where Mr. Tomita's house is?　DAISUKE: Yeah. I checked the map ahead of time, so as not to get lost.

Vocabulary and Grammar 7B

365

三百六十五

command, and it is a paraphrase of a direct quotation of a command. For example, instead of saying,

> カワムラさんに、すぐ横井先生にお話しするように言ってください。
> *Please tell Mr. Kawamura to talk with Professor Yokoi soon.*

you could tell the person the exact words to say:

> カワムラさんに「すぐ横井先生にお話してください」と言ってください。
> *Please say to Mr. Kawamura, "Talk to Professor Yokoi soon."*

Unless you really care about the exact words the person uses to convey your message, the indirect command form is more natural.

39.2 In the following construction, ... ように is used to express a purpose or the manner in which something is to be done.

The plain, nonpast potential form of a verb The plain, nonpast form of a potential verb	ように	Clause
The plain, nonpast, negative form of a verb		

so that; in such a way that

> 日本語が上達するように、毎日練習している。
> *I'm practicing so that I can improve my Japanese.*
> みんなに聞こえるように、マイクを使って話した。
> *I spoke using a microphone so that everyone could hear.*

Note that a purpose is also expressed by ... ために (Chapter 2, **Grammar 10**). The difference between ... ように and ... ために is that the latter expresses a far stronger sense of purpose than the former. Using ... ために indicates that the speaker believes that the action or situation described in the first clause will take place for sure.

> 会議に出るために、大阪へ行った。
> *会議に出るように、大阪へ行った。 (ungrammatical)

In this example, the principal objective of the speaker's going to Osaka was to attend the conference, so only ... ために is grammatical.

> 風邪を引かないように、コートを着た。
> *風邪を引かないために、コートを着た。 (ungrammatical)

By wearing a coat, the speaker might somehow avoid catching a cold, but that is by no means a foolproof method of preventing illness, and the speaker might catch a cold anyway. In this case, then, ... ように is more appropriate.

アクティビティー 10

早く来るように言われた。(*I was told to come early.*)

Fill in the blanks in the first column with the appropriate words from the second column. Each word should be used once.

1. (　　　)に薬を飲むように言われました。
2. (　　　)にスピード違反しないように注意されました。
3. (　　　)に切符を見せるように言われた。
4. (　　　)にノートを貸してくれるように頼まれました。
5. (　　　)にメニューを持ってくるように頼んだ。
6. (　　　)は部下に明日早く会社に来るように命じた (*gave an order*)
7. (　　　)は口をもっと大きく開けるように言った。

a. ウエイター
b. おまわりさん
c. 駅員
d. お医者さん
e. 部長
f. 歯医者さん
g. クラスメート

アクティビティー 11

箱の中を見ないようにしてください。(*Don't look inside the box, please.*)

Fill in the blanks in the first column with the most appropriate phrases from the second column, first changing the phrase from the direct quotation to the indirect quotation form.

[例]　町田さんに(　　　)言われたが、中を見てしまった。
　　　h. 箱の中に何が入っているか見ないように

1. 母に(　　　)頼まれたのを、忘れてしまいました。
2. アメリカ人の友人に(　　　)頼みました。
3. となりの部屋の人に(　　　)言われたので、テレビの音を小さくしました。

a. シートベルトをお締めください。
b. 静かにしてください。
c. 英語の宿題、手伝ってくれないかなあ。
d. もう少し急いでくれませんか。

4. お医者さんが（　　）おっしゃった
ので、コーヒーに砂糖を入れない
ようにしている。

5. スチュワーデスが（　　）言うと、
乗客はみんなそうした。

6. タクシーの運転手は（　　）
言われると、すぐ高速道路に入った。

7. 後ろの人に（　　）言われたので、
そうした。

e. あまり甘いものは食べない
方がいいですよ。

f. 学校の帰りにレタス
を買ってきてね。

g. 座ってくれませんか。

h. 箱の中に何が入っているか
見ないでくださいね。

アクティビティー　12

聞こえるようになりました。(*It became audible.*)

Match each item in the first column with the most appropriate sentence ending
from the second column.

1. 遅れないように
2. 祖母でも読めるように
3. 部屋の中に日が入らないように
4. はっきり聞こえるように
5. 誰も入ってこないように
6. ぐっすり (*soundly*) 眠れるように
7. 彼に知られないように
8. 誰にも気付かれないように

a. 大きな声で話してください。
b. 大きな字で手紙を書いた。
c. ドアの鍵をかけた。
d. 黙って (*not talk*) いてください。
e. 窓から外に出た。
f. 早くうちを出た。
g. ホット・ミルクを飲みなさい。
h. カーテンを閉めてください。

アクティビティー　13

上手に書けるように練習しています。(*I'm practicing so I can get good at
writing.*)

Complete these sentences with something that makes sense.

1. 頭痛が早く治るように、…
2. 両親が喜ぶように、…

3. 日本語が上手に書けるように、…

4. ストレスがたまらない (*not accumulate*) ように…

5. 早く新しい車が買えるように、…

✴ アクティビティー　14

ダイアログ：大切にするように言いましょう。(*I will tell him to make better use of it.*)

カワムラ：こんないい紙を捨てるんですか。

山口：そうね。もったいないわね。大助だわ。

カワムラ：この紙なんか、ほとんど何も書いてありませんよ。

山口：大助にもっと紙を大切にするように言いましょう。

✴ アクティビティー　15

何と言いますか。(*What would you say?*)

What would you say to the following people? Answer in Japanese, following the example.

[例]　ジュースの空き缶 (*empty can*) を捨てている人 →
　　　空き缶をリサイクルするように言います。

1. いつも食べ物を残す人

2. どこへ行くのにも車を使う人

3. いつもハンバーガーばかり食べている人

4. いつも文句 (*complaint*) ばかり言っている人

5. ものぐさ (*lazy*) な人

6. 誰とも付き合わない人 (…と付き合う means *to associate with…*)

7. 好き嫌いの激しい (*having too strong likes and dislikes*) 人

KAWAMURA: Are you going to throw away such good paper?　YAMAGUCHI: You're right. What a waste! It's Daisuke (who is doing that).　KAWAMURA: This paper has almost nothing written on it. YAMAGUCHI: I'll have to tell Daisuke to make better use of paper.

40. It's All Right Not to...: 〜なくてもいい

カワムラ： 古い新聞がたまりましたね。ゴミ回収場所に出して
　　　　　 きましょうか。
山口： ああ、その新聞は出さなくてもいいのよ。
カワムラ： どうしてですか。
山口： チリ紙交換に出すのよ。

On trash collection days, people bring their refuse to designated ゴミ回収場所 found every block or so in residential neighborhoods.

The チリ紙交換 goes around neighborhoods in a loudspeaker truck collecting newspapers and magazines for recycling. People who hand over paper to be recycled receive tissues or toilet paper in return.

The concept of *it is all right not to do* or *one does not have to do* can be expressed with the following construction.

Verb	Negative stem +	
I-adjective	Root + く	なくて（も）いい
Na-adjective/noun	Dictionary form/noun + で（は）	

does not have to; it is all right not to; it is not necessary to; even if

おなかがいっぱいなら、無理して食べなくてもいいです。
If you're full, you don't have to force yourself to eat.

それほどハンサムでなくてもいいから、優しい男の人と結婚したい。
I want to marry a kind man, even if he's not particularly handsome.
　　(Lit., *Because it's all right if he's not particularly handsome, I want to marry a kind man.*)

Remember that 〜なくてはいけない／ならない (see Chapter 1, **Grammar 6**) means *must* or *have to.* A meaning similar to that of 〜なくてもいい can be expressed by the following constructions.

Verb, i-adjective	The nonpast, plain form	必要はない
Na-adjective, noun	Root/noun + である	（必要はありません）

It is not necessary to; there is no need to

KAWAMURA: The old newspapers have accumulated, haven't they? Should I go put them out at the collection site (lit., *put them out and come back*)?　　YAMAGUCHI: Oh, it's all right not to put them out.
KAWAMURA: Why is that?　　YAMAGUCHI: We're going to put them out for the paper recycler.

Nature and Culture

どんなにうるさくても眠れますから、周りが静かである必要は
ありません。

I can fall asleep no matter how noisy it is, so it's not necessary for my surroundings to be quiet.

This construction sounds more formal than ...なくてもいい。

Note that ...必要がある means *it is necessary to...*

我々は省エネに協力する必要がある。

It is necessary for us to cooperate in saving energy.

Another construction that expresses lack of necessity is the nonpast, plain form of the verb plus ことはない (ことはありません).

あんな小さい犬なんて怖がることはないよ。

There's no need to be afraid of a little dog like that.

The literal meaning of both なんか and なんて is *and so on* or *and things like that,* but they can sometimes be used to express a vague contempt.

アクティビティー 16

買い物に行かなくてもいいよ。(*It's OK not to do any shopping.*)

Match each item in the first column with the most appropriate sentence ending from the second column.

1. お金はお母さんから
   いただきましたから、

2. 今日はすることが全然
   ないから、

3. コーヒーはブラックが
   好きだから、

4. 高田さんとはもう
   話したから、

5. 食べる物はたくさん
   あるから、

6. 誰も怒っていないんだから、

7. 本を読んでいるんじゃ
   ないから、

8. 夫婦二人だけだから、

9. お茶であれば、

a. 手紙は出さなくてもいいよ。

b. 買い物に行かなくてもいい。

c. 払わなくても結構です。

d. 熱くなくてもいいです。

e. 家はそんなに広くなくてもいい。

f. 砂糖は入れなくてもいいよ。

g. 電気はそんなに明るくなくても
   いい。

h. 泣かなくてもいい。

i. 来なくてもいい。

アクティビティー　17

どういう人が言ったでしょうか。(*I wonder who said that.*)

Try to imagine who might have said the following sentences to whom. Be creative.

1.　もう明日から会社に出て来なくてもいいわよ。

2.　そんなに大きな声で話さなくてもいいですよ。

3.　ドルでなくてもいいですよ。日本の円でも大丈夫です。

4.　そんなことを言うなら、食べなくてもいい。

5.　もう我慢 (*patience; putting up with something*) しなくてもいいです。
　　よかったですね。

✳ アクティビティー　18

動物園 (*The zoo*)

You have been appointed director of your city's new zoo (動物園長). Following is the layout of your zoo. You have purchased, borrowed from other zoos, or received the following animals as donations. You also have some money to buy more animals or birds of your choice. How will you assign these animals and the new animals to the cages and enclosures?

Animals: パンダ、カバ (*hippopotamus*)、チンパンジー、ライオン、
キリン (*giraffe*)、ペリカン、イルカ (*dolphin*)、ワニ (*crocodile*)、 狼 (*wolf*)、
兎 (*rabbit*)、 狐 (*fox*)

1. Try to satisfy at least the following conditions.
    a. 池が必要な動物と鳥は、池のある檻 (*cage*) に入れる。
    b. 動物園の入口の近くには、子供が好きな動物を入れる。
    c. 動物園の入口には、子供が怖がる (*to be scared*) 動物は入れない。
    d. 食堂や喫茶店のそばの檻には、静かな動物を入れる。
    e. 全ての檻に動物を入れる。

2. After you decide which animals you would put in which enclosures,
   explain your plan, including the rationale behind it, and your purchase
   plan, to your classmates.

3. Look at your classmate's plan, and make comments regarding the
   following items:
    a. 場所を変えたほうがいいのは、どの動物ですか。
    b. 場所を変えなくてもいいのは、どの動物ですか。
    c. 新しく買う動物について、意見 (*opinion*) はありますか。

Vocabulary: Plants (1)

植物	しょくぶつ	plant
草	くさ	grass
盆栽	ぼんさい	**bonsai** (*artificially dwarfed trees grown in containers*)
桜	さくら	cherry tree
梅	うめ	plum tree
菊	きく	chrysanthemum
咲く	さく	to bloom
生える	はえる	to grow; to flourish (*plants and trees*)
枯れる	かれる	to wither; to die (*plants and trees only*)
葉／葉っぱ	は／はっぱ	leaf
花粉	かふん	pollen
土	つち	soil
種	たね	seed
植える	うえる	to plant
松	まつ	pine tree
杉	すぎ	Japanese cedar

Loanwords: カーネーション、ダリヤ、ブーケ、チューリップ
Review: 花、木、庭、花屋

The importance of the cherry blossom in Japanese culture is well known, and the chrysanthemum and pine also play prominent roles in traditional symbolism.

どんな花が好きですか。(*What kind of flower do you like?*)

1. どんな花が好きですか。
2. 母の日にはどんな花をあげますか。
3. ほかにどんなときに花をプレゼントしますか。あなたはよく花を
   プレゼントしますか。
4. 花粉 (*pollen*) アレルギーですか。
5. あなたの家に庭はありますか。どんな花や木がありますか。
6. くだものがなる木にはどんなものがありますか。
7. どんなくだものを食べますか。

Vocabulary Library

Plants (2)

植木	うえき	potted plant
芝生	しばふ	lawn
花壇	かだん	flower bed
石庭	せきてい	rock garden
竹	たけ	bamboo

京都の石庭

41. Coming to a Conclusion: ...わけだ

三村：林さん、最近ウキウキしているみたいだけど、どうしたんですか。
町田：あれ、知らなかったの？林さんとギブソンさん、結婚するんですよ。
三村：そんなわけだったんですか。
町田：ええ、ギブソンさんがようやく「イエス」と言ってくれたから、ウキウキしているわけですよ。

41.1 The noun わけ means *reason, circumstance,* or *meaning,* as shown in the following examples.

なぜ怒っているんですか。わけを聞かせてください。
Why are you angry? Please tell me the reason.

わけの分からないことを言うのはやめてください。
Stop saying things that don't make any sense.

> わけが分からない is an expression meaning *nonsensical.*

41.2 The following construction is used to express the speaker's judgment that a certain circumstance took place as a natural consequence of something. The fact or information that the speaker used to make that judgment is explicitly expressed (in S1 in the box). The information that allows the speaker to make the conclusion can be either auditory or visual. Sometimes the exact nuance is impossible to translate into English and corresponds to the tone of voice that English speakers use when they have just realized something.

S1	S2	
	Plain form of verb and i-adjectives	わけだ（わけです）
	Root of na-adjective ＋ な／だった	
	Noun ＋ という／だった	

It's that; the fact is that; you could say that; so that's why

試験があったんですか。それで、徹夜したわけですか。
You had a test? Is that why you pulled an all-nighter?

MIMURA: Mr. Hayashi seems to be in a very cheerful mood lately. What's going on?　MACHIDA: Oh, didn't you know? Mr. Hayashi and Ms. Gibson are going to get married.　MIMURA: Is that what it was?
MACHIDA: Yes, Ms. Gibson finally said yes, so that's why he's in such a cheerful mood.

Vocabulary and Grammar 7B

375
三百七十五

家計は母が全てやりくりしています。母は我が家の大蔵大臣という
わけです。

*As far as household accounts are concerned, my mother manages
everything. You could say that Mother is our finance minister.*

41.3 わけで, the te-form of わけだ, is used in conjunction with demonstrative
pronouns to form introductory phrases similar in meaning to the English *for this
reason* or *for that reason*.

途中で交通事故がありまして、そんなわけで遅れました。
On the way there was a traffic accident, and for that reason I was late.

Ending a sentence with the plain form of the predicate + というわけだ is
another way of stating a consequence or explaining a situation. It is very similar to
the …のだ construction.

秘密にしてくれと言われたので、誰にも言わなかったというわけです。
Because I was told to keep it a secret, I didn't tell anyone.

～ありまして is the super-
polite form of あって.
People often use these
sorts of very polite forms
when speaking to their
superiors.

41.4 わけではない is used in negative sentences to focus the negation,
particularly when it is necessary to negate someone else's partially correct
supposition. For example, suppose that an acquaintance notices that you no
longer take your morning run. The acquaintance says something indicating an
assumption that you've given up running because you don't like it. In fact, you like
running very much, but your doctor has told you to give it up in favor of
low-impact activities. In such a situation you might be tempted to say,

*嫌いだからやめませんでした。

However, this means something like, *Because I hate it, I didn't quit,* which
sounds strange. What you should say in this situation is

嫌いだからやめたわけではありません。
It isn't the case that I quit because I hate it.

Here are more examples.

三村さんの責任だと言っているわけではありません。
I'm not saying that it's Mr. Mimura's responsibility.

言いわけをするわけではありませんが、お金が足りなかったのです。
It's not that I'm making excuses, but I didn't have enough money.

41.5 The nonpast, plain form of verb + わけに (は) いかない means *it won't do
to…, one ought not to…,* or *it wouldn't be right to…*

あなたからこんな大金をもらうわけにはいかない。

It wouldn't be right for me to receive this large amount of money from you.

町田さんに全部払わすわけにはいかなかった。

It wasn't right to make Ms. Machida pay for the whole thing.

✳ アクティビティー 20

ダイアログ：それで早く咲いたわけですね。(*That's why they've bloomed early, isn't it?*)

山口：いやあ、きれいですね、あの桜は。

カワムラ：ええ。でも、桜の見ごろはまだじゃないんですか。

山口：ええ。でも、今年は冬がとても暖かかったから…

カワムラ：ああ、それで早く咲いたわけですね。

Practice the dialogue, substituting the following expressions for the underlined parts.

1. 今年は冬がとても寒かった
   こんなに遅い

2. 今年の春は暖かい
   もう満開 (*in full bloom*) な

アクティビティー 21

海に行きましたから、日に焼けているわけです。(*I went to the seaside—that's why I got sunburned.*)

Complete the sentences in items **1** through **8** by choosing the appropriate endings from items **a** through **h** on the next page.

1. 泳ぐのが好きだから、

2. お酒が飲めないので、

3. ワープロが使えないので、

4. 料理が好きだったから、

5. 家を買うために、

6. 目が悪い人がいるから、

7. 外でずっと働いていたので、

8. あまり食べないから、

YAMAGUCHI: Hey, aren't they pretty, those cherry blossoms? KAWAMURA: Yes, but isn't the best time to see cherry blossoms later on? (Lit., *Isn't it not yet?*) YAMAGUCHI: Yes, but the winter this year was very warm… KAWAMURA: Oh, that's why they've bloomed early, isn't it?

a. コックになったわけです。

b. そんなにやせているわけですね。

c. 日に焼けた (*got sunburned*) わけ
ですね。

d. 毎日、プールへ行くわけですね。

e. 黒板に大きな字で書いているわけ
ですね。

f. お金を貯めているわけだ。

g. 何でも手書き (*handwritten*)
なわけです。

h. パーティーに出るのがおっくう
(*tiresome*) なわけです。

アクティビティー　22

どういうわけで... (*How did it happen?*)

Complete these sentences by using ...わけだ.

[例] 料理をするのが嫌いだから、————。→
料理をするのが嫌いだから、いつもレストランで食事するわけですね。

1. 日本語が上手になるように、

2. 宿題がむずかしいから、

3. 日本の文化に興味 (*interest*) があるので、

4. 今年は長い休みが取れたから、

5. まだ学生だから、

6. 貝に対して(*toward*) アレルギーがあるから、

CULTURE NOTE • Japanese Poetry

Japanese poems are structured very differently from those found in English or other European languages. They are organized according to syllable count, typically in lines of either five or seven syllables.

By the Heian period (796–1185), one form, the **waka** (和歌), with its 5-7-5-7-7 pattern of syllables, predominated. Composing **waka** was a favorite pastime of the aristocrats, and a necessary social skill learned in childhood. People included original poems in their diaries and personal letters and especially admired the ability to make up impromptu poems in response to the events of the moment.

Creating **renga** (連歌), or "linked verse," was a popular pastime from the fourteenth century on. **Renga** were always composed by two or more people, who took turns writing alternating sets of 7-7 and 5-7-5 lines, ending with a coherent poem.

In the seventeenth century, poets began to write the 5-7-5 poems now known in the West as **haiku** (俳句).

Haiku is still a living tradition in Japan. The best **haiku** either point out a little-noticed but significant detail of the sight described or hint at its emotional or philosophical significance.

Vocabulary and Grammar 7C

Vocabulary and Oral Activities

Culture and Customs

Vocabulary: Culture and Customs

文化	ぶんか	culture
歴史	れきし	history
時代	じだい	era; period
社会	しゃかい	society
習慣	しゅうかん	habit
守る	まもる	to observe (*a custom*); to obey (*a rule*); to protect
みっともない		unseemly; improper; disreputable
おとなしい		proper; well-behaved; mild-mannered
頑張る	がんばる	to do one's best; to hang in there; to come out of a difficult situation all right
我慢する	がまんする	to put up with an unpleasant situation without complaint
お辞儀をする	おじぎをする	to bow
正座(する)	せいざ(する)	sitting traditional style (to sit traditional style) (*on one's heels and keeping one's back straight*)
宗教	しゅうきょう	religion
神	かみ	god; divine being
信じる	しんじる	to believe
仏教	ぶっきょう	Buddhism
仏像	ぶつぞう	Buddhist statue
神道	しんとう	Shintoism
鳥居	とりい	gate of a Shinto shrine
祭り	まつり	festival
御輿	みこし	portable shrine carried during festival processions
キリスト教	キリストきょう	Christianity
ユダヤ教	ユダヤきょう	Judaism
イスラム教／回教	イスラムきょう／かいきょう	Islam
興味(がある)	きょうみ(がある)	interest (to be interested)

Loanwords: タブー、マナー、エチケット

「ワッショイ、ワッショイ」
お祭りで御輿をかついで
います。

※ アクティビティー　**23**

ジェパディー（*Jeopardy*）

What questions would yield the following answers? Use words from the
preceding vocabulary box.

1. 床の上にすわる時、この姿勢（*position*）をとります。
2. 挨拶（*greeting*）する時、これをします。
3. 大変なことがあってもあきらめない（*not give up*）こと。
4. 神社の前にある大きい物。
5. 面白いと思って、もっと知りたいという気持ち。
6. 寺の中、または寺の周りにある物。
7. ヨーロッパから入ってきた宗教。
8. エチケットを守る人はみんなにこう言われるでしょう。
9. 大変なことがあっても、文句（*complaint*）を言わないこと。
10. 日本だけの宗教。

Now make up more questions on Japanese history and culture based on your
personal knowledge, outside reading, or even the 文化ノート in this textbook.
See if you can stump your classmates and instructor.

※ アクティビティー　**24**

習慣、慣例、エチケット（*Customs, formalities, etiquette*）

Discuss in class.

1. あなたの国（文化）にあって、他の国（文化）にない習慣にどんなものがありますか。

2. あなたの国（文化）にはどんなタブーがありますか。

3. 食事をするときにはどんなエチケットを守る必要がありますか。日本ではどんなエチケットを守る必要があるか知っていますか。

4. 他人の家を訪ねる (visit) ときには、どんなエチケットを守らなければなりませんか。

5. 日本人はお正月には神社にお参りし、お葬式はお寺でします。結婚式をキリスト教の教会であげる人もたくさんいます。あなたの国にも、宗教に対してこういう態度 (attitude toward) を取る人はいますか。

CULTURE NOTE • Taboos

Every culture has its own ideas about which actions are socially acceptable and unacceptable. For example, the Japanese consider it rude to blow one's nose in public. Instead, people who have colds or allergies just sniff, sometimes very loudly, until they can get away and blow their noses in private.

There are two taboos connected with chopsticks, both of which derive from Japanese funeral customs. One is that you must never stick your chopsticks upright in your rice bowl but always lay them on the 箸置き（はしおき）, or on the edge of the bowl. Another is that you must never pass food from one set of chopsticks to another.

The idea behind the well-known rule about taking your shoes off before entering a house or temple is that you should not bring the dirt of the outside world into the building. That is why Japanese people do not go barefoot outside, even in the hottest weather.

In connection with this rule, be careful how you dress in hot weather. Both men and women should wear at least a tank top and loosely cut shorts in public on casual occasions, no matter how hot and humid the weather gets. Also keep in mind that what seems like a casual occasion to a North American may be a formal or semiformal occasion by Japanese standards, so if in doubt, ask.

Many North Americans like to be thought of as friendly, so once they have learned how to speak in the plain form, they want to use it with everyone because they think it sounds friendlier. This is inappropriate, because using plain form says either "we are intimates" or "you rank below me," and if neither is the case, the use of the plain form is offensive. When people rank above you, you cannot use the plain form to them, no matter how much you like them or how long you have known them.

There are other taboos as well. Therefore, if you are about to face an unfamiliar formal situation, such as a wedding or a funeral, you should ask someone about the expected etiquette ahead of time. When potentially tricky situations come up unexpectedly, do what the people around you do, especially if there is someone of your age and sex to imitate. Respecting such cultural differences will help make your stay in Japan smooth and productive.

文化ノート

Grammar and Practice Activities

42. Even Though: ...のに

さとみ： お母さん、一万円、貸してくれる？

山口： この間、おこづかいをあげたばかりなのに、また？

さとみ： 新しい服を買ったりして、全部使っちゃったのよ。

山口： あんなにおこづかい、無駄使いしちゃだめだって言ったのに...

さとみ： もう無駄使いしないから、お願い！

山口： あらあら、カワムラさん、ビッショリ濡れてしまって。

カワムラ： ええ、駅を出てしばらくしたら、雨が降ってきちゃって。

山口： 傘を持っていけばよかったのに。

カワムラ： あんなによく晴れていたので、傘はいらないと思ったんですが。

42.1 のに, which combines the nominalizer の and the particle に, expresses meanings such as *in spite of the fact that, contrary to the fact that, even though,* and *although.* The form is constructed as follows.

	S1		
Verbs	Plain form	のに	S2
I-adjectives	Plain form		
Na-adjectives	Dictionary form + な Dictionary form + だった		
Nouns	Noun + な Noun + だった		

Even though S1; in spite of the fact that S1; although S1; contrary to the expectation that S1.

SATOMI: Mom, will you lend me 10,000 yen?   YAMAGUCHI: Again? Even though I just gave you your allowance recently?   SATOMI: I used up my allowance buying new clothes and stuff.
YAMAGUCHI: Even though I told you that it's no good to waste your allowance like that?   SATOMI: I'm not going to waste it anymore, so please!

YAMAGUCHI: My, my, Mr. Kawamura, you're soaking wet!   KAWAMURA: Yes, just a little bit after I left the station, it started raining.   YAMAGUCHI: You should have taken an umbrella.   KAWAMURA: Since (the sky) was really clear, I thought I didn't (lit., *don't*) need an umbrella.

In this construction, the speaker is expressing disbelief, regret, sorrow, surprise, protest, reproach, sarcasm, or frustration that the situation is not turning out or has not turned out as expected.

> まもなくお客さんがいらっしゃるのに、まだそんな格好をしているんですか。
>
> *Even though the guests are coming any minute, you're still dressed like that?*
>
> 彼にプレゼントをあげたのに、お礼の手紙も電話もない。
>
> *In spite of the fact that I gave him a present, he neither (sends) me a thank-you letter nor phones me.*
>
> あんなにむずかしい試験だったのに、全員が満点を取った。
>
> *Even though it was such a difficult test, everyone got a perfect score.*

In conversations, S2 is not often expressed when it is understandable from the context.

> A: カワムラさん、うちにいなかったよ。
>
> *Mr. Kawamura wasn't at home.*
>
> B: せっかく行ったのに？
>
> *Even though you went to all the trouble of going there?*

Also, のに can be added to a sentence to express resentment or disappointment when a promise is broken or one's expectations are otherwise unmet. In these cases, the English equivalent does not necessarily express the idea of *even though*. In fact, the English equivalent is most often an exclamation beginning with *but*.

> あれほど遊園地に連れて行ってくれるって言っていたのに。
>
> *But he kept saying that he would take us to the amusement park!*

Because of the nature of the speaker's involvement discussed here, S2 cannot be a wish, command, request, offer, statement of permission, or statement of intention. In such cases, けれど（も）is used instead of のに.

> ちょっと寒いけれど／*のに、外に出ましょう。
>
> *It's a bit cold, but let's go outside.*
>
> つまらないものだけれど／*なのに、持っていってください。
>
> *It's an insignificant thing, but please take it.*
>
> 遠いけれど／*のに、明日そこに行ってみるつもりです。
>
> *It's far, but I intend to try going there tomorrow.*

42.2 のに is used in contrary-to-fact conditionals to express the speaker's regret about some desirable situation that will most likely not happen or that the speaker wishes would have happened.

To review the conditionals, refer to Chapter 7, **Grammar 42**, in Book 1 for ～たら; Chapter 1, **Grammar 4**, in Book 2 for ...と; and Chapter 6, **Grammar 33**, in Book 2 for ～ば.

Conditional（...と, ～たら, ～ば）	いい／よかった	＋のに

> *It would be good if; I wish it would happen that; It would have been good if; I wish it would have happened that*

Note that this construction is used with the actions of people other than the speaker.

横井先生ともっと（お話しすれば、お話ししたら）よかったのに。
You should have spoken more with Professor Yokoi.
1日が30時間（あれば、あったら）いいのに。
I wish there were thirty hours in a day.
もう少しお金を貯めて（おいたら、おけば）よかったのに。
You should have saved up a little more money.
そんな馬鹿なこと（言わなければ、言わなかったら）よかったのに。
They shouldn't have said such stupid things.

When things that the speaker did are expressed, のに is dropped or is replaced with ...んですが（んだが）or ...んですけど（...だけど）.

夏の間にもっと海に（行っておけば、行っておいたら）よかったんですが...
I should have gone to the coast more during the summer.

だがis considered a masculine form, so female speakers would be well advised to use だけど, which is gender neutral, instead.

The conditional with ...いいのに is often used to give suggestions, but it should be used with caution, because it sounds a bit as if the speaker is scolding the person for doing or having done something contrary to the suggestion.

もっと御飯を食べたらいいのに。
You ought to eat more rice. (The implication is that the person is eating or has eaten something else.)

42.3 There is also a のに construction that is used to express the process required to accomplish some goal. In some cases, it is easily confused with the のに construction meaning *even though*.

S1		
Nonpast, plain verb (= dictionary form)	のに	S2

in order to do; for the purpose of doing

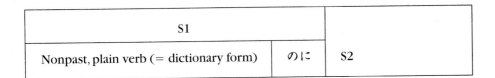

天ぷらを揚げるのに、油が必要です。
*In order to deep-fry **tempura**, you need oil.*
昔はアメリカに行くのに、船で3ヶ月かかりました。
In the old days it took three months by ship to go to America.
きれいな漢字を書くのには筆が一番です。
*In order to write beautiful **kanji**, a writing brush is best.*

* ## アクティビティー　25

ダイアログ：あんなにいやだって言っていたのに (Even though you said that you didn't want to...)

山口：　どうしたんですか。鏡に向かって。

カワムラ：林さんとギブソンさんの結婚式のスピーチの練習をしている
んです。

山口：　あれ、あんなにいやだって言っていたのに、スピーチするん
ですか。

カワムラ：ええ、二人とも親友ですから。

Practice the dialogue, replacing the underlined part with the following
expressions.

人前で話すのは嫌いだといつも言っている

人前で話すのは苦手な

アクティビティー　26

学生なのに人生がよくわかります。(She understands life so well, even though
she's only a student.)

Match each item in the first column with the appropriate sentence ending from
the second column.

1. 波が高いのに、

2. 学生なのに、

3. 日本語を1年しか
勉強しなかったのに、

4. お金があまりなかったのに、

5. ラッシュアワーの時間なのに、

6. もう12時になるのに、

7. 英語を読むのは上手なのに、

8. あの子はさっきまで (until a
little time ago) は静かだったのに、

a. 高いフランス料理の店に入って
しまいました。

b. 父はまだ帰ってこない。

c. 話すのは全くだめだ。

d. 今はとてもうるさい。

e. あまり混んでいません。

f. たくさんの人が泳いでいる。

g. 漢字がたくさん読める。

h. あまり勉強しない。

YAMAGUCHI: What are you doing facing the mirror?　KAWAMURA: I'm practicing the speech for Gibson
and Hayashi's wedding.　YAMAGUCHI: What? Even though you said that you didn't want to (lit., *that it
was that distasteful*), you're giving a speech?　KAWAMURA: Yes, because they're both my friends.

Vocabulary and Grammar 7C

385

三百八十五

せっかく読んだのに... (*After I went to all the trouble of reading it...*)

Complete these sentences.

1. もう梅雨の季節なのに、（　　　）

2. あの家にはガレージがあるのに、（　　　）

3. コートを着ているのに、（　　　）

4. 先月、お金を払ったのに、（　　　）

5. （　　　）、テレビばかり見ている。

6. （　　　）、富士山は見えない。

7. （　　　）、まだ怒っているようだ。

タクシーで来ればよかったのに。(*You could so easily have come by taxi.*)

Complete the dialogues in items **1** through **6** by choosing the appropriate sentences from items **a** through **f**.

1. A: （　　　）
   B: タクシーで来ればよかったのに。

2. A: （　　　）
   B: 少し休むといいのに。

3. A: （　　　）
   B: 予約しておいたらよかったのに。

4. A: （　　　）
   B: 速達で送ればいいのに。

5. A: （　　　）
   B: 部長にお願いしたらいいのに。

6. A: （　　　）
   B: もっと前に座ればよかったのに。

a. 海のそばのホテルは、空室が全然ありませんでした。

b. 駅から歩いて45分もかかるとは知らなかった。

c. 先生の声が小さいので、おっしゃっていることが聞こえなかったよ。

d. この本、田中さんが来週 必要なんだ。

e. 来週、一週間休みを取りたいんだ。

f. ああ、疲れた。

Language Skills

Reading and Writing

Reading 1　ゴルフ場建設反対

Sakura-machi is a small town in a southern prefecture whose main industries are agriculture and fishing. A development company is planning to develop a golf course in the town with backing from the prefectural government. The following is a letter from a resident that appeared in the local paper.

Now Read It!

What do you think are advantages and disadvantages that a golf course on Mt. Moriguchi would present to the residents? Discuss in class.

桜町は自然資源に恵まれた、住みやすい町である。しかし、この町が変わろうとしている。

　最近、桜町の北にある森口山をけずり、ゴルフ場を建設する計画が、南 日本観光開発 会社により発表された。県内各地にヨットハーバー、リゾートランド、マリンランド、キャンプ場、ハンググライダー場などを作り、日本のリゾートの中心にしようとする県もこの計画に賛成のようである。しかし、このゴルフ場建設計画が桜町の自然と環境にどのような影響を与えるか、御存じだろうか。

　先ず、町の北にあって、北風を防いでくれている森口山がなくなると、冬でも暖かい桜町の気候は変わってしまうだろう。また、森口山の樹木は土中深く根を張り、大雨の時も、洪水を防いでくれている。そして、雨の

恵まれる *to be endowed* / しかし *however*

けずる *to whittle away at; to grade (a hill or mountain)* / 建設 *construction* / 計画 *plan*
観光開発会社 *company for the development of tourism* / 県内各地 *in every part of the prefecture*

中心 *center* / 賛成 *agreement*

影響を与える *to have an influence*

深い *deep* / 根を張る *to extend roots* / 洪水 *flood*

降らない時でも、土中の水が川に流れ、森口川の水量を一定に保ってくれる。桜町が洪水や干ばつの被害にあわないのも、森口山のおかげである。

　ゴルフ場が作られると、芝に農薬がまかれ、森口川に流れるおそれがある。農薬で汚れた水は山の麓のミカン、スイカ、トマトの畑や田んぼに流れこむだろう。さらに、この水は海に流れ、桜町沖のハマチ、アサリ、真珠の養殖にも影響を与えるだろう。

　森口山は先祖代々伝わる桜町の宝である。私たちは森口山の春の新緑、秋の紅葉を見て、四季の変化を知ってきた。そして、花見、遠足の場所として、私たちの生活の一部となってきた。この森口山がゴルフ場に変わろうとしている。

　自然破壊、農薬汚染をもたらすゴルフ場の建設に断固反対しよう。6月4日6時から、桜町小学校講堂で反対集会がある。皆さんの参加をお待ちしている。

　　「桜町の自然と環境を守り、ゴルフ場建設に反対する会」

　　　　　　　　　　　　　　　　会長
　　　　　　　　　　　　　　　　吉本太一

一定 *uniform; consistent* / 保つ *to maintain*
干ばつ *drought* / 被害にあう *to sustain damage* / …のおかげで *thanks to…*
芝 *turf; sod* / 農薬をまく *to spread fertilizer* / おそれ *fear*
汚れる *to get dirty* / 田んぼ *rice paddy*
さらに *moreover*

先祖代々伝わる *to be passed down from generations of ancestors* / 宝 *treasure* / 新緑 *spring greenery*
紅葉 *autumn leaves* / 変化 *change* / 遠足 *excursion; outing*

もたらす *to bring about* / 断固 *firm; decisive* / 反対 *opposition*
講堂 *auditorium* / 反対集会 *protest rally* / 参加 *participation*

After You Finish Reading

1. The preceding letter consists of six paragraphs. Summarize the main points of each paragraph in English, following the example.

[例]　Paragraph 1: Introduction to the letter. Sakura-machi, with all its natural beauty, is about to change.

2. According to the letter, what would or could happen to each of the following features of Sakura-machi after the construction of the golf course? Answer in English.

   a. the climate
   b. Moriguchi River
   c. agricultural fields
   d. fisheries

3. Explain what function each of the following words plays in the structure of Mr. Yoshimoto's argument.

   a. paragraph 2 しかし
   b. paragraph 3 先ず
   c. paragraph 3 また
   d. paragraph 4 さらに
   e. paragraph 5 そして

Writing 1

1. Write a letter to support or argue against Mr. Yoshimoto's letter.
2. Write a letter to express your opinion on a current issue that you feel strongly about.

Reading 2 書評
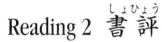

Following is a brief review of a book on Japanese culture.

Before You Read

What stereotypical ideas do people in your country have about Japanese people and their culture? What stereotypical ideas do you think Japanese people have about your country and culture(s)? Discuss in class.

Useful Vocabulary: 日本人論 *discussions about the nature of the Japanese people* (a popular topic for books in Japan), 自ら *self*, 気にする *to give a lot of attention or thought to*, 民族 *ethnic group*, 氏 a title similar in meaning to -さん but used mostly in formal, written contexts, タテ社会の人間関係 lit., *Human Relations in a Vertical Society* (English title: *Japanese Society*), 特に *especially*, 概念 *general concept*, 甘えの構造 lit., *The Structure of Presuming on the Kindness of Superiors* (English title: *The Anatomy of Dependence*), 主張する *to assert*, 両氏 *both of the people mentioned* (This is a very formal expression,

rarely used in conversation.), 共通する *to have traits in common*, 独特の
unique, これに対して *over and against this*, 縮み志向の日本人 lit., *The
Japanese, Who Aim to Shrink Things*, 著者 *author*, 欧米人 *Europeans and North
Americans*, 比較する *to compare*, 独自の *original, peculiar to*, 特性 *unique
characteristic*, 事物を縮小すること *scaling things down*, 扇子 *folding fan*,
機能 *function*, つめこむ *to pack in*, 表れ *expression*, 文字 *written symbol*,
宇宙 *universe*, 歌いこむ *to put all one's poetic expression into something*,
枯山水 *a Japanese-style dry garden*, おしこめる *to push into*, 常に *ordinarily*,
向く *to face toward something*, 西欧 *Western Europe*, 偏重 *over-valuation*,
するどい *sharp*, 警告 *warning*, 是非 *by all means*, すすめる *to suggest, to urge*

Now Read It!

本屋の日本人論のコーナーには、多くの本が並べられている。これは日本人
が自らに興味があり、自らのことをとても気にする民族であるからだろう。

　日本人、日本社会の特性について書かれた本の中では、中根千枝氏の
「タテ社会の人間関係」や土居健郎氏の「甘えの構造」が特に有名である。
中根氏は「タテ社会」の概念により、日本文化のメカニズムを説明しよう
としている。土居氏は日本社会が「タテ社会」なのも、日本人が義理人情を
大切にするのも、「甘え」によると主張している。両氏に共通していること
は「タテ社会」も「甘え」も日本独特の概念であり、外国には見られないと
いうことである。

　これに対して、「縮み志向の日本人」の著者 李御寧氏は、これまでの
日本人論は日本人を欧米人と比較して書かれたものが多く、「タテ社会」も
「甘え」も日本独自のものではなく、韓国にも見られると主張している。

　李氏は日本人の特性は「事物を縮小すること」であると言う。
トランジスタを使った日本の小さいラジオもウォークマンも、この特性に
よるものであると李氏は考える。扇子にいろいろな機能をつめこむのも、
弁当にいろいろなものをつめこむのも、この「縮み」の表れであるし、
17文字の俳句に四季と宇宙を歌いこむのも、盆栽、いけ花、枯山水に自然と
宇宙をおしこめるのも、「縮み」の特性によると言う。

　「縮み」の概念で日本人の特性を説明しようというのも面白いが、常に
文化の中心を欧米と考え、アジアを忘れ、欧米を向いてきた日本人の
西欧文化偏重に対するするどい警告でもある。ぜひ、読むことをすすめたい
本である。

After You Finish Reading

The preceding review consists of five paragraphs. State in English the gist of each paragraph.

Writing 2

Write a review of a book you have read. Before writing, think about what information you would like to include. Some suggestions:

- Information about the author
- Chapter organization (in the case of nonfiction books)
- Short description of the plot (in the case of fiction books)
- Good points about the book
- Points of disagreement with the author
- Whether or not you recommend that others read this book

Language Functions and Situations

Presenting One's Opinion Clearly and Logically

Here are some expressions you can use during discussions.

Clarifying the topic you would like to deal with in your speech:

今日は日本の庭園についてお話ししたいと思います。
Today I want to speak about Japanese gardens.

Starting to state your first point:

まず(最初に)、環境破壊の問題について述べたいと思います。
First I want to discuss the problem of environmental damage.

Moving to the next point:

次に、自然保護についてお話ししたいと思います。
Next, I want to speak about protecting nature.

Explaining in other words:

大気汚染、簡単に言えば、空気がきたなくなることですが...
Air pollution, or, to put it simply, the air becoming dirty...
ゴルフ場の建設は中止になりました。というのは、住民が反対
したからです。
The construction of the golf course was halted. That is to say, it's because residents were opposed.

Comparing:

兵庫県はゴルフ場の数が多い。それに比べて、高知県は少ない。

Hyogo prefecture has a large number of golf courses. Compared with that, Kochi prefecture has a small number.

Citing an example:

いろいろな公害病がおこりました。例えば、富山ではイタイイタイ病が問題となりました。

Various sorts of pollution-caused illnesses arose. For example, in Toyama itai itai disease became a problem.

Citing someone's statement or book:

東京大学の大野先生によると、この問題を無視 (*ignore*) するわけにはいかないそうです。

According to Professor Oono of the University of Tokyo, it won't do to ignore this problem.

Adding a point:

ゴルフ場建設により山がけずられました。さらに、農薬の使用により川も汚染されました。

The mountain was shaved down through the construction of the golf course. Moreover, the river was polluted through the use of fertilizers.

Transition to the next topic:

さて、次の問題に移りたいと思います。

Well then, I think I want to move on to the next problem.

Summarizing:

まとめると、次のようになります。

If we bring everything together, we end up with what follows.

Finishing your speech:

最後に、御清聴、ありがとうございました。

Finally, I thank you for listening to me attentively.

Activity

Make a short presentation on Japan and Japanese culture in class based on research done outside class. Try to use graphs and other visual aids to help clarify your points.

Having a Discussion

Asking for someone's opinion:

どうお考えですか。
What do you think?
御意見をお聞かせください。
Tell me your opinion.

Agreeing:

はい、私もそう思います。
Yes, I think so, too.
はい、賛成（同感）です。
Yes, I agree.

Asking someone if he or she agrees:

その意見に賛成ですか。
Do you agree with this opinion?

Confirming one's position:

では、賛成と考えていいわけですね。
So, it's all right to think of ourselves as being in agreement, right?

Expressing Disagreement

As mentioned in 言語・ノート in Book 1, Japanese are reluctant to refuse a request or express their disagreement directly. This is because いいえ carries a strong connotation of *you are wrong* and is therefore potentially offensive. Maintaining silence, refusing to answer the question, and answering vaguely are the most common means of indirect refusal.

A: 新しいコンピュータを買うことにしましょうよ。
B: 今は何とも言えませんね。
A: *Let's buy a new computer.*
B: *I can't say anything right now.*

A: 新しいコンピュータを買うことにしましょうよ。
B: ええ、まあそうできるといいですけど、...
B: *Yes, it would be good if we could do this, but...*
(Note that this sounds like a *yes* to an English speaker.)

> A: 新しいコンピュータを買うことにしましょうよ。
>
> B: もう少し考えさせてください。
>
> B: *Let me think about it a little more.*

Other common ways of refusing include changing the subject and avoiding the responsibility for answering.

> A: 新しいコンピュータを買うことにしましょうよ。
>
> B: ところで、昼御飯はもう食べましたか。
>
> B: *By the way, have you eaten lunch yet?*

> A: 新しいコンピュータを買うことにしましょうよ。
>
> B: 田中さんに聞いてみてください。
>
> B: *Try asking Mr. Tanaka.*

Agreeing first and then giving a negative qualification is another common strategy for refusing.

> A: 新しいコンピュータを買うことにしましょうよ。
>
> B: ええ、でも、もう少し待ったほうがいいんじゃありませんか。
>
> B: *Yes, but wouldn't it be better to wait a bit?*

Finally, apologizing is another common way to avoid saying *no*.

> A: 新しいコンピュータを買うことにしましょうよ。
>
> B: すみませんが、コンピュータのことはよくわからないんです。
>
> B: *I'm sorry, but I don't know much about computers.*

Activity

Have a discussion in Japanese about some current issues pertinent to you. One of you will play the role of discussion leader or chairman.

Listening Comprehension

1. Five people—Kuriyama, Sasaki, Komada, Matsuno, and Hosokawa—are talking about their hometowns. Listen to their conversation, and write down the most important facts about each person's hometown.
2. Four people—Ichikawa, Mano, Tokuyasu, and Yoshikura—are discussing their experiences with foreign cultures. Write down where each person went and what his or her experience was.

Vocabulary

Geography and Environment

いけ	池	pond
いし	石	stone
おか	丘	hill
かいがん	海岸	beach, shore
かざん	火山	volcano
かんきょう	環境	environment
き	木	tree
こうがい	公害	pollution
しぜん（の）	自然（の）	nature (natural)
しま	島	island
せつやく（する）	節約（する）	economizing; careful use (to economize; to use carefully)
たいりく	大陸	continent
たに	谷	valley
ながれる	流れる	to flow
はやし	林	woods
みずうみ	湖	lake
もり	森	forest
わん	湾	bay

Review: 海（うみ）、川（かわ）、山（やま）、地図（ちず）

Animals and Insects

うさぎ	兎	rabbit
うし	牛	cow; cattle
うま	馬	horse
か	蚊	mosquito
かう	飼う	to keep; to have; to raise (*a pet*)
かえる	蛙	frog
かわいがる		to love, caress, pet
くじら	鯨	whale
くま	熊	bear
ゴキブリ		cockroach
さる	猿	monkey
しか	鹿	deer
せみ	蝉	cicada
ぞう	象	elephant

とら	虎	tiger
とり	鳥	bird
どうぶつ	動物	animal
どうぶつえん	動物園	zoo
ニワトリ	鶏	chicken
はち	蜂	bee
ぶた	豚	pig
へび	蛇	snake
むし	虫	insect

Loanwords: ペット、ゴリラ、パンダ、ライオン
Review: 犬、猫

Plants

うえる	植える	to plant
うめ	梅	plum tree
かれる	枯れる	to wither; to die
きく	菊	chrysanthemum
くさ	草	grass
さく	咲く	to bloom
さくら	桜	cherry tree
しょくぶつ	植物	plant
たね	種	seed
つち	土	soil
は	葉	leaf
ぼんさい	盆栽	**bonsai**
まつ	松	pine tree

Loanwords: カーネーション、ダリヤ、ブーケ
Review: 花、木、庭、花屋

Culture and Customs

エチケット		etiquette
しゃかい	社会	society
しゅうかん	習慣	habit
しゅうきょう	宗教	religion
しんじる	信じる	to believe
しんとう	神道	Shintoism
じだい	時代	era; period
ぶっきょう	仏教	Buddhism
ぶんか	文化	culture
まもる	守る	to observe (*a custom*); to obey (*a rule*); to protect
れきし	歴史	history

Loanwords: タブー、マナー

Miscellaneous

おじぎ（をする）	お辞儀（をする）	(to) bow
がまんする	我慢する	to put up with an unpleasant situation without complaint
がんばる	頑張る	to do one's best; to hang in there; to come out of a difficult situation all right
きょうみ（がある）	興味（がある）	interest (to be interested)
ひつよう（な）	必要（な）	necessary
もったいない		wasteful

Grammar

あるいは	or perhaps		ところで	by the way…
…ことになる	to be decided that…		～なくてもいい	it's all right not to…
そして	and (*connecting verbs*)		…のに	although; even though
それで	and then; therefore		まず	first of all
それとも	or alternatively		または	or
つまり	that is to say…		…ものだ	*adds emotional force*
ところが	but on the contrary…		…わけだ	So it's that…

Kanji

Learn these **kanji:**

然	州	世	最	咲
化	石	界	犬	必
島	岩	昔	馬	要
村	林	害	虫	習
湖	森	例	頼	慣
川	球	他	植	練

チェックリスト

Use this checklist to confirm that you can now

☐ Talk about geography, environment, and nature

☐ Talk about culture and customs

☐ Express a speaker's emotional involvement

☐ Use よう in various ways

☐ Scan letters to the editor in newspapers

☐ Scan book reviews

☐ Present opinions clearly and logically

Review Chapter 7

アクティビティー　1

都会がいいですか。田舎がいいですか。(*Do you prefer the city or the countryside?*)

Work in pairs. Compare the city and the countryside with regard to the following questions. Then discuss what kind of place you would prefer to live in.

1. 空気がきれいか、自然が多いか
2. 買物に便利か
3. 生活のペースが速いか
4. 仕事があるか
5. 人が親切か
6. 交通機関 (*transportation*) が発達 (*development*) しているか
7. 犯罪率 (*crime rate*) が高いか
8. 様々 (*a variety of*) な人がいるか

アクティビティー　2

賛成ですか、反対ですか。(*Do you agree or not?*)

Do you agree with the following statements? Defend your opinions.

1. エネルギーを節約するために、夏はエアコンをできるだけ (*as much as possible*) 使わない方がいい。
2. エネルギーを節約するために、冬は厚着をして、できるだけ暖房 (*heating*) を使わない方がいい。
3. 石油を使うのをやめて、核燃料 (*nuclear power*) を使った方がいい。
4. ゴルフコースは公園に変えた方がいい。
5. 車で会社や学校へ通うのをやめて、公共交通機関 (*public transportation*) を使うべきだ。

6. 公害を引き起こした (bring about) 会社や人は、厳しく (strictly) 罰する (punish) べきだ。

7. 環境の問題も大切だが、経済の発展 (growth) はもっと大切な問題だ。

8. 現在の世界の人口は多過ぎる。人口を増やさないようにするべきだ。

アクティビティー　3

ペットか子供か (A pet or a child?)

Minoru and Megumi Morioka have been married for a year. Megumi thinks that it's time for them to have a baby, while Minoru doesn't want a child and would rather buy a pet. Help them decide which is better for them by listing the advantages and disadvantages of having a pet or a child.

アクティビティー　4

祝日 (Festive occasions)

1. What special day is being described by each of the following sentences?

   a. イエス・キリストの誕生を祝う (to celebrate) 日

   b. 一年の始まりを祝う日

   c. 好きな人にチョコレートをあげる日

   d. アメリカの独立 (independence) を祝う日

2. Explain in Japanese to your classmates which holiday is the most important to you and why.

3. What does the graph tell you about attitudes prevalent among Japanese people? Discuss in Japanese in class.

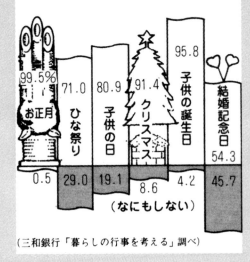

よく行う行事

99.5% お正月 0.5
71.0 ひな祭り 29.0
80.9 子供の日 19.1
91.4 クリスマス 8.6
95.8 子供の誕生日 4.2
結婚記念日 54.3 / 45.7

（なにもしない）

（三和銀行「暮らしの行事を考える」調べ）

結婚記念日 *wedding anniversary*

Appendices

APPENDIX 1: Verb Conjugation

	CLASS 1						
Dictionary Form	会^あう	書^かく	話^{はな}す	立^たつ	死^しぬ*	読^よむ	乗^のる
Root	会(わ)	書	話	立	死	読	乗
Plain, Nonpast, Negative	会わない	書かない	話さない	立たない	死なない	読まない	乗らない
Polite, Nonpast, Affirmative	会います	書きます	話します	立ちます	死にます	読みます	乗ります
ましょう Form (Polite Volitional)	会いましょう	書きましょう	話しましょう	立ちましょう	死にましょう	読みましょう	乗りましょう
たい Form	会いたい	書きたい	話したい	立ちたい	死にたい	読みたい	乗りたい
Command	会いなさい	書きなさい	話しなさい	立ちなさい	死になさい	読みなさい	乗りなさい

	CLASS 1		CLASS 2		CLASS 3	
Dictionary Form	泳ぐ	呼ぶ	How to create forms	食べる	する	来る
Root	泳	呼	Drop る ending	食べ	Irregular	Irregular
Plain, Nonpast, Negative	泳がない	呼ばない	Root + ない	食べない	しない	来ない
Polite, Nonpast, Affirmative	泳ぎます	呼びます	Root + ます	食べます	します	来ます
ましょう Form (Polite Volitional)	泳ぎましょう	呼びましょう	Root + ましょう	食べましょう	しましょう	来ましょう
たい Form	泳ぎたい	呼びたい	Root + たい	食べたい	したい	来たい
Command	泳ぎなさい	呼びなさい	Root + なさい	食べなさい	しなさい	来なさい

	CLASS 1						
Dictionary Form	会う	書く	話す	立つ	死ぬ*	読む	乗る
Potential	会える	書ける	話せる	立てる	死ねる	読める	乗れる
Imperative	会え	書け	話せ	立て	死ね	読め	乗れ
ば Conditional	会えば	書けば	話せば	立てば	死ねば	読めば	乗れば
Volitional	会おう	書こう	話そう	立とう	死のう	読もう	乗ろう
Ta-Form	会った	書いた	話した	立った	死んだ	読んだ	乗った
Te-Form	会って	書いて	話して	立って	死んで	読んで	乗って
たら Conditional	会ったら	書いたら	話したら	立ったら	死んだら	読んだら	乗ったら
Passive	会われる	書かれる	話される	立たれる	死なれる**	読まれる	乗られる
Causative	会わせる	書かせる	話させる	立たせる	死なせる	読ませる	乗らせる
Passive-Causative	会わせられる	書かせられる	話させられる	立たせられる	死なせられる	読ませられる	乗らせられる
Other Verbs	洗う 使う 歌う 買う 手伝う 笑う 言う 習う	聞く 行く† 磨く 働く はく 歩く	探す 直す	持つ 勝つ 待つ		飲む 休む 住む 楽しむ	帰る 入る 知る 降りる 走る 泊まる 止まる 取る 切る 終わる 始まる

---

* 死ぬ is the only verb whose dictionary form ends in ぬ.
† The ta-form and te-form of 行く are 行った and 行って, respectively.
** Used in adversative passive constructions. See **Grammar 32.4**, Chapter 5.

	CLASS 1		CLASS 2		CLASS 3	
Dictionary Form	泳^{およ}ぐ	呼^よぶ		食^たべる	する	来^くる
Potential	泳げる	呼べる	Root ＋ られる	食べられる	できる	来^こられる
Imperative	泳げ	呼べ	Root ＋ ろ	食べろ	しろ	来^こい
ば **Conditional**	泳げば	呼べば	Root ＋ れば	食べれば	すれば	来^くれば
Volitional	泳ごう	呼ぼう	Root ＋ よう	食べよう	しよう	来^こよう
Ta-Form	泳いだ	呼んだ	Root ＋ た	食べた	した	来^きた
Te-Form	泳いで	呼んで	Root ＋ て	食べて	して	来^きて
たら **Conditional**	泳いだら	呼んだら	Root ＋ たら	食べたら	したら	来^きたら
Passive	泳がれる	呼ばれる	Root ＋ られる	食べられる	される	来^こられる
Causative	泳がせる	呼ばせる	Root ＋ させる	食べさせる	させる	来^こさせる
Passive-Causative	泳がせられる	呼ばせられる	Root ＋ させられる	たべさせられる	させられる	来^こさせられる
Other Verbs	脱^ぬぐ 急^{いそ}ぐ	飛^とぶ 遊^{あそ}ぶ		見^みる 起^おきる 寝^ねる 出^でかける 出^でる 着^きる 教^{おし}える 降^おりる All potential verb forms	Nominal verbs (勉^{べん}強^{きょう}する、 洗^{せん}濯^{たく}する)	連^つれてくる 持^もってくる

APPENDIX 2: Adjective and Copula Conjugation

Adjectives

	DICTIONARY FORM	PRENOMIAL	PREDICATE			
			Plain			
			Nonpast		**Past**	
			Affirmative	**Negative**	**Affirmative**	**Negative**
I-Adjectives	赤か 赤い	赤い	赤い	赤くない	赤かった	赤くなかった
	いい	いい	いい	よくない	よかった	よくなかった
Na-Adjectives	しず 静か	静かな	静かだ	静かではない／ 静かじゃない	静かだった	静かではなかった／ 静かじゃなかった

Copula

DICTIONARY FORM	PRENOMIAL	PREDICATE			
		Plain			
		Nonpast		**Past**	
		Affirmative	**Negative**	**Affirmative**	**Negative**
だ	の／である	だ／ である	ではない／ じゃない	だった	ではなかった／ じゃなかった

	PREDICATE			ADVERBIAL
	Te-Form	ば **Conditional**	たら **Conditional**	
I-Adjectives	赤くて	赤ければ	赤かったら	赤く
	よくて	よければ	よかったら	よく
Na-Adjectives	静かで	静かならば／ 静かであれば	静かだったら	静かに

PREDICATE						
Polite				**Te-Form**	ば **Conditional**	たら **Conditional**
Nonpast		**Past**				
Affirmative	**Negative**	**Affirmative**	**Negative**			
です	ではありません／ じゃありません	でした	ではありません でした／ じゃありません でした	で	なら（ば）／ であれば	だったら

Adjective and Copula Conjugation

407

四百七

APPENDIX 3: Kanji List

KANJI	TOTAL NUMBER OF STROKES	RADICAL	NAME OF RADICAL	NUMBER OF STROKES BEYOND THE RADICAL
CHAPTER 1				
京	8	亠	(なべぶた)	6
都	11	阝	(おおざと)	8
社	7	ネ	(しめすへん)	3
内	4	入	(いりがしら)	2
目	5	目	(め)	0
所	8	戸	(と)	4
約	9	糸	(いと)	3
予	4	亅	(はねぼう)	3
車	7	車	(くるま)	0
早	6	日	(ひ)	2
歩	8	止	(とめる)	4
館	16	食	(しょく)	8
乗	9	ノ	(の)	8
待	9	彳	(ぎょうにんべん)	6
駅	14	馬	(うま)	4
止	4	止	(とめる)	0
旅	10	方	(ほう)	6
客	9	宀	(うかんむり)	6
寺	6	寸	(すん)	3
神	9	ネ	(しめす)	5
地	6	土	(つち)	3
図	7	囗	(くにがまえ)	4
海	9	氵	(さんずい)	6
曲	6	日	(ひらび)	2
私	7	禾	(のぎへん)	2
CHAPTER 2				
新	13	斤	(きん)	9
開	12	門	(もん)	4
公	4	八	(はち)	2
園	13	囗	(くにがまえ)	10
住	7	イ	(にんべん)	5
階	13	阝	(こざと)	10
広	5	广	(まだれ)	2
直	8	十	(じゅう)	6
戸	4	戸	(と)	0
古	5	十	(じゅう)	3
門	8	門	(もん)	0
室	9	宀	(うかんむり)	6

	KANJI	TOTAL NUMBER OF STROKES	RADICAL	NAME OF RADICAL	NUMBER OF STROKES BEYOND THE RADICAL
	伝	6	イ	(にんべん)	4
	洗	9	氵	(さんずい)	6
	建	9	廴	(えんにょう)	6
	友	4	又	(また)	2
	貸	11	貝	(かい)	4
	借	10	イ	(にんべん)	8
	置	13	罒	(あみがしら)	8
	静	14	青	(あお)	6
	庭	10	广	(まだれ)	7
	不	4	一	(いち)	3
	便	9	イ	(にんべん)	7
	利	7	刂	(りっとう)	5

CHAPTER 3

	KANJI	TOTAL NUMBER OF STROKES	RADICAL	NAME OF RADICAL	NUMBER OF STROKES BEYOND THE RADICAL
	自	6	自	(みずから)	0
	路	13	足	(あし)	6
	交	6	亠	(なべぶた)	4
	通	10	辶	(しんにゅう)	7
	転	11	車	(くるま)	4
	駐	15	馬	(うま)	5
	教	11	攵	(ぼく)	7
	窓	11	穴	(あな)	6
	閉	11	門	(もん)	3
	消	10	氵	(さんずい)	7
	変	9	夂	(なつあし)	6
	故	9	攵	(ぼく)	5
	横	15	木	(き)	11
	働	13	イ	(にんべん)	11
	工	3	工	(たくみ)	0
	速	10	辶	(しんにゅう)	7
	違	11	辶	(しんにゅう)	9
	反	4	厂	(がんだれ)	2
	差	10	工	(たくみ)	7
	点	9	灬	(れんが)	5
	信	9	イ	(にんべん)	7
	号	5	口	(くち)	2
	走	7	走	(はしる)	0
	帰	10	ヨ	(よ)	7
	注	8	氵	(さんずい)	5
	意	13	心	(こころ)	9

CHAPTER 4

	KANJI	TOTAL NUMBER OF STROKES	RADICAL	NAME OF RADICAL	NUMBER OF STROKES BEYOND THE RADICAL
	体	7	イ	(にんべん)	5
	頭	16	頁	(おおがい)	7

KANJI	TOTAL NUMBER OF STROKES	RADICAL	NAME OF RADICAL	NUMBER OF STROKES BEYOND THE RADICAL
鼻	14	鼻	(はな)	0
式	6	弋	(しきがまえ)	3
耳	6	耳	(みみ)	0
歯	12	歯	(は)	0
御	12	彳	(ぎょうにんべん)	9
首	9	首	(くび)	0
指	9	扌	(て)	6
足	7	足	(あし)	0
毛	4	毛	(け)	0
形	7	彡	(かみかざり)	4
丸	3	、	(てん)	2
角	7	角	(つの)	0
持	9	扌	(て)	6
立	5	立	(たつ)	0
心	4	心	(こころ)	0
配	10	酉	(さけづくり)	3
苦	8	艹	(くさかんむり)	5
死	6	歹	(いちた)	2
元	4	儿	(ひとあし)	2
病	10	疒	(やまいだれ)	5
院	9	阝	(こざと)	7
痛	12	疒	(やまいだれ)	7
熱	15	灬	(れんが)	11
薬	16	艹	(くさかんむり)	13
局	7	尸	(しかばね)	4
顔	18	頁	(おおがい)	9

CHAPTER 5

KANJI	TOTAL NUMBER OF STROKES	RADICAL	NAME OF RADICAL	NUMBER OF STROKES BEYOND THE RADICAL
校	10	木	(き)	6
卒	8	十	(じゅう)	6
業	13	木	(き)	9
仕	5	イ	(にんべん)	3
就	12	亠	(なべぶた)	10
職	18	耳	(みみ)	12
退	8	辶	(しんにゅう)	6
育	8	月	(にくづき)	4
若	8	艹	(くさかんむり)	5
老	6	老	(ろう)	0
愛	13	心	(こころ)	9
恋	10	心	(こころ)	6
初	7	刀	(かたな)	5
結	12	糸	(いと)	6
婚	11	女	(おんな)	8
召	5	口	(くち)	2
様	14	木	(き)	10

KANJI	TOTAL NUMBER OF STROKES	RADICAL	NAME OF RADICAL	NUMBER OF STROKES BEYOND THE RADICAL
研	9	石	（いし）	4
究	7	穴	（あなかんむり）	2
医	7	匸	（はこがまえ）	5
者	8	土	（おいがしら）	4
師	10	巾	（はば）	7
銀	14	金	（かね）	6
亡	3	亠	（なべぶた）	1
忙	6	心	（こころ）	3
知	8	矢	（や）	3
存	6	子	（こ）	3
申	5	田	（た）	0
式	6	弋	（しきがまえ）	3

CHAPTER 6

KANJI	TOTAL NUMBER OF STROKES	RADICAL	NAME OF RADICAL	NUMBER OF STROKES BEYOND THE RADICAL
換	12	扌	（て）	9
際	13	阝	（こざと）	10
留	10	田	（た）	5
守	6	宀	（うかんむり）	3
受	8	爪	（つめ）	4
取	8	又	（また）	6
器	15	口	（くち）	12
報	12	土	（つち）	9
文	4	文	（ぶん）	0
打	5	扌	（て）	2
調	15	言	（ごんべん）	8
英	8	艹	（くさかんむり）	5
映	9	日	（ひ）	5
画	8	凵	（うけばこ）	6
郵	11	阝	（おおざと）	8
紙	10	糸	（いと）	4
送	8	辶	（しんにゅう）	6
達	11	辶	（しんにゅう）	9
宅	6	宀	（うかんむり）	3
重	9	里	（さと）	2
刊	5	刂	（りっとう）	3
雑	14	隹	（ふるとり）	6
誌	14	言	（ごんべん）	7
記	10	言	（ごんべん）	3
放	8	攵	（ぼくづくり）	4
組	11	糸	（いと）	5
試	13	言	（ごんべん）	6
験	18	馬	（うま）	8
困	7	囗	（くにがまえ）	4
志	7	心	（こころ）	3

CHAPTER 7

KANJI	TOTAL NUMBER OF STROKES	RADICAL	NAME OF RADICAL	NUMBER OF STROKES BEYOND THE RADICAL
然	12	灬	(ひ／れんが)	8
化	4	匕	(さじ)	2
島	10	山	(やま)	7
村	7	木	(き)	3
湖	12	氵	(さんずい)	9
川	3	川	(かわ)	0
州	6	川	(かわ)	3
石	5	石	(いし)	0
岩	8	山	(やま)	5
林	8	木	(き)	4
森	12	木	(き)	8
世	5	一	(いち)	4
界	9	田	(た)	4
球	11	玉	(たま)	7
昔	8	日	(ひ)	4
害	10	宀	(うかんむり)	7
例	8	イ	(にんべん)	6
他	5	イ	(にんべん)	3
最	12	日	(いわく)	8
犬	4	犬	(いぬ)	0
馬	10	馬	(うま)	0
虫	6	虫	(むし)	0
頼	16	頁	(おおがい)	7
植	12	木	(き)	8
咲	9	口	(くち)	6
必	5	心	(こころ)	1
要	9	西	(にし)	3
習	11	羽	(はね)	5
練	14	糸	(いと)	8
慣	14	心	(こころ)	11

Japanese-English Glossary

This glossary is not intended to be used as a dictionary. Instead, it lists all Japanese words and phrases that are introduced for the first time in Book 2, with the exception of well-known place names, some proper nouns, conjugated forms, compound words, foreign loanwords that are very similar to the source language, and words and phrases that appeared in the glossary for Book 1. If you try to look up a word appearing in Book 2 and can't find it in this glossary, try the Book 1 glossary.

Entries are arranged in a-i-u-e-o Japanese alphabetical order. As in Japanese dictionaries, each word is presented in hiragana or katakana, followed by the kanji transcription, if appropriate. Compound nouns are grouped together, and phrases containing the same key word are also grouped together.

Verbs and adjectives are cited in their dictionary form except when appearing as part of a set phrase.

Nominal verbs are followed by （する）. I-adjectives are unmarked, but na-adjectives are followed by （な）.

English translations for nouns are given in the singular, and the plural is an option in most cases.

Finally, remember that these translations are not exact equivalents, but only reminders of the meanings you have learned in class. Only real-life contexts and native usage can be relied on to provide the full range of meanings for each word.

The following abbreviations are used:

adv.	word or phrase that functions as an adverb
C1	Class 1 verb
C2	Class 2 verb
C3	Class 3 verb
coll.	colloquial
conj.	conjunction
i-adj.	i-adjective
inf.	informal
interj.	interjection
intr.	intransitive verb
na-adj.	na-adjective
n.v.	noun that can be made into a nominal verb by appending する (both nominal meanings and verbal meanings are given for words with this abbreviation)
part.	particle
pol.	polite
tr.	transitive verb

あ／ア

あいする （愛する） C3, tr. to love （5）
あいて （相手） partner, recipient （6）
あかちゃん （赤ちゃん） baby （5）
あがる （上がる） C1, intr. to rise （3）
あかんぼう （赤ん坊） baby （5）
あきかん （空き缶） empty can （7）
あきる （飽きる） C2, intr. to get bored （6）
あく （開く） C1, intr. to open （3）
アクセル accelerator （3）
あける （開ける） C2, tr. to open （3）
あげる C2, tr. to give (to a second or third person) （2）
あげる （上げる） C2, tr. to raise （3）
あご （顎） jaw （4）
あさがお （朝顔） morning glory （7）
アサリ clam （7）
あし （脚、足） leg, foot; あしくび （足首） ankle; あしのうら （足の裏） sole; あしのゆび （足の指） toe （4）
アスピリン aspirin （4）
アスベスト asbestos （7）
あたえる （与える） C2, tr. to give （5）
あたまがいたい （頭が痛い） one's head hurts （4）
あつかう （扱う） C1, tr. to deal with （5）
あつまる （集まる） C1, intr. to get together, gather （1）; あつめる （集める） C2, tr. to gather, collect (things, people) （3）
あてな （あて名） addressee （6）
あと （で） （後 [で]） after （1）
アナウンサー announcer （5）
アニメ animation （6）
アパート apartment building, complex （2）
あひる duck （7）
あぶない （危ない） i-adj. dangerous （1）
あやまる （謝る） C1, tr. to apologize （7）
あらう （洗う） C1, tr. to wash （2）
あらたまる C1, intr. to be formal or ceremonious （6）
あらわれ （表れ） expression, appearance （7）
あり （蟻） ant （7）
あんき（する） （暗記 [する]） n.v. memorization; to memorize （6）
あんしん（する） （安心 [する]） n.v. peace of mind; to be relieved （4）
あんぜん（な） （安全 [な]） na-adj. safe （2）
アンテナ antenna （3）
あんない（する） （案内 [する]） n.v. guide, information; to guide, lead; あんないこうこく （案内広告） classified ad （6）

い／イ

いいまちがい （言い間違い） slip of the tongue （6）
いけ （池） pond （7）
いけん （意見） opinion （7）
いし （医師）／いしゃ （医者） medical doctor （4）
いし （石） stone （7）

いじ（する） （維持 [する]） n.v. maintenance; to maintain （4）
いじょう （…以上） more than… （2）
いじょうきしょう （異常気象） abnormal weather （7）
いす （椅子） chair （2）
イスラムきょう （イスラム教） Islam （7）
いそいで （急いで） adv. quickly （1）
いたい （痛い） i-adj. painful; いたむ （痛む） C1, intr. to be painful （4）
いたす to do (humble) （5）
いただく to eat （5）; to receive (humble) （2）
いち （位置） position （3）
いちじてき（な） （一時的 [な]） na-adj. temporary （7）
いっしょう （一生） lifetime （5）
いってい （一定） uniform, consistent （7）
いっぱい filled （7）
いっぱくにしょくつき （1泊2食付き） one night's lodging including two meals （1）
いっぽうつうこう （一方通行） one-way traffic （3）
いぬ （犬） dog （7）
いはん（する） （違反 [する]） n.v. violation of rules; to violate rules （3）
いま （居間） living room （2）
いや（な） （嫌 [な]） na-adj. disgusting, disagreeable （3）
いやがらせでんわ （いやがらせ電話） annoying call, crank call （6）
イライラする to be irritated （4）
いらっしゃる to be, come, go (honorific) （5）
いれる （入れる） C2, tr. to put in, insert; to include; to turn on (a switch) （3）
いろいろ（な） na-adj. various （3）
いわ （岩） rock outcropping （7）
いわう （祝う） C1, tr. to celebrate （6）
インコ parakeet （7）
いんさつ（する） （印刷 [する]） n.v. printing; to print; いんさつぶつ （印刷物） printed matter （6）
インタビュー（する） n.v. interview; to interview （6）
インターチェンジ interchange （3）
インターフォン intercom （2）
インドよう （インド洋） Indian Ocean （7）

う／ウ

ウインカー turn signal （3）
うえき （植木） potted plant （7）
うえる （植える） C2, tr. to plant （7）
ウォークマン Walkman （2）
うけとる （受け取る） C1, tr. to receive （6）
うける （受ける） C2, tr. to undergo (surgery, X-rays, an injection) （4）
うごかす （動かす） C1, intr. to set in motion, move (something) （2）; うごく （動く） C1, tr. to be in motion, move （3）
うさぎ （兎） rabbit （7）
うし （牛） cow, cattle （7）
うちゅう （宇宙） outer space, universe （7）; うちゅうひこうし （宇宙飛行士） astronaut （5）

うつくしい （美しい） *i-adj.* beautiful （2）
うつる （移る） *C1, int.* to move, change location （6）
うで （腕） arm （4）
うま （馬） horse （7）
うまれる （生まれる） *C2, int.* to be born; うむ （産む） *C1, tr.* to give birth （5）
うめ （梅） Japanese plum; plum tree （7）
うらない （占い） fortune-telling （7）; うらないし （占師） fortune-teller （7）
うれしい （嬉しい） *i-adj.* happy, delighted （4）
うんが （運河） canal （7）
うんちん （運賃） fare （1）
うんてん(する) （運転 [する]） *n.v.* driving (a car); to drive; うんてんしゅ （運転手） driver; うんてんせき （運転席） driver's seat; うんてんめんきょ（しょう） （運転免許 [証]） driver's license （3）

え／エ

エアコン air conditioner （2）
エイエム AM radio （6）
えいがスター （映画スター） movie star （5）
えいきょう(する) （影響 [する]） *n.v.* influence; to influence; えいきょうをあたえる （影響を与える） have an influence （7）
えいじしんぶん （英字新聞） English-language newspaper （6）
えきいん （駅員） station employee （5）
えきたい （液体） liquid （7）
えきべん （駅弁） box lunch sold at stations （1）
えさ （餌） animal food, bait （7）
えだ （枝） branch （7）
エチケット etiquette （7）
エッセー essay （6）
えどじだい （江戸時代） Edo period (1603–1868) （7）
エヌエチケー NHK (Nippon Hoso Kyokai) （6）
エフエム FM radio （6）
える （得る） *C2, tr.* to obtain （3）
えんか （演歌） enka (*Japanese-style song*) （6）
えんげき （演劇） theatrical performance
エンジン engine; エンジンをかける to start the engine; エンスト engine stall （3）
えんそく （遠足） excursion, outing （7）
えんとつ （煙突） chimney （2）

お／オ

オアシス oasis （7）
おいかける （追いかける） *C2, tr.* to chase （5）
おいこし(する) （追い越し [する]） *n.v.* passing; to pass, overtake （3）
おいでになる to come (*honorific*) （5）
オイル motor oil （3）
おいる （老いる） *C2, intr.* to get old （5）
おいわい （お祝い） celebration （2）
おうせつま [応接間] guest reception room （2）

おうだんほどう （横断歩道） pedestrian crossing; おうだんほどうきょう （横断歩道橋） pedestrian crossing bridge （3）
おうふく(する) （往復 [する]） *n.v.* round trip; to make a round trip （3）; おうふくきっぷ （往復切符） round trip ticket （1）
おうふくはがき （往復葉書） return postal card （6）
おうべい （欧米） Europe and America （4）; おうべいじん （欧米人） Europeans and North Americans （4）
おうぼ(する) （応募 [する]） *n.v.* application; to apply; おうぼようし （応募用紙） application form （5）
おえる （終える） *C2, tr.* to end （3）
オーエル OL ("office lady" or female worker) （5）
オーエー OA (office automation) （5）
おおかみ （狼） wolf （7）
オートバイ motorcycle （3）
オーブン oven （2）
オーム parrot （7）
おおやさん （大家さん） property or apartment owner （2）
おか （丘） hill （7）
おき （沖） offing, open sea near a coast （7）
おく （置く） *C1, tr.* to put, place （2）
おくりもの （贈り物） gift （1）
おくる （送る） *C1, tr.* to send （6）
おくれる （遅れる） *C2, intr.* to be late, to be delayed （1）
おこなう （行なう） *C1, tr.* to carry out （7）
おこる （起こる） *C1, intr.* to happen, take place （6）
おこる （怒る） *C1, tr.* to get angry （4）
おしいれ （押入） futon closet （2）
おじぎをする （お辞儀をする） to bow （7）
おじゃまする （お邪魔する） to visit (*humble*) （5）
おしり （お尻） *pol.* buttocks （4）
おす （押す） *C1, tr.* to push （3）; おしこめる *C2, tr.* to push into （7）
おせん(する) （汚染 [する]） *n.v.* pollution; to pollute （7）
おそれ fear （7）
オゾン ozone （7）
おちる （落ちる） *C2, intr.* to fall (from a height) （3）
おつかい errand （6）
おっしゃる to say (*honorific*) （5）
おてあらい （お手洗い） *pol.* rest room, toilet （2）
おとこのこ （男の子） boy （5）
おとす （落とす） *C1, tr.* to drop （3）
おとなしい *i-adj.* quiet, well-behaved （6）
おとなり （お隣） *pol.* next-door neighbor （2）
おどる （踊る） *C1, tr.* to dance （1）
おどろく （驚く） *C1, intr.* to be surprised （4）
おなか *pol.* belly, stomach （4）; おなかがすく to get hungry （1）
おなくなりになる to die (*honorific*) （5）
おなじ （同じ） same （2）
おふろ （お風呂） bath （1）
おへそ （お臍） *pol.* navel （4）
おぼえる （覚える） *C2, tr.* to learn （6）
おみこし （お御輿） *pol.* portable festival shrine （7）

おみまい （お見舞い） *pol.* condolence; visit to the sick （6）

おみやげ souvenir （1）

おめしになる （お召しになる） to wear (*honorific*) （5）

おめにかかる （お目にかかる） to see, meet (*humble*); おめにかける （お目にかける） to show (*humble*) （5）

おも（な） （主［な］） *na-adj.* main, major, chief （3）; おもに （主に） *adv.* mainly （5）

おもさ （重さ） weight; おもさをはかる （重さを計る） to weigh （6）

オランウータン orangutan （7）

おり （檻） cage （7）

おりる （降りる） *C2, tr.* to get off (*a vehicle*) （1）

おる *C1, intr.* to be (*humble*) （5）

おわび （お詫び） apology （6）

おわる （終わる） *C1, intr.* to come to an end （3）

おんがくか （音楽家） musician （5）; おんがくばんぐみ （音楽番組） music show (*on television*) （6）

おんしつ （温室） greenhouse （7）

おんせん （温泉） hot spring （1）

おんだんか （温暖化） global warming; greenhouse effect （7）

おんなのこ （女の子） girl （5）

か／カ

か （蚊） mosquito （7）

カー・エアコン car air conditioner; カー・ステレオ car stereo; カー・ラジオ car radio （3）; カーホン cellular car phone （6）; カーレーサー car racer （5）

カーテン curtain （2）

ガードレール guard rail （3）

カーネーション carnation （7）

カーブ curve （3）

カーペット carpet （2）

かいがいりょこう （海外旅行） travel abroad （1）

かいがん （海岸） beach, shore （7）

かいぎ （会議） meeting, conference （1）

かいきょう （海峡） channel, straits （7）

かいけいし （会計士） accountant （5）

かいけつ（する） （解決［する］） *n.v.* solution; to solve （7）

がいこうかん （外交官） diplomat （5）

かいさつぐち （改札口） turnstile gate in station （3）

かいしゃ （会社） company; かいしゃいん （会社員） company employee （5）; かいしゃけいえいしゃ （会社経営者） company manager （5）

かいすうけん （回数券） multiride ticket (*for train or bus*) （3）

かいそう （海草） seaweed （4）

〜かいだて （〜階建て） 〜storey-building （2）

かいだん （階段） stairway, steps （2）

かいちょう （会長） chairman （5）

ガイド guide; ガイドブック guidebook （1）

がいねん （概念） general concept （7）

かいはつ（する） （開発［する］） *n.v.* development; to develop （7）

かいもの（する） （買い物［する］） *n.v.* shopping; to shop （2）

かいりゅう （海流） ocean current （7）

かう （飼う） *C1, tr.* to raise or keep an animal （7）

かえる （蛙） frog （7）

かえる （変える） *C2, tr.* to change (something) （3）

かお （顔） face （4）

がか （画家） painter （5）

かがくしゃ （科学者） scientist （5）

かかと （踵） heel (*of foot*) （4）

かがみ （鏡） mirror （2）

かかりちょう （係長） subsection chief （5）

かき （夏期） summertime; summer term （1）

かきどめ （書留） registered mail （6）

かぎをかける （鍵をかける） to lock （2）

かく （掻く） to scratch （4）

かぐ （家具） furniture （2）

かぐ （嗅ぐ） to perceive a smell （4）

がくれき （学歴） education history （5）

がけ （崖） cliff （7）

かける （掛ける） *C2, tr.* to hang (something) up （4）; エンジンをかける to start an engine （3）; でんわ（電話）をかける to make a phone call （6）; アイロンをかける to iron (something) （2）; おめ（目）にかける to show (*humble*) （5）; かぎ（鍵）をかける to lock （2）; かけなお（直）す to call back （6）

かこむ （囲む） *C1, tr.* to surround （5）

かざん （火山） volcano （7）

かじ （家事） housework, household chores （2）

かじ （火事） fire （6）

かじつ （果実） fruit （7）

かしべっそう （貸し別荘） vacation rental （2）

かしゅ （歌手） singer （5）

かじる *C1, tr.* to bite, chew （4）

かす （貸す） *C1, tr.* to rent out, to lend （2）

かず （数） number （5）

ガスレンジ gas stove （2）

かぜをひく （風邪をひく） to catch a cold or the flu; かぜぐすり （風邪薬） cold medicine （4）

かせいふ （家政婦） housekeeper （5）

ガソリン gasoline; ガソリン・スタンド gas station （3）

かた （肩） shoulder （4）

かた〜 （片〜） one (*of something that comes in pairs*); かたて （片手） one hand （4）; かたみちきっぷ （片道切符） one-way ticket （1）

かたち （形） shape （4）

かたづける （片付ける） *C2, tr.* to straighten up; to clean off; to put away （2）

かだん （花壇） flower bed （7）

かちく （家畜） domestic animal, livestock （7）

かちょう （課長） section chief （5）

がちょう goose （7）

かつお bonito （7）

がっかりする to be disappointed （4）

カッコいい *i-adj.* good looking （3）

かっこう（学校）school （5）
かってぐち（勝手口）back or side door （2）
かつやく（する）（活躍［する］）n.v. being active; to play an active role, to be prominent （5）
かていらん（家庭欄）home section (of a newspaper) （6）
かど（角）corner （2）
かなしい（悲しい）i-adj. sad; かなしむ（悲しむ）C1, tr. to be sad （4）
カナリア canary （7）
かのうせい（可能性）possibility （7）
カバ hippopotamus （7）
かびん（花瓶）vase （2）
かぶしきがいしゃ（株式会社）incorporated company （5）
かふん（花粉）pollen （7）
かべ（壁）wall; かべがみ（壁紙）wallpaper （2）
かまう C1, tr. to mind, be bothered （6）
がまん（する）（我慢［する］）n.v. patience, endurance; to put up with （3）
かむ C1, tr. to bite （5）
カメラ camera （6）
かゆい i-adj. itchy （7）
かようきょく（歌謡曲）kayookyoku, (Japanese-style popular song) （6）
カラス crow （7）
からだ（体）body （4）
カラーテレビ color TV （6）
かりる（借りる）C2, tr. to rent, to borrow （2）
カルテ patient's chart （4）
かれさんすい（枯山水）Japanese-style dry garden （7）
かれる（枯れる）C2, intr. to wither, die (plants) （7）
ガレージ garage （2）
かわ（川）river （2）
かわいがる C1, tr. to treat with affection, cuddle （7）
かわかす（乾かす）C1, tr. to dry (something) （2）
かわる（変わる）C1, intr. to undergo change, change （3）
かん（間）during, for; interval （1）
かんがえ（考え）idea （2）
かんがえる（考える）C2, tr. to think, to ponder （2）
かんきょう（環境）circumstances; environment （5）; かんきょうはかい（環境破壊）environmental damage; かんきょうほご（環境保護）protection of the environment （7）
かんけつ（な）（簡潔［な］）na-adj. brief （6）
かんこう（する）（観光［する］）n.v. sightseeing, touring; to sightsee, tour; かんこうあんないしょ（観光案内所）tourist information center; かんこうきゃく（観光客）sightseer, tourist; かんこうち（観光地）tourist site （1）; かんこうバス（観光バス）sightseeing bus, tour bus （3）; かんこうりょこう（観光旅行）sightseeing trip （1）
かんごふ（看護婦）nurse （4）
かんじゃ（患者）patient （4）
かんしゅう（慣習）custom （7）
かんじょう（感情）feeling, emotion （4）
かんじる（感じる）C2, tr. to feel (an emotion) （4）

かんぜい（関税）tariff （6）
かんそうき（乾燥機）drier （2）
かんぬし（神主）Shinto priest （5）
かんばつ（旱魃）drought （7）
がんばる（頑張る）C1, intr. to do one's best, hang in, persevere （7）
かんめい（する）（感銘［する］）n.v. impression, admiration; to be impressed, struck with admiration （5）

き／キ

きえる（消える）C2, intr. to go off, go out (lights, fire, etc.); disappear （3）
きがるに（気軽に）adv. feeling free （6）
きかん（期間）period, length （5）
ききまちがい（聞き間違い）hearing error （6）
きぎょう（企業）enterprise, company （5）
きく（菊）chrysanthemum （7）
きげん（機嫌）mood, state of mind （4）
きし（岸）shore, riverbank （7）
ぎし（技師）engineer （5）
きしゃ（記者）reporter （6）
きしゃかいけん（する）（記者会見［する］）n.v. press conference; to have a press conference （6）
ぎせい（犠牲）sacrifice （7）
きつえんせき（喫煙席）smoking seat （1）
きづく（気づく）C1, intr. to notice （6）
きってをはる（切手を貼る）to affix a stamp （6）
きつね（狐）fox （7）
きっぷ（切符）ticket （1）
きにする（気にする）to give a lot of attention or thought to （7）; きになる（気になる）to be worried about, be nervous about （3）; きをつける（気をつける）to watch for （1）
きにゅう（する）（記入［する］）n.v. filling in; to fill in (a form) （5）
きねんきって（記念切手）commemorative stamp （6）
きのう（する）（機能［する］）n.v. function; to function （7）
きぼう（する）（希望［する］）n.v. wish, desire; to desire （5）
きほんてき（な）（基本的［な］）na-adj. basic （6）
きめる（決める）C2, tr. to decide （6）
きもち（気持ち）feeling, mood, atmosphere （4）
きゃくしつ（客室）guest room （1）
ぎゃくたい（する）（虐待［する］）n.v. cruel treatment, abuse; to treat cruelly, abuse （7）
きゃくま（客間）room for entertaining guests, parlor （2）
きゃっかんてき（な）（客観的［な］）na-adj. objective, detached （7）
キャッシャー cashier （1）
キャリアウーマン career woman （5）
キャンセル（する）n.v. cancellation; to cancel （1）
きゅうか（休暇）vacation, break （1）
きゅうきゅうしゃ（救急車）ambulance （4）
きゅうこう（急行）express train （1）
きゅうこん（球根）bulb (in plants) （7）
きゅうじんこうこく（求人広告）help wanted ad （5）

きゅうりょう（給料）salary （5）
ぎょう（行）line （6）
きょういく（する）（教育［する］）*n.v.* education; to educate （5）; きょういくばんぐみ（教育番組）educational program (*on television*) （6）
きょうかしょ（教科書）textbook （6）
きょうし（教師）schoolteacher （5）
きょうじゅ（教授）college professor （5）
きょうつう（する）（共通［する］）*n.v.* common factor; to have something in common （7）
きょうりょく（する）（協力［する］）*n.v.* assistance, cooperation; to cooperate （4）
ぎょぎょう（漁業）commercial fishing （7）
きょく（曲）tune, melody （5）
キリストきょう（キリスト教）Christianity （7）
きりぬき（切り抜き）newspaper clipping （6）
キリン giraffe （7）
きる（切る）*C1, tr.* to turn off (a switch), cut （2）; きれる（切れる）*C2, intr.* to be cut, be used up （3）
きんえんせき（禁煙席）non-smoking seat （1）
ぎんこう（銀行）bank; ぎんこういん（銀行員）bank employee （5）
きんじょ（近所）neighborhood （2）
きんにく（筋肉）muscle （4）
きんむじかん（勤務時間）working hours （5）

く／ク

クイズばんぐみ（クイズ番組）quiz show (*on television*) （6）
くうき（空気）air （2）
くうこう（空港）airport （1）
くうしつ（空室）vacant room （1）
クーペ coupe （3）
クーラー air conditioner, cooler （2）
くさ（草）grass （7）
くさばな（草花）flowering plant （7）
くじら（鯨）whale （7）
くずいれ（屑入れ）trash basket （2）
くずす *C1, tr.* to change, break （6）
くすり（薬）medicine; くすりをのむ（薬を飲む）to take medicine; くすりや（薬屋）pharmacy （4）
くださる *C1, tr.* to give (*honorific*) （5）
くだり（下り）going away from Tokyo (*by train*) （1）
くち（口）mouth （4）
くちひげ（口髭）moustache （4）
くちびる（唇）lip （4）
くつばこ（靴箱）shoe cabinet （2）
くつみがき（靴みがき）polishing shoes; a person who shines shoes （5）
くに（国）country, nation （7）
くび（首）neck （4）
くびにする（首にする）to fire; くびになる（首になる）to be fired （5）
くま（熊）bear （7）
くみあい（組合）union （5）
クラクション horn (*automobile*) （3）
クラッチ clutch (*automobile*) （3）
グラビア photogravure （6）
グラブコンパートメント glove compartment （3）

グリーン・ハウス・エフェクト greenhouse effect （7）
グリーンせき（グリーン席）first-class (lit., *green*) seat （1）
くるしい（苦しい）*i-adj.* oppressively painful （4）
くるま（車）car （3）
くれる *C2, tr.* to give (*to speaker or speaker's in-group*) （2）
クロゼット closet （2）
ぐんじん（軍人）soldier （5）

け／ケ

け（毛）hair, strand of hair, fur （4）
けいえい（する）（経営［する］）*n.v.* management; to manage, own a company （5）
けいけん（する）（経験［する］）*n.v.* experience; to experience （5）
けいこうとう（蛍光灯）fluorescent light （2）
けいこく（する）（警告［する］）*n.v.* warning; to warn （7）
けいざいてき（な）（経済的［な］）*na-adj.* economical （3）
けいざいらん（経済欄）economic section (*of a newspaper*) （6）
けいさつかん（警察官）policeman （5）
けいしき（形式）form （6）
げいじゅつか（芸術家）artist （5）
けが（怪我）injury; けがをする（怪我をする）to get injured （4）
けがわ（毛皮）fur （7）
ケシ poppy （7）
けしょうひん（化粧品）cosmetics （6）
けす（消す）*C1, tr.* to turn off, extinguish （3）
けずる *C1, tr.* to whittle away at, grade (a hill or mountain) （7）
げた *geta* (wooden clogs) （3）
けつえきがた（血液型）blood type （4）
けっか（結果）result （5）
げっかんし（月刊誌）monthly magazine （6）
げっきゅう（月給）monthly salary （5）
けっこん（する）（結婚［する］）*n.v.* marriage; to marry; けっこんきねんび（結婚記念日）wedding anniversary; けっこんしき（結婚式）wedding ceremony （5）
けっちゅう（血中）in the blood （4）
げり（下痢）diarrhea; げりをする（下痢をする）to have diarrhea （4）
けわしい（険い）*i-adj.* steep （7）
～けん（～軒）counter for houses （2）
げんいん（原因）cause （4）
げんかん（玄関）entry hall, foyer （2）
けんきゅうしゃ（研究者）researcher; けんきゅうじょ（研究所）research laboratory （5）
げんきんかきどめ（現金書留）registered money order （6）
けんこう（な）（健康［な］）*na-adj.* health （4）
けんさ（する）（検査［する］）*n.v.* test (*medical*); to test （4）
げんざい（現在）*adv.* at present （5）
げんさく（原作）original work, the original （6）

けんじ （検事） prosecutor （5）
げんじつ （現実） reality （7）
げんしりょく （原子力） nuclear power （7）
けんせつ（する） （建設［する］） *n.v.* construction; to construct （7）
げんだいじん （現代人） people of the modern age （4）
けんちくか （建築家） architect （2）
けんばいき （券売機） ticket vending machine （1）
けんぶつ（する） （見物［する］） *n.v.* sightseeing; to sightsee （1）
けんりょく （権力） authority, power （5）

こ／コ

こい （濃い） *i-adj.* thick, dense （2）
こいびと （恋人） boyfriend, girlfriend （5）
こういん （工員） factory worker （5）
こうがい （公害） pollution; public nuisance （7）
こうがい （郊外） the suburbs （2）
こうぎ （講義） lecture （7）
こうくうしょかん （航空書簡） aerogram （6）
こうくうびん （航空便） airmail （6）
ごうけい （合計） total （3）
こうげん （高原） plateau （2）
こうこう （高校） high school （5）
こうこく（する） （広告［する］） *n.v.* advertisement; to advertise; こうこくらん （広告欄） advertisement section (*of a newspaper*); こうこくをだす （広告を出す） to place an advertisement （6）
こうさい（する） （交際［する］） *n.v.* socializing; to be socialized （5）
こうさてん （交差点） intersection （1）
こうじちゅう （工事中） under construction （3）
こうしゅうでんわ （公衆電話） public phone （6）
こうしょう（する） （交渉［する］） *n.v.* negotiation; to negotiate （7）
こうじょう （工場） factory （5）
こうずい （洪水） flood （2）
こうそくどうろ （高速道路） freeway （3）
こうつう （交通） traffic, transportation; こうつういはん （交通違反） traffic violation; こうつうきかん （交通機関） means of transportation; こうつうじこ （交通事故） traffic accident; こうつうじゅうたい （交通渋滞） traffic jam; こうつうしんごう （交通信号） traffic light; こうつうひょうしき （交通標識） road sign, traffic sign （3）
こうどう （講堂） auditorium （7）
こうどく（する） （購読［する］） *n.v.* subscription; to subscribe （6）
こうぶざせき （後部座席） rear seat （3）
こうへい（な） （公平［な］） *na-adj.* fair （6）
こうむいん （公務員） public office worker, civil servant （5）
こうよう （紅葉） autumn leaves （7）
こえる （超える） *C2, tr.* to exceed （2）
こおる （凍る） *C1, intr.* to freeze （1）
ごかい（する） （誤解［する］） *n.v.* misunderstanding; to misunderstand （6）
ゴキブリ cockroach （7）
こきょう （故郷） hometown （7）

こくさいでんわ （国際電話） international call （6）
こくないりょこう （国内旅行） domestic travel （1）
こころ （心） mind, feeling, heart （4）; こころをこめる （心をこめる） to be sincere （6）
こし （腰） waist, hips （4）; こしかける （腰かける） *C2, intr.* to sit down, take a seat （3）
ごじ （誤字） misspelling, wrong letter （6）
ゴシップ gossip （6）
こしょう（する） （故障［する］） *n.v.* mechanical breakdown; to be out of order, have a mechanical breakdown （3）
ごぞんじだ （ご存じだ） to know (*honorific*) （5）
こたつ table with built-in heater （2）
コック cook （5）
こづつみ （小包） package （6）
こと (abstract) thing, matter, concept; 〜ことがある there are occasions when ... （6）; 〜ことにする to decide on ... （1）; 〜ことになる to be decided that ... （7）
こども （子供） child （5）; こどもべや （子供部屋） child's room （2）
ことわる （断る） *C1, tr.* to reject （5）
コピーマシン photocopier （5）
ごふくや （呉服屋） Japanese kimono store （5）
こふんじだい （古墳時代） Kofun period (3rd through 6th century) （7）
コマーシャル commercial （6）
こまる （困る） *C1, intr.* to have difficulty, be troubled （4）
ごみ （塵） garbage, trash （7）; ゴミや （ゴミ屋） trash collector （5）
こむ *C1, intr.* to be crowded （2）
コメディー sitcom （6）
ごらんになる （ご覧になる） to look at (*honorific*) （5）
ゴリラ gorilla （7）
こる *C1, intr.* to become stiff （4）
コレクトコール collect call （6）
ころす （殺す） *C1, tr.* to kill （7）
こわい （怖い） *i-adj.* frightening, afraid; こわがる （怖がる） *C1, tr.* to be frightened （4）
こわす *C1, tr.* to break; こわれる *C2, intr.* to become broken （3）
コンドミニアム condominium （2）
コンピュータ computer （2）
こんやく（する） （婚約［する］） *n.v.* engagement; to get engaged; こんやくしゃ （婚約者） fiancé(e) （5）
コーヒーメーカー coffeemaker （2）

さ／サ

サービス・ステーション service station; サービスエリア service area （3）; サービスりょう （サービス料） service charge （1）
さいこう （最高） most, best （2）
さいごに （最後に） *adv.* lastly, finally （3）
ざいさん （財産） property （5）
さいてい （最低） least, worst （2）
サイドブレーキ parking brake （3）
さいばんかん （裁判官） judge （5）

さがる（下がる）*C1, intr.* to come/go down; to dangle （3）

さかん（な） *na-adj.* prevalent, abundant （7）

さきゅう（砂丘） sand dune （7）

さく（咲く）*C1, intr.* to bloom （7）

さくいん（索引） index （6）

さくら（桜） cherry tree （7）

さけ（鮭） salmon （1）

さけよいうんてん（する）（酒酔い運転［する］）*n.v.* drunk driving; to drive drunk （3）

さげる（下げる）*C2, tr.* to lower (something) （3）

さしあげる *C2, tr.* to give (*humble*) （2）

さしだしにん（差出人） sender （6）

さそい（誘い） invitation （7）

〜さつ（〜冊） counter for books （6）

さっか（作家） author （5）

ざっし（雑誌） magazine （6）

さばく（砂漠） desert （7）

さびしい（寂しい）*i-adj.* lonely （4）

ざぶとん（座布団） floor cushion （2）

さら（皿） plate （2）

さらに *adv.* furthermore, moreover （2）

さる（猿） monkey （7）

さわやかな *na-adj.* fresh, refreshing （6）

さわる（触る）*C1, intr.* to touch （4）

さんか（する）（参加［する］）*n.v.* participation; to participate （7）

さんかく（三角） triangle; さんかくの（三角の） triangular （4）

さんぎょう（産業） industry; さんぎょうこうがい（産業公害） industrial pollution （7）

ざんぎょう（残業） overtime （5）

さんこうしょ（参考書） reference book （6）

さんごしょう（珊瑚礁） coral reef （7）

さんせい（する）（賛成［する］）*n.v.* agreement; to agree （7）

さんちょう（山頂） mountain peak; さんみゃく（山脈） mountain range （7）

さんめんきじ（三面記事） social news, gossip （6）

し／シ

し（死） death （5）

し（氏） Mr., Ms. (*formal*) （6）

しあわせ（な）（幸せ［な］）*na-adj.* happy （5）

シーエム CM (commercial message), commercial （6）

シーディープレーヤー（CDプレーヤー） CD player （2）

シート・ベルト seat belt （3）

シェーバー shaver （2）

しおれる *C2, intr.* to wither, fade, droop （7）

しか（鹿） deer （7）

しか…ない only, not except for （2）

しかいしゃ（司会社） master of ceremonies （6）

しがいつうわ（市外通話） long-distance call; しがいきょくばん（市外局番） area code （6）

しかく（四角） rectangle, square; しかくい（四角い）*i-adj.* rectangular, square （4）

じかようしゃ（自家用車） private or family car （3）

しかる（叱る）*C1, tr.* to scold （5）

じきゅう（時給） hourly wage （5）

じぎょう（事業） enterprise, business （5）

しげん（資源） resources （7）

じけん（事件） event, incident （6）

じこ（事故） accident; じこにあう（事故にあう） to get involved in an accident; じこをおこす（事故を起こす） to cause an accident （3）

じこくひょう（時刻表） timetable （1）

しごと（仕事） job, work （1）

ししゃ（支社） company branch office （5）

じしょ（辞書） dictionary （6）

ししょばこ（私書箱） P.O. box （6）

しぜん（自然） nature; しぜんはかい（自然破壊） destroying nature （7）

じそく（時速） speed per hour （3）

した（舌） tongue （4）

じだい（時代） era, period （7）

じだいげき（時代劇） samurai drama （6）

したがう（従う）*C1, intr.* to follow (a command, etc.) （7）

しちめんちょう（七面鳥） turkey （7）

しっかり *adv.* firmly （3）

しつぎょう（する）（失業［する］）*n.v.* unemployment; to lose one's employment （5）

じつげん（する）（実現［する］）*n.v.* realization; to realize （5）

じつは（実は） actually, to tell the truth （4）

しっぱい（する）（失敗［する］）*n.v.* failure; to fail （5）

しつれい（な）（失礼［な］）*na-adj.* impolite, rude （6）

していせき（指定席） reserved seat （1）

してつ（私鉄） private railway （1）

してん（支店） branch store, bank branch （5）

じてん（事典） encyclopedia （6）

じてん（辞典） dictionary （6）

じてんしゃ（自転車） bicycle （3）

じどうしゃ（自動車） automobile, car （3）

しな（品） item, product （2）

しないつうわ（市内通話） local call （6）

じなん（次男） second son （5）

しぬ（死ぬ）*C1, intr.* to die （5）

しば（芝） turf, sod （7）

しばい（芝居） theatrical play （7）

しばふ（芝生） lawn （7）

しばらく *adv.* for a while （2）

じぶつ（事物） things （7）

じぶん（自分） oneself, self （1）

しほうしけん（司法試験） bar exam （5）

しま（島） island （7）

しまる（閉まる）*C1, intr.* to shut off, close, be closed （1）; しめる（閉める）*C2, tr.* to close (something) （3）

じむしつ（事務室） office; じむしょ（事務所） office; じむいん（事務員） office clerk （5）

ジャーナリズム journalism （6）

しゃいん（社員） company employee; しゃちょう（社長） company president （5）

しゃかい（社会） society （5）; しゃかいらん（社会欄） society section (*of a newspaper*) （6）

しゃくやにん（借家人） tenant （2）

しゃこ（車庫） garage, carport （2）

しゃしょう（車掌） conductor （1）

しゃしんか　（写真家）　photographer　(5)
しゃせつ　（社説）　editorial　(6)
しゃどう　（車道）　road　(3)
ジャングル　jungle　(7)
しゅう　（州）　state (*U.S., Australia*), province (*Canada*)　(7)
しゅうかん　（習慣）　habit　(7)
しゅうかんし　（週刊誌）　weekly magazine　(6)
しゅうきょう　（宗教）　religion　(7)
ジューサー　juicer　(2)
じゅうしょ　（住所）　address　(2)
しゅうしょく（する）　（就職［する］）　*n.v.* getting a job; to get a job　(5)
じゆうせき　（自由席）　nonreserved seat　(1)
じゅうたく　（住宅）　residence, housing;　じゅうたくち （住宅地）　residential area　(2)
しゅうちゅうりょく　（集中力）　ability to concentrate　(4)
じゆうに　（自由に）　*adv.* freely　(3)
じゅうぶん（な）　（十分［な］）　*na-adj.* sufficient　(3)
じゅうやく　（重役）　executive　(1)
じゅうよう（な）　（重要［な］）　*na-adj.* important　(7)
しゅうり（する）　（修理［する］）　*n.v.* repair; to repair　(3)
しゅうりこう　（修理工）　mechanic　(3)
じゅく　（塾）　cram school　(4)
しゅくしょう（する）　（縮小［する］）　*n.v.* reduction; to reduce　(7)
しゅくでん　（祝電）　congratulatory telegram　(6)
しゅくはく（する）　（宿泊［する］）　*n.v.* lodging; to stay, lodge;　しゅくはくりょう （宿泊料）　room charge, hotel charges　(1)
じゅけん（する）　（受験［する］）　*n.v.* taking an examination; to take an examination　(4)
しゅざい（する）　（取材［する］）　*n.v.* news coverage; to cover, collect information　(6)
しゅじゅつ　（手術）　surgery　(4)
しゅだん　（手段）　means　(6)
しゅちょう（する）　（主張［する］）　*n.v.* assertion; to assert, claim　(7)
しゅつえん（する）　（出演［する］）　*n.v.* appearance on TV, stage, etc.; to appear, perform　(6)
しゅっきん（する）　（出勤［する］）　*n.v.* coming to work; to come to work　(5)
しゅっさん（する）　（出産［する］）　*n.v.* giving birth; to have a baby　(5)
しゅっせき（する）　（出席［する］）　*n.v.* attendance; to attend　(5)
しゅっちょう（する）　（出張［する］）　*n.v.* business trip; to go on a business trip　(1)
しゅっぱん（する）　（出版［する］）　*n.v.* publication; to publish;　しゅっぱんしゃ （出版社）　publisher　(6)
しゅふ　（主婦）　housewife　(5)
じゅもく　（樹木）　trees and shrubs　(7)
じゅわき　（受話器）　telephone receiver;　じゅわきをとる （受話器を取る）　to pick up the receiver　(6)
じゅんび（する）　（準備［する］）　*n.v.* preparation; to prepare　(3)
しょうエネ　（省エネ）　saving energy　(7)
しょうがっこう　（小学校）　grade school　(5)
じょうきゃく　（乗客）　passenger　(1)

じょうけん　（条件）　condition　(5)
じょうざい　（錠剤）　pill　(4)
しょうじ　（障子）　shoji (screen made of translucent paper)　(2)
じょうし　（上司）　superior, supervisor　(5)
しょうしゃ　（商社）　trading company　(5)
じょうしゃけん　（乗車券）　ticket (*transportation*)　(3)
しょうじょ　（少女）　girl　(5)
しょうしん（する）　（昇進［する］）　*n.v.* promotion; to promote　(5)
しょうせつ　（小説）　novel　(6)
しょうとつ（する）　（衝突［する］）　*n.v.* collision; to collide　(3)
しょうねん　（少年）　boy　(5)
じょうほう　（情報）　information　(3)
しょうぼうし　（消防士）　firefighter　(5);　しょうぼうしゃ （消防車）　fire engine　(3)
じょうもんじだい　（縄文時代）　*Jomon* period (prehistoric times until the 3rd century B.C.)　(7)
じょうようしゃ　（乗用車）　passenger car　(3)
しょうらい　（将来）　future　(7)
しょくぎょう　（職業）　occupation　(5)
しょくせいかつ　（食生活）　diet, eating habits;　しょくぜん （食前）　before meals;　しょくご （食後）　after meals　(4)
しょくどうしゃ　（食堂車）　dining car　(1)
しょくば　（職場）　working place　(5)
しょくぶつ　（植物）　plant　(7)
しょくよく　（食欲）　appetite;　しょくよくがある （食欲がある）　to have an appetite　(4)
しょくれき　（職歴）　employment history　(5)
じょこう（する）　（徐行［する］）　*n.v.* going slowly; to go slowly　(3)
しょさい　（書斎）　study room　(2)
しょるい　（書類）　document, paper　(5)
しらせる　（知らせる）　*C2, tr.* to notify　(2)
しる　（知る）　*C1, tr.* to know　(1)
シロップ　syrup, liquid medicine　(4)
しんかんせん　（新幹線）　bullet train　(1)
シングル　single room　(1)
しんごう　（信号）　traffic light　(1)
じんこうようしょく　（人工養殖）　artificial culturing (*fish, etc.*)　(7)
しんこく（な）　（深刻［な］）　*na-adj.* serious　(7)
しんこんりょこう　（新婚旅行）　honeymoon　(5)
しんさつ（する）　（診察［する］）　*n.v.* medical examination; to perform a medical examination　(4)
しんしつ　（寝室）　bedroom　(2)
じんじぶ　（人事部）　personnel department　(5)
しんじゅ　（真珠）　pearl　(7)
しんじる　（信じる）　*C2, tr.* to believe　(7)
じんせい　（人生）　life　(5)
しんせき　（親戚）　relative, kinfolk　(5)
しんせん（な）　（新鮮［な］）　*na-adj.* fresh　(5)
しんだいしゃ　（寝台車）　sleeping car　(1)
しんちょう　（身長）　height (body)　(4)
しんとう　（神道）　Shintoism　(7)
しんぱい（する）　（心配［する］）　*n.v.* worry; to be worried　(4)
しんぷ　（神父）　Catholic priest　(5)

しんぶん（新聞）newspaper; しんぶんきじ（新聞記事）newspaper article (6); しんぶんきしゃ（新聞記者）journalist (5); しんぶんしゃ（新聞社）newspaper company; しんぶんにのる（新聞に載る）to appear in a paper; しんぶんをとる（新聞をとる）to subscribe to a newspaper (6)

しんぽ（する）（進歩［する］）*n.v.* progress; to progress (7)

しんやほうそう（深夜放送）midnight broadcast (6)

しんりょく（新緑）spring greenery (7)

しんりん（森林）forest (7)

す／ス

す（巣）nest (7)

スイート suite (1)

すいおんけい（水温計）water temperature gauge (3)

スイカ watermelon (7)

すいしつおせん（水質汚染）water pollution (7)

スイッチ switch; スイッチをいれる（スイッチを入れる）to turn on a switch; スイッチをきる（スイッチを切る）to turn off a switch (2)

すいはんき（炊飯器）rich cooker (2)

すいへいせん（水平線）horizon (7)

スカンク skunk (7)

すぎ（杉）Japanese cedar (7)

すごく *adv.* terribly (6)

すずめ（雀）sparrow (7)

すすめる *C2, tr.* to suggest, recommend (4)

スタジオ studio (6)

スタンド floor lamp, desk lamp (2)

～ずつ each..., per... (2)

ずつうがする（頭痛がする）to have a headache (4)

スッキリする to feel refreshed (4)

ずっと *adv.* without interruption, all the way (1)

スト（ライキ）strike (5)

すな（砂）sand (7)

すなお（な）（素直［な］）*na-adj.* gentle, mild (6)

すなはま（砂浜）sandy beach (7)

すね（脛）shin (4)

ズバリ *adv.* boldly, decisively (6)

スピード speed; スピードいはん（スピード違反）speeding violation; スピードメーター speedometer; スピードをおとす（スピードを落とす）to decrease speed; スピードをだす（スピードを出す）to increase speed (3)

スポーツし（スポーツ紙）sports paper (6); スポーツせんしゅ（スポーツ選手）athlete (5); スポーツばんぐみ（スポーツ番組）sports program; スポーツらん（スポーツ欄）sports section (of a newspaper) (6)

スポンサー sponsor (6)

すませる *C2, tr.* to get along, manage (6)

スミレ violet (7)

すむ（住む）*C1, intr.* to reside, live (2)

スモッグ smog (7)

するどい *i-adj.* sharp (7)

スーツケース suitcase (1)

せ／セ

せいおう（西欧）Western Europe (7)

せいかつ（する）（生活［する］）*n.v.* life; to lead life (6)

せいき（世紀）century (7)

せいけいしゅじゅつ（整形手術）cosmetic surgery (4)

せいげんそくど（制限速度）speed limit (3)

せいざ（する）（正座［する］）sitting formally; to sit in formal position (7)

せいさん（する）（生産［する］）*n.v.* production; to produce (5)

せいじか（政治家）politician (5)

せいじらん（政治欄）politics section (of a newspaper) (6)

せいねん（成年）majority age (5)

せいねん（青年）young people (5)

せいねんがっぴ（生年月日）birth date (5)

セールスマン salesperson (5)

せおう（背負う）*C1, tr.* to carry on one's back (5)

せかい（世界）world (7); せかいてき（な）（世界的［な］）*na-adj.* worldwide (5)

せき（席）seat (1); せきをゆずる（席を譲る）to give up one's seat (3)

せきがでる（咳が出る）to have a cough; せきをする（咳をする）to cough (4)

せきてい（石庭）rock garden (7)

せきどう（赤道）equator (7)

せきにん（責任）responsibility (5)

セダン sedan (3)

せっかく long-awaited, after much trouble (3)

せっけい（する）（設計［する］）*n.v.* architectural design; to design buildings (2)

せっけん（石鹸）soap (7)

ぜったいに（絶対に）*adv.* absolutely (4)

せつめい（する）（説明［する］）*n.v.* explanation; to explain (5)

せつやく（する）（節約［する］）*n.v.* saving, economizing; to save, economize (7)

せなか（背中）back (4)

ぜひ（是非）*adv.* by all means (5)

せまい（狭い）*i-adj.* narrow, not spacious (2)

せみ（蝉）cicada (7)

セロテープ adhesive tape (5)

せわ（する）（世話［する］）*n.v.* care; to care for (2)

ぜんこく（全国）all over the country (1)

ぜんしゅう（全集）complete works (6)

せんす（扇子）folding fan (7)

せんそう（戦争）war; せんご（戦後）after a war (5)

センターライン center line (3)

せんたく（する）（洗濯［する］）*n.v.* laundry; to do laundry; せんたくき（洗濯機）washing machine; せんたくもの（洗濯物）things to be laundered (2)

せんぷうき（扇風機）electric fan (2)

ぜんぶざせき（前部座席）front seat (3)

ぜんぶで（全部で）in total (2)

せんむとりしまりやく（専務取締役）managing director (5)

せんめんじょ（洗面所）washstand, sink (2)

そ／ソ

ぞう （象） elephant （7）
ぞう （像） statue （1）
そう （な） *na-adj.* looking like, looking as if （4）
そうじ（する） （掃除［する］） *n.v.* cleaning; to do cleaning; そうじき （掃除機） vaccum cleaner （2）; そうじふ （掃除夫） sweeper （5）
そうしき （葬式） funeral （5）
そうだん（する） （相談［する］） *n.v.* consultation; to consult （3）
そうだんしつ （相談室） consulting room （6）
そうりょ （僧侶） Buddhist priest or monk （5）
そくたつ （速達） express mail （6）
そくど （速度） speed （3）
そせん （祖先） ancestor(s) （5）
そだつ （育つ） *C1, intr.* to grow up （5）
そつぎょう（する） （卒業［する］） *n.v.* graduation; to graduate （5）
ソファー sofa （2）
そろばん abacus （5）
ぞんじる （存じる） *C2, tr.* to think, know (*humble*) （5）

た／タ

たいいん（する） （退院［する］） *n.v.* release from hospital; to be discharged from the hospital （4）
たいおん （体温） body temperature （4）; たいおんけい （体温計） clinical thermometer
だいがくいん （大学院） graduate school （5）
たいきおせん （大気汚染） air pollution （7）
だいきぎょう （大企業） large enterprise （5）
だいく （大工） carpenter （2）
たいじゅう （体重） weight (body) （4）
だいじょうぶ（な） （大丈夫［な］） *na-adj.* all right, no problem （2）
たいしょく（する） （退職［する］） *n.v.* retirement; to retire （5）
たいせいよう （大西洋） Atlantic Ocean （7）
たいせつ（な） （大切［な］） *na-adj.* important （4）
たいだんばんぐみ （対談番組） interview show （6）
だいち （台地） plateau （7）
たいど （態度） attitude （7）
だいなし （台無し） totally spoiled （3）
ダイニング・キッチン eat-in kitchen (lit., *dining-kitchen*) （2）
ダイニング・ルーム dining room （2）
たいふう （台風） typhoon （7）
タイプライター typewriter; タイプをうつ （タイプを打つ） to type （5）
たいへいよう （太平洋） Pacific Ocean （7）
たいへん（な） （大変［な］） *na-adj.* troublesome （4）
タイヤ tire; タイヤをかえる to change a tire （3）
ダイヤル dial; ダイヤルつうわ （ダイヤル通話） direct dialing （6）
たいりく （大陸） continent （7）
たいりょうせいさん （大量生産） mass production （5）
タウンハウス townhouse （2）
だえん （楕円） *noun* oval （4）

たおす （倒す） *C1, tr.* to knock over, set back （3）
たか （鷹） hawk, falcon （7）
たかさ （高さ） height （7）
たかめる （高める） *C2, tr.* raise （5）
たから （宝） treasure （7）
たき （滝） waterfall （7）
タクシー taxi （3）
たくはいびん （宅配便） door-to-door package delivery （6）
たけ （竹） bamboo （7）
〜だけでなく not only... （4）
タコメーター tachometer （3）
たしかめる （確かめる） *C2, tr.* to make sure （3）
たしょう （多少） *adv.* more or less （7）
だす （出す） *C1, tr.* to send out, put out （3）
たずねる *C2, tr.* to ask, inquire （1）
ただいま （只今） *adv.* right now （2）
ただしく （正しく） *adv.* correctly （6）
たたみ （畳） *tatami* (woven reed mat) （2）
たつ （発つ） *C1, intr.* to leave （1）
たつ （立［建］つ） *C1, intr.* to be built, stand （3）; たてる （建てる） *C2, tr.* to build （2）
だつじ （脱字） missing letter （6）
ダッシュボード dashboard （3）
たてつぼ （建坪） floor space, floor area （2）
たとえば （例えば） for example （3）
たな （棚） shelf （2）
たに （谷） valley （7）
たね （種） seed （7）
たのしい （楽しい） *i-adj.* enjoyable, fun （4）
たのしみ （楽しみ） pleasure （2）
たはた （田畑） rice paddies and dry fields （7）
タブー taboo （7）
ダブル double room with one bed （1）
ため （に） for the purpose of, for the sake of （2）
ためる （貯める） *C2, tr.* to save （5）
たもつ （保つ） *C2, tr.* to maintain （7）
ダリヤ dahlia （7）
タレント TV personality （6）
だんこ （断固） firm, decisive （7）
たんこうぼん （単行本） book (not magazine) （6）
たんじょうび （誕生日） birthday （1）
たんす chest of drawers, wardrobe （2）
たんだい （短大） junior college （5）
だんたいりょこう （団体旅行） group travel （1）
だんだん *adv.* gradually （2）
だんち （団地） housing development （2）
たんぱ （短波） short-wave （6）
ダンプカー dump truck （3）
たんぼ （田んぼ） rice paddy （7）

ち／チ

ちい （地位） position, status （5）
チェック（する） *n.v.* check; to check （3）
チェックアウト（する） *n.v.* check-out; to check out of hotel; チェックイン（する） *n.v.* check-in; to check into hotel （1）
チェンジレバー gear shift lever （3）

ちかづく （近づく） *C1, intr.*　to approach, draw close　(3)

ちかみち （近道）　shortcut　(3)

ちきゅう （地球）　earth　(7)

ちこく（する） （遅刻[する]） *n.v.*　late for work; to be late for work　(5)

ちじん （知人）　acquaintance　(6)

ちず （地図）　map　(1)

チャーター　charter (*flight, bus, etc.*)　(1)

ちゃくりく（する） （着陸[する]）　landing; to land　(1)

チャンネル　TV channel;　チャンネルをかえる （チャンネルを変える）　to change channels　(6)

ちゅう （中）　during, in the middle　(2)

ちゅうい（する） （注意[する]） *n.v.*　attention; to watch out, be cautious, take care　(3)

ちゅういりょく （注意力）　attentiveness　(3)

ちゅうがっこう （中学校）　middle school　(5)

ちゅうけい（する） （中継[する]） *n.v.*　telecast; to telecast　(6)

ちゅうこ （中古）　secondhand, used　(2)

ちゅうこく（する） （忠告[する]） *n.v.*　advice; to advise　(1)

ちゅうしゃ （注射）　injection　(4)

ちゅうしゃきんし （駐車禁止）　no parking;　ちゅうしゃじょう （駐車場）　parking lot　(3)

ちゅうしょうきぎょう （中小企業）　small business　(5)

ちゅうしん （中心）　center　(1)

ちゅうねん （中年）　middle age　(5)

チューリップ　tulip　(7)

ちょう （蝶）　butterfly　(7)

ちょうかん （朝刊）　morning paper　(6)

ちょうきょりでんわ （長距離電話）　long-distance call　(6)

ちょうさ（する） （調査[する]） *n.v.*　investigation; to investigate　(3)

ちょうじょう （頂上）　mountain peak　(7)

ちょうしんき （聴診器）　stethoscope　(4)

ちょうでん （弔電）　telegram of condolence　(6)

ちょうなん （長男）　oldest son　(5)

ちょうりし （調理師）　cook　(5)

ちょきん（する） （貯金[する]） *n.v.*　savings; to save (money)　(2)

ちょくせつに （直接に） *adv.*　directly　(6)

ちょしゃ （著者）　author　(7)

ちょっとした　simple, easy　(4)

ちり （地理）　geography　(7)

ちりょう（する） （治療[する]）　medical treatment; to give medical treatment　(4)

ちる （散る） *C1, intr.*　to fall (leaves), be scattered　(7)

チンパンジー　chimpanzee　(7)

つ／ツ

ツアー　package tour　(1)

ツアー・コンダクター　tour guide　(1)

ついとつ（する） （追突[する]） *n.v.*　rear-end collision; to rear-end　(3)

ツイン　room with twin beds　(1)

つうきん（する） （通勤[する]） *n.v.*　commuting to work; to commute to work　(6)

つうやく（する） （通訳[する]） *n.v.*　interpreter; to interpret　(5)

つうわ （通話）　telephone call, talking over the phone;　つうわりょう （通話料）　telephone charge　(6)

つかまる （捕まる） *C1, intr.*　to be caught; to be arrested　(3)

つかむ　*C1, tr.*　to grab, hold, catch　(4)

つかれる （疲れる） *C2, intr.*　to get tired　(1)

つき （月）　moon　(7)

つぎに （次に）　next;　つぎの （次の）　following　(3)

つく （着く） *C1, intr.*　to arrive　(1)

つく （付く） *C1, intr.*　to become attached, to go on (lights, appliances, etc.)　(2);　つける （付ける） *C2, tr.*　to attach, turn on　(3)

つくえ （机）　desk　(2)

つけね （つけ根）　base, root　(4)

つける （着ける） *C2, tr.*　to attach, buckle up　(3)

つたえる （伝える） *C2, tr.*　to report, convey information　(6)

つち （土）　soil　(7)

つづける （続ける） *C2, tr.*　to continue　(3)

つなぐ　*C1, tr.*　to link　(6)

つねに （常に） *adv.*　ordinarily　(7)

つばさ （翼）　wing　(7)

つばめ　swallow　(7)

つぶれる　*C2, intr.*　to go under　(5)

つまさき （爪先）　tip of the toe　(4)

つめ （爪）　nail (finger or toe)　(4)

つめこむ　*C1, tr.*　to pack in　(7);　つめる　*C1, tr.*　to pack　(1)

つれていく （連れていく） *C1, tr.*　to take (people)　(1)

つれてくる （連れてくる） *C3, tr.*　to bring (people)　(1)

て／テ

て （手）　hand　(4)

ディージェー　deejay (disc jockey)　(6)

ていえん （庭園）　garden　(7)

ていきけん （定期券）　monthly commuter pass　(3);　ていきけんしん （定期検診）　regular health check-up;　ていきてき（な） （定期的[な]） *na-adj.*　periodic, regular　(4);　ていきてんけん （定期点検）　regular check-up　(3)

ていりゅうじょ （停留所）　bus or tram stop　(1)

ディレクター　director　(6)

てがみ （手紙）　letter　(6)

てきせい （適性）　aptitude　(5)

てくび （手首）　wrist　(4)

デザイナー　designer　(5)

てつだう （手伝う） *C1, tr.*　to help, assist　(2)

てっぺん　top of the head　(4)

でも　or something like that　(1)

テレックス　telex　(5)

テレビ　TV　(2)

てん （点）　point　(3)

てんいん （店員）　store clerk　(5)

でんき （電気）　light, electricity;　でんきせいひん （電気製品）　electric appliance;　でんきゅう （電球）　lightbulb;　でんきをけす （電気を消す）　to turn off a light; でんきをつける（電気をつける）to turn on a light *(2)*

てんきよほう（天気予報）weather forecast *(6)*

てんきん（する）（転勤［する］）*n.v.* transfer; to transfer *(5)*

てんけん（する）（点検［する］）*n.v.* check; to spot-check *(3)*

でんごん（伝言）message *(6)*

でんしゃ（電車）train, tram car *(3)*

てんじょう（天井）ceiling *(2)*

てんじょういん（添乗員）tour conductor *(5)*

てんしょくする（転職する）to change jobs *(5)*

でんしレンジ（電子レンジ）microwave oven *(2)*

でんせつ（伝説）legend *(7)*

でんたく（電卓）electric calculator *(5)*

でんぽう（電報）telegram, wire; でんぶん（電文）telegram message; でんぽうきょく（電報局）telegram office; でんぽうようし（電報用紙）telegram blank; でんぽうりょう（電報料）telegram fee; でんぽうをうつ（電報を打つ）to telegraph, send a telegram *(6)*

てんもんがく（天文学）astronomy *(7)*

でんわ（電話）telephone *(2)*; でんわ（を）する（電話［を］する）*n.v.* to make a call; でんわきょく（電話局）telephone company; でんわちょう（電話帳）telephone directory; でんわばんごうあんない（電話番号案）directory assistance; でんわボックス（電話ボックス）telephone booth; でんわりょう（電話料）telephone charge; でんわをかける（電話をかける）to make a call; でんわをきる（電話を切る）to hang up a phone *(6)*

テーブル table *(2)*

と／ト

と（戸）door; ドア door *(2)*

といあわせる（問い合わせる）*C2, tr.* to inquire *(6)*

トイレ rest room, toilet *(2)*

とうげ（峠）mountain pass *(7)*

どうしても by all means *(1)*

とうしょ（する）（投書［する］）*n.v.* sending a letter to the editor; to send a letter to the editor *(6)*

とうしょらん（投書欄）letters-to-the-editor section *(6)*

どうとく（道徳）morality *(7)*

どうぶつ（動物）animal; どうぶつえん（動物園）zoo *(7)*

どうよう（同様）in the same way *(6)*

どうりょう（同僚）colleague *(5)*

どうろ（道路）street, road *(3)*

どうろちず（道路地図）road map *(3)*

どうわ（童話）story, tale *(6)*

とおす（通す）*C1, tr.* to send through; とおる（通る）*C1, intr.* to go through, to go along (a street) *(3)*

トースター toaster *(2)*

とかげ lizard *(7)*

ドキュメンタリー documentary *(6)*

どくじの（独自の）original, peculiar to *(7)*

どくしゃ（読者）reader *(6)*

とくしゅう（特集）special feature, special collection *(6)*

どくしん（独身）single *(5)*

とくせい（特性）unique characteristic *(7)*

どくとくの（独特の）unique *(7)*

とくに（特に）*adv.* especially *(7)*

とくはいん（特派員）special correspondent *(6)*

とくべつ（な）（特別［な］）*na-adj.* special *(5)*

どくりつ（する）（独立［する］）*n.v.* independence; to become independent *(5)*

とこのま（床の間）alcove *(2)*

ところ point in time *(2)*

としをとる（齢をとる）to get old, age *(5)*

～として as... *(5)*

とじる（閉じる）*C2, tr.* to close *(4)*

とち（土地）land, locale *(2)*

とちゅう（途中）on the way *(3)*

とっきゅう（特急）super express train *(1)*

とっておき *C1, tr.* best, treasured, valuable *(6)*

とどける（届ける）*C2, tr.* to deliver *(5)*

どの...も each *(2)*

どのように how, in what way *(1)*

とぶ（飛ぶ）*C1, intr.* to fly, jump *(1)*

とまる（止まる）*C1, intr.* to come to a stop *(3)*

とまる（泊まる）*C1, intr.* to stay overnight *(1)*

とら（虎）tiger *(7)*

ドライブ（する）*n.v.* drive; to drive *(3)*

ドライヤー hair dryer *(2)*

トラクター tractor *(3)*

トラック truck *(3)*

トラベラーズ・チェック travelers' check *(1)*

ドラマ drama *(6)*

トランク trunk *(3)*

とり（鳥）bird *(7)*

とりい（鳥居）gate of a Shinto shrine *(7)*

どりょく（する）（努力［する］）*n.v.* effort; to make an effort *(5)*

トレーラー trailer *(3)*

トローリーバス trolley bus *(3)*

とんぼ dragonfly *(7)*

とんや（問屋）wholesale store *(5)*

な／ナ

ないせん（内線）extension *(6)*

ないよう（内容）content(s) *(6)*

なおす（直す）*C1, tr.* to repair, mend *(2)*; なおる（直る）*C1, intr.* to get better, recover *(3)*

ながし（流し）sink *(2)*

ながでんわ（長電話）long phone call *(6)*

ながめ（眺め）view *(2)*

ながもちする（長持ちする）durable *(3)*

ながれる（流れる）*C2, intr.* to flow *(4)*

なく（泣く）*C1, intr.* to cry, weep *(4)*

なくす *C1, tr.* to lose *(3)*

なくてもいい it's all right not to... *(7)*

なくなる to get lost, disappear *(3)*

など etc. *(1)*

なまの（生の）raw (fish), unboiled (water) *(1)*

なまほうそう（する）（生放送［する］）*n.v.* live broadcast; to broadcast live *(6)*

なみ 波 wave *(7)*

なめる　*C2, tr.*　to lick　(4)
なやみごと　悩みごと　worries, troubles　(6)
なやむ　（悩む）　*C1, intr.*　to suffer from　(5)
ならう　（習う）　*C1, tr.*　to learn　(5)
ならじだい　（奈良時代）　*Nara* period (710-796)　(7)
ならぶ　（並ぶ）　*C1, intr.*　to line up　(1)；　ならべる
　（並べる）　*C2, tr.*　to line (something) up　(3)
なる　（鳴る）　*C1, intr.*　to ring　(6)
なれる　（慣れる）　*C2, intr.*　to get used to　(5)
なわとび　jumping rope　(4)
なんきょく　（南極）　South Pole　(7)
ナンバープレート　license plate　(3)

に／ニ

～にかんする　（～に関する）　regarding…　(6)
にぎる　（握る）　*C1, tr.*　to grip, hold　(3)
～にちがいない　there is no doubt that…　(6)
にちじょうせいかつ　（日常生活）　daily life　(2)
にっか　（日課）　daily schedule　(5)
にっかんし　（日刊紙）　daily paper　(6)
にっき　（日記）　diary　(5)
にぶる　*C1, intr.*　to decline　(3)
にほんま　（日本間）　Japanese-style room　(2)
にもつ　（荷物）　luggage　(1)
にゅういん（する）　（入院［する］）　*n.v.*　hospitalization;
　to be hospitalized　(5)
にゅうがく（する）　（入学［する］）　*n.v.*　entering a
　school; to enter school　(5)
にゅうしゃ（する）　（入社［する］）　*n.v.*　entering a
　company; to start working for a company　(5)
ニュース　news　(6)
にわ　（庭）　garden, yard；　にわいじりをする
　（庭いじりをする）　to do gardening　(2)
ニワトリ　chicken　(7)
にんぎょう　（人形）　doll　(7)
にんしん（する）　（妊娠［する］）　*n.v.*　pregnancy; to get
　pregnant　(5)

ぬ／ヌ

ぬう　（縫う）　*C1, tr.*　to sew；　ぬいものをする
　（縫い物をする）　to do sewing　(2)
ぬま　（沼）　marsh　(7)

ね／ネ

ねをはる　（根を張る）　to extend roots　(7)
ねがう　（願う）　*C1, tr.*　to request　(5)
ねかす　（寝かす）　*C1, tr.*　to put to bed；　ねる（寝る）
　C1, tr.　to go to sleep, go to bed　(3)
ねこ　（猫）　cat　(7)
ねずみ　（鼠）　mouse, rat　(7)
ねつ　（熱）　fever　(4)
ねったいうりん　（熱帯雨林）　tropical rain forest　(7)
ねむい　（眠い）　*i-adj.*　sleepy　(3)
ねんがじょう　（年賀状）　New Year's card　(6)
ねんじゅうぎょうじ　（年中行事）　annual events　(7)

ねんりょうけい　（燃料計）　fuel gauge　(3)
ねんれい　（年齢）　age　(5)

の／ノ

のうみん　（農民）　farmer　(5)
のうやくをまく　（農薬をまく）　to spread fertilizer　(7)
～のおかげで　thanks to…　(7)
～のかわりに　in place of…　(6)
のこす　（残す）　*C1, tr.*　to leave behind　(3)
のこり　（残り）　remainder, the rest　(5)；　のこる（残る）
　C1, intr.　to be left over, remain　(3)
のせる　（乗せる）　*C2, tr.*　to put on a vehicle, give a ride
　to　(3)
のど　（喉）　throat　(4)；　のどがかわく　（喉がかわく）
　to get thirsty　(1)
～のに　*conj.*　although…　(7)
のばす　（伸ばす）　*C1, tr.*　to extend or stretch
　(something)　(4)
のはら　（野原）　field, meadow　(7)
～のほかに　in addition to…　(4)
のぼり　（上り）　going toward Tokyo (by train)　(1)
のみ　flea　(7)
のり　（海苔）　seaweed　(2)
のる　（乗る）　*C1, intr.*　to board a vehicle, ride；
　のりかえる　（乗り換える）　*C2, tr.*　to transfer
　(vehicles)；　のりもの　（乗り物）　vehicles　(1)
のる　（載る）　*C1, intr.*　to be covered (*in a newspaper*)
　(6)
ノロノロうんてん　（ノロノロ運転）　sluggish traffic　(3)

は／ハ

は　（歯）　tooth　(4)；　はいしゃ　（歯医者）　dentist　(5)
は　（葉）　leaf；　はっぱ　（葉っぱ）　leaf　(7)
パーツ　part (of a mechanical object)　(3)
バーテンダー　bartender　(5)
ハートがた　（ハート形）　heart-shaped　(4)
パートタイム　part-time job, part-timer　(5)
はいきぶつ　（廃棄物）　industrial waste　(7)
はいく　（俳句）　haiku poetry　(7)
はいけん（する）　（拝見［する］）　*n.v.*　taking a look; to
　look at (*humble*)　(5)
はいざら　（灰皿）　ashtray　(2)
はいしゃく（する）　（拝借［する］）　*n.v.*　borrowing; to
　borrow (*humble*)　(5)
はいたつ（する）　（配達［する］）　*n.v.*　delivery; to
　deliver　(6)
バイパス　bypass　(3)
はいゆう　（俳優）　actor, actress (cf. 女優)　(5)
はいる　（入る）　*C1, intr.*　to enter, go; come in, be
　included　(3)
パイロット　pilot　(1)
はう　（這う）　*C1, intr.*　to creep, crawl　(4)
はえ　（蝿）　housefly　(7)
はえる　（生える）　*C2, intr.*　to grow, flourish
　(*plants*)　(7)
はか　（墓）　grave, tomb　(5)
はがき　（葉書）　postcard　(6)

ばかり　only　(2)

はかる　(計る)　C1, tr.　to weigh　(6)

はきけ　(吐き気)　nausea;　はきけがする
　(吐き気がする)　to be nauseated;　はく　C1, tr.
　to vomit, spit　(4)

はく　(掃く)　C1, tr.　to sweep (with a broom)　(2)

はくちょう　(白鳥)　swan　(7)

はこぶ　(運ぶ)　C1, tr.　to transport, carry (a large
　object)　(2)

はし　(橋)　bridge　(1)

はじまる　(始まる)　C1, intr.　to begin;　はじめる
　(始める)　C2, tr.　to begin　(3)

はしら　(柱)　pillar　(2)

バス　bus　(3)

はず　expectation　(4)

バス・ガイド　tour bus guide　(3)

はずかしい　(恥ずかしい)　i-adj.　shameful,
　embarrassed　(4)

はずす　(外す)　C1, tr.　to release, undo　(3)

パスポート　passport　(1)

はだ　(肌)　skin　(4)

はたらきざかり　(働き盛り)　the prime of life　(5)

はたらく　(働く)　C1, intr.　to work　(3)

はち　(蜂)　wasp　(7)

はちゅうるい　(爬虫類)　reptile　(7)

はっきり　(と)　adv.　clearly　(6)

バック・ミラー　rearview mirror　(3)

はつこい　(初恋)　first love　(5)

はっしゃ　(する)　(発車[する])　to start a car　(3)

はったつ　(する)　(発達[する])　n.v.　development; to
　develop, evolve　(7)

バッテリー　battery　(3)

はってん　(する)　(発展[する])　n.v.　development; to
　develop　(7)

はつばいちゅう　(発売中)　on sale　(2)

はっぴょう　(する)　(発表[する])　n.v.　announcement;
　to announce　(6)

はつめい　(する)　(発明[する])　n.v.　invention; to
　invent　(5)

はと　(鳩)　pigeon, dove　(7)

パトカー　patrol car, police car　(3)

はな　(鼻)　nose　(4)

はなしちゅう　(話し中)　the line is busy　(6)

はなす　(放す)　C1, tr.　to release　(3)

はなす　(離す)　C1, tr.　to detach　(4);　はなれる
　(離れる)　C2, tr.　to leave, to be away　(3)

はなやか　(な)　(華やか[な])　na-adj.　spectacular,
　showy　(5)

はば　(幅)　width　(1)

ハマチ　yellowtail (fish)　(7)

はやく　(早く)　adv.　early, quickly　(1)

はやし　(林)　woods　(7)

ばら　(薔薇)　rose　(7)

はらう　(払う)　C1, tr.　to pay　(1)

バラエティー・ショー　variety show　(6)

はる　(貼る)　C1, tr.　to paste　(6)

バルコニー　balcony　(2)

はんが　(版画)　woodblock print　(7)

パンク（する)　n.v.　flat tire; to get a flat tire　(3)

ばんぐみ　(番組)　(TV, radio) program　(6)

ばんごうちがい　(番号違い)　wrong number　(6)

はんざい　(犯罪)　crime　(7)

パンダ　panda　(7)

はんたい　(する)　(反対[する])　n.v.　opposition; to
　oppose　(7)

はんとう　(半島)　peninsula　(7)

ハンドブレーキ　hand break　(3)

ハンドル　steering wheel;　ハンドルをきる
　(ハンドルを切る)　to turn the wheel;
　ハンドルをにぎる　(ハンドルを握る)　to take the
　wheel　(3)

バンパー　bumper　(3)

ひ／ヒ

ヒーター　heater　(2)

ビールス　virus　(4)

ひがいにあう　(被害にあう)　to sustain damage　(7)

ひかく　(する)　(比較[する])　n.v.　comparison; to
　compare　(7)

ひきずる　C1, tr.　to drag　(4)

ひきだし　(引き出し)　drawer　(2)

ひげ　(髭)　beard　(4)

ひこうき　(飛行機)　airplane　(1)

ひごろ　(日頃)　daily　(4)

ひざ　(膝)　knee　(4)

ビザ　visa　(1)

ひじ　(肘)　elbow　(4)

ひしがた　(菱形)　lozenge, diamond shape　(4)

ビジネスマン　businessman　(5)

ひしょ　(秘書)　secretary　(1)

ひしょち　(避暑地)　summer resort　(1)

ひたい　(額)　forehead　(4)

ひだり　(左)　left (direction)　(4);　ひだりがわ　(左側)
　left side　(1);　ひだりがわつうこう　(左側通行)
　driving on the left　(3);　ひだりきき　(左利き)
　left-handed;　ひだりて　(左手)　left hand　(4)

びっくりする　to be surprised　(4)

ひっこす　(引っ越す)　C1, intr.　to move (from one
　address to another)　(2)

ひつじ　(羊)　sheep　(7)

ヒッチハイク　hitchhiking　(1)

ひつよう　(な)　(必要[な])　na-adj.　necessary　(7)

ビデオ　video　(6);　ビデオレコーダー　VCR　(2)

ひとりたび　(一人旅)　traveling alone, solo trip　(1)

ひふ　(皮膚)　skin, skin surface　(4)

ひま　(な)　(暇[な])　na-adj.　free, with time to
　spare　(5)

ひまわり　(向日葵)　sunflower　(7)

ひょう　(豹)　panther, leopard　(7)

びょういん　(病院)　hospital　(4)

ひょうが　(氷河)　glacier　(7)

びょうき　(病気)　sick, sickness;　びょうきになる
　(病気になる)　to get sick　(4)

ひょうこう　(標高)　height above sea level　(7)

ひょうさつ　(表札)　nameplate　(2)

びようし　(美容師)　hairstylist　(5)

ひょうろんか　(評論家)　critic　(6)

ひよこ（雛） baby chick　(7)
ひらしゃいん（平社員） rank and file　(5)
ひろい（広い） *i-adj.* wide, spacious　(2)
びんせん（便箋） letter pad, letter paper　(6)

ふ／フ

～ぶ（～部） counter for newspapers　(6)
ファイル file　(5)
ファクシミリ facsimile　(5)；　ファックス fax　(6)
ファッション・モデル fashion model　(5)
ブーケ bouquet　(7)
ふうとう（封筒） envelope　(6)
フェリーボート ferry　(1)
ふえる（増える） *C2, intr.* to increase, become greater　(4)
フェンダー fender　(3)
ぶか（部下） subordinate　(5)
ふかい（深い） *i-adj.* deep　(7)；　ふかさ（深さ） depth　(3)
ふく（拭く） *C1, tr.* to wipe　(2)
ふくさよう（副作用） side effect　(4)
ふくしゃき（複写機） photocopier　(5)
ふくしゃちょう（副社長） vice president　(5)
ふくそう（服装） clothes　(5)
ふくつう（腹痛） stomachache　(4)
ふくろう owl　(7)
ふしぎ（な）（不思議［な］） *na-adj.* weird, amazing　(7)
ふじゆう（な）（不自由［な］） *na-adj.* poor; handicapped; inconvenient　(5)
ふすま sliding door of opaque paper　(2)
ふせぐ（防ぐ） *C1, tr.* to prevent, ward off　(7)
ぶた（豚） pig　(7)
ふだん *adv.* usually　(6)
ぶちょう（部長） department head　(5)
ふつうしゃ（普通車） coach, regular car；　ふつうせき（普通席） regular-class seat；　ふつうれっしゃ（普通列車） local train　(1)
ぶつかる *C1, intr.* to run into, collide with, be hit；　ぶつける *C2, tr.* to hit (something), throw at forcefully　(3)
ぶっきょう（仏教） Buddhism；　ぶつぞう（仏像） statue of the Buddha　(7)
プッシュフォン push-button telephone　(6)
ふどうさんや（不動産屋） real estate agency or agent　(2)
ふとりすぎ（太り過ぎ） overweight　(4)
ふとんをあげる（ふとんを上げる） to put the futon away　(4)
ふなびん（船便） surface mail　(6)
ふね（船） ship　(1)
ぶひん（部品） part (*of a mechanical object*)　(3)
ふむ（踏む） *C1, tr.* to step on, to pedal　(3)
ふもと（麓） foot of a mountain　(7)
ふやす（増やす） *C1, tr.* to increase (something)　(4)
フライト flight　(1)
ブラインド blind　(2)
プランをたてる to make a plan　(1)
フリーザー freezer　(2)

ふりむく *C1, intr.* to look back　(4)
プリンタ printer　(5)
ふる（振る） *C1, tr.* to shake (something)　(4)
ブルドーザー bulldozer　(3)
ブレーキ brake；　ブレーキをかける to put on the brakes　(3)
プログラマー programmer　(5)
プロデューサー producer　(6)
プロポーズ（する） *n.v.* proposal (marriage); to propose marriage　(5)
フロント front desk　(1)
フロント・ガラス windshield　(3)
ふんか（する）（噴火［する］） *n.v.* eruption; to erupt　(7)
ぶんか（文化） culture　(7)
ぶんこぼん（文庫本） paperback, pocket book　(6)
ぶんしょ（文書） document, paper　(5)
ぶんや（分野） field of endeavor　(5)

へ／ヘ

ヘアードレッサー hairdresser　(5)
へい（塀） wall, fence　(2)
へいあんじだい（平安時代） *Heian* period (796-1185)　(7)
へいきん（平均） average　(7)
へいや（平野） plains　(7)
ページ page　(6)
べっそう（別荘） vacation home　(2)
ベッド bed　(2)
ペット pet　(7)
ヘッドライト headlight　(3)
へび（蛇） snake　(7)
へや（部屋） room; counter for rooms　(2)
へらす（減らす） *C1, tr.* to decrease　(4)
ベランダ verandah　(2)
ペリカン pelican　(7)
ベル doorbell　(2)
へる（減る） *C1, intr.* to decrease　(4)
へんか（する）（変化［する］） *n.v.* change; to change　(4)
べんきょうべや（勉強部屋） child's study room　(2)
べんごし（弁護士） lawyer；　べんごしじむしょ（弁護士事務所） law office　(5)
へんじ（返事） reply；　へんじをかく（返事を書く） to write a reply　(6)
へんしゅうちょう（編集長） editor in chief　(6)
へんちょう（する）（偏重［する］） *n.v.* overvaluation; overvalue　(7)
べんぴ（する）（便秘［する］） *n.v.* constipation; to be constipated　(4)

ほ／ホ

ほいくえん（保育園） day nursery　(5)
～ほうがいい it's better to...　(2)
ほうげん（方言） dialect　(1)
ほうそう（する）（放送［する］） *n.v.* broadcast; to broadcast　(5)
ほうそうきょく（放送局） broadcasting station　(6)

ほうっておく （放っておく） *C1, tr.* to leave as is （4）

ほうどう(する) （報道［する］） *n.v.* report, news; to report, inform （6）

ぼうりょく （暴力） violence （7）

ほお （頬） cheek; ほっぺた cheek （4）

ボーナス bonus （5）

ホーム platform （1）

ほかの （他の） other （6）

ポケベル beeper, pager （6）

ほけん （保険） insurance （1）; ほけんじょ （保健所） public health insurance office （4）

ほご(する) （保護［する］） *n.v.* protection; to protect （7）

ほこうしゃ （歩行者） pedestrian （3）

ほし （星） star （7）

ぼしゅう(する) （募集［する］） enrollment; to enroll （5）

ほす （干す） *C1, tr.* to air-dry (something), to air (something) out （4）

ほっきょく （北極） North Pole （7）

ホッチキス stapler （5）

〜ほど approximately… （2）

ほどう （歩道） sidewalk （3）

ほにゅうどうぶつ （哺乳動物） mammal （7）

ほね （骨） bone （4）

ほぼ （保母） nursery caretaker （5）

ほめる *C2, tr.* to praise （7）

ほん （本） book （6）

ぼんさい （盆栽） bonsai (*artificially dwarfed trees*) （7）

ほんしゃ （本社） company headquarters （5）

ほんだな （本棚） bookshelf （2）

ぼんち （盆地） basin, valley surrounded by mountains （7）

ほんてん （本店） main store; bank headquarters （5）

ボンネット hood （3）

ほんや （本屋） bookstore （6）

ほんやく(する) （翻訳［する］） *n.v.* translation; to translate （6）; ほんやくしゃ （翻訳者） translator （5）

ま／マ

〜ま （〜間） counter for rooms （2）

マイク microphone （6）

マイクロバス minibus （3）

まいる （参る） *C1, intr.* to go (*humble*) （5）

まえ(に) （前［に］） before （1）

まがる （曲がる） *C1, intr.* to turn (in a direction) （1）

まぐろ tuna （7）

まげる （曲げる） *C2, tr.* to bend (something) （4）

まごつく *C1, intr.* to be bewildered （4）

マスコミ mass communication （6）

ますます *adv.* increasingly （7）

まちあいしつ （待ち合い室） waiting room （1）

まちがう （間違う） *C1, tr.* to be in error; まちがえる （間違える） *C1, tr.* to make a mistake (about something) （3）; まちがいでんわ （間違い電話） wrong (phone) number （6）

まつ （松） pine tree （7）

まつげ （睫） eyelashes （4）

まっすぐ *adv.* straight （1）

まで *part., conj.* until （1）

までに by (the time) （1）

まとめる *C2, tr.* to summarize, compile （6）

マナー manner （7）

まねく （招く） *C1, tr.* to invite （2）

まねる （真似る） *C2, tr.* to imitate （4）

マフラー muffler （3）

まま while 〜ing, without change （6）

まもる （守る） *C1, tr.* to keep, maintain, observe (a custom), obey (a rule), protect （6）

まゆげ （眉毛） eyebrow （4）

まる （丸） circle; まるい （丸い） *i-adj.* round （4）

まるで *adv.* just like （4）

まわる （回る） *C1, intr.* to turn around, go around; まわりみち （回り道） detour; まわす （回す） *C1, tr.* to turn (something), to send around （3）

まんが （漫画） comic book, comic magazine, cartoon （6）

まんかい （満開） full bloom （7）

マンション apartment building, condominium （2）

まんなか （真ん中） middle （1）

み／ミ

み （実） berry, fruit; みがなる （実がなる） to bear fruit （7）

みあげる （見上げる） *C2, tr.* to look upward （4）

みがく （磨く） *C1, tr.* to polish, wipe clean （2）

みき （幹） trunk （7）

みぎ （右） right (*direction*) （4）; みぎがわ （右側） right side （1）; みぎきき （右利き） right-handed; みぎて （右手） right hand （4）

ミキサー blender （2）

みさき （岬） cape, promontory （7）

ミシン sewing machine （2）

みずをまく （水をまく） to sprinkle water （2）

みずうみ （湖） lake （7）

みずから （自ら） *adv.* by oneself （7）

みせいねん （未成年） minor, underage person （5）

みせる （見せる） *C2, tr.* to show （2）

みぞ （溝） (tire) tread （3）

みたい(な) *na-adj.* like… （4）

みだし （見出し） headline （6）

みちにまよう （道に迷う） to lose one's way （3）

みつ （蜜） honey, nectar （7）

みつける （見つける） *C2, tr.* to find; みつかる （見つかる） *C1, intr.* to be found （3）

みっともない *i-adj.* unseemly, improper, disreputable （7）

みつばち （蜜蜂） bee （7）

みつりん （密林） jungle （7）

みなと （港） harbor, port （1）

みならい （見習い） apprentice （5）

みまい(にいく) （見舞い［に行く］） (to pay) a visit to a sick person （4）

みみ （耳） ear; みみたぶ （耳たぶ） earlobe （4）

みんしゅく （民宿） Japanese-style bed and breakfast （1）

みんぞく （民族） ethnic group （7）

みんぽう （民放） commercial broadcasting （6）

みんよう （民謡） folk song （6）

む／ム

むかえる（迎える）*C2, tr.*　to invite, receive　*(6)*
むかし（昔）olden days　*(7)*
むく（向く）*C1, intr.*　to be fit for, be suitable, face toward something　*(5)*
むくち（な）（無口［な］）*na-adj.*　taciturn　*(6)*
むし（虫）insect　*(7)*
むし（する）（無視［する］）*n.v.*　negligence; to ignore, to neglect　*(2)*
むね（胸）chest　*(4)*
むろまちじだい（室町時代）*Muromachi* period (1336–1568)　*(7)*

め／メ

め（芽）sprout, shoot, seedling　*(7)*
〜め（〜目）~th (*cardinal numbers*)　*(1)*
め（目）eye　*(4)*
めいしょ（名所）sights, famous places　*(1)*
めいよ（名誉）prestige, honor　*(5)*
メカニック　mechanic　*(5)*
めぐまれる（恵まれる）*C1, intr.*　to be blessed with　*(5)*
めざましどけい（目覚し時計）alarm clock　*(2)*
めしあがる（召し上がる）*C1, tr.*　to eat (*honorific*)　*(5)*
メロドラマ　soap opera　*(6)*
めんする（面する）*C3, intr.*　to face toward　*(7)*
めんせき（面積）area, land area　*(7)*
めんせつ（する）（面接［する］）*n.v.*　job interview; to interview (for a job)　*(5)*
メンテナンス　maintenance　*(3)*

も／モ

もうしあげる（申し上げる）*C2, tr.*　to say (*humble*)　もうす（申す）*C1, tr.*　to say (*humble*)　*(5)*
もくじ（目次）table of contents　*(6)*
もくてき（目的）objective, goal　*(3)*
もじ（文字）written symbol　*(7)*
もたらす　*C1, tr.*　to bring about　*(7)*
もちろん　*adv.*　of course　*(2)*
もったいない　*i-adj.*　wasteful　*(7)*
もっていく（持っていく）*C1, tr.*　to take (things); もってくる（持ってくる）*C3, tr.*　to bring (things)　*(1)*
モデルルーム　model room　*(2)*
もどす　*C1, tr.*　to vomit　*(4)*
もどる（戻る）*C1, intr.*　to return, come back　*(3)*; もどす（戻す）*C1, tr.*　to return something to its previous place　*(4)*
もの　things　*(5)*
ものおき（物置）storeroom　*(2)*
ものぐさ（な）*na-adj.*　lazy　*(7)*
モノレール　monorail　*(3)*
モペット　moped　*(3)*
もも（腿）thigh　*(4)*
もよう（模様）situation, appearance　*(6)*
もらう　*C1, tr.*　to receive (*from an equal or inferior*)　*(2)*

もり（森）forest　*(7)*
もんく（文句）complaint　*(7)*

や／ヤ

やぎ（山羊）goat　*(7)*
やく（役）role　*(5)*
やくしょ（役所）government office　*(5)*
やくにたつ（役に立つ）to be useful　*(6)*
やすむ（休む）*C1, intr.*　to rest, to be absent　*(4)*
やちん（家賃）rent (*money*)　*(2)*
やっきょく（薬局）pharmacy　*(4)*
やど（宿）lodgings　*(1)*
やとう（雇う）*C1, tr.*　to hire　*(1)*
やぬし（家主）property or apartment owner (*formal*)　*(2)*
やね（屋根）roof　*(2)*
やめる　*C1, tr.*　to quit, stop　*(1)*
やよいじだい（弥生時代）*Yayoi* period (3rd century B.C. to A.D. 3rd century)　*(7)*
やる　*C1, tr.*　to give (*to a social inferior*)　*(2)*

ゆ／ユ

ゆうかん（夕刊）evening paper　*(6)*
ユース・ホステル　youth hostel　*(1)*
ユーターン（U-ターン）U-turn; ユーターンきんし（U-ターン禁止）no U-turn　*(3)*
ゆうびん（郵便）mail　*(6)*; ゆうびんうけ（郵便受け）mailbox or slot (*for receiving mail*)　*(2)*; ゆうびんかわせ（郵便為替）postal money order; ゆうびんきょく（郵便局）post office; ゆうびんきょくいん（郵便局員）post office clerk; ゆうびんちょきん（郵便貯金）postal savings; ゆうびんはいたつ（郵便配達）mail delivery, mail carrier　*(6)*; ゆうびんはいたつにん（郵便配達人）mail carrier　*(5)*; ゆうびんばんごう（郵便番号）ZIP code; ゆうびんポスト（郵便ポスト）mailbox (*for public use*); ゆうびんりょうきん（郵便料金）postage; ゆうびんをだす（郵便を出す）to mail　*(6)*
ゆか（床）floor　*(2)*
ゆけつ（する）（輸血［する］）*n.v.*　blood transfusion; to give a blood transfusion　*(4)*
ゆしゅつ（する）（輸出［する］）*n.v.*　export; to export　*(5)*
ユダヤきょう（ユダヤ教）Judaism　*(7)*
ゆっくり　*adv.*　leisurely　*(1)*
ゆび（指）finger　*(4)*
ゆめ（夢）dream　*(5)*
ゆり（百合）lily　*(7)*

よ／ヨ

よう　appearance, seems　*(7)*; よう（な）*na-adj.*　like, appearance　*(4)*
ようい（する）（用意［する］）*n.v.*　preparation; to prepare　*(1)*
ようじ（幼児）infant　*(5)*
ようしつ（洋室）Western-style room; ようま（洋間）Western-style room　*(2)*

ようちえん （幼稚園） kindergarten （5）
〜ようにする to make an effort to...; 〜ようになる
to start 〜ing （5）
ようぼう（する） （要望［する］） *n.v.* request; to request
（6）
ようやく（する） （要約［する］） *n.v.* summary;
to summarize （6）
よく *adv.* often, well （1）
よくしつ （浴室） room with bathtub/shower （2）
よごれる （汚れる） *C2, intr.* to get dirty （7）
よてい （予定） plan, schedule （1）
よぶ （呼ぶ） *C1, tr.* to summon （1）
よぶん（な） （余分［な］） *na-adj.* excessive, extra
（4）
よやく（する） （予約［する］） *n.v.* reservation; to make
a reservation （1）
よろこぶ （喜ぶ） *C1, tr.* to be delighted （4）

ら／ラ

ライオン lion （7）
らくてんてき（な） （楽天的［な］） *na-adj.*
optimistic （5）
〜らしい *i-adj.* it seems that..., the word is （4）
ラジエーター radiator （3）
ラジオ radio （2）
ラン orchid （7）

り／リ

りかい（する） （理解［する］） *n.v.* understanding; to
understand （5）
リクラニング・シート reclining seat （3）
りこん（する） （離婚［する］） *n.v.* divorce; to get
divorced （5）
リサイクル（する） *n.v.* recycling; to recycle （7）
リゾート resort （1）
リビング・ルーム living room （2）
りゆう （理由） reason （6）
りゅうがく（する） （留学［する］） *n.v.* study abroad; to
study abroad （5）
りよう（する） （利用［する］） *n.v.* use; make use
of （2）
りょう （量） amount （3）
りょう〜 （両〜） both... （4）; りょうて （両手）
both hands （4）
りょうきん （料金） fee, charge （1）
りょうし （漁師） fisherman （5）
りようし （理容師） barber （5）
りょうし （猟師） hunter （5）
りょうり（する） （料理［する］） *n.v.* cook; to cook （2）;
りょうりのほん （料理の本） cookbook;
りょうりばんぐみ （料理番組） cooking show （6）
りょかん （旅館） Japanese-style inn （1）

りょこう（する） （旅行［する］） *n.v.* travel; to travel
（1）
りょこうしゃ （旅行者） traveler （1）
りょひ （旅費） travel expense(s) （1）
りりく（する） （離陸［する］） take-off; to take off （1）
りれきしょ （履歴書） résumé （5）

る／ル

ルームサービス room service （1）
るすばんでんわ （留守番電話） answering machine （2）

れ／レ

れきし （歴史） history （7）
レジ cash register （5）
レポーター reporter （5）
れんあい （恋愛） love （5）
れんぞくドラマ （連続ドラマ） drama sequel （6）
レンタカー rental car （1）
レントゲンをとる （レントゲンを撮る） to take X-rays
（4）
れんらく（する） （連絡［する］） *n.v.* contact; to
contact （2）

ろ／ロ

ろうか （廊下） hallway （2）
ろうじん （老人） old person, old people （5）
ろうねん （老年） aged （5）
ろくおん（する） （録音［する］） *n.v.* recording; to
record sound （6）
ろくが（する） （録画［する］） *n.v.* videotaping; to
videotape （6）
ロッカー locker （5）
ロバ donkey （7）

わ／ワ

ワードプロセッサー word processor （5）
ワイパー (windshield) wiper （3）
わか （和歌） waka poetry （7）
わかれる （別れる） *C2, intr.* to separate （5）
わくせい （惑星） planet （7）
〜わけだ that's why..., so it's that... （7）
わし （鷲） eagle （7）
わしつ （和室） Japanese-style room （2）
わたす （渡す） *C1, tr.* to hand over （4）
わたる （渡る） *C1, intr.* to cross （1）
わらう （笑う） *C1, tr.* to laugh, smile （4）
わる （割る） *C1, tr.* to break (something) into pieces;
われる （割れる） *C2, intr.* to break, become broken,
shatter （3）
わるい （悪い） *i-adj.* bad, at fault （7）
わん （湾） bay （7）
ワンマンバス bus without a conductor （3）

Glossary

English-Japanese Glossary

Abbreviations used in this glossary are explained at the beginning of the Japanese-English Glossary.

A

abacus　（そろばん）（5）
abnormal weather　（異常気象）いじょうきしょう（7）
absent (be absent)　（休む）やすむ　C1, intr.　（4）
absolutely　（絶対に）ぜったいに　adv.　（4）
abundant　さかん（な）na-adj.　（7）
abuse; to abuse　（虐待［する］）ぎゃくたい（する）
　n.v.　（7）
accelerator　アクセル（3）
accident　（事故）じこ；to cause an accident
　（事故を起こす）じこをおこす；to get involved in an
　accident（事故にあう）じこにあう（3）
accountant　（会計士）かいけいし（5）
acquaintance　（知人）ちじん（6）
acting; performance　（演劇）えんげき（7）
activity; to be active　（活躍［する］）かつやく（する）
　n.v.　（5）
actor, actress　（俳優）はいゆう（5）
actually　（実は）じつは（4）
address　（住所）じゅうしょ（2）
addressee　（あて名）あてな（6）
adhesive tape　セロテープ（5）
admiration; admire　（感銘［する］）かんめい（する）
　n.v.　（5）
advancement; advance, evolve　（発達［する］）
　はったつ（する）n.v.　（7）
advertisement; advertise　（広告［する］）こうこく（する）
　n.v.;　advertisement section (of a newspaper)
　（広告欄）こうこくらん；place an advertisement
　（広告を出す）こうこくをだす（6）
advice; advise　（忠告［する］）ちゅうこく（する）
　n.v.　（1）
aerogram　（航空書簡）こうくうしょかん（6）
afraid　（怖い）こわい　i-adj.　（4）
after (doing)…　〜てから（1）
after meals　（食後）しょくご（4）
age　（年齢）ねんれい（5）
age (to get old)　（齢をとる）としをとる（5）
aged　（老年）ろうねん（5）
agreement; agree　（賛成［する］）さんせい（する）
　n.v.　（7）
air　（空気）くうき（5）
air conditioner　エアコン（2）
airmail　（航空便）こうくうびん（6）
air out, air-dry　（干す）ほす　C1, tr.　（2）

airplane　（飛行機）ひこうき（1）
air pollution　（大気汚染）たいきおせん（7）
airport　（空港）くうこう（1）
alarm clock　（目覚し時計）めざましどけい（2）
alcove　（床の間）とこのま（2）
all right, no problem　（大丈夫［な］）だいじょうぶ（な）
　na-adj.　（2）
although　のに　conj.　（7）
AM (radio)　エイエム（6）
ambulance　（救急車）きゅうきゅうしゃ（3）
amount　（量）りょう（3）
ancestor　（祖先）そせん（5）
angry (get angry)　（怒る）おこる　C1, tr.　（4）
animal　（動物）どうぶつ；domestic animal（家畜）
　かちく；animal food（餌）えさ（7）
animation　アニメ（6）
ankle　（足首）あしくび（4）
announcement; announce　（発表［する］）
　はっぴょう（する）n.v.　（6）
announcer　アナウンサー（5）
annoying call　（いやがらせ電話）いやがらせでんわ（6）
annual event　（年中行事）ねんじゅうぎょうじ（7）
answering machine　（留守番電話）るすばんでんわ（2）
ant　（蟻）あり（7）
antenna　アンテナ（3）
apartment complex　アパート（2）
apartment building (condominium)　マンション（2）
apartment owner　（家主）やぬし（formal）;
　（大家さん）おおやさん（inf.）（2）
apologize　（謝る）あやまる　C1, tr.　（7）
apology　（お詫び）おわび（6）
appear　（出る）でる　C2, intr.　（3）
appearance; appear (on TV, stage, etc.)　（出演［する］）
　しゅつえん（する）n.v.　（6）
appearance　（模様）もよう（6）
appetite　（食欲）しょくよく（4）
application; apply　（応募［する］）おうぼ（する）n.v.;
　application form（応募用紙）おうぼようし（5）
apprentice　（見習い）みならい（5）
approach, draw close　（近づく）ちかづく　C1, intr.　（3）
approximately, extent　ほど（2）
aptitude　（適性）てきせい（5）
architect　（建築家）けんちくか（2）
architectural design; to design buildings　（設計［する］）
　せっけい（する）n.v.　（2）
area, land area　（面積）めんせき（7）

area code　（市外局番）しがいきょくばん　(6)
arm　（腕）うで　(4)
arrive　（着く）つく　*C1, intr.*　*(1)*
artificial culturing　（人工養殖）じんこうようしょく　(7)
artist　（芸術家）げいじゅつか　(5)
as...　として　(5)
asbestos　アスベスト　(7)
ashtray　（灰皿）はいざら　(2)
ask, inquire　たずねる　*C2, tr.*　*(1)*
aspirin　アスピリン　(4)
assertion; assert　（主張［する］）しゅちょう（する）
　　n.v.　(7)
assist, help　（手伝う）てつだう　*C1, tr.*　(2)
assistance, cooperation; assist, cooperate　（協力［する］）
　　きょうりょく（する）*n.v.*　(4)
astronaut　（宇宙飛行士）うちゅうひこうし　(5)
astronomy　（天文学）てんもんがく　(7)
athlete　（スポーツ選手）スポーツせんしゅ　(5)
Atlantic Ocean　（大西洋）たいせいよう　(7)
atmosphere　（気持ち）きもち　(4)
attach　（着ける／付ける）つける　*C2, tr.*　(3);
　　be attached　（付く）つく　*C1, intr.*　(2)
attendance; attend　（出席［する］）しゅっせき（する）
　　n.v.　(5)
attention; pay attention　（注意［する］）ちゅうい
　　（する）*n.v.*;　attentiveness　（注意力）ちゅういりょく
　　(3);　give a lot of attention to　（気にする）きにする
　　(7)
attitude　（態度）たいど　(7)
auditorium　（講堂）こうどう　(7)
author　（作家）さっか　(5);　（著者）ちょしゃ　(7)
authority, power　（権力）けんりょく　(5)
automobile　（自動車）じどうしゃ　(3)
autumn leaves　（紅葉）こうよう　(7)
average　（平均）へいきん　(7)
away (be separated)　（離れる）はなれる　*C2, tr.*　(3)
awkward　ぎこちない　*i-adj.*　(6)

B

baby　（赤ちゃん）あかちゃん;　（赤ん坊）あかんぼう
　　(5)
back (*body part*)　（背中）せなか　(4)
back or side door　（勝手口）かってぐち　(2)
bad　（悪い）わるい　*i-adj.*　(7)
bait　（餌）えさ　(7)
balcony　バルコニー　(2)
bamboo　（竹）たけ　(7)
bank　（銀行）ぎんこう;　bank employee　（銀行員）
　　ぎんこういん　(5)
bar exam　（司法試験）しほうしけん　(5)
bartender　バーテンダー　(5)
barber　（理容師）りようし　(5)
base　（つけ根）つけね　(6)
basic　（基本的［な］）きほんてき（な）*na-adj.*　(6)
basin　（盆地）ぼんち　(7)
bath　（お風呂）おふろ　*(1)*
bathroom (with a bathtub/shower)　（浴室）よくしつ
　　(2)
battery　バッテリー　(3)
bay　（湾）わん　(7)

be　いらっしゃる　(*honorific*)　*C1, intr.*;　be　おる
　　(*humble*)　*C1, intr.*　(5)
beach　（海岸）かいがん　(7)
bear　（熊）くま　(7)
bear fruit　（実がなる）みがなる　(7)
beard　（髭）ひげ　(4)
beautiful　（美しい）うつくしい　*i-adj.*　(2)
bed　ベッド;　bedroom　（寝室）しんしつ　(2);　go to
　　bed　（寝る）ねる　*C1, tr.*　(3)
bee　（蜜蜂）みつばち　(7)
beeper　ポケベル　(6)
before　（前［に］）まえ（に）　*(1)*
before meals　（食前）しょくぜん　(4)
begin　（始まる）はじまる　*C1, intr.*;　（始める）
　　はじめる　*C2, tr.*　(3)
believe　（信じる）しんじる　*C2, tr.*　(7)
belly　おなか　(4)
bend　（曲げる）まげる　*C2, tr.*　(4)
berry　（実）み　(7)
best　（最高）さいこう　(2)
better (it's better to...)　～ほうがいい　(2)
better (to get better)　（直る）なおる　*C1, intr.*　(3)
bewilder (to be bewildered)　まごつく　*C1, intr.*　(4)
bicycle　（自転車）じてんしゃ　(3)
bird　（鳥）とり　(7)
birth; give birth　（出産［する］）しゅっさん（する）
　　n.v.　(5);　give birth　（産む）うむ　*C1, tr.*　(5)
birth date　（生年月日）せいねんがっぴ　(5)
birthday　（誕生日）たんじょうび　*(1)*
bite　（かむ）*C1, tr.*　(5);　bite, chew　（かじる）
　　C1, tr.　(4)
blender (*electric*)　ミキサー　(2)
bless (to be blessed with)　（恵まれる）めぐまれる
　　C1, intr.　(7)
blind　ブラインド　(2)
blood (in the blood)　（血中）けっちゅう;　blood
　　transfusion; carry out blood transfusion　（輸血［する］）
　　ゆけつ（する）*n.v.*;　blood type　（血液型）けつえ
　　きがた　(4)
bloom　（咲く）さく　*C1, intr.*　(7)
board (*a vehicle*)　（乗る）のる　*C1, intr.*　*(1)*
body　（体）からだ;　body temperature　（体温）
　　たいおん　(4)
boldly　ズバリ　*adv.*　(6)
bone　（骨）ほね　(4)
bonito　かつお　(7)
bonus　ボーナス　(5)
book　（本）ほん;　bookstore　（本屋）ほんや　(6);
　　bookshelf　（本棚）ほんだな　(2)
book (*not magazine*)　（単行本）たんこうぼん　(6)
bored (get bored)　（飽きる）あきる　*C2, intr.*　(6)
born (be born)　（生まれる）うまれる　*C2, intr.*　(5)
borrow　（借りる）かりる　*C2, tr.*　(2);　（拝借する）
　　はいしゃくする　(*humble*)　(5)
both　（両）りょう　(4);　both hands　（両手）
　　りょうて　(3)
bouquet　ブーケ　(7)
bow (from waist)　（お辞儀をする）おじぎをする
　　(7)
box lunch (*sold at stations*)　（駅弁）えきべん　*(1)*
boy　（男の子）おとこのこ;　（少年）しょうねん　(5)

Glossary

433

四百三十三

boyfriend, girlfriend （恋人）こいびと (5)

brake　ブレーキ;　to put on the brakes
　ブレーキをかける;　hand brake　ハンドブレーキ;
　parking brake　サイドブレーキ (3)

branch (*of tree*) （枝）えだ (7)

branch store or office （支店）してん (5)

break, smash　こわす　*C1, tr.*;　be broken　こわれる
　C2, intr. (3)

break, crack （割れる）われる　*C2, intr.*;　divide into
　pieces （割る）わる　*C1, tr.* (3)

break, change for smaller money　くずす　*C1, tr.* (6)

bridge （橋）はし (1)

brief （簡潔[な]）かんけつ(な)　*na-adj.* (6)

bring (*things*) （持ってくる）もってくる　*C3, tr.*;　bring
　(*people*) （連れてくる）つれてくる　*C3, tr.* (1)

bring about　もたらす　*C1, tr.* (7)

broadcast; to broadcast （放送[する]）ほうそう(する)
　n.v. (5);　broadcasting station （放送局）
　ほうそうきょく;　live broadcast （生放送）
　なまほうそう　*n.v.* (6)

buckle up （着ける）つける　*C2, tr.* (3)

Buddhism （仏教）ぶっきょう (7);　Buddhist monk
　（僧侶）そうりょ (5)

build （建てる）たてる　*C2, tr.* (2);　built (be built)
　（立[建]つ）たつ　*C1, intr.* (3)

bulb (*of plant*) （球根）きゅうこん (7)

bulldozer　ブルドーザー (3)

bullet train （新幹線）しんかんせん (1)

bumper　バンパー (3)

bus guide　バス・ガイド (3)

business （事業）じぎょう (5)

business trip; go on a business trip （出張[する]）
　しゅっちょう(する)　*n.v.* (1)

businessman　ビジネスマン (5)

butterfly （蝶）ちょう (7)

buttocks （お尻）おしり (4)

by (the time)　までに (1)

by all means　どうしても (1);　（是非）ぜひ　*adv.* (5)

bypass (road)　バイパス (3)

C

cage （檻）おり (7)

call back （かけ直す）かけなおす　*C1, tr.* (6)

camera　カメラ (6)

canal （運河）うんが (7)

canary　カナリア (7)

cancellation; to cancel　キャンセル(する)　*n.v.* (1)

cape, promontory （岬）みさき (7)

car （車）くるま;　car air conditioner　カー・エアコン
　(3);　car racer　カーレーサー (5);　car radio
　カー・ラジオ;　car stereo　カー・ステレオ (3)

care; care for （世話[する]）せわ(する)　*n.v.* (2)

career woman　キャリアウーマン (5)

carnation　カーネーション (7)

carpenter （大工）だいく (2)

carpet　カーペット (2)

carport （車庫）しゃこ (2)

carry (*large object*) （運ぶ）はこぶ　*C1, tr.* (2)

carry (*on one's back*) （背負う）せおう　*C1, tr.* (5)

carry out （行なう）おこなう　*C1, tr.* (7)

cartoon （漫画）まんが (6)

cash register　レジ (5)

cash sent by registered mail （現金書留）
　げんきんかきとめ (6)

cashier　キャッシャー (1)

cat （猫）ねこ (7)

catch　つかむ　*C1, tr.* (4);　to be caught （捕まる）
　つかまる　*C1, intr.* (3)

cattle （牛）うし (7)

cause （原因）げんいん (4)

caution; be cautious （注意[する]）ちゅうい(する)
　n.v. (4)

CD player　シーディープレーヤー (2)

ceiling （天井）てんじょう (2)

celebrate （祝う）いわう　*C1, tr.* (6);　celebration
　（お祝い）おいわい (2)

cellular car phone　カーホン (6)

center （中心）ちゅうしん (1)

center line　センターライン (3)

century （世紀）せいき (7)

chair （椅子）いす (2)

chairman （会長）かいちょう (5)

change money （くずす）*C1, tr.* (6)

change, become different （変わる）かわる
　C1, intr. (3)

change; to change （変化[する]）へんか(する)
　n.v. (7)

change a tire　タイヤをかえる (3)

change channels (*on TV*) （チャンネルを変える）
　チャンネルをかえる (6)

change jobs （転職する）てんしょくする (5)

channel　チャンネル (6)

channel (*ocean*) （海峡）かいきょう (7)

charge (*amount of money*) （料金）りょうきん (1)

charter (*flight, bus, etc.*)　チャーター (1)

chase （追いかける）おいかける　*C2, tr.* (5)

check; to spot-check （点検[する]）てんけん(する) (3)

check-in; check into hotel　チェックイン(する)
　n.v. (3)

check-out; check out of hotel　チェックアウト(する)
　n.v. (1)

check up on　チェックする (3)

cheek　ほっぺた;　（頬）ほお (4)

cherry tree （桜）さくら (7)

chest, breast （胸）むね (4)

chest of drawers　たんす (2)

chicken　ニワトリ;　baby chick （雛）ひよこ (7)

chief （主[な]）おも(な)　*na-adj.* (3)

child （子供）こども (5);　child's room （子供部屋）
　こどもべや;　child's study room （勉強部屋）
　べんきょうべや (2)

chimney （煙突）えんとつ (2)

chimpanzee　チンパンジー (7)

Christianity （キリスト教）キリストきょう (7)

chrysanthemum （菊）きく (7)

cicada （蝉）せみ (7)

circle （丸）まる (4)

circumstances （環境）かんきょう (5)

civil servant （公務員）こうむいん (5)

claim; to claim　（主張［する］）しゅちょう（する）
　n.v.　(7)

clam　アサリ　(7)

classified ad　（案内広告）あんないこうこく　(6)

cleaning; to clean　（掃除［する］）そうじ（する）
　n.v.

clean off　（片付ける）かたづける　*C2, tr.*　(2)

clearly　はっきり（と）　*adv.*　(6)

cliff　（崖）がけ　(7)

clock　（時計）とけい　(2)

close　（閉じる）とじる　*C2, tr.*　(4)；（閉まる）しまる
　C1, intr.　(1)；（閉める）しめる　*C2, tr.*　(3)

closet　クロゼット　(2)

clothes　（服装）ふくそう　(3)

clutch　クラッチ　(3)

coach, regular car　（普通車）ふつうしゃ　(1)

cockroach　ゴキブリ　(7)

coffeemaker　コーヒーメーカー　(2)

cold (to catch a cold)　（風邪をひく）かぜをひく；cold
　medicine　（風邪薬）かぜぐすり　(4)

colleague　（同僚）どうりょう　(5)

collect　（集める）あつめる　*C2, tr.*　(3)

collect call　コレクトコール　(6)

college professor　（教授）きょうじゅ　(5)

collision; collide　（衝突［する］）しょうとつ（する）
　n.v.

color TV　カラーテレビ　(6)

come　いらっしゃる　(*honorific*)；おいでになる
　(*honorific*)

come down　（下がる）さがる　*C1, intr.*　(3)

come in　（入る）はいる　*C1, intr.*　(3)

come near　（近づく）ちかづく　*C1, intr.*　(4)

come out　（出る）でる　*C2, intr.*　(3)

come to an end　（終わる）おわる　*C1, tr.*　(3)

comic book, magazine　（漫画）まんが　(6)

commemorative stamp　（記念切手）きねんきって　(6)

commercial message (CM)　コマーシャル，
　シーエム　(6)

commercial broadcasting　（民放）みんぽう　(6)

common factor, to have something in common
　（共通［する］）きょうつう（する）*n.v.*　(7)

commuting; commute　（通勤［する］）つうきん（する）
　n.v.　(6)

company　（会社）かいしゃ；（企業）きぎょう；
　company branch office　（支社）ししゃ；company
　employee　（会社員）かいしゃいん，（社員）しゃいん；
　company headquarters　（本社）ほんしゃ　(5)；
　company owner　（会社経営者）かいしゃけいえいしゃ
　(6)

comparison; compare　（比較［する］）ひかく（する）
　n.v.　(7)

compile　まとめる　*C2, tr.*　(6)

complaint　（文句）もんく　(7)

completed works　（全集）ぜんしゅう　(6)

computer　コンピュータ　(2)

concentration　（集中力）しゅうちゅうりょく　(4)

concerned (be concerned)　（気になる）きになる　(3)

condition　（条件）じょうけん　(5)

condolence　（お見舞い）おみまい　(6)

condominium　コンドミニアム，マンション　(2)

conductor　（車掌）しゃしょう　(1)

conference　（会議）かいぎ　(1)

congratulatory telegram　（祝電）しゅくでん　(6)

consistent, fixed　（一定）いってい　(7)

constipation　（便秘）べんぴ　(4)

construction; construct　（建設［する］）けんせつ（する）
　n.v.　(7)

consultation; consult　（相談［する］）そうだん（する）
　n.v.　(3)；consulting room　（相談室）そうだんしつ
　(6)

contact; to contact　（連絡［する］）れんらく（する）
　n.v.　(2)

content　（内容）ないよう　(6)

continent　（大陸）たいりく　(7)

continue　（続ける）つづける　*C2, tr.*　(3)

convey information　（伝える）つたえる　*C2, tr.*　(6)

cook　コック；（調理師）ちょうりし　(5)

cooking; to cook　（料理［する］）りょうり（する）
　n.v.　(2)；cookbook　（料理の本）りょうりのほん；
　cooking show　（料理番組）りょうりばんぐみ　(6)

cooler (air conditioner)　クーラー　(2)

cooperation; cooperate　（協力［する］）きょうりょく
　（する）*n.v.*　(4)

coral reef　（珊瑚礁）さんごしょう　(7)

corner　（角）かど　(2)

correctly　（正しく）ただしく　*adv.*　(6)

cosmetic surgery　（整形手術）せいけいしゅじゅつ
　(4)

cosmetics　（化粧品）けしょうひん　(6)

couch　ソファー　(2)

cough (to cough)　（咳をする）せきをする；to have a
　cough　（咳が出る）せきがでる　(4)

counter for books　（〜冊）さつ　(6)

counter for newspapers　（部）ぶ　(6)

counter for rooms　（〜間）ま；（部屋）へや　(2)

country　（国）くに　(7)；all over the country　（全国）
　ぜんこく　(1)

coupe　クーペ　(3)

coupon ticket　（回数券）かいすうけん　(3)

cover (*in a newspaper*)　（載る）のる　*C1, intr.*　(6)

cow　（牛）うし　(7)

cram school　（塾）じゅく　(4)

crank phone call　（いやがらせ電話）いやがらせでんわ
　(6)

crawl, creep　（這う）はう　*C1, intr.*　(4)

crime　（犯罪）はんざい　(7)

critic　（評論家）ひょうろんか　(6)

cross　（渡る）わたる　*C1, intr.*　(1)

crow　カラス　(7)

crowd (to be crowded)　こむ　*C1, intr.*　(2)

cruel treatment; to treat cruelly　（虐待［する］）
　ぎゃくたい（する）*n.v.*　(7)

cry　（泣く）なく　*C1, intr.*　(4)

culture　（文化）ぶんか　(7)

curtain　カーテン　(2)

curve　カーブ　(3)

custom　（慣習）かんしゅう　(7)

customary diet　（食生活）しょくせいかつ　(4)

cut　（切る）きる　*C1, tr.*；to be cut　（切れる）きれる
　C2, intr.　(3)

D

dahlia ダリヤ (7)
daily （日頃）ひごろ (4)
daily life （日常生活）にちじょうせいかつ (2)
daily paper （日刊紙）にっかんし (6)
daily schedule （日課）にっか (5)
damage (sustain damage) （被害にあう）ひがいにあう (7)
dance （踊る）おどる C1, tr. (1)
dangerous （危ない）あぶない i-adj. (1)
dangle （下がる）さがる C1, intr. (3)
dashboard ダッシュボード (3)
day nursery （保育園）ほいくえん (5)
deal with （扱う）あつかう C1, tr. (5)
death （死）し (5)
decide （決める）きめる C2, tr. (6)
decisive （断固）だんこ (7); decisively ズバリ adv. (6)
decline, get dull （にぶる）にぶる C1, intr. (3)
decrease （減らす）へらす C1, tr.; （減る）へる C1, intr. (4)
deejay (disc jockey) ディージェー (6)
deep （深い）ふかい i-adj. (7)
deer （鹿）しか (7)
delay (be delayed) （遅れる）おくれる C2, intr. (1)
delight (be delighted) （喜ぶ）よろこぶ C1, tr.; delighted （嬉しい）うれしい i-adj. (4)
deliver （届ける）とどける C2, tr. (5)
delivery; deliver (a baby) （出産［する］）しゅっさん（する）n.v. (5)
delivery; deliver （配達［する］）はいたつ（する）n.v. (6)
dense （濃い）こい i-adj. (2)
dentist （歯医者）はいしゃ (5)
department head （部長）ぶちょう (5)
depth （深さ）ふかさ (3)
desert （砂漠）さばく (7)
design for building; design buildings （設計［する］）せっけい（する）n.v. (2)
designer デザイナー (5)
desire; to desire, want （希望［する］）きぼう（する）n.v. (5)
desk （机）つくえ (2)
desk lamp スタンド (2)
destroying nature （自然破壊）しぜんはかい (7)
detach （離す）はなす C1, tr. (4)
detour （回り道）まわりみち (3)
development; develop （開発［する］）かいはつ（する）n.v. (7)
development, growth; develop, grow （発達［する］）はったつ（する）n.v. (7)
development; develop, progress （発展［する］）はってん（する）n.v. (7)
dial ダイヤル (6)
dialect （方言）ほうげん (1)
diamond shape （菱形）ひしがた (4)
diarrhea (to have diarrhea) （下痢をする）げりをする (4)

diary （日記）にっき (5)
dictionary （辞書）じしょ; （辞典）じてん (6)
die （死ぬ）しぬ C1, intr.; おなくなりになる (honorific) (5)
die; wither (plants) （枯れる）かれる C2, intr. (7)
dining car （食堂車）しょくどうしゃ (1)
dining room ダイニング・ルーム (2)
diplomat （外交官）がいこうかん (5)
direct dialing （ダイヤル通話）だいやるつうわ (6)
directly （直接）ちょくせつ adv. (6)
director ディレクター (6)
directory assistance （電話番号案内）でんわばんごうあんない (6)
dirty (get dirty) （汚れる）よごれる C2, intr. (7)
disagreeable （嫌［な］）いや（な）na-adj. (3)
disappear なくなる; （消える）きえる C2, intr. (3)
disappoint (be disappointed) がっかりする (4)
disgusting （嫌）いや（な）na-adj. (3)
disreputable みっともない i-adj. (7)
divorce; get divorced （離婚［する］）りこん（する）n.v. (5)
do する; なさる (honorific); いたす (humble) (5)
do one's best （頑張る）がんばる C1, intr. (7)
doctor (medical) （医師）いし (4)
document （書類）しょるい; document, paper （文書）ぶんしょ (5)
documentary ドキュメンタリー (6)
dog （犬）いぬ (7)
doll （人形）にんぎょう (7)
donkey ロバ (7)
door ドア; （戸）と (2)
doorbell ベル (2)
door-to-door package delivery （宅配便）たくはいびん (6)
double room ダブル (1)
dove （鳩）はと (7)
drag ひきずる C1, tr. (4)
dragonfly とんぼ (7)
drama ドラマ; drama sequel （連続ドラマ）れんぞくドラマ (6)
drawer （引き出し）ひきだし (2)
dream （夢）ゆめ (5)
drier （乾燥機）かんそうき (2)
drive; drive (a car) ドライブ（する）, （運転［する］）うんてん（する）n.v.; driver （運転手）うんてんしゅ; driver's license （運転免許［証］）うんてんめんきょ（しょう）; driver's seat （運転席）うんてんせき; driving on the left （左側通行）ひだりがわつうこう; drunk driving （酒酔い運転）さけよいうんてん C2, tr. (3)
droop しおれる C2, intr. (7)
drop （落とす）おとす C1, tr. (3)
drought （旱魃）かんばつ (7)
dry （乾かす）かわかす C1, tr. (2)
duck あひる (7)
dump truck ダンプカー (3)
durable （長持ちする）ながもちする (3)
during （間）かん (1); （中）ちゅう (2)

E

each..., per...　〜ずつ　(2)
eagle　(鷲)　わし　(7)
ear　(耳)　みみ;　earlobe　(耳たぶ)　みみたぶ　(4)
early　(早く)　はやく　adv.　(1)
earth　(地球)　ちきゅう　(7)
easy　ちょっとした　(4)
eat　いただく　(humble);　(召し上がる)　めしあがる
　(honorific)　C1, tr.　(5)
eat-in kitchen　ダイニング・キッチン　(2)
economical　(経済的[な])　けいざいてき(な)
　na-adj.　(3)
economy section　(of a newspaper)　(経済欄)
　けいざいらん　(6)
editorial　(社説)　しゃせつ　(6)
editor in chief　(編集長)　へんしゅうちょう　(6)
education; educate　(教育[する])　きょういく(する)
　n.v.;　education history　(学歴)　がくれき　(5);
　educational program　(TV)　(教育番組)
　きょういくばんぐみ　(6)
effort; make an effort　(努力[する])　どりょく(する)
　n.v.　(5)
elbow　(肘)　ひじ　(4)
electric appliance　(電気製品)　でんきせいひん　(2)
electric calculator　(電卓)　でんたく　(5)
electric fan　(扇風機)　せんぷうき　(2)
elephant　(象)　ぞう　(7)
embarrassed　(恥ずかしい)　はずかしい　i-adj.　(4)
emotion　(感情)　かんじょう　(4)
employment history　(職歴)　しょくれき　(5)
empty can　(空き缶)　あきかん　(7)
encyclopedia　(事典)　じてん　(6)
end　(終える)　おえる　C2, tr.　(3)
endurance; to put up with　(我慢[する])　がまん(する)
　n.v.　(3)
engagement; get engaged　(婚約[する])　こんやく(する)
　n.v.　(5)
engine　エンジン;　start the engine　エンジンをかける;
　engine stall　エンスト　(3)
engineer　(技師)　ぎし　(5)
English-language newspaper　(英字新聞)
　えいじしんぶん　(6)
enjoyable　(楽しい)　たのしい　i-adj.　(4)
enrollment; enroll　(募集[する])　ぼしゅう(する)
　n.v.　(5)
enter　(入る)　はいる　C1, intr.　(3)
entering a school; enter school　(入学[する])
　にゅうがく(する)　n.v.　(5)
entering a company; enter a company　(入社[する])
　にゅうしゃ(する)　n.v.　(5)
enterprise, company　(企業)　きぎょう　(5)
enterprise, work　(事業)　じぎょう　(5)
entry hall, foyer　(玄関)　げんかん　(2)
envelope　(封筒)　ふうとう　(6)
environment　(環境)　かんきょう　(5);　environmental
　damage　(環境破壊)　かんきょうはかい　(7)
equator　(赤道)　せきどう　(7)
era　(時代)　じだい　(7)
err (be in error)　(間違う)　まちがう　C1, tr.　(3)

errand　おつかい　(6)
eruption; erupt　(噴火[する])　ふんか(する)　n.v.　(7)
especially　(特に)　とくに　adv.　(7)
essay　エッセー　(6)
etc.　など　(1)
ethnic group　(民族)　みんぞく　(7)
etiquette　エチケット　(7)
Europe and North America　(欧米)　おうべい　(4);
　Europeans and North Americans　(欧米人)
　おうべいじん　(7)
evening paper　(夕刊)　ゆうかん　(6)
event　(事件)　じけん　(6)
every　どの...も　(2)
examination; take an examination　受験[する]
　じゅけん(する)　n.v.　(4)
exceed　(超える)　こえる　C2, tr.　(2)
excessive　(余分[な])　よぶん(な)　na-adj.　(4)
excursion　(遠足)　えんそく　(7)
executive　(重役)　じゅうやく　(1)
experience; to experience　(経験[する])
　けいけん(する)　n.v.　(5)
explanation; explain　(説明[する])　せつめい(する)
　n.v.　(5)
export; to export　(輸出[する])　ゆしゅつ(する)
　n.v.　(5)
express　(急行)　きゅうこう　(1)
expression　(表れ)　あらわれ　(7)
express mail　(速達)　そくたつ　(6)
extend　(伸ばす)　のばす　C1, tr.　(4)
extend roots　(根を張る)　ねをはる　(7)
extension　(telephone)　(内線)　ないせん　(6)
extinguish　(消す)　けす　C1, tr.　(3)
extra　(余分[な])　よぶん(な)　na-adj.　(4)
eye　(目)　め;　eyebrow　(眉毛)　まゆげ;　eyelashes
　(睫)　まつげ　(4)

F

face　(顔)　かお　(4)
face, confront　(面する)　めんする　C3, intr.　(7)
face toward　(向く)　むく　C1, intr.　(7)
facsimile　ファクシミリ　(5);　ファックス　(6)
factory　(工場)　こうじょう;　factory worker　(工員)
　こういん　(5)
fade　しおれる　C2, intr.　(7)
failure; fail　(失敗[する])　しっぱい(する)　n.v.　(5)
fair　(公平[な])　こうへい(な)　na-adj.　(6)
fall down　(落ちる)　おちる　C2, intr.　(3)
fall (leaves)　(散る)　ちる　C1, intr.　(7)
fare　(運賃)　うんちん　(1)
farmer　(農民)　のうみん　(5)
fashion model　ファッション・モデル　(5)
father (Catholic priest)　(神父)　しんぷ　(5)
faulty　(悪い)　わるい　i-adj.　(7)
fear　おそれ　(7)
fee　(料金)　りょうきん　(1)
feel emotion　(感じる)　かんじる　C2, tr.　(4)
feeling　(感情)　かんじょう　(4)
feeling, mood　(気持ち)　きもち　(4)
fender　フェンダー　(3)

ferry　フェリーボート　(1)
fertilizer　(農薬)　のうやく　(7)
fever　(熱)　ねつ　(7)
fiancé(e)　(婚約者)　こんやくしゃ　(5)
field of endeavor　(分野)　ぶんや　(5)
field, meadow　(野原)　のはら　(7)
file　ファイル　(5)
notation; fill in (*form*)　(記入[する])　きにゅう(する)
　n.v.　(5)
filled, full　いっぱい　(7)
find　(見つける)　みつける　*C2, tr.*;　find (be found)
　(見つかる)　みつかる　*C1, intr.*　(3)
finger　(指)　ゆび　(4)
fire, force to resign　(首にする)　くびにする;　be fired
　(首になる)　くびになる　(5)
fire　(火事)　かじ　(6);　fire engine　(消防車)
　しょうぼうしゃ　(3);　firefighter　(消防士)
　しょうぼうし　(5)
firm, decisive　(断固)　だんこ　(7)
firmly　しっかり　*adv.*　(3)
first love　(初恋)　はつこい　(5)
first-class seat (*on train*)　(グリーン席)　グリーンせき
　(1)
fisherman　(漁師)　りょうし　(5)
fishing, commercial　(漁業)　ぎょぎょう　(7)
fit (be fit for)　(向く)　むく　*C1, intr.*　(5)
flat tire; get a flat tire　パンク(する)　*n.v.*　(3)
flea　のみ　(7)
flight　フライト　(1)
flood　(洪水)　こうずい　(7)
floor　(床)　ゆか　(2)
floor cushion　(座布団)　ざぶとん　(2)
floor lamp　スタンド　(2)
floor space, floor area　(建坪)　たてつぼ　(2)
flourish (*plants*)　(生える)　はえる　*C2, intr.*　(7)
flow　(流れる)　ながれる　*C2, intr.*　(4)
flower bed　(花壇)　かだん　(7)
flowering plant　(草花)　くさばな　(7)
flu (to catch the flu)　(風邪をひく)　かぜをひく　(4)
fluorescent light　(蛍光灯)　けいこうとう　(2)
fly　(飛ぶ)　とぶ　*C1, intr.*　(1)
FM (*radio*)　エフエム　(6)
folding fan　(扇子)　せんす　(7)
folk song　(民謡)　みんよう　(6)
follow (*a command, etc.*)　(従う)　したがう
　C1, intr.　(6)
following, next　(次の)　つぎの　(3)
foot　(脚、足)　あし　(4)
for (*duration*)　(間)　かん　(1)
for a while　しばらく　(2)
forehead　(額)　ひたい　(4)
forest　(森)　もり;　(森林)　しんりん　(7)
for example　(例えば)　たとえば　(3)
form, shape　(形式)　けいしき　(6)
formal (be formal)　あらたまる　*C1, intr.*　(6)
fortune-teller　(占師)　うらないし　(5);　fortune-telling
　(占い)　うらない　(7)
fox　(狐)　きつね　(7)
free, with time to spare　(暇[な])　ひま(な)
　na-adj.　(5)

freely　(自由に)　じゆうに　*adv.*　(3)
freeway　(高速道路)　こうそくどうろ　(3)
freeze　(凍る)　こおる　*C1, intr.*　(1)
freezer　フリーザー　(2)
fresh, sparking　さわやかな　*na-adj.*　(6)
fresh, new　(新鮮[な])　しんせん(な)　*na-adj.*　(5)
frighten (be frightened)　(怖がる)　こわがる　*C1, tr.*;
　frightening　(怖い)　こわい　*i-adj.*　(4)
frog　(蛙)　かえる　(7)
front desk　フロント　(1)
front seat　(前部座席)　ぜんぶざせき　(3)
fruit　(果実)　かじつ　(7)
fruit, berry　(実)　み　(7)
fuel gauge　(燃料計)　ねんりょうけい　(3)
full bloom　(満開)　まんかい　(7)
fun　(楽しい)　たのしい　*i-adj.*　(4)
function; to function　(機能[する])　きのう(する)
　n.v.　(7)
funeral　(葬式)　そうしき　(5)
fur　(毛皮)　けがわ　(7)
furniture　(家具)　かぐ　(2)
furthermore　さらに　*adv.*　(2)
futon closet　(押入)　おしいれ　(2)
future　(将来)　しょうらい　(7)

G

garage　ガレージ;　(車庫)　しゃこ　(2)
garbage　(塵)　ごみ　(7);　garbage collector　(ゴミ屋)
　ゴミや　(5)
garden　(庭園)　ていえん　(7);　garden, yard　(庭)
　にわ;　do gardening　(庭いじりをする)
　にわいじりをする　(2)
gasoline　ガソリン;　gas station　ガソリン・スタンド
　(3);　gas stove　ガスレンジ　(2)
gather　(集まる)　あつまる　*C1, intr.*　(1);　gather,
　collect　(集める)　あつめる　*C2, tr.*　(3)
gear shift lever　チェンジレバー　(3)
general concept　(概念)　がいねん　(7)
gentle, mild　(素直[な])　すなお(な)　*na-adj.*　(6)
geography　(地理)　ちり　(7)
get along, manage　すませる　*C2, tr.*　(6)
get off (*a vehicle*)　(降りる)　おりる　*C2, tr.*　(1)
get together, gather　(集まる)　あつまる　*C1, intr.*　(1)
get used to　(慣れる)　なれる　*C2, intr.*　(5)
gift　(贈り物)　おくりもの　(1)
giraffe　キリン　(7)
girl　(女の子)　おんなのこ;　(少女)　しょうじょ　(5)
girlfriend, boyfriend　(恋人)　こいびと　(5)
give (*to a second or third person*)　あげる　*C2, tr.*;
　(*to speaker or speaker's in-group*)　くれる　*C2, tr.*;
　さしあげる (*humble*)　*C2, tr.*;　(*to a social inferior*)
　やる　*C1, tr.*　(2)
give, convey　(与える)　あたえる　*C2, tr.*　(5)
glacier　(氷河)　ひょうが　(7)
global warming (greenhouse effect)　(温暖化)
　おんだんか　(7)
glove compartment　グラブコンパートメント　(3)
go　(参る)　まいる (*humble*)　*C1, intr.*;
　いらっしゃる (*honorific*)　(5)

go along (*a street*), go through （通る）とおる
  C1, intr. (*3*)
go around （回る）まわる *C1, intr.* (*3*)
go down （下がる）さがる *C1, intr.* (*3*)
go in （入る）はいる *C1, intr.* (*3*)
go off (*lights, fire, etc.*) （消える）きえる *C2, intr.* (*3*)
go on (*lights, appliances, etc.*) （付く）つく
  C1, intr. (*2*)
go out (*lights, fire, etc.*), disappear （消える）きえる *C2, intr.* (*3*)
go under つぶれる *C2, intr.* (*5*)
goat （山羊）やぎ (*7*)
going slowly, to go slowly （徐行［する］）じょこう（する）
  n.v. (*3*)
good looking カッコいい *i-adj.* (*3*)
goose がちょう (*7*)
gorilla ゴリラ (*7*)
gossip ゴシップ (*6*)
government office （役所）やくしょ (*5*)
grab つかむ *C1, tr.* (*4*)
grade, scrape (*a hill or mountain*) けずる *C1, tr.* (*7*)
grade school （小学校）しょうがっこう (*5*)
gradually だんだん *adv.* (*2*)
graduate school （大学院）だいがくいん (*5*)
grass （草）くさ (*7*)
grave, tomb （墓）はか (*5*)
greenhouse （温室）おんしつ (*7*)
greenhouse effect グリーン・ハウス・エフェクト (*7*)
grip （握る）にぎる *C1, tr.* (*4*)
group travel （団体旅行）だんたいりょこう (*1*)
grow (*plants*) （生える）はえる *C2, intr.* (*7*)
grow up （育つ）そだつ *C1, intr.* (*5*)
guard rail ガードレール (*3*)
guest reception room （応接間）おうせつま (*2*)
guest room （客室）きゃくしつ (*1*)
guide ガイド; guidebook ガイドブック (*1*)
guide; guide, show around （案内［する］）
  あんない（する）*n.v.* (*6*)

H

habit （習慣）しゅうかん (*7*)
haiku （俳句）はいく (*7*)
hair, strand of hair, fur （毛）け (*4*)
hairdresser ヘアードレッサー (*5*)
hair dryer ドライヤー (*2*)
hairstylist （美容師）びようし (*5*)
hallway （廊下）ろうか (*2*)
hand （手）て (*4*)
handicapped （不自由［な］）ふじゆう（な）*na-adj.* (*5*)
hand over, pass （渡す）わたす *C1, tr.* (*4*)
hang in, strive （頑張る）がんばる *C1, intr.* (*7*)
hang up （掛ける）かける *C2, tr.* (*4*)
happen （起こる）おこる *C1, intr.* (*6*)
happy, glad （嬉しい）うれしい *i-adj.* (*4*)
happy, lucky （幸せ［な］）しあわせ（な）*na-adj.* (*5*)
harbor （港）みなと (*1*)
have in common, share （共通する）きょうつうする
  (*7*)
hawk, falcon （鷹）たか (*7*)

headache (have a headache) （頭が痛い）
  あたまがいたい; （頭痛がする）ずつうがする (*4*)
headlight ヘッドライト (*3*)
headline （見出し）みだし (*6*)
headquarters （本店）ほんてん (*5*)
health （健康［な］）けんこう（な）*na-adj.* (*4*)
hearing error （聞き間違い）ききまちがい (*6*)
heart-shaped （ハート形）ハートがた (*4*)
heater ヒーター (*2*)
heel （踵）かかと (*4*)
height （高さ）たかさ (*7*); (*of body*) （身長）
  しんちょう (*4*)
height above sea level （標高）ひょうこう (*7*)
high school （高校）こうこう (*5*)
hill （丘）おか (*7*)
hippopotamus カバ (*7*)
hips （腰）こし (*4*)
hire （雇う）やとう *C1, tr.* (*1*)
history （歴史）れきし (*7*)
hit ぶつける *C2, tr.*; be hit ぶつかる *C1, intr.* (*3*)
hitchhike ヒッチハイク (*1*)
hold, grip つかむ *C1, tr.* (*4*)
holiday （休暇）きゅうか (*1*)
home section (*of a newspaper*) （家庭欄）かていらん
  (*6*)
hometown （故郷）こきょう (*7*)
honey, nectar （蜜）みつ (*7*)
honeymoon （新婚旅行）しんこんりょこう (*5*)
honor （名誉）めいよ (*5*)
hood (*of car*) ボンネット (*3*)
horizon （水平線）すいへいせん (*7*)
horn (*of car*) クラクション (*3*)
horse （馬）うま (*7*)
hospital （病院）びょういん; hospitalization; be
  hospitalized （入院［する］）にゅういん（する）*n.v.*;
  be discharged from hospital （退院［する］）
  たいいん（する）*n.v.* (*4*)
hot spring （温泉）おんせん (*1*)
hourly wage （時給）じきゅう (*5*)
housefly （蝿）はえ (*7*)
housekeeper （家政婦）かせいふ (*5*)
housewife （主婦）しゅふ (*5*)
housework （家事）かじ (*2*)
housing （住宅）じゅうたく; housing development
  （団地）だんち (*2*)
how どのように (*1*)
hungry (to get hungry) おなかがすく (*1*)
hunter （猟師）りょうし (*5*)

I

idea （考え）かんがえ (*2*)
imitate （真似る）まねる *C2, tr.* (*4*)
impolite, rude （失礼［な］）しつれい（な）*na-adj.* (*6*)
important （重要［な］）じゅうよう（な）*na-adj.* (*7*);
  大切［な］たいせつ（な）*na-adj.* (*4*)
impression; impress (be impressed) （感銘［する］）
  かんめい（する）*n.v.* (*5*)
improper みっともない *i-adj.* (*7*)
in addition to のほかに (*4*)

in place of... ～のかわりに (6)
in the same way （同様）どうよう (6)
incident （事件）じけん (6)
include （入れる）いれる *C2, tr.*; be included （入る）
　はいる *C1, intr.* (3)
incorporated company （株式会社）かぶしきがいしゃ
　(5)
increase, proliferate （増える）ふえる *C2, intr.*;
　increase (something) （増やす）ふやす *C1, tr.* (4)
increasingly ますます *adv.* (6)
independence; become independent （独立［する］)
　どくりつ（する）*n.v.* (5)
index （索引）さくいん (6)
industry （産業）さんぎょう; industrial pollution
　（産業公害）さんぎょうこうがい; industrial waste
　（廃棄物）はいきぶつ (7)
infant （幼児）ようじ (3)
influence; exert influence （影響［する］)
　えいきょう（する）*n.v.*; have influence
　（影響を与える）えいきょうをあたえる (7)
inform (*news*) （報道する）ほうどうする (6)
information （情報）じょうほう (3)
injection （注射）ちゅうしゃ (4)
injury （怪我）けが; get injured （怪我をする）
　けがをする (4)
inquire, ask　たずねる　*C2, tr.* (1)
inquire, question （問い合わせる）といあわせる
　C2, tr. (6)
insect （虫）むし (7)
insert （入れる）いれる *C2, tr.* (3)
insurance （保健）ほけん (1);　public health insurance
　office （保険所）ほけんじょ (4)
interchange　インターチェンジ (3)
intercom　インターフォン (2)
interpreter; interpret （通訳［する］)つうやく（する）
　n.v. (5)
intersection （交差点）こうさてん (1)
interview; have an interview　インタビュー［する］*n.v.*;
　interview show （対談番組）たいだんばんぐみ (6)
invention; invent （発明［する］)はつめい（する）
　n.v. (5)
investigation; investigate （調査［する］)ちょうさ（する）
　n.v. (3)
invitation （誘い）さそい (7)
invite, engage （迎える）むかえる *C2, tr.* (6)
invite, beckon （招く）まねく *C1, tr.* (2)
iron　アイロン (2)
irritated　イライラする (4)
Islam （イスラム教）イスラムきょう (7)
island （島）しま (7)
itchy　かゆい　*i-adj.* (7)
item （品）しな (2)

J

Japanese cedar （杉）すぎ (7)
Japanese kimono store （呉服屋）ごふくや (5)
Japanese plum （梅）うめ (7)
Japanese-style inn （旅館）りょかん (1)
Japanese-style room （和室）わしつ (2)

Japanese-style song （演歌）えんか (6)
jaw （顎）あご (4)
job （仕事）しごと (5)
job-seeking; get a job （就職［する］)しゅうしょく（する）
　n.v.;　job interview （面接［する］)めんせつ（する）
　n.v. (5)
journalism　ジャーナリズム (6);　journalist
　（新聞記者）しんぶんきしゃ (5)
Judaism （ユダヤ教）ユダヤきょう (7)
judge （裁判官）さいばんかん (5)
juicer　ジューサー (2)
jump （跳ぶ）とぶ *C1, intr.* (4)
jumping rope　なわとび (4)
jungle　ジャングル; （密林）みつりん (7)
junior college （短大）たんだい (5)
just like　まるで　*adv.* (4)

K

keep （守る）まもる *C1, tr.* (6)
keep an animal （飼う）かう *C1, tr.* (7)
kill （殺す）ころす *C1, tr.* (7)
kindergarten （幼稚園）ようちえん (5)
knee （膝）ひざ (4)
knock over （倒す）たおす (3)
know （ご存じだ）ごぞんじだ (*honorific*);
　（存じている）ぞんじている　(*humble*) (5)

L

lake （湖）みずうみ (7)
land （土地）とち (2)
landing; to land （着陸［する］)ちゃくりく（する）
　n.v. (1)
large enterprise （大企業）だいきぎょう (5)
lastly （最後に）さいごに　*adv.* (3)
late (to be late) （遅れる）おくれる *C2, intr.* (1);
　lateness; be late for work （遅刻［する］)ちこく（する）
　n.v. (5)
laugh （笑う）わらう *C1, tr.* (4)
laundry; do laundry （洗濯［する］)せんたく（する）
　n.v.;　things to be laundered （洗濯物）せんたくもの
　(2)
law office （弁護士事務所）べんごしじむしょ (5)
lawn （芝生）しばふ (7)
lawyer （弁護士）べんごし (5)
lay down, put to sleep （寝かす）ねかす *C1, tr.* (3)
lazy　ものぐさ（な）*na-adj.* (7)
leaf （葉）は; （葉っぱ）はっぱ (7)
learn （覚える）おぼえる *C2, tr.* (6)
least, worst （最低）さいてい (2)
leave, depart （発つ）たつ *C1, intr.* (1)
leave, separate from （離れる）はなれる *C2, tr.* (3)
leave (be left over) （残る）のこる *C1, intr.* (3)
leave as is （放っておく）ほうっておく *C1, tr.* (4)
leave behind （残す）のこす *C1, tr.* (3)
lecture （講義）こうぎ (7)
left （左）ひだり; left hand （左手）ひだりて (4);
　left side （左側）ひだりがわ (1);　left-handed
　（左利き）ひだりきき (4)

leg, foot　（脚、足）　あし　(4)

leisurely　ゆっくり　*adv.*　(1)

lend　（貸す）　かす　*C1, tr.*　(2)

length　（期間）　きかん　(5)

leopard　（豹）　ひょう　(7)

letter　（手紙）　てがみ　(6)

letter paper, stationery　（便箋）　びんせん　(6)

letters-to-the-editor section　（投書欄）　とうしょらん;
　writing to the editor; write to the editor
　（投書［する］）　とうしょ（する）　*n.v.*　(6)

license plate　ナンバープレート　(3)

lick　なめる　*C2, tr.*　(4)

life　（人生）　じんせい　(5); life, living　（生活）
　せいかつ　*n.v.*　(1); life; lead one's life　（生活［する］）
　せいかつ（する）　*n.v.*　(6); lifetime　（一生）
　いっしょう　(5)

light, lamp, electricity　（電気）　でんき; turn off a light
　（電気を消す）　でんきをけす; turn on a light
　（電気をつける）　でんきをつける; lightbulb　（電球）
　でんきゅう　(2)

like...　みたい（な）　*na-adj.*　(4)

lily　（百合）　ゆり　(7)

line, row　（行）　ぎょう　(6)

line up　（並ぶ）　ならぶ　*C1, intr.*　(1); （並べる）
　ならべる　*C2, tr.*　(3)

link　つなぐ　*C1, tr.*　(6)

lion　ライオン　(7)

lip　（唇）　くちびる　(4)

liquid　（液体）　えきたい　(7)

live, reside　（住む）　すむ　*C1, intr.*　(2)

livestock　（家畜）　かちく　(7)

living room　リビング・ルーム; （居間）　いま　(2)

lizard　とかげ　(7)

locker　ロッカー　(5)

lock up　（鍵をかける）　かぎをかける　(2)

lodging; stay overnight　（宿泊［する］）　しゅくはく（する）
　n.v.; lodgings　（宿）　やど; lodging charges　（宿泊料）
　しゅくはくりょう　(1)

lonely　（寂しい）　さびしい　*i-adj.*　(4)

long-awaited, after much trouble　せっかく　(3)

look, look at　（拝見［する］）　はいけん（する）　*(humble)*
　n.v.; look at　（ご覧になる）　ごらんになる
　(honorific)　(5)

look back　ふりむく　*C1, intr.*　(4)

look upward　（見上げる）　みあげる　*C2, tr.*　(4)

lose　なくす　*C1, tr.*　(3)

lose (get lost)　なくなる; lose one's way　（道に迷う）
　みちにまよう　(3)

love　（愛する）　あいする　*C3, tr.*; be enamored　（恋愛）
　れんあい　(5)

lower　（下げる）　さげる　(3)

lozenge-shaped　（菱形）　ひしがた　(4)

luggage　（荷物）　にもつ　(1)

M

mail　（郵便）　ゆうびん　(6); mail carrier　（郵便配達人）
　ゆうびんはいたつにん　(5); mail delivery
　（郵便配達）　ゆうびんはいたつ; mailbox (for public
　use)　（郵便ポスト）　ゆうびんポスト　(6); mailbox
　(for receiving mail)　（郵便受け）　ゆうびんうけ　(2)

main, major　（主［な］）　おも（な）　*na-adj.*　(3)

mainly　（主に）　おもに　*adv.*　(5)

main store　（本店）　ほんてん　(5)

maintain, protect　（守る）　まもる　*C1, tr.*　(6)

maintenance　メンテナンス　(3); maintenance; to
　maintain　（維持［する］）　いじ（する）　*n.v.*　(4)

make sure　（確かめる）　たしかめる　*C2, tr.*　(3)

mammal　（哺乳動物）　ほにゅうどうぶつ　(7)

manage, get along　すませる　*C2, tr.*　(6)

management, administration; manage, administer
　（経営［する］）　けいえい（する）　*n.v.*　(5)

managing director　（専務取締役）
　せんむとりしまりやく　(5)

manner　マナー　(7)

map　（地図）　ちず　(1)

marriage; marry　（結婚［する］）　けっこん（する）
　n.v.　(5)

marsh　（沼）　ぬま　(7)

mass communication　マスコミ　(6)

mass production　（大量生産）　たいりょうせいさん　(5)

master of ceremonies　（司会者）　しかいしゃ　(6)

means　（手段）　しゅだん　(6)

mechanic　メカニック　(5); （修理工）
　しゅうりこう　(5)

mechanical breakdown; have a mechanical breakdown
　（故障［する］）　こしょう（する）　*n.v.*　(3)

medical doctor　（医者）　いしゃ　(4)

medical examination; perform a medical examination
　（診察［する］）　しんさつ（する）　*n.v.*　(4)

medical treatment　（治療）　ちりょう　(4)

medicine　（薬）　くすり　(4)

meet　（お目にかかる）　おめにかかる　*(humble)*　(5)

memorization; memorize　（暗記［する］）　あんき（する）
　n.v.　(6)

mend, fix　（直す）　なおす　*C1, tr.*　(2)

message　（伝言）　でんごん　(6)

microphone　マイク　(6)

microwave oven　（電子レンジ）　でんしレンジ　(2)

middle (in the middle)　（中）　ちゅう　(2)

middle age　（中年）　ちゅうねん　(5)

middle school　（中学校）　ちゅうがっこう　(5)

midnight broadcast　（深夜放送）　しんやほうそう　(6)

mind, be bothered　かまう　*C1, tr.*　(6)

mind, feeling, heart　（心）　こころ　(4)

minibus　マイクロバス　(3)

minor, underage person　（未成年）　みせいねん　(5)

mirror　（鏡）　かがみ　(4)

missing letter　（脱字）　だつじ　(6)

misspelling　（誤字）　ごじ　(6)

mistake (make a mistake)　（間違える）　まちがえる
　C1, tr.　(3)

misunderstanding; misunderstand　（誤解［する］）
　ごかい（する）　*n.v.*　(6)

modern people　（現代人）　げんだいじん　(4)

monkey　（猿）　さる　(7)

monorail　モノレール　(3)

monthly commuter pass　（定期券）　ていきけん　(3)

monthly magazine　（月刊誌）　げっかんし　(6)

monthly salary　（月給）　げっきゅう　(5)

mood, state of mind　（機嫌）　きげん; mood, atmosphere
　（気持ち）　きもち　(4)

moon　（月）つき　(7)

moped　モペット　(3)

morality　（道徳）どうとく　(7)

more or less　（多少）たしょう　adv.　(7)

moreover　さらに　adv.　(7)

more than…　（…以上）いじょう　(2)

morning glory　（朝顔）あさがお　(7)

morning paper　（朝刊）ちょうかん　(6)

mosquito　（蚊）か　(7)

most, best　（最高）さいこう　(2)

motor oil　オイル　(3)

motorcycle　オートバイ　(3)

mountain pass　（峠）とうげ;　mountain peak　（山頂）
　さんちょう, （頂上）ちょうじょう;　mountain range
　（山脈）さんみゃく;　foot of a mountain　（麓）
　ふもと　(7)

mouse　（鼠）ねずみ　(7)

moustache　（口髭）くちひげ　(4)

mouth　（口）くち　(4)

move　（移る）うつる　C1, int.　(6);　move something,
　set in motion　（動かす）うごかす　C1, tr.　(2);
　move, be in motion　（動く）うごく　C1, intr.　(3)

move residence　（引っ越す）ひっこす　C1, intr.　(2)

movie star　（映画スター）えいがスター　(5)

Mr., Ms.　（氏）し　（formal）　(6)

muscle　（筋肉）きんにく　(4)

music show　（音楽番組）おんがくばんぐみ　(6);
　musician　（音楽家）おんがくか　(5)

N

nail (finger or toe)　（爪）つめ　(4)

nameplate　（表札）ひょうさつ　(2)

nation　（国）くに　(7)

nature　（自然）しぜん　(7)

nausea (be nauseated)　（吐き気がする）
　はきけがする　(4)

navel　お臍　おへそ　pol.　(4)

necessary　（必要[な]）ひつよう（な）　na-adj.　(7)

neck　（首）くび　(4)

negligence; neglect, ignore　（無視[する]）むし（する）
　n.v.　(2)

negotiation; negotiate　（交渉[する]）こうしょう（する）
　n.v.　(7)

nervous, care about　（気になる）きになる　(3)

nest　（巣）す　(7)

news coverage; to cover, collect information　（取材[する]）
　しゅざい（する）　n.v.　(6)

news report　（報道）ほうどう　(6)

newspaper article　（新聞記事）しんぶんきじ;
　newspaper clipping　（切り抜き）きりぬき;
　newspaper company　（新聞社）しんぶんしゃ　(6);
　appear in a newspaper　（新聞に載る）しんぶんにのる
　(6)

New Year's card　（年賀状）ねんがじょう　(6)

next　（次に）つぎに　(3)

next-door neighbor　お隣　おとなり　pol.　(2)

Nippon Hoso Kyokai (NHK)　エヌエチケー　(6)

nonreserved seat　（自由席）じゆうせき　(1)

nonsmoking seat　（禁煙席）きんえんせき　(1)

no parking　（駐車禁止）ちゅうしゃきんし　(3)

North Pole　（北極）ほっきょく　(7)

nose　（鼻）はな　(4)

not only… but also　だけでなく　(4)

notice　（気づく）きづく　C1, intr.　(6)

notify　（知らせる）しらせる　C2, tr.　(2)

novel　（小説）しょうせつ　(6)

nuclear power　（原子力）げんしりょく　(7)

number　（数）かず　(5)

nurse　（看護婦）かんごふ　(4)

nursery school teacher　（保母）ほぼ　(5)

O

oasis　オアシス　(7)

obey a rule, observe a custom　（守る）まもる
　C1, tr.　(6)

objective, unbiased　（客観的[な]）きゃっかんてき（な）
　na-adj.　(7)

objective, goal　（目的）もくてき　(3)

obtain　（得る）える　C2, tr.　(3)

occupation　（職業）しょくぎょう　(5)

ocean current　（海流）かいりゅう　(7)

of course　もちろん　adv.　(2)

office　（事務室）じむしつ;　（事務所）じむしょ
　(5)

office automation (OA)　オーエー;
　office clerk　（事務員）じむいん;
　OL (lit., office lady)　オーエル　(5)

offing (from coast)　（沖）おき　(7)

old people　（老人）ろうじん　(5)

olden days　（昔）むかし　(7)

oldest son　（長男）ちょうなん　(5)

one hand　（片手）かたて　(4)

one-way traffic　（一方通行）いっぽうつうこう
　(3)

oneself　（自分）じぶん　(1);　oneself (by oneself)
　（自ら）みずから　adv.　(7)

only, none except…　しか…ない;　ばかり　(2)

open, be open　（開く）あく　C1, intr.;　（開ける）
　あける　C2, tr.　(3)

opinion　（意見）いけん　(7)

opposition; oppose　（反対[する]）はんたい（する）
　n.v.　(7)

optimistic　（楽天的[な]）らくてんてき（な）
　na-adj.　(5)

orangutan　オランウータン　(7)

orchid　ラン　(7)

ordinarily　（常に）つねに　adv.　(7)

original work　（原作）げんさく　(6)

original, unique　（独自の）どくじの　(7)

other　（他の）ほかの　(6)

outer space　（宇宙）うちゅう　(7)

out of order (be out of order)　（故障する）
　こしょうする　(3)

oval (noun)　（楕円）だえん　(4)

oven　オーブン　(2)

overtime　（残業）ざんぎょう　(5)

over valuation; overvalue　（偏重[する]）
　へんちょう（する）　n.v.　(7)

overweight （太り過ぎ）ふとりすぎ （4）
owl ふくろう （7）
ozone オゾン （7）

P

pack in つめこむ *C1, tr.* （7）; つめる *C1, tr.* （1）
Pacific Ocean （太平洋）たいへいよう （7）
package （小包）こづつみ （6）
page ページ （6）
painful （痛い）いたい *i-adj.*; be painful, hurt （痛む）
いたむ *C1, intr.*; painful, agonizing （苦しい）
くるしい *i-adj.* （4）
painter （画家）がか （5）
panda パンダ （7）
panther （豹）ひょう （7）
paper (document) （書類）しょるいー （5）
paperback （文庫本）ぶんこぼん （6）
parakeet インコ （7）
parking lot （駐車場）ちゅうしゃじょう （3）
parlor （客間）きゃくま （2）
parrot オーム （7）
part (*of a mechanical object*) （部品）ぶひん;
パーツ （3）
participation; participate （参加［する］）さんか（する）
n.v. （7）
partner （相手）あいて （6）
part-time job, part-timer パートタイマー （5）
passing; pass (overtake) （追い越し［する］）
おいこし（する）*n.v.* （3）
paste （貼る）はる *C1, tr.* （6）
passenger （乗客）じょうきゃく （1）; passenger car
（乗用車）じょうようしゃ （3）
passport パスポート （1）
patience, endurance; put up with （我慢［する］）がまん
（する）*n.v.* （4）
patient （患者）かんじゃ （4）
patrol car パトカー （3）
pay （払う）はらう *C1, tr.* （1）
peace of mind （安心）あんしん （4）
pearl （真珠）しんじゅ （7）
peculiar, characteristic （独自の）どくじの （7）
pedal, step on （踏む）ふむ *C1, tr.* （3）
pedestrian （歩行者）ほこうしゃ; pedestrian crossing
（横断歩道）おうだんほどう; pedestrian bridge
（横断歩道橋）おうだんほどうきょう （3）
pelican ペリカン （7）
peninsula （半島）はんとう （7）
performance; perform (*on stage, TV, etc.*) （出演［する］）
しゅつえん（する）*n.v.* （6）
period, duration （期間）きかん （5）
period, era （時代）じだい （7）
periodic （定期的［な］）ていきてき（な）*na-adj.* （4）
personnel ad （求人広告）きゅうじんこうこく （5）
personnel department （人事部）じんじぶ （5）
pet ペット （7）
pharmacy （薬屋）くすりや; （薬局）やっきょく （4）
photocopier コピーマシン; （複写機）ふくしゃき
（5）
photographer （写真家）しゃしんか （5）
photogravure グラビア （6）

pig （豚）ぶた （7）
pigeon （鳩）はと （7）
pill （錠剤）じょうざい （4）
pillar （柱）はしら （2）
pilot パイロット （1）
pine tree （松）まつ （7）
place, put （置く）おく *C1, tr.* （2）
plains （平野）へいや （7）
plans, schedule （予定）よてい; make a plan
プランをたてる （1）
planet （惑星）わくせい （7）
plant (*in soil*) （植える）うえる *C2, tr.* （7）
plant, vegetation （植物）しょくぶつ （7）
plate （皿）さら （2）
plateau. （高原）こうげん （2）
plateau, heights （台地）だいち （7）
platform ホーム （1）
pleasure （楽しみ）たのしみ （2）
plum tree （梅）うめ （7）
P.O. box （私書箱）ししょばこ （6）
point （点）てん （3）
police car パトカー （3）
policeman （警察官）けいさつかん （5）
polish, wipe （磨く）みがく *C1, tr.* （2）
politician （政治家）せいじか （5）
politics section (*of a newspaper*) （政治欄）
せいじらん （6）
pollen （花粉）かふん （7）
pollution; pollute （汚染［する］）おせん（する）
n.v. （7）
pollution (*environmental*), nuisance （公害）こうがい
（7）
pond （池）いけ （7）
poppy ケシ （7）
popular song (*traditional*) （歌謡曲）かようきょく
（6）
port （港）みなと （1）
position （位置）いち （3）
position, status （地位）ちい （5）
possibility （可能性）かのうせい （7）
post office （郵便局）ゆうびんきょく; post office clerk
（郵便局員）ゆうびんきょくいん; postage
（郵便料金）ゆうびんりょうきん; postal money order
（郵便為替）ゆうびんかわせ; postal savings
（郵便貯金）ゆうびんちょきん （6）
postcard （葉書）はがき （6）
potted plant （植木）うえき （7）
power, authority （権力）けんりょく （5）
praise ほめる *C2, tr.* （7）
pregnancy; get pregnant （妊娠［する］）にんしん（する）
n.v. （5）
preparation; prepare （準備［する］）じゅんび（する）*n.v.*
（6）; preparation; prepare, get ready
（用意［する］）ようい（する）*n.v.* （1）
presently, at present （現在）げんざい *adv.* （5）
president (*of company*) （社長）しゃちょう （5）
press conference; have a press conference
（記者会見［する］）きしゃかいけん（する）*n.v.* （6）
prestige （名誉）めいよ （5）
prevalent, common さかん（な）*na-adj.* （7）
prevent （防ぐ）ふせぐ *C1, tr.* （7）

Glossary

443

prime of life （働き盛り） はたらきざかり （5）

printing; print （印刷[する]） いんさつ（する） n.v.;
printed matter （印刷物） いんさつぶつ （6）;
printer プリンタ （5）

private (family) car （自家用車） じかようしゃ （3）

private railway （私鉄） してつ （1）

production; produce （生産[する]） せいさん（する）
n.v. （5）

producer プロデューサー （6）

product, goods （品） しな （2）

program (TV, radio) （番組） ばんぐみ （6）

programmer プログラマー （5）

progress; to progress （進歩[する]） しんぽ（する）
n.v. （7）

prominence; be prominent, active （活躍[する]）
かつやく（する） n.v. （5）

promotion; promote (in job) （昇進[する]）
しょうしん（する） n.v. （5）

property （財産） ざいさん （5）; property owner
（家主） やぬし （formal）; （大家さん） おおやさん
（inf.） （2）

proposal (marriage); propose プロポーズ（する）
n.v. （5）

prosecutor （検事） けんじ （5）

protect, maintain （守る） まもる C1, tr. （6）

protection; protect, guard （保護[する]） ほご（する）
n.v. （7）

protection of the environment （環境保護）
かんきょうほご （7）

province (in Canada) （州） しゅう （7）

public phone （公衆電話） こうしゅうでんわ （6）

publication; publish （出版[する]） しゅっぱん（する）
n.v.; publishing company （出版社） しゅっぱんしゃ
（6）

purpose （目的） もくてき （3）

push （押す） おす C1, tr. （3）

push-button telephone プッシュフォン （6）

push into おしこめる C2, tr. （7）

put on a vehicle （乗せる） のせる C2, tr. （3）

put away, clean up （片付ける） かたづける C2, tr. （2）

put in （入れる） いれる C2, tr. （3）

Q

quickly （急いで） いそいで adv. （1）

quiet, well-behaved おとなしい i-adj. （6）

quit やめる C1, tr. （1）

quiz show (on television) （クイズ番組）
クイズばんぐみ （6）

R

rabbit （兎） うさぎ （7）

radio ラジオ （2）

raise an animal （飼う） かう C1, tr. （7）

raise, elevate （高める） たかめる C2, tr. （5）

raise up （上げる） あげる C2, tr. （3）

rank-and-file worker （平社員） ひらしゃいん （5）

rat （鼠） ねずみ （7）

raw, uncooked （生の） なまの （1）

reader （読者） どくしゃ （6）

real estate agency, agent （不動産屋） ふどうさんや （2）

reality （現実） げんじつ （7）

realization; realize （実現[する]） じつげん（する）
n.v. （5）

rear-end collision; collide at rear （追突[する]）
ついとつ（する） n.v. （3）

rear seat （後部座席） こうぶざせき （3）

rearview mirror バック・ミラー （3）

reason （理由） りゆう （7）

receive いただく （humble）; (from an equal or
inferior) もらう C1, tr. （2）; （受け取る） うけとる
C1, tr. （6）

receiver (phone) （受話器） じゅわき; pick up the
receiver （受話器を取る） じゅわきをとる （6）

reclining seat リクライニング・シート （3）

recommend すすめる C2, tr. （4）

recording; record (on tape, etc.) （録音[する]）
ろくおん（する） n.v. （6）

recover （直る） なおる C1, intr. （3）

rectangle （四角） しかく; rectangular （四角い）
しかくい i-adj. （4）

recycling; recycle リサイクル[する] n.v. （7）

reduction; reduce （縮小[する]） しゅくしょう（する）
n.v. （7）

reference book （参考書） さんこうしょ （6）

refreshed (feel) スッキリする （4）

refreshing さわやかな na-adj. （6）

regarding… （〜に関する） にかんする （6）

registered mail （書留） かきどめ （6）

regular （定期的[な]） ていきてき（な） na-adj. （4）;
regular check （定期点検） ていてんけん （3）;
regular health check-up （定期検診）
ていきけんしん （4）

regular-class seat （普通席） ふつうせき （1）

reject, refuse （断る） ことわる C1, tr. （5）

relative (family) （親戚） しんせき （5）

relaxed （気軽に） きがるに adv. （6）

release （外す） はずす C1, tr.; （放す） はなす
C1, tr. （3）

relief; be relieved （安心[する]） あんしん（する）
n.v. （4）

religion （宗教） しゅうきょう （7）

remain （残る） のこる C1, intr. （3）; remainder, the
rest （残り） のこり （5）

rent （家賃） やちん （2）

rent, borrow （借りる） かりる C2, tr. （2）

rental car レンタカー （1）

rent out （貸す） かす C1, tr. （2）

repairs; repair （修理[する]） しゅうり（する） n.v. （3）

repair, fix （直す） なおす C1, tr. （2）

reply （返事） へんじ; (write a reply) （返事を書く）
へんじをかく （6）

report, tell （伝える） つたえる C2, tr. （6）

report; report (news) （報道[する]） ほうどう（する）
（6）

reporter （記者） きしゃ （6）; レポーター （5）

reptile （爬虫類） はちゅうるい （7）

request, wish （願う） ねがう C1, tr. （5）

request; request, ask for　（要望［する］）　ようぼう（する）
　　n.v.　(6)
research laboratory　（研究所）　けんきゅうじょ;
　　researcher　（研究者）　けんきゅうしゃ　(5)
reservation; make a reservation　（予約［する］）
　　よやく（する）　*n.v.*　(1)
reserved seat　（指定席）　していせき　(1)
rest　（休む）　やすむ　*C1, intr.*　(4)
reside　（住む）　すむ　*C1, intr.*;　residence　（住宅）
　　じゅうたく;　residential area　（住宅地）
　　じゅうたくち　(2)
resort　リゾート　(1)
resources (natural)　（資源）　しげん　(7)
responsibility　（責任）　せきにん　(5)
rest room　（お手洗い）　おてあらい　(*pol.*);　トイレ　(2)
result　（結果）　けっか　(5)
résumé　（履歴書）　りれきしょ　(5)
retirement; retire　（退職［する］）　たいしょく（する）
　　n.v.　(5)
return, send back　（戻す）　もどす　*C1, tr.*　(4);　return,
　　come back　（戻る）　もどる　*C1, intr.*　(1)
return postcard　（往復葉書）　おうふくはがき　(6)
rice cooker　（炊飯器）　すいはんき　(2)
rice paddy　（田んぼ）　たんぼ;　rice paddies and dry
　　fields　（田畑）　たはた　(7)
ride (*on vehicle*)　（乗る）　のる　*C1, intr.*　(1);　give a
　　ride　（乗せる）　のせる　*C2, tr.*　(3)
right-hand side　（右）　みぎ;　right hand　（右手）
　　みぎて　(4);　right side　（右側）　みぎがわ　(1);
　　right-handed　（右利き）　みぎきき　(4)
right now　（只今）　ただいま　*adv.*　(2)
ring (*telephone*)　（鳴る）　なる　*C1, intr.*　(6)
rise, get up　（上がる）　あがる　(*C1, intr.*)　(3)
river　（川）　かわ　(2)
riverbank　（岸）　きし　(7)
road　（車道）　しゃどう;　（道）　みち;　road map
　　（道路地図）　どうろちず;　road sign　（交通標識）
　　こうつうひょうしき　(3)
rock　（岩）　いわ　(7)
rock garden　（石庭）　せきてい　(7)
role　（役）　やく　(5)
roof　（屋根）　やね　(2)
room　（部屋）　へや　(2)
room charge　（宿泊料）　しゅくはくりょう　(1)
room service　ルームサービス　(1)
root　（つけ根）　つけね　(4)
rose　（薔薇）　ばら　(7)
round　（丸い）　まるい　*i-adj.*　(4)
round trip; make a round trip　（往復［する］）
　　おうふく（する）　*n.v.*　(3);　round trip ticket
　　（往復切符）　おうふくきっぷ　(1)
run into　ぶつかる　*C1, intr.*　(3)

S

sacrifice　（犠牲）　ぎせい　(7)
sad　（悲しい）　かなしい　*i-adj.*;　be sad　（悲しむ）
　　かなしむ　*C1, tr.*　(4)
safe　（安全［な］）　あんぜん（な）　*na-adj.*　(2)
sake (for the sake of)　ために　(2)

salary　（給料）　きゅうりょう　(5)
sale (on sale)　（発売中）　はつばいちゅう　(2)
salesperson　セールスマン　(5)
salmon　（鮭）　さけ　(1)
same　（同じ）　おなじ　(2)
sand　（砂）　すな;　sand dune　（砂丘）　さきゅう;　sandy
　　beach　（砂浜）　すなはま　(7)
save, collect　（貯める）　ためる　*C2, tr.*　(5)
saving, economizing; save, economize　（節約［する］）
　　せつやく（する）　*n.v.*　(7)
saving energy　（省エネ）　しょうエネ　(7)
savings (money); save (money)　（貯金［する］）
　　ちょきん（する）　*n.v.*　(2)
say　おっしゃる　(*honorific*)　(5)
say, speak　（申し上げる）　もうしあげる　(*humble*)
　　C2, tr.;　（申す）　もうす　(*humble*)　*C1, tr.*　(5)
school　（学校）　がっこう　(5)
schoolteacher　（教師）　きょうし　(5)
scientist　（科学者）　かがくしゃ　(5)
scold　（叱る）　しかる　*C1, tr.*　(5)
scratch　（掻く）　かく　(4)
seat　（席）　せき　(1);　take a seat　（腰かける）
　　こしかける　*C2, intr.*;　seat belt　シート・ベルト
　　(3)
seaweed　（海草）　かいそう　(4);　（海苔）　のり　(2)
secondhand　（中古）　ちゅうこ　(2)
second son　（次男）　じなん　(5)
secretary　（秘書）　ひしょ　(1)
section chief　（課長）　かちょう　(5)
sedan　セダン　(3)
see, meet　（お目にかかる）　おめにかかる　(*humble*)
　　(5)
seed　（種）　たね　(7)
seedling　（芽）　め　(7)
self　（自分）　じぶん　(1)
send　（送る）　おくる　*C1, tr.*　(6)
send around, turn around　（回す）　まわす　*C1, tr.*　(3)
send out　（出す）　だす　*C1, tr*　(3)
sender　（差出人）　さしだしにん　(6)
send through　（通す）　とおす　*C1, tr.*　(3)
separate　（別れる）　わかれる　*C2, intr.*　(5)
serious　（深刻［な］）　しんこく（な）　*na-adj.*　(7)
service area　サービスエリア　(3)
service charge　（サービス料）　サービスりょう　(1)
service station　サービス・ステーション　(3)
sew　（縫う）　ぬう　*C1, tr.*;　do sewing　（縫い物をする）
　　ぬいものをする;　sewing machine　ミシン　(2)
shake　（振る）　ふる　*C1, tr.*　(4)
shameful, embarrassing　（恥ずかしい）　はずかしい
　　i-adj.　(4)
shape　（形）　かたち　(4)
sharp　（するどい）　*i-adj.*　(7)
shatter　（割れる）　われる　*C2, intr.*　(3)
shaver　シェーバー　(2)
sheep　（羊）　ひつじ　(7)
shelf　（棚）　たな　(2)
shin　（臑）　すね　(4)
Shinto priest　（神主）　かんぬし　(5);　Shintoism　（神道）
　　しんとう　(7)
ship　（船）　ふね　(1)

shoe cabinet （靴箱） くつばこ （2）;　person who shines shoes （靴みがき） くつみがき （5）

shoot (sprout) （芽） め （7）

shopping; go shopping （買い物［する］） かいもの（する） n.v. （2）

shore, beach （海岸） かいがん （7）

shortcut （近道） ちかみち （3）

short-wave （短波） たんぱ （6）

shoulder （肩） かた （4）

show （お目にかける） おめにかける （humble） （5）; （見せる） みせる C2, tr. （2）

showy （華やか［な］） はなやか（な） na-adj. （5）

shut off （閉まる） しまる C1, intr. （1）

sick, sickness （病気） びょうき;　get sick （病気になる） びょうきになる （4）

side effect （副作用） ふくさよう （4）

sidewalk （歩道） ほどう （3）

sights, famous places （名所） めいしょ （1）

sightseeing, touring; sightsee, tour （観光［する］） かんこう（する） n.v.;　sightseeing bus （観光バス） かんこうバス;　sightseeing trip （観光旅行） かんこうりょこう;　sightseer （観光客） かんこうきゃく （1）

sightseeing; sightsee （見物［する］） けんぶつ（する） n.v. （1）

simple ちょっとした （4）

singer （歌手） かしゅ （5）

single （独身） どくしん （5）

single room シングル （1）

sink （流し） ながし （2）

sit down （腰かける） こしかける C2, intr. （3）

sit formally (kneeling) （正座する） せいざする （7）

sitcom コメディー （6）

situation （模様） もよう （6）

skin （肌） はだ （4）

skin, skin surface （皮膚） ひふ （4）

skunk スカンク （7）

sleep (go to sleep) （寝る） ねる C1, tr. （3）

sleeping car （寝台車） しんだいしゃ （1）

sleepy （眠い） ねむい i-adj. （3）

sliding door of opaque paper （障子） しょうじ （2）

slip of the tongue （言い間違い） いいまちがい （6）

small business （中小企業） ちゅうしょうきぎょう （5）

smell （嗅ぐ） かぐ C1, tr. （4）

smile （笑う） わらう C1, tr. （4）

smog スモッグ （7）

smoking seat （喫煙席） きつえんせき （1）

snake （蛇） へび （7）

soap （石鹸） せっけん （2）

soap opera メロドラマ （6）

socializing; socialize （交際［する］） こうさい（する） n.v. （5）

society （社会） しゃかい （5）

society section (of a newspaper) （社会欄） しゃかいらん （6）

soil （土） つち （7）

soldier （軍人） ぐんじん （5）

sole of foot （足の裏） あしのうら （4）

solution; solve （解決［する］） かいけつ（する） n.v. （7）

soon すぐ adv. （2）

South Pole （南極） なんきょく （7）

souvenir おみやげ （1）

space heater ストーブ （2）

sparrow （雀） すずめ （7）

special （特別［な］） とくべつ（な） na-adj. （5）

special correspondent （特派員） とくはいん （6）

special feature, special collection （特集） とくしゅう （6）

spectacular （華やか［な］） はなやか（な） na-adj. （5）

speed （速度） そくど;　スピード;　decrease speed （スピードを落とす） スピードをおとす;　increase speed （スピードを出す） スピードをだす;　speed limit （制限速度） せいげんそくど;　speed per hour （時速） じそく;　speeding violation （スピード違反） スピードいはん;　speedometer スピードメーター （3）

sponsor スポンサー （6）

sports car スポーツカー （3）;　sports paper （スポーツ紙） スポーツし;　sports program （スポーツ番組） スポーツばんぐみ;　sports section (of a newspaper) （スポーツ欄） スポーツらん （6）

spot-check; spot-check （点検［する］） てんけん（する） n.v. （3）

spring greenery （新緑） しんりょく （7）

sprinkle water （水をまく） みずをまく （2）

square （四角） しかく;　（四角い） しかくい i-adj. （4）

stairway, steps （階段） かいだん （2）

stamp, affix a stamp （切手を貼る） きってをはる （6）

stapler ホッチキス （5）

star （星） ほし （7）

start a car （発車する） はっしゃする （3）

state (in U.S., Australia) （州） しゅう （7）

station employee （駅員） えきいん （5）

statue （像） ぞう （1）

statue of the Buddha （仏像） ぶつぞう （7）

stay overnight （泊まる） とまる C1, intr. （1）

steep （険い） けわしい i-adj. （7）

steering wheel ハンドル （3）

step on （踏む） ふむ C1, tr. （3）

stethoscope （聴診器） ちょうしんき （4）

stiff (become stiff) こる C1, intr. （4）

stomachache （腹痛） ふくつう （4）

stone （石） いし （7）

stop やめる C1, tr. （1）;　stop (come to a stop) （止まる） とまる C1, intr. （3）

stop (bus or tram) （停留所） ていりゅうじょ （1）

store clerk （店員） てんいん （5）

storeroom （物置） ものおき （2）

storey (~storey-building) （~階建て） ~かいだて （2）

story, tale （童話） どうわ （6）

straight まっすぐ adv. （1）

straits （海峡） かいきょう （7）

street, road （道路） どうろ （3）

stretch （伸ばす） のばす C1, tr. （4）

strike スト（ライキ） （5）

studio スタジオ （6）

study, den （書斎） しょさい （2）

study abroad; to study abroad （留学［する］）
りゅうがく（する）　*n.v.*　(5)
subordinate　（部下）ぶか　(5)
subsection chief　（係長）かかりちょう　(5)
subscription; subscribe　（購読［する］）こうどく（する）
n.v.　(6)
subscribe to a newspaper　（新聞をとる）しんぶんをとる
(6)
suburbs　（郊外）こうがい　(2)
suffer　（悩む）なやむ　*C1, intr.*　(5)
sufficient　（十分［な］）じゅうぶん（な）　*na-adj.*　(3)
suggest, recommend　すすめる　*C2, tr.*　(4)
suitable (to be suitable)　（向く）むく　*C1, intr.*　(5)
suitcase　スーツケース　(1)
suite　スイート　(1)
summarize, recap　まとめる　*C2, tr.*　(6)
summary; summarize　（要約［する］）ようやく（する）
n.v.　(6)
summer resort　（避暑地）ひしょち　(1)
summertime; summer term　（夏期）かき　(1)
summon, call　（呼ぶ）よぶ　*C1, tr.*　(1)
sunflower　（向日葵）ひまわり　(7)
super express　（特急）とっきゅう　(1)
superior, supervisor　（上司）じょうし　(5)
surface mail　（船便）ふなびん　(6)
surgery　（手術）しゅじゅつ　(4)
surprise (be surprised)　びっくりする；（驚く）おどろく
C1, intr.　(4)
surround　（囲む）かこむ　*C1, tr.*　(5)
swallow　つばめ　(7)
swan　（白鳥）はくちょう　(7)
sweep (*with a broom*)　（掃く）はく　*C1, tr.*　(2)
sweeper　（掃除夫）そうじふ　(5)
switch off　（スイッチを切る）スイッチをきる；switch
on　（スイッチを入れる）スイッチをいれる　(2)
syrup　シロップ　(4)

T

table with built-in heater　こたつ　(2)
table of contents　（目次）もくじ　(6)
taboo　タブー　(7)
tachometer　タコメーター　(3)
taciturn　（無口［な］）むくち（な）　*na-adj.*　(6)
take (thing)　（持っていく）もっていく　*C1, tr.*　(1)
take (person)　（連れていく）つれていく　*C1, tr.*　(1)
take out　（出す）だす　*C1, tr.*　(3)
take-off; to take off　（離陸［する］）りりく（する）*n.v.*
(1)
take place　（起こる）おこる　*C1, intr.*　(6)
tariff　（関税）かんぜい　(6)
telecasting; telecast　（中継［する］）ちゅうけい（する）
n.v.　(6)
telegram, wire　（電報）でんぽう；send a telegram
（電報を打つ）でんぽうをうつ；telegram charge
（電報料）でんぽうりょう；telegram of condolence
（弔電）ちょうでん；telegram form　（電報用紙）
でんぽうようし; telegram message　（電文）でんぶん；
telegram office　（電報局）でんぽうきょく　(6)

telephone　（電話）でんわ　(2)；telephone booth
（電話ボックス）でんわボックス；telephone charge
（通話料）つうわりょう，（電話料）でんわりょう；
telephone company　（電話局）でんわきょく；
telephone directory　（電話帳）でんわちょう；
international call　（国際電話）こくさいでんわ；local
call　（市内通話）しないつうわ；long phone call
（長電話）ながでんわ；long-distance call
（市外通話）しがいつうわ；（長距離電話）
ちょうきょりでんわ；make a call
（電話［を］する）でんわ（を）する　(6)
telephone conversation　（通話）つうわ　(6)
telex　テレックス　(5)
temporary　（一時的［な］）いちじてき（な）　*na-adj.*　(7)
tenant　（借家人）しゃくやにん　(2)
terribly　すごく　*adv.*　(6)
test (medical); make a (medical) test　（検査［する］）
けんさ（する）　*n.v.*　(4)
textbook　（教科書）きょうかしょ　(6)
~th (with cardinal numbers)　（目）め　(1)
thanks to...　のおかげで　(7)
theatrical play　（芝居）しばい　(7)
thermometer (body)　（体温計）たいおんけい　(4)
thick, dense　（濃い）こい　*i-adj.*　(2)
thigh　（腿）もも　(4)
things　（事物）じぶつ　(7)；もの　(5)
think, ponder　（考える）かんがえる　*C2, tr.*　(2)；give
a lot of thought　（気にする）きにする　(7)
think, have an opinion　（存じる）ぞんじる　(*humble*)
C2, tr.　(5)
thirsty, get thirsty　（喉がかわく）のどがかわく　(1)
throat　（喉）のど　(4)
throw (at forcefully)　ぶつける　*C2, tr.*　(3)
ticket　（切符）きっぷ　(1)；(for riding train, bus, etc.)
（乗車券）じょうしゃけん　(3)；one-way ticket
（片道切符）かたみちきっぷ；ticket vending machine
（券売機）けんばいき　(1)
tiger　（虎）とら　(7)
timetable　（時刻表）じこくひょう　(1)
tire　タイヤ　(3)
tired, get tired　（疲れる）つかれる　*C2, intr.*　(1)
toaster　トースター　(2)
toe　（足の指）あしのゆび；tip of the toe　（爪先）
つまさき　(4)
tongue　（舌）した　(4)
tooth　（歯）は　(4)
top of the head　てっぺん　(4)
total; tally up　（合計［する］）ごうけい（する）　*n.v.*　(3)
total (in total)　（全部で）ぜんぶで　(2)
totally spoiled　（台無し）だいなし　(3)
touch　（触る）さわる　*C1, intr.*　(4)
tour, package tour　ツアー　(1)
tour guide　ツアー・コンダクター　(1)；（添乗員）
てんじょういん　(5)
tourist information center　（観光案内所）
かんこうあんないしょ；tourist site　（観光地）
かんこうち　(1)
townhouse　タウンハウス　(2)
tractor　トラクター　(3)

trading company　（商社）しょうしゃ　(5)

traffic　（交通）こうつう;　sluggish traffic
（ノロノロ運転）ノロノロうんてん;　traffic accident
（交通事故）こうつうじこ;　traffic jam
（交通渋滞）こうつうじゅうたい;　traffic light
（交通信号）こうつうしんごう　(3),（信号）しんごう
(1);　traffic sign　（交通標識）こうつうひょうしき;
traffic violation　（交通違反）こうつういはん　(3)

trailer　トレーラー　(3)

train, tram car　（電車）でんしゃ　(3);　local train
（普通列車）ふつうれっしゃ;　train going toward
Tokyo　（上り）のぼり;　train moving away from
Tokyo　（下り）くだり　(1)

transfer (*vehicles*)　（乗り換える）のりかえる
C2, tr.　(1)

transfer; transfer (*on the job*)　（転勤［する］）
てんきん（する）*n.v.*　(5)

translation; translate　（翻訳［する］）ほんやく（する）
n.v. (6);　translator　（翻訳者）ほんやくしゃ　(5)

transport　（運ぶ）はこぶ　*C1, tr.*　(2)

transportation (means of transportation)　（交通機関）
こうつうきかん　(3)

trash basket　（屑入れ）くずいれ　(2)

travel, trip; travel, go on a trip　（旅行［する］）
りょこう（する）*n.v.*;　travel abroad　（海外旅行）
かいがいりょこう;　travel expense(s)　（旅費）りょひ;
traveler　（旅行者）りょこうしゃ;　travelers' check
トラベラーズ・チェック;　domestic travel　（国内旅行）
こくないりょこう　(1)

traveling alone　（一人旅）ひとりたび　(1)

tread (tire)　（溝）みぞ　(3)

treasure　（宝）たから　(7)

treasured, valuable　（とっておきの）(6)

treat with affection, coddle　かわいがる　*C1, tr.*　(7)

treatment (medical)　（治療）ちりょう　(4)

trees and shrubs　（樹木）じゅもく　(7)

triangle　（三角）さんかく;　triangular　（三角の）
さんかくの　(4)

trolley bus　トローリーバス　(3)

tropical rain forest　（熱帯雨林）ねったいうりん　(7)

troublesome　（大変［な］）たいへん（な）*na-adj.*　(4)

truck　トラック　(3)

trunk　トランク　(3)

trunk (tree)　（幹）みき　(7)

truth (to tell the truth)　（実は）じつは　(4)

tulip　チューリップ　(7)

tuna　まぐろ　(7)

tunes　（曲）きょく　(5)

turf　（芝）しば　(7)

turkey　（七面鳥）しちめんちょう　(7)

turn (*knob, wheel*)　（回す）まわす　*C1, tr.*;　turn
around　（回る）まわる　*C1, intr.*　(3)

turn (*in a direction*)　（曲がる）まがる　*C1, intr.*　(1)

turn off (*light, etc.*)　（消す）けす　*C1, tr.*;　turn on (*light,
etc.*)　（付ける）つける　*C2, tr.*　(3)

turn off (*switch*)　（切る）きる　*C1, tr.* (2);　turn on
(*switch*)　（入れる）いれる　*C2, tr.*　(3)

turn signal　ウインカー　(3)

turnstile gate in station　（改札口）かいさつぐち　(3)

TV　テレビ　(2)

TV personality　タレント　(6)

twin-bed hotel room　ツイン　(1)

type　（タイプを打つ）タイプをうつ;　typewriter
タイプライター　(5)

typhoon　（台風）たいふう　(7)

U

under construction　（工事中）こうじちゅう　(3)

undergo (medical procedure)　（受ける）うける
C2, tr.　(4)

understanding; understand　（理解［する］）りかい（する）
n.v.　(5)

undo, unfasten　（外す）はずす　*C1, tr.*　(3)

unemployment; become unemployed　（失業［する］）
しつぎょう（する）*n.v.*　(5)

uniform, consistent　（一定）いってい　(7)

union　（組合）くみあい　(5)

unique　（独特の）どくとくの　(7)

unique characteristic　（特性）とくせい　(7)

universe　（宇宙）うちゅう　(7)

university　（大学）だいがく　(5)

unseemly　みっともない　*i-adj.*　(7)

until　まで　*part., conj.*　(1)

use; make use of　（利用［する］）りよう（する）*n.v.*　(2)

used, secondhand　（中古）ちゅうこ　(2)

used up　（切れる）きれる　(3)

usually　ふだん　*adv.*　(6)

U-turn; make a U-turn　（U-ターン［する］）
ユーターン（する）*n.v.*　(3)

V

vacant room　（空室）くうしつ　(1)

vacation, break　（休暇）きゅうか　(1)

vacation home　（別荘）べっそう;　vacation rental
（貸し別荘）かしべっそう　(2)

vacuum cleaner　（掃除機）そうじき　(2)

valley　（谷）たに　(7)

various　いろいろ（な）*na-adj.*　(3)

vase　（花瓶）かびん　(2)

VCR　ビデオレコーダー　(2)

vehicle(s)　（乗り物）のりもの　(1)

verandah　ベランダ　(2)

vice president (*company*)　（副社長）ふくしゃちょう
(5)

video　ビデオ;　videotaping; videotape　（録画［する］）
ろくが（する）*n.v.*　(6)

view　（眺め）ながめ　(2)

violation; violate (rules)　（違反する）いはん（する）
n.v.　(3)

violence　（暴力）ぼうりょく　(7)

violet (*flower*)　スミレ　(7)

virus　ビールス　(4)

visa　ビザ　(1)

visit, interrupt　（お邪魔する）おじゃまする
(*humble*)　(5)

visit (pay a visit to a sick person)　（見舞い［に行く］）
みまい（にいく）(4)

volcano　（火山）　かざん　（7）
vomit　はく　*C1, tr.*;　もどす　*C1, tr.*　（4）

W

waist　（腰）　こし　（4）
waiting room　（待ち合い室）　まちあいしつ　（1）
wall, fence　（塀）　へい　（2）
wall　（壁）　かべ;　wallpaper　（壁紙）　かべがみ　（2）
war　（戦争）　せんそう;　after a war　（戦後）
　せんご　（5）
ward off　（防ぐ）　ふせぐ　*C1, tr.*　（7）
wardrobe, chest of drawers　たんす　（2）
warning; warn　（警告［する］）　けいこく（する）　*n.v.*　（7）
wash　（洗う）　あらう　*C1, tr.*;　washing machine
　（洗濯機）　せんたくき　（2）
washstand　（洗面所）　せんめんじょ　（2）
wasp　（蜂）　はち　（7）
wasteful　もったいない　*i-adj.*　（7）
watch for, be careful　（気をつける）　きをつける　（1）
watch out　（注意［する］）　ちゅうい（する）　*n.v.*　（3）
water pollution　（水質汚染）　すいしつおせん　（7）
waterfall　（滝）　たき　（7）
watermelon　スイカ　（7）
wave　（波）　なみ　（7）
way (on the way)　（途中）　とちゅう　（3）
wear　（お召しになる）　おめしになる　（*honorific*）　（5）
weather forecast　（天気予報）　てんきよほう　（6）
wedding　（結婚式）　けっこんしき;　wedding anniversary
　（結婚記念日）　けっこんきねんび　（5）
weekly magazine　（週刊誌）　しゅうかんし　（6）
weep　（泣く）　なく　*C1, intr.*　（4）
weigh　（計る）　はかる　*C1, tr.*;　（重さを計る）
　おもさをはかる　（6）
weight　（重さ）　おもさ　（6）
weight (body)　（体重）　たいじゅう　（4）
weird　（不思議［な］）　ふしぎ（な）　*na-adj.*　（7）
well　よく　*adv.*　（1）
Western European　（西欧）　せいおう　（7）
Western-style room　（洋間）　ようま;　（洋室）
　ようしつ　（2）
whale　（鯨）　くじら　（7）
wheel　ハンドル;　take the wheel　（ハンドルを握る）
　ハンドルをにぎる;　turn the wheel　（ハンドルを切る）
　ハンドルをきる　（3）
while ~ing　まま　（6）

whittle away at　けずる　*C1, tr.*　（7）
wholesale store　（問屋）　とんや　（5）
wide, spacious　（広い）　ひろい　*i-adj.*　（2）
width　（幅）　はば　（1）
windshield　フロントガラス　（3）
wing　（翼）　つばさ　（7）
wipe　（拭く）　ふく　*C1, tr.*　（2）
wiper (windshield)　ワイパー　（3）
wish　（希望）　きぼう　*n.v.*　（5）
wither　しおれる　*C2, intr.*;　（*plants*）　（枯れる）
　かれる　*C2, intr.*　（7）
without interruption, all the way　ずっと　*adv.*　（1）
wolf　（狼）　おおかみ　（7）
woodblock print　（版画）　はんが　（7）
wooden clogs　げた　（3）
woods　（林）　はやし　（7）
word processor　ワードプロセッサー　（5）
work　（仕事）　しごと　（5）;　（働く）　はたらく　*C1, intr.*
　（3）;　going to work; go to work　（出勤［する］）
　しゅっきん（する）　*n.v.*;　working hours　（勤務時間）
　きんむじかん;　working place　（職場）　しょくば
　（5）
world　（世界）　せかい　（7）;　worldwide　（世界的［な］）
　せかいてき（な）　*na-adj.*　（5）
worries, troubles　（悩みごと）　なやみごと　（6）
worry; be worried　（心配［する］）　しんぱい（する）
　n.v.　（4）
wrist　（手首）　てくび　（4）
written symbol, letter　（文字）　もじ　（7）
wrong number　（番号違い）　ばんごうちがい　（6）

X

X-ray (to take)　（レントゲンを撮る）　レントゲンをとる
　（4）

Y

yellowtail　ハマチ　（7）
young people　（青年）　せいねん　（5）
youth hostel　ユース・ホステル　（1）

Z

ZIP code　（郵便番号）　ゆうびんばんごう　（6）
zoo　（動物園）　どうぶつえん　（7）

Index

Index

四百五十一

Grateful acknowledgment is made for use of the following:

Photographs: *Page 1* © Andy Sacks/Tony Stone Images; *14* © D. F. Cox/Tony Stone Images; *56* © Fujifotos/The Image Works; *61* © Yutaka Imamura/Amana Corporation; *76* © Don Smeizer/Tony Stone Images; *101* © Fujifotos/The Image Works; *135* © Adina Tovy/Photo 20-20; *190* © Tony Stone Images; *243* © Charles Gupton/Tony Stone Images; *246* © Cameramann/The Image Works; *254* © D. H. Hessell/Stock Boston; © *296* Sonia Katchian/Photo Shuttle: Japan; *298* © Photo Shuttle: Japan or © David Ryan/Photo 20-20; *334* © P. Perrin/Sygma; *350* © Robert E. Schwerzel/Stock Boston; *374* © Rich Iwasaki/Tony Stone Images; *380* © Sonia Kachian/Photo Shuttle: Japan

Realia: *Page 9* Coffee Shop Parador; *21* Nihon Ryoko, Akai Husen Ryokobu; *22* J. R. Kosai Shuppansha; *65* Reprinted by courtesy of Shobunsha, © Shobunsha Publication, Inc., 1998, E-037; *69* Japan Railways; *79* Token Sangyoo; *89* Co-op Tokyo; *136* From *Zukai Gairaigo Jiten* by Norio Toshizawa (Tokyo: Kadowawa Shoten); *141* Toyota Parking Network; *168* Tokyo-to Kotsukyoku; *177* Reprinted with permission of Japan Traffic Safety Association; *180* Japanese Automobile Federation; *267* © Natsume Fusanosuke Office, Ltd.; *289* Kokuyo Company; *314* Tokyo Chuo Yubinkyoku; *324* The Yomiuri Shimbun, April, 1994; *331* © 1995 Msao Yajima/Kenshi Hirokane/Shogakukan, Inc.; *399* Sanwa Bank Ltd.; *349* JOB

にほんちず
日本地図

0   100   200 km

にほんかい
日本海

つしま
対馬

おきしょとう
隠岐諸島

ちゅうごく ち ほう
中国地方

ちゅうぶ ち ほう
中部地方

まつえ
松江

さが
佐賀

ふくおか
福岡

やまぐち
山口

しまね
島根

とっとり
鳥取

かなざわ
金沢

とやま
富山

ながさき
長崎

佐賀

福岡

山口

ひろしま
広島

おかやま
岡山

鳥取

ふくい
福井

いしかわ
石川

富山

長崎

くまもと
熊本

おおいた
大分

福岡

広島

岡山

ひょうご
兵庫

きょうと
京都

福井

ぎふ
岐阜

ながの
長野

長崎

熊本

まつやま
松山

かがわ
香川

たかまつ
高松

京都

しが
滋賀

岐阜

かごしま
鹿児島

えひめ
愛媛

こうち
高知

こうべ
神戸

おおさか
大阪

おおつ
大津

なごや
名古屋

こうふ
甲府

くまもと
熊本

大分

香川

とくしま
徳島

徳島

大阪

奈良

なごや

あいち
愛知

やまなし
山梨

みやざき
宮崎

高知

わかやま
和歌山

なら
奈良

みえ
三重

愛知

しずおか
静岡

かごしま
鹿児島

宮崎

しこく ち ほう
四国地方

和歌山

奈良

三重

静岡

きゅうしゅう ち ほう
九州地方

きんき ち ほう
近畿地方

かながわ
神奈川

やくしま
屋久島

たいへいよう
太平洋

いずしょとう
伊豆諸島

神奈川